Incisive Research On AI And Law

Advanced Series On
Artificial Intelligence (AI)
And Law

Dr. Lance B. Eliot, MBA, PhD

Disclaimer: This book is presented solely for educational and entertainment purposes. The author and publisher are not offering it as legal, accounting, or other professional services advice. The author and publisher make no representations or warranties of any kind and assume no liabilities of any kind with respect to the accuracy or completeness of the contents and specifically disclaim any implied warranties of merchantability or fitness of use for a particular purpose. Neither the author nor the publisher shall be held liable or responsible to any person or entity with respect to any loss or incidental or consequential damages caused, or alleged to have been caused, directly or indirectly, by the information or programs contained herein. Every company is different and the advice and strategies contained herein may not be suitable for your situation.

 First Edition.

ISBN: 978-1-73-630311-5

DEDICATION

To my incredible daughter, Lauren, and my incredible son, Michael.

Forest fortuna adiuvat (from the Latin; good fortune favors the brave).

CONTENTS

Note: Visuals are collected together in Appendix B, rather than being interjected into the chapter contents, for ease of reading, enhanced flow, and to see the visuals altogether.

ACKNOWLEDGMENTS

I have been the beneficiary of advice and counsel by many friends, colleagues, family, investors, and many others. I want to thank everyone that has aided me throughout my career. I write from the heart and the head, having experienced first-hand what it means to have others around you that support you during the good times and the tough times.

To renowned scholar and colleague, Dr. Warren Bennis, I offer my deepest thanks and appreciation, especially for his calm and insightful wisdom and support.

To billionaire and university trustee, Mark Stevens and his generous efforts toward funding and supporting the Stevens Center for Innovation.

To Peter Drucker, William Wang, Aaron Levie, Peter Kim, Jon Kraft, Cindy Crawford, Jenny Ming, Steve Milligan, Chis Underwood, Frank Gehry, Buzz Aldrin, Steve Forbes, Bill Thompson, Dave Dillon, Alan Fuerstman, Larry Ellison, Jim Sinegal, John Sperling, Mark Stevenson, Anand Nallathambi, Thomas Barrack, Jr., and many other innovators and leaders that I have met and gained mightily from doing so.

Thanks to Ed Trainor, Kevin Anderson, James Hickey, Wendell Jones, Ken Harris, DuWayne Peterson, Mike Brown, Jim Thornton, Abhi Beniwal, Al Biland, John Nomura, Eliot Weinman, John Desmond, and many others for their unwavering support during my career.

Thanks goes to the Stanford University CodeX Center for Legal Informatics and the Stanford University Computer Science department for their generous support, and for the insightful and inspirational discussions and feedback from my many fellow colleagues there.

And most of all thanks as always to Lauren and Michael, for their ongoing support and for having seen me writing and heard much of this material during the many months involved in writing it. To their patience and willingness to listen.

CHAPTER 1

INTRODUCTION TO AI AND LAW

This book provides a series of in-depth research papers encompassing the burgeoning field of AI and the law.

These research papers are ostensibly standalone and do not require any prior familiarity with the AI and law topic. You are welcome to read the chapters in whichever order you might prefer. The chapters have been numbered and sequenced for ease of referring to the discussions and not due to any need to read one before another.

This research collection provides a helpful entry point into the scholarly field of AI and law. You will find that these papers are written in a decidedly academic style and can be somewhat initially off-putting if you are not already comfortable with such an approach. Nonetheless, slog through it and you will undoubtedly find the journey worthwhile. The chosen topics entail the latest and hottest trends in the AI and law arena.

For those of you that are potentially interested in knowing more about AI and the law, you might consider my three other books:

- *"AI and Legal Reasoning Essentials"* by Dr. Lance Eliot
- *"Artificial Intelligence and LegalTech Essentials"* by Dr. Lance Eliot
- *Decisive Essays on AI and Law"* by Dr. Lance Eliot

The first two are akin to textbook-style orientations to the AI and the law field, and the third is a collection of breezy essays. All three books are available on Amazon and at major bookseller sites.

One of the most frequent questions that I get asked during my webinars, seminars, and college courses about AI and the law consists of what the phrase "AI and the law" actually refers to.

That is a fair question and deserves a useful answer. In a moment, I will borrow from my other books to provide an explanation about the meaning of "AI and the law" and then dovetail into a brief indication about each of the research papers contained in this collection.

Per the research papers selected for this book, you'll end up seeing that there is a great deal of enthusiastic spirit for AI and the law, and likewise a sizable dollop of angst and trepidation about the intertwining of the two. In my view, whether you love it or hate it, there is no stopping the steamroller moving ahead that is going to infuse AI together with the law.

I would urge that any lawyer worth their salt ought to be learning about AI and the law. This will assuredly be especially important for those that are just now starting their legal careers, which I mention because the odds are that the convergence of AI and the law will have an especially pronounced effect throughout your lifelong legal efforts.

For those of you that might be going a more so academic route in the legal realm, rather than being a practitioner of the law per se, the beauty of AI and the law is that there is ample room for new research and a grand opportunity to make a demonstrative mark on the field.

Despite the fact that the field of AI and the law has been studied for many years, dating back to the beginning of the AI field itself, please be aware that we have only scratched the surface on this interweaving. Anyone with a desire to push the boundaries of these two realms will readily find plenty of rampways to do so.

If you are keenly interested in the possible research avenues to pursue, make sure to take a look at my book on *AI and Legal Reasoning Essentials* since it provides a solid foundation on the history, present, and future of such research activities.

AI And Law

In my viewpoint, Artificial Intelligence (AI) and the field of law are synergistic partners. The intertwining of AI and Law can generally be categorized into two major approaches:

- **AI as applied to Law**
- **Law as applied to AI**

Let us consider each of those two approaches.

AI As Applied To Law

AI as applied to law consists of trying to utilize AI technologies and AI techniques for the embodiment of law, potentially being able to perform legal tasks and undertake legal reasoning associated with the practice of law. Those scholars, experts, and practitioners that have this focus are using AI to aid or integrate artificial intelligence into how humans practice law, either augmenting lawyers and other legal professionals or possibly replacing them in the performance of various legal tasks.

Crafting such AI is especially hard to accomplish, problematic in many ways, and there have been and continue to emerge a myriad of attempts to achieve this difficult goal or aspiration. The rise of LegalTech and LawTech, which is modern digital technology used to support and enable lawyers, law offices, and the like throughout the practice of law are gradually and inexorably being bolstered by the addition of AI capabilities.

There are many indications already of this trend rapidly expanding in the existing and growing LegalTech and LawTech marketplace. Notably, the potent AI and LegalTech/LawTech combination has been drawing the rapt attention of Venture Capitalists (VCs). According to figures by the National Venture Capital Association (NVCA), the last several years have witnessed VC's making key investments of over one billion dollars towards law-related tech startups, many of which have some form of an AI capability involved.

Most of the AI developed so far for LegalTech and LawTech is only able to assist lawyers and legal professions in rather modest and simplistic ways. For example, AI might speed-up the search for documents during e-discovery or might enhance the preparation of a contract by identifying pertinent contractual language from a corpus of prior contracts.

Where the field of applying AI to law is seeking to head involves having AI that can perform legal minded tasks that human lawyers and other legal professionals perform. In essence, creating AI systems that can undertake legal reasoning. This is commonly referred to as AI for Legal Reasoning (AILR).

In a sense, legal reasoning goes to the core of performing legal tasks and is considered the ultimate pinnacle as it were for the efforts to try and apply AI to law. It is undoubtedly one of the most exciting areas of the AI-applied-to-law arena and one that holds both tremendous promise and perhaps some angst and possible somber qualms.

Law As Applied To AI

The other major approach that combines AI and law focuses on the law as applied AI. This is an equally crucial perspective on the AI and law topic.

Sometimes this is also referred to as the **Governance of AI**, though there are those that believe that to be a somewhat narrower perspective on the topic. In any case, the focus is primarily on the governance of AI and how our laws might need to be revised, updated, or revamped in light of AI systems.

You likely already know that AI is experiencing quite a resurgence and has become a key focus of the tech field, along with gaining attention throughout society. AI is being rapidly infused into a wide variety of industries and domain specialties, including AI in the financial sector, AI in the medical domain, and so on.

This rapid pace of AI adoption has opened the eyes of society about the benefits of AI but also has gradually brought to the forefront many of the costs or negative aspects that AI can bring forth. Some assert that our existing laws are insufficient to cope with the advances that AI is producing.

Thus, the need to closely examine our existing laws and possibly revamp them for an era and future of ubiquitous AI.

Expected Impacts

Let's consider how AI and the law can impact those in the AI field, and also contemplate how it can impact those in the field of law.

If you are an AI specialist, you should certainly be interested in the AI and law topic, either due to the possibilities of advancing AI by discovering how to leverage AI into the legal domain or due to the potential of how existing and future laws are going to impact the exploration and fielding of AI systems.

If you are a lawyer or legal specialist, you ought to be interested in the AI and law topic too, for the same reasons as the AI specialist, though perhaps with some added stake in the game.

What is the added stake?

If AI can ultimately become advanced enough to practice law, there is concern by some that it could potentially replace the need for human lawyers and other human legal-related law practitioners.

Some liken this to the famous and telling remark about commitment as exhibited via a chicken and a pig. A chicken and a pig are walking along and discussing what they might do together, and the chicken offers that perhaps they ought to open a restaurant that serves ham-n-eggs. Upon a moment of reflection, the pig speaks up and says that if they did so, the chicken would only be involved (making the eggs), while the pig would end-up being fully committed (being the bacon).

In that sense, AI specialists in this topic are involved, while legal specialists and lawyers are committed.

Meanwhile, for those of you squarely in the field of law, lest you think that AI specialists are to be spared the same fate of being overtaken by AI, you will be perhaps surprised to know that there are efforts underway to craft AI that makes AI, such as in the field of Machine Learning (ML), a specialty known as AutoML, which could potentially put human developers of AI out of a job.

What is good for the goose is good for the gander. Or, it might be that what is bad for the goose is equally bad for the gander.

About These Research Papers

Now that you've gotten an initial synopsis regarding the topic of AI and law, let's take a moment to briefly take a look at the research papers assembled for this incisive collection.

Chapter 1 – Introduction To AI And Law

Key briefing points about this chapter:

- This book is a collection of important research papers about AI and the law
- The papers are provided as numbered chapters (the sequence is not essential)
- AI and the law consist of two key facets
- One facet is AI as applied to the law (a mainstay of this collection)
- The other facet is applying the law to AI (i.e., governance of AI)

Chapter 2 – Framework for Autonomous Legal Reasoning

Key abstract about this chapter:

> A framework is proposed that seeks to identify and establish a set of robust autonomous levels articulating the realm of Artificial Intelligence and Legal Reasoning (AILR). Doing so provides a sound and parsimonious basis for being able to assess progress in the application of AI to the law, and can be utilized by scholars in academic pursuits of AI legal reasoning, along with being used by law practitioners and legal professionals in gauging how advances in AI are aiding the practice of law and the realization of aspirational versus achieved results. A set of seven levels of autonomy for AI and Legal Reasoning are meticulously proffered and mindfully discussed.

Chapter 3 – AI Turing Test and the Practice of Law

Key abstract about this chapter:

> Artificial Intelligence (AI) is increasingly being applied to law and a myriad of legal tasks amid attempts to bolster AI Legal Reasoning (AILR) autonomous capabilities. A major question that has generally been unaddressed involves how we will know when AILR has achieved autonomous capacities. The field of AI has grappled with similar quandaries over how to assess the attainment of Artificial General Intelligence (AGI), a persistently discussed issue among scholars since the inception of AI, with the Turing Test communally being considered as the bellwether for ascertaining such matters. This paper proposes a variant of the Turing Test that is customized for specific use in the AILR realm, including depicting how this famous gold standard of AI fulfillment can be robustly applied across the autonomous levels of AI Legal Reasoning.

Chapter 4 – Dualism of Moral Agency and AI Legal Reasoning

Key abstract about this chapter:

A neglected dualism is occurring in AI for Social Good involving the lack of encompassing both the role of artificial moral agency and artificial legal reasoning in advanced AI systems. Efforts by AI researchers and AI developers have tended to focus on how to craft and embed artificial moral agents to guide moral decision making when an AI system is operating in the field but have not also focused on and coupled the use of artificial legal reasoning capabilities, which is equally necessary for robust moral and legal outcomes. This paper addresses this problematic neglect and offers insights to overcome a substantive prevailing weakness and vulnerability.

Chapter 5 – Unauthorized Practice of Law (UPL) and AI

Key abstract about this chapter:

Advances in Artificial Intelligence (AI) and Machine Learning (ML) that are being applied to legal efforts have raised controversial questions about the existent restrictions imposed on the practice-of-law. Generally, the legal field has sought to define Authorized Practices of Law (APL) versus Unauthorized Practices of Law (UPL), though the boundaries are at times amorphous and some contend capricious and self-serving, rather than being devised holistically for the benefit of society all told. A missing ingredient in these arguments is the realization that impending legal profession disruptions due to AI can be more robustly discerned by examining the matter through the lens of a framework utilizing the autonomous levels of AI Legal Reasoning (AILR). This paper explores a newly derived instrumental grid depicting the key characteristics underlying APL and UPL as they apply to the AILR autonomous levels and offers key insights for the furtherance of these crucial practice-of-law debates.

Chapter 6 – Multidimensionality of AI Legal Singularity

Key abstract about this chapter:

> Legal scholars have in the last several years embarked upon an ongoing discussion and debate over a potential Legal Singularity that might someday occur, involving a variant or law-domain offshoot leveraged from the Artificial Intelligence (AI) realm amid its many decades of deliberations about an overarching and generalized technological singularity (referred to classically as The Singularity). This paper examines the postulated Legal Singularity and proffers that such AI and Law cogitations can be enriched by these three facets addressed herein: (1) dovetail additionally salient considerations of The Singularity into the Legal Singularity, (2) make use of an in-depth and innovative multidimensional parametric analysis of the Legal Singularity as posited in this paper, and (3) align and unify the Legal Singularity with the Levels of Autonomy (LoA) associated with AI Legal Reasoning (AILR) as propounded in this paper.

Chapter 7 – Principles of Justice and AI Legal Reasoning

Key abstract about this chapter:

> Efforts furthering the advancement of Artificial Intelligence (AI) will increasingly encompass AI Legal Reasoning (AILR) as a crucial element in the practice of law. It is argued in this research paper that the infusion of AI into existing and future legal activities and the judicial structure needs to be undertaken by mindfully observing an alignment with the core principles of justice. As such, the adoption of AI has a profound twofold possibility of either usurping the principles of justice, doing so in a Dystopian manner, and yet also capable to bolster the principles of justice, doing so in a Utopian way. By examining the principles of justice across the Levels of Autonomy (LoA) of AI Legal Reasoning, the case is made that there is an ongoing tension underlying the efforts to develop and deploy AI that can demonstrably determine the impacts and sway upon each core principle of justice and the collective set.

Chapter 8 – AI-Enabled Legal Micro-Directives

Key abstract about this chapter:

Recent research by legal scholars suggests that the law might inevitably be transformed into legal micro-directives consisting of legal rules that are derived from legal standards or that are otherwise produced automatically or via the consequent derivations of legal goals and then propagated via automation for everyday use as readily accessible lawful directives throughout society. This paper examines and extends the legal micro-directives theories in three crucial respects: (1) By indicating that legal micro-directives are likely to be AI-enabled and evolve over time in scope and velocity across the autonomous levels of AI Legal Reasoning, (2) By exploring the trade-offs between legal standards and legal rules as the imprinters of the micro-directives, and (3) By illuminating a set of brittleness exposures that can undermine legal micro-directives and proffering potential mitigating remedies to seek greater robustness in the instantiation and promulgation of such AI-powered lawful directives.

Chapter 9 – AI Legal Sentiment Analysis and Opinion Mining

Key abstract about this chapter:

An expanding field of substantive interest for the theory of the law and the practice-of-law entails Legal Sentiment Analysis and Opinion Mining (LSAOM), consisting of two often intertwined phenomena and actions underlying legal discussions and narratives: (1) Sentiment Analysis (SA) for the detection of expressed or implied sentiment about a legal matter within the context of a legal milieu, and (2) Opinion Mining (OM) for the identification and illumination of explicit or implicit opinion accompaniments immersed within legal discourse.

Efforts to undertake LSAOM have historically been performed by human hand and cognition, and only thinly aided in more recent times by the use of computer-based approaches.

> Advances in Artificial Intelligence (AI) involving especially Natural Language Processing (NLP) and Machine Learning (ML) are increasingly bolstering how automation can systematically perform either or both of Sentiment Analysis and Opinion Mining, all of which is being inexorably carried over into engagement within a legal context for improving LSAOM capabilities. This research paper examines the evolving infusion of AI into Legal Sentiment Analysis and Opinion Mining and proposes an alignment with the Levels of Autonomy (LoA) of AI Legal Reasoning (AILR), plus provides additional insights regarding AI LSAOM in its mechanizations and potential impact to the study of law and the practicing of law.

Chapter 10 – Anticipating the Fourth Era of the Law

Key abstract about this chapter:

> Legal scholars have postulated that there have been three eras of American law to-date, consisting in chronological order of the initial Age of Discovery, the Age of Faith, and then the Age of Anxiety. An open question that has received erudite attention in legal studies is what the next era, the fourth era, might consist of, and for which various proposals exist including examples such as the Age of Consent, the Age of Information, etc. There is no consensus in the literature as yet on what the fourth era is, and nor whether the fourth era has already begun or will instead emerge in the future. This paper examines the potential era-elucidating impacts amid the advent of autonomous Artificial Intelligence Legal Reasoning (AILR), entailing whether such AILR will be an element of a fourth era or a driver of a fourth, fifth, or perhaps the sixth era of American law. Also, a set of meta-characteristics about the means of identifying a legal era changeover are introduced, along with an innovative discussion of the role entailing legal formalism versus legal realism in the emergence of the American law eras.

Chapter 11 – Legal Judgment Prediction (LJP) and AI

Key abstract about this chapter:

> Legal Judgment Prediction (LJP) is a longstanding and open topic in the theory and practice-of-law. Predicting the nature and outcomes of judicial matters is abundantly warranted, keenly sought, and vigorously pursued by those within the legal industry and also by society as a whole. The tenuous act of generating judicially laden predictions has been limited in utility and exactitude, requiring further advancement. Various methods and techniques to predict legal cases and judicial actions have emerged over time, especially arising via the advent of computer-based modeling. There has been a wide range of approaches attempted, including simple calculative methods to highly sophisticated and complex statistical models. Artificial Intelligence (AI) based approaches have also been increasingly utilized. In this paper, a review of the literature encompassing Legal Judgment Prediction is undertaken, along with innovatively proposing that the advent of AI Legal Reasoning (AILR) will have a pronounced impact on how LJP is performed and its predictive accuracy. Legal Judgment Prediction is particularly examined using the Levels of Autonomy (LoA) of AI Legal Reasoning, plus, other considerations are explored including LJP probabilistic tendencies, biases handling, actor predictors, transparency, judicial reliance, legal case outcomes, and other crucial elements entailing the overarching legal judicial milieu.

Chapter 12 – AI and Legal Argumentation

Key abstract about this chapter:

Legal argumentation is a vital cornerstone of justice, underpinning an adversarial form of law, and extensive research has attempted to augment or undertake legal argumentation via the use of computer-based automation including Artificial Intelligence (AI). AI advances in Natural Language Processing (NLP) and Machine Learning (ML) have especially furthered the capabilities of leveraging AI for aiding legal professionals, doing so in ways that are modeled here as *CARE*, namely Crafting, Assessing, Refining, and Engaging in legal argumentation. In addition to AI-enabled legal argumentation serving to augment human-based lawyering, an aspirational goal of this multi-disciplinary field consists of ultimately achieving autonomously effected human-equivalent legal argumentation. As such, an innovative meta-approach is proposed to apply the Levels of Autonomy (LoA) of AI Legal Reasoning (AILR) to the maturation of AI and Legal Argumentation (AILA), proffering a new means of gauging progress in this ever-evolving and rigorously sought domain.

More About This Book

For anyone opting to use this book in a class or course that pertains to these topics, note that Appendix A contains suggestions about how to use the book in a classroom setting.

Furthermore, Appendix B contains a set of slides that depict many of the salient points made throughout the book.

In some of my prior books, I've interspersed the slides into the chapter contents, but feedback by readers has generally been that readers prefer to not have the textual flow become disrupted by the slides, and instead prefer to have the supplemental material assembled altogether into an appendix.

To make sure that you are aware of those added materials, you'll notice that the ending of each chapter provides a quick reminder about the visual depictions that are available in Appendix B.

And so, with this overall orientation to the nature and structure of this book in mind, please proceed to read the research papers and learn about the field of AI and law.

I'm truly hoping that you'll find the research papers mentally engaging and stimulative to the nature of how the law is being changed and what the future of the law might become.

Note: *For supplemental materials depicting the aspects discussed in this chapter, refer to Appendix B, which contains various augmented diagrams, charts, and additional related facets of relevance.*

CHAPTER 2

FRAMEWORK FOR AUTONOMOUS AI LEGAL REASONING

Abstract

A framework is proposed that seeks to identify and establish a set of robust autonomous levels articulating the realm of Artificial Intelligence and Legal Reasoning (AILR). Doing so provides a sound and parsimonious basis for being able to assess progress in the application of AI to the law, and can be utilized by scholars in academic pursuits of AI legal reasoning, along with being used by law practitioners and legal professionals in gauging how advances in AI are aiding the practice of law and the realization of aspirational versus achieved results. A set of seven levels of autonomy for AI and Legal Reasoning are meticulously proffered and mindfully discussed.

Section 1: Background and Context

Interest in applying Artificial Intelligence (AI) to the law has been existent since the early days of AI research [7] [15] [26] [31], having been variously attempted even during the initial formulation of computer-based AI capabilities, and continues earnestly today with ongoing efforts in a multitude of forums, including by AI development labs, by law scholars, by progressive law practices, by legal systems providers, and the like [8] [32] [45].

The field of AI and law has been populated over the years with numerous experimental systems that set new ground and inched forward progress in applying AI to the legal domain, notably TAXMAN [47], HYPO [2], CATO [6], and others [3] [54] have provided a foundation for incremental advancements. Despite these notable accomplishments, there is still much unexplored and unattained in terms of applying AI to the law. As eloquently phrased in the 1950s by Supreme Court Justice William Douglas [61]: "The law is not a series of calculating machines where answers come tumbling out when the right levers are pushed." His insightful remarks were true then and remain still true to this day.

At the core of the law is the human cognitive aspects for legal reasoning [62], and it is presumed that legal reasoning ultimately underlies all the salient acts of studying, conveying, and undertaking the practice of law [35] [36]. As such, AI as applied to the law is predominantly about the nature of legal reasoning and how this cognitive act can be undertaken by a computer-based system. Aptly stated by Ghosh [33]: "AI & Law is a subfield of AI research that focuses on designing computer programs, or computational models, that perform or simulate legal reasoning. In other words, AI & Law is the field of modeling computationally the legal reasoning for the purpose of building tools for legal practice."

1.1 Defining Automation versus Autonomy

It is customary in the legal reasoning context to divide the use of AI and computer-based systems into two focuses, one being the application of *automation* to the act of legal reasoning, which primarily then serves as an adjunct or augmentation to human legal reasoning efforts, and the other being the goal of achieving *autonomous* legal reasoning that consists of computer-based systems able to perform legal reasoning unaided by human legal reasoners and that can operate autonomously with respect to the practice of law. As per Galdon [30]: "Automation is defined as a system with a limited set of pre-programmed supervised tasks on behalf of the user. Autonomy, on the other hand, is defined as a technology designed to carry out a user's goals without supervision with the capability of learning and changing over time."

Law practices and legal professionals routinely today make use of *automation* in the performance of their needed tasks involving legal activities. A modern-day law office might use e-Discovery software as part of their case discovery pursuits and be perhaps crafting new contracts via the use of an online cloud-based service that pieces together prior contracts from a corpus established to enable reuse. Generally, the appropriate adoption of law-related computer-based systems has significantly aided lawyers and legal staff in undertaking their efforts, oftentimes cited as boosting efficiency and effectiveness accordingly. The automation being used for these purposes is not considered autonomous as yet, though advancements in these systems are being fostered by infusing AI capabilities to someday achieve autonomous operation.

A significant body of research exists on attempts to clarify what autonomy or autonomous operations consist of [42] [43]. There is much debate regarding the particulars of autonomy and different viewpoints ascribe differing qualities to the matter.

For example, Sifakis [60] defines that "autonomy is the capacity of an agent to achieve a set of coordinated goals by its own means (without human intervention) adapting to environment variations. It combines five complementary aspects: Perception e.g. interpretation of stimuli, removing ambiguity/vagueness from complex input data and determining relevant information; Reflection e.g. building/updating a faithful environment run-time model; Goal management e.g. choosing among possible goals the most appropriate ones for a given configuration of the environment model; Planning to achieve chosen goals; Self-adaptation e.g. the ability to adjust behavior through learning and reasoning and to change dynamically the goal management and planning processes."

Rather than weighing in herein on trying to pinpoint what autonomy entails per se, it is sufficient for the purposes of this discussion to consider that an *autonomous* computer-based system in this context would be one that can perform legal reasoning on its own, doing so without the aid of a human, and essentially perform legal reasoning that is on par with that of a human versed in legal reasoning [25] [26] [28].

Furthermore, it is prudent to refrain from discussing herein any indication about the AI techniques and technologies that might be required or employed to autonomously undertake the legal reasoning task, since doing so would tend to muddle the matter of concern. In essence, AI techniques and technologies are in a continual state of flux, being adjusted, refined, and at times formed a new, and the discussion herein might inadvertently get mired in AI that is known today but that might very well be improved or advanced tomorrow.

An exemplar would be the case of today's versions of Machine Learning (ML), and that Sifakis [60] emphasizes: "A main conclusion is that autonomy should be associated with functionality and not with specific techniques. Machine learning is essential for removing ambiguity from complex stimuli and coping with uncertainty of unpredictable environments. Nonetheless, it can be used to meet only a small portion of the needs implied by autonomous system design."

1.2 Establishing the Framework

The purpose of this paper is to identify and establish a set of automation and autonomous levels that can be applied to the law and therefore would articulate a framework for aiding and bolstering the realm of Artificial Intelligence (AI) and Legal Reasoning (AILR). There does not exist today an established taxonomy or framework that provides a set of autonomous levels for AILR [13] [26] [51].

This crucial point comes as a surprise to some that assumed or presumed that such a framework already existed. The lack of an established framework could be argued as an omission that has at times allowed for specious claims about what AI systems can do in the case of AILR and permitted misleading and at times outright false assertions by vendors or others, of which will likely inexorably further worsen as AI is increasingly infused into computer-based legal systems into the future.

Consider then these bases for justifying the formulation and promulgation of a bona fide set of autonomous levels for instituting a viable apples-to-apples depiction of the act of practicing law and the embodiment of AI-powered legal reasoning:

- Vendor offerings could be rated as to what level of automation or autonomy their wares truly provide, overcoming vacuous and otherwise unsubstantiated claims, allowing for easier and fair game comparisons.

- Law practices seeking to acquire or make use of legal systems would readily have the means to gauge what capabilities the automation or autonomy provides in those systems, and knowingly ascertain what they are getting and how to best implement such systems in their practices.

- Lawyers would be better informed as to the capabilities of AI-enabled legal systems, along with being able to assess the progress of automation that might serve either as an augmentation to their efforts or could potentially be an autonomous replacement for their efforts.

- Researchers and scholars would be able to ascertain what progress is being made in applying AI to the law, showcasing aspects that require further research and advancement and rely upon a validated framework as a barometer measuring the totality of the state of AILR.

- And so on.

In recap, there seems ample rationalization for putting in place an acknowledged and practical set of autonomous levels for AILR that would, therefore, provide a sound and robust basis for being able to assess progress in the application of AI to the law.

Accordingly, a framework consisting of a set of seven levels of autonomy for AI Legal Reasoning is proffered in this paper, accompanied by a carefully elucidated explanation that explicitly states the foundations used to formulate the framework. By including essential underpinnings, it is hoped that readers will be thusly cognizant of why the structure is shaped as so proposed (else it might seem haphazard or enigmatic as to the basis employed) and will also ensure a kind of open access for those that desire to refine or otherwise augment the draft framework.

Section 2: Levels of Autonomy (LoA) Approaches

The notion of crafting a set of Levels of Autonomy (LoA) is not unheard of, indeed, there have been many earnest attempts and equally varied outcomes that have occurred over time to derive LoA's, as will be briefly examined next.

One perspective is that a generic LoA should be formulated and then applied "as is" to any domain seeking to embrace a set of levels of autonomous operations within that specific realm. Others argue that each domain dictates a tailored assessment of what an appropriate LoA ought to look like to adequately meet the needs of that sphere or discipline, and thus by implication that a wholly brand-new set of LoA should be handcrafted for that particular milieu. A modicum of middle ground consists of taking a prior LoA, even one that might already be grounded in a specific domain, and mindfully adapting the LoA to a new area or as yet unspecified domain.

In short, the varied approaches seem to consist of:

- Seek a generic LoA and apply it to a target domain Y, or
- Take a generic LoA, adjust and reshape it, then fit the result to a target domain Y, or
- Start entirely fresh for a target domain Y and create an LoA from scratch for it, or
- Reuse a domain-specific LoA of X, and transform as warranted to apply to a different domain Y

In theory, whichever path is undertaken does not especially matter, as long as the final result is an appropriate LoA for the target domain of interest. Though that declaration seems perhaps obvious, the concerns oft-expressed are that the starting point can potentially adversely influence the ending point, such that there is a heightened chance of infusing ill-advised or unwelcomed artifacts into an LoA that otherwise via taking an alternative approach would not have been inadvertently enmeshed. This precautionary warning is properly taken for this proposed framework.

In devising a framework of LoA for the law domain and AILR, let's consider this to be the domain Y, a reuse of salient prior efforts has been undertaken for this framework and thusly benefits from lessons gleaned by those prior accomplishments, doing so with a viewpoint of averting being tainted by such precedents. To a great extent, the reuse of a prior domain-specific LoA is extensively relied upon, aptly justified by its widely accepted use and acclaim as a "gold standard" for LoA's, namely the Society for Automotive Engineers (SAE) J3016 *Taxonomy and Definitions for Terms Related to Driving Automation Systems for On-Road Motor Vehicles* [58], which is known globally and accepted worldwide as a standard LoA for Autonomous Vehicles (AVs) and especially self-driving cars [22] [24].

Consider some key facets of the SAE LoA, which posits these six levels of autonomy [58]:

- Level 0: No Driving Automation
- Level 1: Driver Assistance
- Level 2: Partial Driving Automation
- Level 3: Conditional Driving Automation
- Level 4: High Driving Automation
- Level 5: Full Driving Automation

Some notable aspects that will be further addressed in the next section of this paper encompass that the numbering scheme ranges from a low-to-high indication, the numbering starts with zero, there are six designated levels, the naming of the levels is intended to approximately reflect succinctly the nature of the levels, and each level per the details of the standard is considered separate and distinct from the other levels (we will momentarily return to further inspection of this SAE standard). It is worth noting that core guiding principles were underlying the formulation of the SAE standard, stated as [58]:

"1. Be descriptive and informative rather than normative.
2. Provide functional definitions.
3. Be consistent with current industry practice.
4. Be consistent with prior art to the extent practicable.
5. Be useful across disciplines, including engineering, law, media, public discourse.
6. Be clear and cogent and, as such, it should avoid or define ambiguous terms."

Note that the fifth guiding principle mentions that the SAE standard was intended to be used across disciplines, including the law domain. As such, this framework explicitly leverages the SAE standard and does so with appreciation that those having formulated the SAE standard had the forethought to anticipate the added value of their LoA being reused accordingly, avoiding the need to perhaps reinvent the wheel, as it were.

As an example of an effort at reusing the SAE LoA, consider this indication by Yang et al [69] in the context of creating an LoA for the domain of medical robots: "The regulatory, ethical, and legal barriers imposed on medical robots necessitate careful consideration of different levels of autonomy, as well as the context for use. For autonomous vehicles, levels of automation for on-road vehicles are defined, yet no such definitions exist for medical robots. To stimulate discussions, we propose six levels of autonomy for medical robotics as one possible framework."

Here are the six levels that were postulated [69]:

"Level 0: No Autonomy

This level includes tele-operated robots or prosthetic devices that respond to and follow the user's command.

Level 1: Robot Assistance

The robot provides some mechanical guidance or assistance during a task while the human has continuous control of the system

Level 2: Task Autonomy

The robot is autonomous for specific tasks initiated by a human.

Level 3: Conditional Autonomy

A system generates task strategies but relies on the human to select from among different strategies or to approve an autonomously selected strategy.

Level 4: High Autonomy

The robot can make medical decisions but under the supervision of a qualified doctor

Level 5: Full Autonomy

This is a "robotic surgeon" that can perform an entire surgery."

Yet another example consists of efforts by Galdon et al [30] in the use case of Virtual Assistants:

Level 1: No Autonomy
Level 2: Assistance
Level 3: Partial Autonomy
Level 4: Conditional Autonomy
Level 5: Relational Autonomy
Level 6: High Autonomy
Level 7: Full Autonomy

Parasuraman et al [53] had before the SAE standard sought to indicate a generic LoA, consisting of these ten levels:

1. The computer offers no assistance, human must take all decision and actions
2. The computer offers a complete set of decision/action alternatives
3. Narrows the selection down to a few
4. Suggests one alternative
5. Executes that suggestion if the human approves
6. Allows the human a restricted time to veto before automatic execution
7. Exercise automatically, then necessarily informs the human
8. Informs the human only if asked
9. Informs the human only if it, the computer, decides to
10. The computer decides everything, acts autonomously, ignoring the human

As generally might be evident, by-and-large, the number of autonomous levels is usually in the five to ten range, and the preponderance of the approaches conforms to a low-to-high convention. An important feature of the SAE standard that might not be immediately apparent is the concept of an Operational Design Domain (ODD). An ODD is defined by the SAE standard as this [58]: "Operating conditions under which a given driving automation system or feature thereof is specifically designed to function, including, but not limited to, environmental, geographical, and time-of-day restrictions, and/or the requisite presence or absence of certain traffic or roadway characteristics."

The significance of this crucial concept is that it allows for a subdividing of a domain into those portions that might be amenable to autonomous capabilities or that sooner might be amenable. Without such a proviso, it would tend to hamstring a set of levels in an LoA to require that either autonomy is entirely and completely the case at a given level or it is not at all at that level. This kind of take-it-or-leave-it conundrum was a stumbling block to the acceptability of some other LoA's and represented a subtle but vital form of progression in the formulation of an LoA.

The ODD concept will be instrumental into providing a similar benefit for the LoA of this proposed framework, as will be discussed in the next section.

Briefly, here are the SAE standard levels with an indication of their short-form definitional aspects, notably focused on the driving task (referred to as the DDT or Dynamic Driving Task), incorporating an Automated Driving System (ADS), and expected to provide an OEDR (Object and Event Detection and Response) [58]:

- Level 0: No Driving Automation

"The performance by the driver of the entire DDT, even when enhanced by active safety systems."

- Level 1: Driver Assistance

"The sustained and ODD-specific execution by a driving automation system of either the lateral or the longitudinal vehicle motion control subtask of the DDT (but not both simultaneously) with the expectation that the driver performs the remainder of the DDT."

- Level 2: Partial Driving Automation

"The sustained and ODD-specific execution by a driving automation system of both the lateral and longitudinal vehicle motion control subtasks of the DDT with the expectation that the driver completes the OEDR subtask and supervises the driving automation system."

- Level 3: Conditional Driving Automation

"The sustained and ODD-specific performance by an ADS of the entire DDT with the expectation that the DDT fallback-ready user is receptive to ADS-issued requests to intervene, as well as to DDT performance-relevant system failures in other vehicle systems, and will respond appropriately."

- Level 4: High Driving Automation

"The sustained and ODD-specific performance by an ADS of the entire DDT and DDT fallback, without any expectation that a user will respond to a request to intervene."

- Level 5: Full Driving Automation

"The sustained and unconditional (i.e., not ODD-specific) performance by an ADS of the entire DDT and DDT fallback without any expectation that a user will respond to a request to intervene."

For further details about the SAE standard, including its various limitations and weaknesses, see the in-depth analysis of Eliot [22]. Salient aspects of the SAE standard, considered a specific-domain LoA, will be reused and transformed for purposes of devising the LoA for AILR, as will be indicated in the next sections.

One additional aspect to be covered briefly, particularly when discussing an LoA for the law, entails whether it might be feasible to reuse an existent accepted overarching ontology of the law. Thus, just as reusing an LoA offers merits, so too would reusing an overarching ontology of the law. For clarification, the meaning of ontology in this context is as per Neches et al [52]: "An ontology defines the basic terms and relations comprising the vocabulary of a topic area as well as the rules for combining terms and relations to define extensions to the vocabulary."

As legal scholars are aware, there is not a single unified ontology of the law, though many efforts have been undertaken to form such a taxonomy. For a detailed explanation of ontologies associated with the law, including their strengths and limitations, see [26] [56] [57] [65].

Section 3: Foundation for LoA Framework Robustness

In this section, a discussion about the key characteristics that are advisably used when creating a set of autonomy levels is undertaken and includes an examination of how those factors are salient to be used in devising a set of levels of autonomy in the matter of AI Legal Reasoning.

3.1 Key Characteristics

When defining levels of autonomy, there is a multitude of factors that should be employed, doing so to systematically arrive at a parsimonious set that is logically sound and inherently robust. Any notable facets that are omitted or skirted, whether inadvertently or by intent, could undermine the veracity of the definition and thus weaken or entirely vacate the utility of the resulting taxonomy.

Utilized here is a bounded set of ten specific characteristics that are significant overall, and for which have been contributory in deriving the levels of autonomy for AI Legal Reasoning. Note that each such characteristic is valuable on its own merits and the listing of them in a numbered or sequenced fashion is not done to showcase priority or ranking, and instead merely showcased for ease of reference.

Those ten key characteristics are:

1. Scope
2. Sufficiency of Reason
3. Completeness
4. Applicability
5. Usefulness
6. Understandability
7. Foolproofness
8. Observe Occam's Razor
9. Differentiable
10. Logical Progression

3.1.1 Scope

Scope is a crucial factor since the nature of the underlying act or tasks that are being subject to autonomous operation must be relatively well-stated and apparent to those that seek to rely upon or apply a framework embodying levels of autonomy.

Here, the scope consists of all forms of legal reasoning. This is readily stated but certainly less amenable to being entirely articulated.

Some have argued for example that legal reasoning is essentially that which lawyers do, and therefore the presumed scope would be those acts or effort for which attorneys undertake [9] [10]. But this raises the question of whether an attorney that is say calculating the number of billable hours on a legal case is performing a legal reasoning task, which on the surface does not seem so, and yet falls within the broad interpretation of suggesting that legal reasoning is scoped as that which lawyers are apt to perform.

One remedy would seem to be the addition of a qualifier that legal reasoning is that which lawyers do *when it comes to the practice of law.* This aspect is illuminated via the ABA model definition of the practice of law [68]: "The 'practice of law' is the application of legal principles and judgment with regard to the circumstances or objectives of a person that require the knowledge and skill of a person trained in the law."

Though seemingly somewhat self-referential and thus a bit unclear, the ABA model is further clarified by its attempt to specify the acts or tasks involved in the practice of law, consisting of these four stipulations [68]: "(1) Giving advice or counsel to persons as to their legal rights or responsibilities or to those of others; (2) Selecting, drafting, or completing legal documents or agreements that affect the legal rights of person; (3) Representing a person before an adjudicative body, including, but not limited to, preparing or filing documents or conducting discovery; or (4) Negotiating legal rights or responsibilities on behalf of a person."

For the moment, assume that this provides a general semblance of the scope as it applies to the legal reasoning undertaken by those that formally practice the law as attorneys.

There is still the matter of legal reasoning as utilized by others, including for example judges, which herein is assumed to also be within the scope of these levels of autonomy.

Plus, there is the notion of legal reasoning as used by juries.

Some argue fervently that jurors are not an instance of bona fide legal reasoning per se, apparently being something else instead, perhaps exercising solely common-sense reasoning and not considered equated to the domain-specific elements of legal reasoning [63]. Nonetheless, one can easily argue that there is some form of legal reasoning being relied upon by jurors, regardless of any lack of training in the law or being certified in the law, and therefore it would seem fallacious to excise jurors as legal reasoners altogether.

This discussion raises too the fluency and fluidity properties underlying legal reasoning. A juror might not be entirely fluent in the law and can only muster say a small percentage of their reasoning as being within the realm of legal reasoning when acting in their juror capacity. Does a minimal composition of the harking of legal reasoning somehow play into whether legal reasoning is being deployed, or will any amount, even if infinitesimal, be considered as substantive to being encompassed within the legal reasoning captive?

Such arduous and contentious questions are covered in other versed discussions [46] [50] [61] [66] and are too lengthy to try and settle herein, thus let's proceed to stipulate that any smattering of legal reasoning, regardless of in-the-small or in-the-large, ultimately is considered within the confines of the levels of autonomy for legal reasoning for purposes of the framework being outlined in this paper.

3.1.2 Sufficiency of Reason

Sufficiency of reason is a factor entailing whether the levels of autonomy can abide by the Leibniz-like notion of modus ponens inference, generally meaning that each of the asserted levels must have a sufficient explanation for why it is said to be needed or occur.

Any level that does not have adequate justification or rationale would seem unneeded and therefore has no rightful place in the set of levels.

3.1.3 Completeness

Completeness is a factor that necessitates assuring that the levels of autonomy can provide a totality of coverage over the realm being subsumed.

If the set of levels does not adequately encompass the scope, this means that the autonomy description is unable to express a fullness of coverage and will suffer accordingly, i.e., by leaving out portions or failing to cope with all that which needs to be specified. The autonomy levels need to embody the entirety of the scope and not have any omitted or overlooked aspects.

That being said, it is equally crucial and certainly preferential to not overshoot the scope and thus by design or by an ill-devised scheme draw into the levels of autonomy those matters that are not in the realm of that which is at hand.

3.1.4 Applicability

Applicability refers to an assurance that the levels of autonomy are applicable or practical in their application. If a set of levels of autonomy are exclusively abstract and unable to be applied, they would seem less valuable than otherwise might be the case. Though such a set might be handy for scholarly pursuits and conceptual analyses, it is argued here that the levels of autonomy have to also be seen as and must readily be able to be applied to that which is considered usable in the real world.

In this case, herein, the levels of autonomy need to be applicable to the day-and-day matters of legal reasoning and be similarly applicable to the broader acts of conceptualizing legal matters too that might arise in academic pursuits regarding the law and legal reasoning.

3.1.5 Usefulness

Usefulness is an additive on top of the factor that the levels of autonomy need to be applicable and augments that the set also needs to be useful in its application.

In other words, it might be possible to apply something, and yet it in the end provides little utility in doing so. The consideration here is that the levels must also rise to the occasion and provide usefulness that is part-and-parcel of their existence.

For example, in the case of AI Legal Reasoning, given the existing confusion and confounding state of affairs regarding what vendor offerings provide in the way of computer-based legal reasoning capacities, a set of levels of autonomy could aid in clarifying such matters and therefore serve a quite useful purpose.

Likewise, for those scholars striving to devise advances in AI Legal Reasoning, a set of levels of autonomy that is useful would provide guidance as to where the state-of-the-art presently resides and where the future direction of new efforts can potentially aim.

3.1.6 Understandability

Understandability is the nature of how readily comprehended or conveyed the levels of autonomy are.

If the levels are arcane or obtuse, the eventual applicability and usefulness are most likely undermined. In turn, this suggests that the levels of autonomy would not gain awareness and nor take hold as a viable means of defining autonomous operations.

That being said, some might argue that there is not a need for a set of autonomy levels to be popular and that undue admiration toward seeking popularity might water down or subvert a rigorous approach. In one sense, those kinds of arguments can be a false portrayal of a misleadingly alluded to mutually exclusive condition. The implication is that rigor can only exist when there is not popularity, while that which is popular cannot somehow include rigor. This presumption needs to be rejected. Instead, the merits of the set of levels of autonomy can be assessed on both its semblance of rigor and its semblance of popularity, both of which can very well co-exist, and perhaps more so if the levels of autonomy are particularly well-designed accordingly (rather than by happenstance).

3.1.7 Foolproofness

Foolproofness is a factor that attempts to indicate whether the levels of autonomy can be too readily distorted or twisted to accommodate those that might wish to subvert the set, or in the counter, whether the levels are strongly devised to reduce the ease of subversions.

This is a fundamental recognition that there will be those that wish to misuse the levels for purposes of making claims beyond which they should not be allowed to do. Certainly, such claims are going to be made, no matter how foolproof the structure might be, nonetheless, the notion is to try and anticipate such untoward efforts and prevent or at least diminish the ease of enabling those saboteurs from doing so.

For example, someone claiming to have an AI legal reasoning system at level Z, while in fact only a level less than Z has been achieved, ought to have hurdles or other barriers that make such a claim readily shown to be false and inappropriate. This capacity can then be handy for revealing those that are making false claims and would undoubtedly be instrumental in aiding those that sincerely are desirous of abiding by the set and not accidentally misjudge the nature of the levels.

3.1.8 Observe Occam's Razor

As William of Ockham succinctly stated [67], "plurality should not be posited without necessity," which has become widely known as Occam's razor. In short, everything else being equal, the simpler of two competing approaches ought to weigh toward the favor of that which is the simpler and thus accordingly cast into disfavor that which is not so.

The set of levels of autonomy should be held to the test that it proffers the simplest possible rendering, without loss of other factors, and that anything that is otherwise overcomplicated should be further reduced into simplicity if at all feasible.

As an example, if a set of levels of autonomy were initially devised to be twenty such levels, and if there was a means to reduce the set to say ten, doing so without losing or undermining the set, there would be a preference toward the set of ten in lieu of the larger set of twenty, under the belief that the set of ten is the simpler of the two competing approaches (everything else being equal).

Of course, it is crucial to not blindly seek Occam's razor and neglect to uphold the key premise that everything else being equal overrides the simplicity goal. Sometimes there is an inadvertent race to the bottom, as it were, failing to realize that along the way there has been a substantive loss in other merits of the structure.

3.1.9 Differentiable

Differentiable is a factor that involves the clarity of separation or distinction between the levels of autonomy that are being stated.

Suppose there was a level M and a separate level O in a given defined set of levels of autonomy. If there was no ready means to differentiate between level M and level O, this would suggest that there is truly no need for two such levels and they could be consolidated into one level (this abides by the Occam's razor).

Indeed, if the set is allowed to exist with the two separate levels, M and O, yet they are indistinguishable from each other, it would indubitably create confusion as to whether a claimant is rightfully using level M or rightfully using level O, which presumably they could use either one as they so wish, but this then decreases the efficacy of the levels.

Each level ought to stand on its own, separately and distinctly, and not be readily muddled into another level.

3.1.10 Logical Progression

Logical progression is perhaps one of the most controversial of these ten factors and entails the supposition that the levels of autonomy should have a preponderance toward a progression or advancement of autonomous capacities.

Suppose that we had a set of autonomous levels that consisted of ten levels. Presumably, the ten levels could be scrambled and placed into any order one might so wish. They essentially could be randomly arrayed.

But this would seem to undercut several of the other factors already mentioned herein, such that if there was a means to sequence or order the levels, it might make the set more readily useful, applicable, etc. This does not imply that a force fit is appropriate, and a false or forced effort to arrange the levels is little better than a random arrangement, one would so argue (perhaps worse so).

It would be preferential to have the levels of autonomy arranged into a logical profession, making the set easier to assimilate and apply.

This might be arrayed from low to high, or from high to low, and does not materially make a difference, though it can be said that prior sets of autonomy have typically gone from low to high, establishing a kind of default approach that is more likely to resonate for any subsequent sets of autonomy.

On an allied aspect, there is also the matter of whether to number the levels or assign them letters of the alphabet or use some other means to designate that the levels are an ordered set and range from low to high or from high to low. Providing an indicator of their respective positioning is abundantly helpful as an aid in referring to the various levels. A preference herein is given to the use of numbering, though one could make use of some other method if so desired.

Part of the handiness of numbering is that we already arithmetically accept and immediately comprehend that numbers illustrate a progression. There is little cognitive effort in making that kind of mental leap and tends to make the set more intelligible and easier to refer to.

When using numbers, the question seems to arise repeatedly about the use of the number zero. In essence, some dislike the use of a zero within the levels of autonomy and suggest it is an artifact of those that are computer-versed that they oft include the number zero (a bits and bytes mindset, as it were), whereas presumably, it is customary that people start usually a counting sequence with the number one, rather than starting at the number zero.

On the other hand, it can be argued that the use of zero is intuitively useful since if it is used to denote that there is no semblance of autonomy, and those that use the set will readily grasp why the set starts with the number zero. This matter about the use of zero might seem like a mundane debate and unworthy of consideration, but do not downplay the significance of how important the numbering can become. By-and-large, most sets of autonomy become known by their numbering scheme, even more so than any naming or descriptor that is associated with each of the levels.

Another seemingly debated topic is whether the levels should have numbers-only or whether they should have names or descriptors only. Again, this seems to be a false dichotomy. Nothing is preventing the use of both numbers and a name or descriptor, and indeed this is generally customary as an approach, and suitable too as it provides the convenience and shortcut use of a number to denote a level, along with allowing for a name or descriptor that can provide more substance.

The naming or descriptor has to also be carefully worded and be mindfully expressed. If the words used to name or describe a level are inexpressive, they can undermine the entire set and also create confusion over the significance of the numbering scheme being used. Thus, the wording should succinctly designate the overarching significance of the level, using as few words as possible, and the right words, and not use overloaded words or be superfluous in the wording.

One additional concern has to do with the logical progression and whether the stepwise movement from one level to the next is somehow a simple linear movement. The problem with numbers is that we typically think of the number 2 as simply one more than the number 1, and the number 3 to be simply two more than the number 1, and so on. This causes difficulty in expressing for example the magnitude of earthquakes, which the famous Richter scale attempts to do, and for which the numbers though seemingly progressing one at a time represent a much larger magnitude in jumps.

Some would assert that the numbering ought to convey magnitudes of degree or change when it is so built-in to the levels, and therefore that perhaps instead of numbering 1, 2, 3, 4, and so on, the numbering should be something like 1, 20, 100, etc., attempting to immediately illustrate the magnitude differences. Unfortunately, this attempt at overcoming one facet then introduces other problems, such as the difficulty of people remembering what the numbers of the levels are and tends to undermine their use accordingly. As such, the convention seems to be that the use of ordinary counting numbers is easiest to be conveyed and be remembered, and meanwhile, there should be an ongoing effort to try and communicate that the levels are of increasing orders of magnitude.

Section 4: Autonomous Levels of AI Legal Reasoning

In this section, a proposed framework for the autonomous levels of AI legal reasoning is depicted. In addition to the depiction, there is also an indication of how the devised autonomous levels conform to the key characteristics discussed in the prior section, providing a rationale for understanding the basis of the formulated levels and what they portend to provide.

The proposed levels are as follows:

Level 0: No Automation for AI Legal Reasoning

Level 1: Simple Assistance Automation for AI Legal Reasoning

Level 2: Advanced Assistance Automation for AI Legal Reasoning

Level 3: Semi-Autonomous Automation for AI Legal Reasoning

Level 4: Domain Autonomous for AI Legal Reasoning

Level 5: Fully Autonomous for AI Legal Reasoning

Level 6: Superhuman Autonomous for AI Legal Reasoning

4.1 Background and Rationale

A fundamental question involves how many levels ought to be used for adequately depicting the levels of autonomy of AI Legal Reasoning.

We can begin by first stating the seemingly obvious, namely that there would certainly seem to be at least two such levels, namely a level of which there is no legal reasoning and a second level in which there is in fact some amount of legal reasoning. In that sense, the minimum set would be at two levels.

It is possible to try and argue that there only needs to be one level and that the absence of autonomy for legal reasoning is implied, but this seems somewhat disingenuous as an assertion and preferably better handled explicitly rather than by implicit default or base assumption.

Beyond the core of the two foundational levels, the second level consisting of the legal reasoning of some amount could readily be argued as worthy of further subdivision. Furthermore, if the full set is to be considered complete, it would seem logical to suggest that there should be a topmost level. In that way of thinking, the levels now should be a set of three, consisting of a level of no legal reasoning, a level of some amount of legal reasoning, and a third or uppermost level of full legal reasoning or a pinnacle level.

This then arrives at a minimum set of three levels. Are there are more levels needed? Abiding by the earlier desire to observe Occam's razor, any additional levels would need to be carefully and thoughtfully proffered, assuming that three levels alone might be accommodating to the matter. Simplicity is the watchword.

One especially salient aspect that has arisen in the AI field is whether there will be the chance that AI will surpass human intelligence and proceed into some form of superhuman intelligence level [23] [28]. Though this is certainly debatable, it would seem prudent to prepare the levels of autonomy for such a possibility, regardless of whether it might be viable in the near-term or not, and thus be prepared for the long-term in case the superhuman facets materialize.

In that case, it would be prudent to add a fourth level, a superhuman level of autonomy to the set of AI legal reasoning levels. As might be evident, this now suggests that the minimum set of levels is four.

One quick aside is that some might have qualms over this kind of logical bottoms-up construction of the levels and want to declare summarily that the levels are the levels, meaning that a top-down approach should be utilized instead. This presumably implies that we can merely inspect the legal reasoning realm and will somehow naturally divine the appropriate number of levels. It will accountably appear by the act of inspection alone.

This top-down perspective as a starting point is worthy of consideration, though if the bottoms-up method arrives at ultimately the same set, it would seem to not make any substantive of a difference as to how the set was arrived at. Whichever approach is undertaken, the other approach would be a helpful double-check. If one wants to try and make the case that one approach is more intrinsically advantageous or quicker to the answer being sought, that's fine, though it does not materially impact the result and indeed should have no effect whatsoever.

With four levels now in hand, once again the question arises as to whether this is sufficient, complete, understandable, applicable, and so on. Let's consider these facets.

One of the greatest downsides of any set of levels of autonomy is the confluence of everyday *automation* with the kind of automation intended via the use of AI. The very act of saying that there is a level of autonomy does tend to imply that *autonomous* effort is present, and regrettably introduces confusion and the potential for untoward uses of the set.

It is helpful for the factors of at least understandability and applicability to try and separate the levels containing autonomy from those that do not. In that sense, we now need five levels, namely one with no automation, one with everyday automation, one with autonomy at some level, one with full autonomy equivalent to human intelligence, and one at a superhuman level.

This aids in abiding by the factors, but then opens the question about the possible subdivisions within the notion of everyday automation. As advances are made in non-AI automation, it would seem unruly to cast all such automation as essentially being the same. As such, it would be prudent to add a level to allow for stipulating a simple variant of everyday automation and an additional level for more advanced automation.

For those levels that are lacking in AI autonomous capacities, the assumption is that the automation will be assistive rather than performing autonomously, which makes definitional sense herein. In that vein, the naming or descriptor for those levels should be careful in not conflating the notion of *automation* versus the notion of *autonomy*.

In the case of full autonomy, the requirement of AI to achieve full autonomy is undeniably aspirational in this context. To aid in the levels providing coverage for that which is less than full autonomy, we will add another level. This additional level will allow for domain-specific AI legal reasoning instantiations, similar to the earlier discussed ODDs in the case of AV's.

Finally, there is the situation of AI that is semi-autonomous. Some would argue, at times persuasively, that there should not be a level or category known as semi-autonomous. The argument goes that this is a slippery middle ground and lends itself to being misused. A viewpoint taken is that something is either autonomous or it is not and trying to split hairs by including a semi-autonomous grouping is perilous and unsettling.

Those are valued words of caution. Nonetheless, in a practical sense, there is a gray area into which there is some amount of AI that goes beyond ordinary automation, and then there is more robust AI that takes the realm into the autonomous sphere. Somehow, the gray area needs to be included and not omitted.

Thus, though freely acknowledging the potential drawbacks, it seems more so beneficial to include a semi-autonomous category than to exclude it.

This brings up an allied topic which is that there will inexorably over time be a shift of what we all accept as ordinary automation versus that which is considered AI. In that way, any set of levels of autonomy might very well need to be refined and adjusted, though that will play out over a lengthy period and does not negate or undermine the value of the levels at a point in time.

All told, based on the foregoing, these again are the proposed levels:

Level 0: No Automation for AI Legal Reasoning

Level 1: Simple Assistance Automation for AI Legal Reasoning

Level 2: Advanced Assistance Automation for AI Legal Reasoning

Level 3: Semi-Autonomous Automation for AI Legal Reasoning

Level 4: Domain Autonomous for AI Legal Reasoning

Level 5: Fully Autonomous for AI Legal Reasoning

Level 6: Superhuman Autonomous for AI Legal Reasoning

4.2 Explanation of the Levels

There are seven levels in the proposed framework.

In the matter of whether this is possibly excessive, and a lesser number of levels might be more readily grasped, the aspect that the levels are at the count of seven is in conformance with the well-known so-called magical number 7 and plus-or-minus 2, a longstanding classic rule-of-thumb established in research on human psychology by Miller [48]. Also, each of the levels is justifiable on a standalone basis and the levels are progressively arranged in a logical order from low to high in terms of autonomous capabilities, thus proffering a relatively easily understood structure.

It could be argued that there is a somewhat natural flow and coherence to the devised levels and that it abides by the "Goldilocks principle" of just the right number of levels, none less so and none more so.

As an aside, it is acknowledged that one minor problem associated with starting the autonomous levels numbering at the number zero is that it inadvertently creates some potential confusion over how many levels there are. With similar such numbering, it is easy for many to simply look at the highest number of the levels, in this case, the number six, and assume therefore that there are only six levels. This is a recurring aggravation and source of some mild disorientation for other instances of the use of zero as a starting point. In any case, it can be argued that the use of level zero is still of merit and those that misquote or misstate the number of levels are doing so by lack of awareness, plus it does not necessarily hamper or undermine the set, other than at times sparking modest confusion about how many levels there are in the set.

In terms of the levels, Level 0 is the special case of no automation, meaning that there is no notable automation involved in undertaking AI and legal reasoning.

The basis for stating that there is no notable automation stems from a debate over whether say a fax machine used in transmitting legal documents fits into Level 0 or would fit into Level 1. Strictly speaking, since a fax machine could be envisioned as a form of automation, it would seemingly belong in Level 1, though others contend that a fax machine does not rise to the notion of automation and should, therefore, be cast into Level 0. This overarching question about the boundaries and assessing fit for clarity is addressed in the respective subsections.

Level 1 and Level 2 entail automation of an ordinary manner that would be hard-pressed to be described as AI capabilities, while Level 3 is the in-between state of automation that is approaching AI-like capacities, yet still not within the realm of autonomy.

Level 4 is the first of the designated autonomous levels and consists of allowed-for constraints upon the range or scope of the autonomy, indicating that within a specified subdomain of law the AI legal reasoning can operate autonomously. Level 5 is considered full autonomy in terms of AI legal reasoning across all domains of the law and encompassing an entirely autonomous operation. Level 6 is the superhuman autonomous level of the law as undertaken by AI legal reasoning, and for which it is unknown if any such autonomous capability will ever be achieved but has nonetheless been included for completeness' sake.

See Figure 1 and Figure 2 for a summary chart depicting the autonomous levels of AI Legal Reasoning.

Figure 1 indicates via rows of the chart the successive levels of the framework and then depicts the main name or descriptor, followed by an exemplar short set, and then a brief indication of the automation capacity that is then followed by the latest status. The latest status column will naturally change over time in terms of its contents (due to advancements in technology and usage), while the other columns will remain static and are deemed definitional and unchanging thereof.

Figure 2 is similar to Figure 1, though showcases the same material via placing the levels upon the columns. This alternative portrayal is intended merely to help present the same information in a different format, a convenience of presentation or display, and not meant to introduce any new or differing facets or content. In that manner, the two figures are wholly consistent and aligned with each other.

4.2.1 Level 0: No Automation for AI Legal Reasoning

Level 0 is considered the no automation level. Legal reasoning is carried out via manual methods and principally occurs via paper-based methods.

This level is allowed some leeway in that the use of say a simple handheld calculator or perhaps the use of a fax machine could be allowed or included within this Level 0, though strictly speaking it could be said that any form whatsoever of automation is to be excluded from this level.

If purity of exclusion helps to avoid attempts at misusing the Level 0, it would seem prudent to take such a stark position, though there is a balance required between being dogmatic and yet allowing for some flexibility in the spirit and denotation of the levels. It seems doubtful though, in any case, that many would seek to argue about Level 0 versus Level 1, since those levels are rather straightforward and without particular acclaim, and thus the need to bear down on being strictly stipulated would not seem especially bothersome or significant to be entertained for these ascertained levels.

On a related aspect, keep in mind that the levels can apply to different facets of the act of practicing law. For example, within a law office, there might be some tasks done entirely by manual and paper-based methods, while other tasks being carried via presumed forms of automation. Some would be falsely quick to ascribe that the law office is to be rated as at a Level 0 of the levels of autonomy since there are some instances of no use of automation. Others might insist that since there is some amount of presumed bona fide automation in use, the entirety of the law office should be given a Level 1 rather than a Level 0 designation.

This is an unfortunate misreading and misinterpretation of the intentions of the levels of autonomy. It would be expected that those tasks of the law office without the use of automation are considered at a Level 0 and meanwhile, simultaneously, the other tasks of the law office using automation might very well be at Level 1 or perhaps Level 2, or higher. There is nothing inconsistent or incoherent about the application of the levels as being applied to particular segments or portions of activity.

In that same vein, clarification is perhaps for the viewpoint of that which is an instance versus that which is a generalized facet. For example, suppose a law office is performing a task via manual methods, doing so by their choice to do so, and yet suppose further that there is automation that could be applied to those tasks, but the law office has not yet opted to adopt such automation. It would be a mischaracterization to then say that those tasks are Level 0 per se since there is in fact (we are assuming) automation available that could carry out or assist in those tasks.

As such, it would be preferred that the use of the autonomous levels be used in a generalized fashion, demarking the state of the whole, rather than being used in the assessment of a particular practice or usage.

4.2.2 Level 1: Simple Assistance Automation for AI Legal Reasoning

Level 1 consists of simple assistance automation for AI legal reasoning.

Examples of this category encompassing simple automation would include the use of everyday computer-based word processing, the use of everyday computer-based spreadsheets, the access to online legal documents that are stored and retrieved electronically, and so on. By-and-large, today's use of computers for legal activities is predominantly within Level 1. It is assumed and expected that over time, the pervasiveness of automation will continue to deepen and widen, and eventually lead to legal activities being supported and within Level 2, rather than Level 1.

The demarcation between Level 1 and Level 0 has been discussed in the Level 0 subsection, while the demarcation between Level 1 and Level 2 is discussed next in the Level 2 subsection.

4.2.3 Level 2: Advanced Assistance Automation for AI Legal Reasoning

Level 2 consists of advanced assistance automation for AI legal reasoning.

Examples of this notion encompassing advanced automation would include the use of query-style Natural Language Processing (NLP), Machine Learning (ML) for case predictions, and so on.

Gradually, over time, it is expected that computer-based systems for legal activities will increasingly make use of advanced automation. Law industry technology that was once at a Level 1 will likely be refined, upgraded, or expanded to include advanced capabilities, and thus be reclassified into Level 2.

The demarcation between Level 1 and Level 2 is undoubtedly likely to spur great debate and consternation. Vendors of legal technology are more desirous of having their wares classified as Level 2 versus at Level 1. To try and prevent or head-off this difficulty, it would certainly be preferable to have an ironclad set of metrics or stipulations that would rule out that which is attempting to misleadingly attempt to be labeled as Level 2 when it is more reasonably stated as Level 1.

One approach to coping with this dilemma would be to enumerate all possible kinds of legal technology that falls within Level 1 and within that of Level 2, thus, it would be a simple matter of ensuring that a given legal technology either matched to those listed in the Level 1 definition or matched to those in the Level 2 definition.

This same debate arises in trying to discern Level 2 versus Level 3, and therefore is a recurring problematic consideration that permeates not only this set of autonomous levels but generally occurs in any set of autonomous levels.

In essence, autonomous levels tend to defy any simple indication of metrics or enumeration that could delineate indisputable crafting of scope and boundaries that manifestly distinguishes one level versus another.

For the moment, we will lean into the use of a reasonableness test, namely that some semblance of reasonableness concerning the overall spirit and intent of the levels of autonomy is to be observed. This is an open research question too as to how it can be ultimately finitely resolved, if it can, and might consist of some anointed standards bodies that ascertain the specifics of what constitutes each level and rates or judges submissions of legal technology that is seeking a form of certification for their claimed achieved level. For those seeking a more precise and perhaps mathematical or formulaic distinction, this topic is certainly a worthwhile research pursuit to determine if such an approach is potentially viable and workable.

4.2.4 Level 3: Semi-Autonomous Automation for AI Legal Reasoning

Level 3 consists of semi-autonomous automation for AI legal reasoning.

Examples of this notion encompassing semi-autonomous automation would include the use of Knowledge-Based Systems (KBS) for legal reasoning, the use of Machine Learning and Deep Learning (ML/DL) for legal reasoning, and so on.

Today, such automation tends to exist in research efforts or prototypes and pilot systems, along with some commercial legal technology that has been infusing these capabilities too.

All told, there is increasing effort to add such capabilities into legal technology and thus it is anticipated that many of today's Level 2 will inevitably be refined or expanded to then be classifiable into Level 3.

The same debate about what belongs in Level 2 versus Level 3 is akin to the debate about what belongs in Level 1 versus Level 2 and has been covered ergo in the discussion about Level 2 (see prior subsection). Once again, the answer, in brief, is that there is a reasonableness test to be assumed and that for now, there is no formulaic or precise demarcation, subject to further research and consideration.

4.2.5 Level 4: Domain Autonomous for AI Legal Reasoning

Level 4 consists of domain autonomous computer-based systems for AI legal reasoning.

This level reuses the conceptual notion of Operational Design Domains (ODDs) as utilized in the autonomous vehicles and self-driving cars levels of autonomy, though in this use case it is being applied to the legal domain.

Essentially, this entails any AI legal reasoning capacities that can operate autonomously, entirely so, but that is only able to do so in some limited or constrained legal domain.

Some elaboration on these aspects might help ensure that Level 4 is well understood.

First, unfortunately, there is no globally accepted standardized way to stipulate what the legal domains per se consist of.

Efforts to ontologically specify law have been made repeatedly, and there are many approaches to choose from, but there does not seem to be one wholly accepted and nor fully adopted taxonomy that could be leveraged for this Level 4 definition, particularly without lively debate and inexorably falling into a related but not integral definitional abyss that would tend to undermine the overarching aspirations of this framework, needlessly so.

As an example of what types of legal domains might be construed, consider these [27]:

- Animal law
- Admiralty law
- Bankruptcy law
- Banking law
- Civil Rights law
- Constitutional law
- Corporate law
- Criminal law
- Education law
- Entertainment law
- Employment law
- Environmental law
- Family law
- Health law
- Immigration law
- International law
- IP law
- Military law
- Personal injury law
- Real Estate law
- Tax law
- Etc.

The indicated list of potential legal domains is not exhaustive and could readily be further expanded and refined. Another perspective on legal domains could be by delineating the type of task performed, such as these functional areas of law practices [27]:

- Case Management
- Contracts
- Courts/Trials
- Discovery
- Documents/Records
- IP
- Law Office/Practice
- Lawyer & Client Interaction
- Legal Assistants
- Legal Collaboration
- Legal Research
- Legal Workflow
- Legal Writing
- Professional Conduct

There is also the matter of what is a domain in terms of its degree of magnitude. For example, would Case Management for Real Estate law to be considered a domain or a subdomain? This raises the question about the extent of domains and also the extent of subdomains, along with the perhaps ad infinitum possibility of subdomains within subdomains, etc. Envision a subdomain of a subdomain of a subdomain of a subdomain that is so narrow in scope that it would perhaps be easy or nearly trivial to claim that there is autonomous AI legal reasoning that someone has crafted for that tiny milieu.

In brief, this is an open question as to what the domains or subdomains would consist of, and thus further research is desired and necessary to aid in pinning down the particulars for Level 4. That being said, it is worth noting that the autonomous vehicles and self-driving cars ODD is similarly without definitive stipulation about the parameters of the domains, and yet the autonomous levels and Level 4 are generally considered agreed to and put into use. The point is that even if part of a framework is left open, for now, this does not negate the framework in any demonstrative way and instead simply leaves available the utility of closing the gap by rendering some later specificity to the matter.

4.2.6 Level 5: Fully Autonomous for AI Legal Reasoning

Level 5 consists of fully autonomous computer-based systems for AI legal reasoning.

In a sense, Level 5 is the superset of Level 4 in terms of encompassing all possible domains as per however so defined ultimately for Level 4. The only constraint, as it were, consists of the facet that the Level 4 and Level 5 are concerning human intelligence and the capacities thereof. This is an important emphasis due to attempting to distinguish Level 5 from Level 6 (as will be discussed in the next subsection)

It is conceivable that someday there might be a fully autonomous AI legal reasoning capability, one that encompasses all of the law in all foreseeable ways, though this is quite a tall order and remains quite aspirational without a clear cut path of how this might one day be achieved. Nonetheless, it seems to be within the extended realm of possibilities, which is worthwhile to mention in relative terms to Level 6.

4.2.7 Level 6: Superhuman Autonomous for AI Legal Reasoning

Level 6 consists of superhuman autonomous computer-based systems for AI legal reasoning.

In a sense, Level 6 is the entirety of Level 5 and adds something beyond that in a manner that is currently ill-defined and perhaps (some would argue) as yet unknowable. The notion is that AI might ultimately exceed human intelligence, rising to become superhuman, and if so, we do not yet have any viable indication of what that superhuman intelligence consists of and nor what kind of thinking it would somehow be able to undertake.

Whether a Level 6 is ever attainable is reliant upon whether superhuman AI is ever attainable, and thus, at this time, this stands as a placeholder for that which might never occur. In any case, having such a placeholder provides a semblance of completeness, doing so without necessarily legitimatizing that superhuman AI is going to be achieved or not. No such claim or dispute is undertaken within this framework.

4.3 Magnitudes of the Levels

As earlier stated, there is always a complication that using a numbering scheme of simple integers for a set of autonomous levels can convey an implied equal magnitude difference between the levels. It is overly easy for someone to construe that say Level 2 is merely one more than Level 3, thus the leap or jump is of some unstated magnitude, and that likewise the movement from say Level 3 to Level 4 is the equal amount of a shift or step-up increment when perhaps the chasm between those respective levels is uneven and dramatically differs. Trying to use the numbering scheme to suggest magnitudes is unfortunately overloading that then tends to undermine the simplicity and ease of conveying what the levels are.

The numbering for this framework falls within that same approach of using simple incremental integers, and yet the magnitude between the levels is uneven per each jump from level to level.

As illustrative of the span between the steps see Figure 3.

Figure 3 is not drawn to scale and merely anecdotally is presented to suggest that there are magnitudes of difference between each step.

The curve shown could be redrawn in a multitude of ways, and there is an argument to be made that Level 6 might be so far off the chart that you would need to shrink the rest of the graph into a tiny smidgen to get Level 6 onto the chart at all.

In any case, the point is that it is vital to realize that there are varying magnitudes of difference between each of the levels and it is not a simple linear progression among them.

4.4 Conformance to Key Characteristics of Autonomy Levels

Recall that the earlier portion of this section proffered these suggested key characteristics that a sound and robust set of autonomy levels should aspire to attain:

1. Scope
2. Sufficiency of Reason
3. Completeness
4. Applicability
5. Usefulness
6. Understandability
7. Foolproofness
8. Observe Occam's Razor
9. Differentiable
10. Logical Progression

In a recap of the seven proposed autonomous levels for AI Legal Reasoning, it is hoped that the preceding discussion about the levels is adequate to showcase conformance to those key characteristics. The scope was directly discussed, as were the reasons for each level and the entire set, plus a semblance of completeness, applicability, usefulness, understandability, foolproofness, application of Occam's razor, differentiability, and logical progression were indicated.

That being the case, and for clarification, meeting those characteristics to whatever degree has been achieved does not necessarily mean that for all intent and purposes that a framework is settled or somehow conclusively stated.

That is decidedly not the case herein, and much additional work and open questions are still to be addressed, but this is to be realized and does not impinge or undermine the essence of the framework and nor hamper or mar its initial introduction and formulation.

Section 5: Additional Considerations and Future Research

In this final section, coverage of additional facets is included and so too are some strident calls for future research for the furtherance of this important topic.

First, note that the framework is considered descriptive rather than prescriptive.

Second, nothing about the levels and nor the framework is intended to suggest that legal reasoning autonomy will indeed be achieved via AI. Some are predicting that a so-called *legal singularity* will someday arise, purportedly denoting a time at which the laws are entirely established and adjudicated via AI autonomous systems. Within those predictions, there is a concern that the law might inevitably become cast in stone, unchanging and unwavering, or that the law will be so stipulated and codified that all legal uncertainty is excised and thus the entirety of legal outcomes is perfectly predictable.

This framework is neither supportive of such assertions and nor a denier of such theories. In a sense, the framework is the framework, intending simply to provide a means of identifying and distinguishing levels of autonomy concerning the law and AI legal reasoning. Whether such autonomy is achieved, or when it might be achieved, does not bear on the nature of the framework. For example, it could very well be that no AI system ever is sufficiently capable to be considered at a Level 5, but that does not negate the value of having a Level 5 as part of the framework.

Likewise, for those that especially eschew the concept of a superhuman AI capability, having included this element as a cornerstone of Level 6 is not somehow a testament that superhuman AI will be reached.

Construe Level 6 as a future placeholder, potentially sitting empty for a time to come, yet nonetheless available if the day should ever arrive for its use.

On a related theme, there is much discussion in and beyond the law industry concerning whether lawyers and legal professionals will ultimately be replaced by AI autonomous legal reasoning. This kind of societal consideration is again another aspect that is not within the purview of this framework. No commentary or weighing in about the matter is substantive to the rendering and applicability of this LoA. That's not to suggest that such a topic is not erstwhile, only that it is not pertinent to the formulation of this specific matter at hand.

In terms of scope of this LoA, those in the field of law are at times focused on what is somewhat euphemistically referred to as the shadow of the law [49], and as such, there might be a question as to whether this particular dimension of the law is also within the scope of the framework. In short, yes, the shadow of the law would also be encompassed to the degree that it involves the crucial ingredient that underlies all facets of the intended scope, namely the instantiation of legal reasoning.

For each of the levels, an attempt has been made to showcase that each level is distinct from the other levels. One of the frequently raised questions about any LoA is whether it is possible to be a partial member of a given level, sometimes denoted by a fractional amount. For example, perhaps a legal system software is within Level 2, but the system is nearing to Level 3, thus, the inclination is to proffer that the software is a Level 2.5 or some akin fractional amount. This is decidedly *not* the nature of this framework and typically disallowed indeed by most such frameworks, including the SAE standard for AVs.

Next, consider some typical questions disclosed when evaluating a legal industry LoA.

One concern is whether adopting this kind of framework for the legal industry will expose those using the LoA to a form of *alluring legal liability*.

Suppose that a vendor Q opts to claim that their AI legal system is rated at a Level 4. In terms of potential legal liability, some question whether this opens the vendor to potential legal exposures if it can be later shown that the system was not qualified for a Level 4 rating. In that sense, the preference by some, such as vendors, might be to avoid using the framework, for angst of incurring a legal exposure.

Some are also concerned that a framework such as this LoA might be unduly codified into the law itself, perhaps becoming a regulation that is lawful to be observed. On the one hand, this could be said to provide teeth to any such LoA and aid in promulgating it, but at the same time perhaps serve in an overbearing or stifling manner. Indeed, there are reservations about the potential heralding of a Collingridge dilemma [17] by enacting any such framework. This refers to a postulated theory by researcher Collingridge that suggests if structures and potential burdens are placed onto an innovation before it has a chance to breathe, or maturely innovate and gain traction, this can inadvertently quash or delay the innovation.

Also, a more detailed specification for the nature of each level would be another viable and fruitful avenue of additional research. Doing so is evocative of the likeliest controversy for this kind of LoA, as is similarly the case for most any LoA, which typically comes down to trying to ascertain the veracity of a claim that an AI system has earned its way into a particular level. The tighter that such a measuring mechanism can be devised, presumably it will be easier for those using the framework to accurately and readily select the appropriate level, and also more expediently unmask false designations. As the acclaimed management theorist Peter Drucker has been oft-quoted as asserting [19], you cannot manage that which you cannot measure.

For far too long, the legal industry has been without an accepted and robust Levels of Autonomy (LoA) measuring tool for AILR which this framework proposes a draft formulation of, serving as a potential and earnest step in that needed direction. Additional research is welcomed and highly encouraged in this hoped-for valued contribution to the future of law and aims to provide a potential impetus for or otherwise aid in the advent of automation and autonomy of the law via AI and Legal Reasoning.

References

1. Alarie, Benjamin (2016). "The Path of the Law: Toward Legal Singularity," May 27, 2016, SSRN, University of Toronto Faculty of Law and Vector Institute for Artificial Intelligence.

2. Aleven, Vincent (1997). "Teaching Case-Based Argumentation Through a Model and Examples," Ph.D. Dissertation, University of Pittsburgh.

3. Aleven, Vincent (2003). "Using Background Knowledge in Case-Based Legal Reasoning: A Computational Model and an Intelligent Learning Environment," Artificial Intelligence.

4. Amgoud, Leila (2012). "Five Weaknesses of ASPIC+," Volume 299, Communications in Computer and Information Science (CCIS).

5. Antonious, Grigoris, and George Baryannis, Sotiris Batsakis, Guido Governatori, Livio Robaldo, Givoanni Siragusa, Ilias Tachmazidis (2018). "Legal Reasoning and Big Data: Opportunities and Challenges," August 2018, MIREL Workshop on Mining and Reasoning Legal Texts.

6. Ashley, Kevin (1991). "Reasoning with Cases and Hypotheticals in HYPO," Volume 34, International Journal of Man-Machine Studies.

7. Ashley, Kevin, and Karl Branting, Howard Margolis, and Cass Sunstein (2001). "Legal Reasoning and Artificial Intelligence: How Computers 'Think' Like Lawyers," Symposium: Legal Reasoning and Artificial Intelligence, University of Chicago Law School Roundtable.

8. Baker, Jamie (2018). "A Legal Research Odyssey: Artificial Intelligence as Disrupter," Law Library Journal.

9. Batsakis, Sotiris, and George Baryannis, Guido Governatori, Illias Tachmazidis, Grigoris Antoniou (2018). "Legal Representation and Reasoning in Practice: A Critical Comparison," Volume 313, Legal Knowledge and Information Systems.

10. Bench-Capon, Trevor (2004). "AGATHA: Automation of the Construction of Theories in Case Law Domains," January 2004, Legal Knowledge and Information Systems Jurix 2004, Amsterdam.

11. Bench-Capon, Trevor (2012). "Representing Popov v Hayashi with Dimensions and Factors," March 2012, Artificial Intelligence and Law.

12. Bench-Capon, Trevor and Givoanni Sartor (2003). "A Model of Legal Reasoning with Cases Incorporating Theories and Values," November 2013, Artificial Intelligence.

13. Breuker, Joost (1996). "A Functional Ontology of Law," October 1996, ResearchGate.

14. Bruninghaus, Stefanie, and Kevin Ashley (2003). "Combining Case-Based and Model-Based Reasoning for Predicting the Outcome of Legal Cases," June 2003, ICCBR'03: Proceedings of the 5th International Conference on Case-based reasoning: Research and Development.

15. Buchanan, Bruce, and Thomas Headrick (1970). "Some Speculation about Artificial Intelligence and Legal Reasoning," Volume 23, Stanford Law Review.

16. Chagal-Feferkorn, Karni (2019). "Am I An Algorithm or a Product: When Products Liability Should Apply to Algorithmic Decision-Makers," Stanford Law & Policy Review.

17. Collingridge, David (1980). The Social Control of Technology. St. Martin's Press.

18. Douglas, William (1948). "The Dissent: A Safeguard of Democracy," Volume 32, Journal of the American Judicature Society.

19. Drucker, Peter (1963). "Managing for Business Effectiveness," May 1963, Harvard Business Review.

20. Dung, P, and R. Kowalski, F. Toni (2006). "Dialectic Proof Procedures for Assumption-Based Admissible Argumentation," Artificial Intelligence.

21. Eliot, Lance (2016). AI Guardian Angels for Deep AI Trustworthiness. LBE Press Publishing.

22. Eliot, Lance (2017). New Advances in AI Autonomous Driverless Self-Driving Cars. LBE Press Publishing.

23. Eliot, Lance (2018). "AI Arguing Machines," November 7, 2018, AI Trends.

24. Eliot, Lance (2019). "Explaining Level 4 and Level 5 of Self-Driving Cars," December 20, 2019, Forbes.

25. Eliot, Lance (2020). "The Neglected Dualism of Artificial Moral Agency and Artificial Legal Reasoning in AI for Social Good." Harvard University, Harvard Center for Research on Computation and Society, AI for Social Good Conference, July 21, 2020.

26. Eliot, Lance (2020). AI and Legal Reasoning Essentials. LBE Press Publishing.

27. Eliot, Lance (2019). Artificial Intelligence and LegalTech Essentials. LBE Press Publishing.

28. Eliot, Lance (2020). "FutureLaw 2020 Showcases How Tech is Transforming The Law, Including the Impacts of AI," April 16, 2020, Forbes.

29. Erdem, Esra, and Michael Gelfond, Nicola Leone (2016). "Applications of Answer Set Programming," AI Magazine.

30. Galdon, Fernando, and Ashley Hall, Stephen Jia Wang (2020). "Designing Trust in Highly Automated Virtual Assistants: A Taxonomy of Levels of Autonomy," Artificial Intelligence in Industry 4.0: A Collection of Innovative Research Case-Studies.

31. Gardner, Anne (1987). Artificial Intelligence and Legal Reasoning. MIT Press.

32. Genesereth, Michael (2009). "Computational Law: The Cop in the Backseat," Stanford Center for Legal Informatics, Stanford University.

33. Ghosh, Mirna (2019). "Automation of Legal Reasoning and Decision Based on Ontologies," Normandie Universite.

34. Grabmair, Matthias (2017). "Predicting Trade Secret Case Outcomes using Argument Schemes and Learned Quantitative Value Effect Tradeoffs," IJCAI June 12, 2017, London, United Kingdom.

35. Hage, Jaap (1996). "A Theory of Legal Reasoning and a Logic to Match," Volume 4, Artificial Intelligence and Law.

36. Hage, Jaap (2000). "Dialectical Models in Artificial Intelligence and Law," Artificial Intelligence and Law.

37. Hage, Japp, and Ronald Leenes, Arno Lodder (1993). "Hard Cases: A Procedural Approach," Artificial Intelligence and Law.

38. Hobbes, Thomas (1651). The Matter, Form and Power of a Common-Wealth Ecclesiasticall and Civil.

39. Holmes, Oliver (1897). "The Path of the Law," Volume 10, Harvard Law Review.

40. Katz, Daniel, and Michael Bommarito, Josh Blackman (2017). "A General Approach for Predicting the Behavior of the Supreme Court of the United States," April 12, 2017, PLOS ONE.

41. Kowalski, Robert, and Francesca Toni (1996). "Abstract Argumentation," AI-Law96.

42. Laswell, Harold (1955). "Current Studies of the Decision Process: Automation Creativity," Volume 8, Western Political Quarterly.

43. Libal, Tomer, and Alexander Steen (2019). "The NAI Suite: Drafting and Reasoning over Legal Texts," October 15, 2019, arXiv.

44. Lipton, Zachary (2017). "The Mythos of Model Interpretability," March 6, 2017, arXiv.

45. Markou, Christopher, and Simon Deakin (2020). "Is Law Computable? From Rule of Law to Legal Singularity," May 4, 2020, SSRN, University of Cambridge Faculty of Law Research Paper.

46. Martin, Andrew, and Kevin Quinn, Theodore Ruger, Pauline Kim (2004). "Competing Approaches to Predicting Supreme Court Decision Making," December 2014, Symposium on Forecasting U.S. Supreme Court Decisions.

47. McCarty, Thorne (1977). "Reflections on TAXMAN: An Experiment in Artificial Intelligence and Legal Reasoning," January 1977, Harvard Law Review.

48. Miller, George (1956). "The Magical Number Seven, Plus Or Minus Two: Some Limits On Our Capacity For Processing Information." Volume 63, Number 2, Psychological Review.

49. Mnookin, Robert, and Lewis Kornhauser (1979). "Bargaining in the Shadow of the Law," Volume 88, Number 5, April 1979, The Yale Law Review.

50. Modgil, Sanjay, and Henry Prakken (2013). "The ASPIC+ Framework for Structured Argumentation: A Tutorial," December 16, 2013, Argument & Computation.

51. Mowbray, Andrew and Philip Chung, Graham Greenleaf (2019). "Utilising AI in the Legal Assistance Sector," LegalAIIA Workshop, ICAIL, June 17, 2019, Montreal, Canada.

52. Neches, Robert and Richard Fikes, Tim Finn, Thomas Gruber, Ramesh Patil, Ted Senator, William Swartout (1991). "Enabling Technology for Knowledge Sharing," Fall 1991, Volume 12, Number 3, AI Magazine.

53. Parasuraman, Raja, and Thomas Sheridan, Christopher Wickens (2000). "A Model for Types and Levels of Human Interaction with Automation," May 2000, IEEE Transactions on Systems, Man, and Cybernetics.

54. Popple, James (1993). "SHYSTER: A Pragmatic Legal Expert System," Ph.D. Dissertation, Australian National University.

55. Prakken, Henry, and Giovanni Sartor (2015). "Law and Logic: A Review from an Argumentation Perspective," Volume 227, Artificial Intelligence.

56. Rissland, Edwina (1988). Artificial Intelligence and Legal Reasoning: A Discussion of the Field and Gardner's Book," Volume 9, AI Magazine.

57. Rissland, Edwina (1990). "Artificial Intelligence and Law: Stepping Stones to a Model of Legal Reasoning," Yale Law Journal.

58. SAE (2018). Taxonomy and Definitions for Terms Related to Driving Automation Systems for On-Road Motor Vehicles, J3016-201806, SAE International.

59. Searle, John (1980). "Minds, Brains, and Programs," Volume 3, Behavioral and Brain Sciences.

60. Sifakis, Joseph (2018). "Autonomous Systems: An Architectural Characterization." arXiv: 1811:10277.

61. Sunstein, Cass (2001). "Of Artificial Intelligence and Legal Reasoning," University of Chicago Law School, Public Law and Legal Theory Working Papers.

62. Sunstein, Cass, and Kevin Ashley, Karl Branting, Howard Margolis (2001). "Legal Reasoning and Artificial Intelligence: How Computers 'Think' Like Lawyers," Symposium: Legal Reasoning and Artificial Intelligence, University of Chicago Law School Roundtable.

63. Surden, Harry (2014). "Machine Learning and Law," Washington Law Review.

64. Surden, Harry (2019). "Artificial Intelligence and Law: An Overview," Summer 2019, Georgia State University Law Review.

65. Valente, Andre, and Joost Breuker (1996). "A Functional Ontology of Law," Artificial Intelligence and Law.

66. Waltl, Bernhard, and Roland Vogl (2018). "Explainable Artificial Intelligence: The New Frontier in Legal Informatics," February 2018, Jusletter IT 22, Stanford Center for Legal Informatics, Stanford University.

67. Wittgenstein, Ludwig (1953). Philosophical Investigations. Blackwell Publishing.

68. Wolfman, Zack. ABA Model Definition of the Practice of Law, American Bar Association.

69. Yang, Guang, and James Cambias, Kevin Cleary, Eric Daimler, James Drake, Pierre Dupont, Nobuhiko Hata, Peter Kazanzides, Sylvain Martel, Rajni Patel, Veronica Santos, Russell Taylor (2017). "Medical Robots: Regulatory, Ethical, and Legal Considerations for Increasing Levels of Autonomy," March 15, 2017, Science Robotics.

Note: *For supplemental materials depicting the aspects discussed in this chapter, refer to Appendix B, which contains various augmented diagrams, charts, and additional related facets of relevance*

CHAPTER 3

AI TURING TEST AND THE PRACTICE OF LAW

Abstract

Artificial Intelligence (AI) is increasingly being applied to law and a myriad of legal tasks amid attempts to bolster AI Legal Reasoning (AILR) autonomous capabilities. A major question that has generally been unaddressed involves how we will know when AILR has achieved autonomous capacities. The field of AI has grappled with similar quandaries over how to assess the attainment of Artificial General Intelligence (AGI), a persistently discussed issue among scholars since the inception of AI, with the Turing Test communally being considered as the bellwether for ascertaining such matters. This paper proposes a variant of the Turing Test that is customized for specific use in the AILR realm, including depicting how this famous "gold standard" of AI fulfillment can be robustly applied across the autonomous levels of AI Legal Reasoning.

Section 1: Background and Context

Artificial Intelligence (AI) is increasingly being applied to law and legal tasks amid attempts to bolster AI Legal Reasoning (AILR) autonomous capabilities [1] [5] [11] [17]. The use of Machine Learning (ML) and Deep Learning (DL) has significantly aided in making improvements and advances in AILR systems [27] [31]. Also, ML/DL in Natural Language Processing (NLP) has made tremendous strides in computational fluency and semantic analysis performance that has bolstered the use of LegalTech for e-Discovery, contract creation, searches of a large corpus of court cases, and the like [14] [26] [40].

A major question that has generally been unaddressed involves how we will know when AILR has achieved autonomous capacities. So far, AI as applied to the legal profession has primarily consisted of aiding or supporting the legal work of human lawyers but has not reached the capability of being able to autonomously perform legal tasks. A base assumption is that inexorably there will be advances made in AI that will boost AILR systems and ultimately transcend them into having autonomous capacities, but there does not yet exist any bona fide and nor rigorous means to viably attest to whether such AILR autonomy has been achieved [44].

Without an acknowledged and universally accepted method or means of attesting to AILR autonomy, a vacuum remains that will likely stoke false claims and confound those within the law industry and those outside the legal field. Vendors providing AILR systems will continue to be able to assert they have been able to develop autonomous AILR, doing so with shallow assertions buoyed-up by whatever obtuse measures they wish to stake such a claim on. Likewise, AI and law researchers that are striving to make scholarly foundational advances in AILR will lack any viable means to discern the pace and scope of progress in creating AILR autonomous functionality.

The overarching field of AI has grappled with alike quandaries concerning how to assess the attainment of Artificial General Intelligence (AGI). AGI refers to the goal of seeking to achieve AI that can be on par with human intelligence and thus convincingly demonstrate the same caliber and depth of reasoning as that of human cognition. Discussion and debates over how to assess whether AGI has been attained have permeated the field of AI since its very inception. Generally, the Turing Test [52] has commonly been considered the bellwether for ascertaining such matters and is known worldwide as a method or approach to the testing of AI, having been devised by the famous mathematician Alan Turing in 1950 [39] [41] [47] [51].

This paper proposes a variant of the Turing Test that is customized for specific use in the AILR realm, including depicting how this renowned "gold standard" of AI fulfillment can be robustly applied to AILR.

Also, the paper makes use of a framework of autonomous levels of AI Legal Reasoning [20] [21] [24], indicating how the Turing Test applies at each successive level of AILR autonomy. The proposed grid and discussion are intended to contribute to the study of AI & Law as this burgeoning realm seeks to identify and mature a method or means to suitably determine and formally assess AI Legal Reasoning autonomous systems.

This paper consists of five sections:

- Section 1: Background and Context
- Section 2: Key Elements of the Turing Test
- Section 3: Autonomous Levels of AI Legal Reasoning
- Section 4: Turing Test Grid Integrating Autonomous Levels of AILR
- Section 5: Additional Considerations and Future Research

In Section 1, an overall background about the Turing Test is provided. Section 2 then goes into a further in-depth analysis of the Turing Test and identifies the key elements involved. In Section 3, an overview is provided on the autonomous levels of AI Legal Reasoning, which is crucial to then understanding Section 4. Section 4 proposes a grid that aligns the Turing Test elements with the autonomous levels of AI Legal Reasoning. Section 5 is a discussion of additional considerations and also offers suggested avenues for future research on these matters.

1.1 Overview of the Turing Test

Noted mathematician Alan Turing proposed the Turing Test in 1950 when trying to address the question of whether machines can think [52]. He was desirous of avoiding getting mired in debates about what thinking consists of, which can readily get hindered in the murky and unknown underpinnings of the brain and cognition. Note that even today, some 70 years later, the means of how we think are still largely undetermined.

The overarching notion by Turing was to treat thinking as a black box and thus not need to ascertain the internal mechanisms.

He conceived of a testing approach that would avert relying upon how thinking is derived, and instead be aimed at the resultant behavior that thinking produces. He also wanted to separate the physical aspects of thinking from the intellectual aspects. In essence, a thinking machine does not necessarily need to have a human body or any semblance of a body and might instead be encapsulated in a computer-based system that does not showcase itself in a human-like way (i.e., it does not need to be a robot that has the appearance of a human figure).

Some immediately criticized the Turing Test for averting the ongoing question of mind-body, whereby some theorists suggest that the human mind and the act of thinking are intertwined, and it is not possible to separate the two [41] [55]. This criticism though is addressed by the simple fact that the test as devised would presumably lead to a failure on the part of the AI if indeed a mind-body composition is an absolute requirement for the act of thinking since the AI would assuredly be unable to demonstrate thinking as it has no such body or encasement included.

Per Turing [52], he stated that "It is natural that we should wish to permit every kind of engineering technique to be used in our machines," and thus he wanted to devise a test that would not limit how a thinking machine could be developed. He also anticipated the retort that if any machine is allowed, potentially a person might be cloned via biological techniques, and this "machine" considered a form of AI due to it being "engineered" into existence. Turing [52] remarked that "To do so would be a feat of biological technique deserving of the very highest praise, but we would not be inclined to regard it as a case of 'constructing a thinking machine.'"

Therefore, it is assumed that for the sake of the Turing Test, a reasonableness perspective be taken about the AI and how it is embodied and that it somehow is considered to be commonly denoted as a "machine" and not a biological person (trying to definitively define the meaning of "machine" can in itself be a significant burden).

The Turing Test that he devised consists of a person that takes the role of conducting an interrogation, asking questions of two subjects or participants, one being a human and the other being a (potential) thinking machine, and neither is visible to the interrogator. Imagine that the two subjects are hidden behind a curtain on a stage and that the interrogator can only interact indirectly via speaking or writing a message to them but cannot see them directly. This hiding of the subjects aids in what otherwise would be a rather perfunctory exercise of merely looking at the participants and visually ascertaining which is the human and which is the machine (assuming that the machine is not a robot fashioned to look identically like a human).

The interrogator does not know beforehand which of the two is the human and nor which of the two is the AI. For sake of convenience, label one of them as X and the other as Y. The interrogator asks questions or makes queries of the X and Y, and at some point, ascertains that the effort should be concluded. Upon so ending the effort, the interrogator is then to state whether X is the human or whether Y is the human, which alternatively could be stated by indicating whether X is the AI or whether Y is the AI.

Turing referred to this test as the "imitation game" since it involves the AI attempting to imitate the human, though this might or might not be the intention per se of the AI. It could be that the AI has been devised to be a thinking machine, and thus it "mimics" the act of human thinking. Whether this kind of thinking is the same as human thinking is a longstanding open debate, therefore that can be somewhat sidestepped by suggesting that the AI is mimicking human thinking, regardless of whether it is, in fact, identical in how it thinks or does so in an entirely different manner.

Many prefer to refer to the imitation game as the Turing Test, rather than mentioning that it is a game, which perhaps undermines the cogent value of the approach. When considering games or contests, we might be quick to dismiss them as nothing of worthwhile consequence. Some suggest too that the Turing Test is more so an experimental arrangement, and thusly refer to the human participant and the AI as subjects, akin to the phrasing used in scientific experiments.

The aim of the Turing Test is that if the interrogator is unable to differentiate between the two subjects, presumably the AI is thusly indistinguishable from the human, in terms of thinking, and thus we can conclude that the AI has achieved the equivalence of human intelligence. This greatly simplifies the seemingly intractable problem of trying to define what human intelligence consists of. If the AI can demonstrate intelligence to the same degree as a human, it can be said to be a thinking machine.

When pursuing the consideration of human intelligence, Turing envisioned that a question and answer dialogue would be a key means for the integrator to try and separate the chaff from the wheat, so to speak, and assumed that the interrogator is sufficiently capable undertaking the interrogation, and ultimately able to reach a reasoned conclusion about which is the human and which is the AI. Turing suggested that the interrogator might ask the subjects to write poetry, or play chess, or do whatever kinds of mentally engaging tasks that might be deemed worthwhile for purposes of conducting the test.

The Turing Test has been pervasive in the field of AI over the many years since it was first proposed and continues today as a commonly referred to "standard" of how to assess the achievement of machine-based human-like intelligence [3] [4] [39]. Various tournaments have taken place using the Turing Test, along with prizes offered for being able to devise AI that can succeed at winning a Turing Test. It is crucial though to realize that none of these various Turing Tests were of the variety envisioned by Turing, and instead are extremely reduced versions, oftentimes limiting the test to a pre-determined scope or a set time limit. Thus, there is not yet any AI that has been able to successfully win or pass a Turing Test of an unencumbered nature that was robustly attempting to ascertain general intelligence.

Some have used the Turing Test to examine AI in specific disciplines. For example, in the medical field, there are AI systems that purportedly exhibit human intelligence capacities when analyzing an X-ray or MRI, and thus a type of Turing Test can be set up to try and determine the veracity of such medically specialized claims [42] [57]. Note that this is not the same as determining general intelligence and instead of a focus on so-called narrow AI.

In the field of law, efforts to apply AI to legal reasoning have also at times referred to the Turing Test, proposing that it be utilized for ascertaining the capabilities of AI LegalTech systems. Such suggestions have not been laid out in specified detail and are typically an overall reference to the importance and potential applicability of using the Turing Test in the application of AI to the law [41] [45].

In an unusual and intriguing perspective about the Turing Test, Reinbold [44] discusses the Turing Test in the context of patents. Currently, the United States does not allow AI to be considered a patent inventor, but some argue that AI ought to be permitted to hold a patent. Reinbold suggests that the Turing Test could be used to aid in deciding whether AI should be eligible for being granted a patent [44]: "Principally, AI that passes the Turing Test constitutes 'inventive AI' and likely produces unpatentable inventions under 35 U.S.C. § 103. In contrast, AI that fails the Turing Test permits user control and influence over the inventive process and may result in patentable 'AI-assisted inventions.'" In short, if the AI passes the Turing Test, it cannot be granted a patent under existing provisions, while if it fails then it could potentially be considered an AI-assisted invention.

Overall, there is a gap or opening within the field of AI and law that leaves unstated how we will know when AI has reached a sufficiency of being able to practice law and thus might be permitted to do so, autonomously rather than via working solely on a human attorney-assisted basis. This paper proposes that the Turing Test be tailored to the discipline of law, and by doing so would provide a means to assess AI applications purporting to perform legal reasoning.

In the next section, this paper identifies the key elements involved in the Turing Test and discusses how those elements can be tailored or customized to the assessment of AI-based Legal Reasoning.

Section 2: Key Elements of the Turing Test

In this section, the key elements of the Turing Test are identified. An explanation for each key element is provided. This will be crucial for then applying these elements to the autonomous levels of AILR.

2.1 Turing Test and Key Elements

The key elements are depicted in the below short-form descriptors that are considered suitable for use in a grid and consist of keywords to represent each element. The key elements consist of:

- The Inquirer
- Human Participant
- AI-Based Legal Reasoner
- Queries of the Turing Test
- Answers to the Turing Test
- Rules of the Turing Test
- Potential Observers
- Conclusion Reached
- Reverse Turing Test

In the subsections, each key element will be briefly explained and explored.

2.2 Details Underlying Key Elements

For each of the key elements, it is foundational to explain the nature and scope of the element, doing so to ensure that each is representative of its focused intent.

2.2.1 Element "The Inquirer"

The person that asks the questions of the Turing Test participants is customarily known as the interrogator, which was the wording originally used by Turing in describing the overall arrangement. Since the word "interrogator" can have varied connotations associated with it, which invokes for some a semblance of antagonism or other definitional baggage, the person in the role of conducting the inquiry has oft been coined as the inquirer. There are additional wording variations such as being referred to as the evaluator, sometimes also referred to as the judge, and so on.

For purposes of this study, the word "inquirer" is utilized.

Doing so is for purposes of seeking to avoid any otherwise distracting confusion or confounding considerations about the role. The word "inquirer" is presumed to be less likely to trigger any adverse reactions about the nature of the role and thus is considered a relatively neutral phrasing. Regardless of the phrasing chosen, the role is still the same role as originally envisioned.

One question to be considered about the inquirer is whether this is denoted as one person or whether it could be more than one. The original portrayal implied it would be one person, though this was not an aspect that garnered particular attention or was raised as a potential consideration in the initial arrangement.

The viewpoint taken here is that it would be feasible to have a Turing Test with more than one inquirer, which is a reasonable stance given that the role of the inquiry overall is to try and assess the full range of human intelligence and whether the AI can exhibit that entire range. It would seem problematic to assume that one person alone in the inquirer role could cover the varied breadth and depth of human intelligence, and as such, there might be multiple inquirers employed for the role. Ideally, the number of inquirers would be kept to a reasonable number and there would be cogent coordination among the inquirers too. This concept of multiple persons in the inquirer role is deserving of additional research and will be mentioned further in Section 5. When using the word "inquirer," henceforth herein this is intended to indicate the role of the inquirer and for which it might be one or more persons.

Another aspect of the inquirer role is that it is a multi-faceted role. As originally described, the inquirer asks questions of the participants, acting in a somewhat prosecutorial manner, and simultaneously is gauging the answers, acting in a somewhat judicial manner, along with ultimately rendering a decision as to the outcome of the Turing Test. Whether this is an unduly overloaded role has been previously questioned.

Likewise, this brings up the corresponding concern that having one person that serves essentially as a mix of a prosecutor, judge, and jury would seem inherent to have the undue potential for problematic sway including incurring cognitive biases as the inquirer (an inquirer might be swayed by their own choice of questions, whereas if there was a separate evaluator they might independently be better served at assessing the answers of the participants, and so on). This matter is not addressed per se in this study and merely noted as a consideration about the nature of the Turing Test and for purposes of potentially spurring further research on the matter.

All told, the person that undertakes the inquirer role is notably significant since how the person conducts the Turing Test is tantamount to shaping the worth of the effort and its outcome. Someone that is insufficiently capable in this role would undeniably undercut the significance of the Turing Test.

In the overarching Turing Test, the inquirer is covering all facets of general intelligence. For purposes of the Turing Test utilization in the context of this study, the inquirer is focused on the discipline of legal reasoning.

2.2.2 Element "Human Participant"

The human participant is the barometer against which the AI system is being compared, and therefore it is essential to the Turing Test that the human participant be sufficiently capable in this role.

As similarly discussed in the prior subsection about the inquirer, the human participant was originally depicted as one person rather than being multiple people at once. The underlying question arises regarding whether it is reasonable to expect that one person alone would be capable of serving in this crucial barometer capacity. As such, it is conceivable that the human participant could consist of one or more humans and that they would need to be coordinated in their efforts thereto. This is a concept deserving of additional research and will be so mentioned in Section 5.

Another facet of the human participant is the base assumption that the human participant will genuinely perform when undertaking the Turing Test. If the human participant is insincere in their effort, it would undoubtedly undermine the nature of the testing activity. There is a counterargument sometimes made that this could also be a ploy by the AI, attempting to portray itself in a human-like manner. In that same logical vein, the human participant could attempt to masquerade as the AI, if one assumes that the AI can be so mimicked.

Yet another aspect involves whether the human participant can be equipped with the use of a computer. Purists would tend to argue that the human should be entirely unaided and be acting solely based on their own intellect. Where this comes to play would involve the aspect of the inquirer asking each of the subjects to calculate a large value, and when one of them is unable to do so or takes a long time to do so, the human participant is revealed. To solve this, the belief is that the human participant should be permitted to use a computer. But this introduces additional complications, such as if the computer is running the same AI as the AI being used for the comparator, does the Turing Test make any reasonable sense when the human participant is armed with the same AI. For purposes of this study, the viewpoint is taken that the human participant would likely need to have available some computer-based capacities due to the nature of the context yet would need to be limited in having access to the AI per se (this is a matter mentioned further in Section 5 for future research exploration).

In the overarching Turing Test, the human participant is expected to cover all facets embodying general intelligence. For purposes of the Turing Test utilization in the context of this study, the human participant is focused on the discipline of legal reasoning.

2.2.3 Element "AI-Based Legal Reasoner"

The computer-based AI is the comparator to the human participant.

In the overarching Turing Test, the AI is intended to cover all facets of general intelligence. For purposes of the Turing Test utilization in the context of this study, the AI is focused on the discipline of legal reasoning and will be denoted as the AI-based Legal Reasoner.

Referring to AI overall has an implied monolithic insinuation, which should not be necessarily taken or interpreted in that manner. It could be that the AI is a federated system with numerous components that work in conjunction with each other. Note that however the AI is formed, including the underpinnings of technology used, does not bear on the Turing Test in any substantive way. The Turing Test is essentially technology agnostic and there is no indication and nor assertion as to what or how the AI is composed and undertaken.

Another aspect of the AI involves whether the AI might be devised to attempt trickery at mimicking the human participant or the nature of human responses. Some have labeled this ploy as a form of Artificial Stupidity, arising from the notion that if the AI is asked to calculate a complex equation, and arrives at an answer with fifty digits, this perhaps gives away the AI, and thus the AI might purposely act as though it only knows a few of the digits, or perhaps even offers the digits erroneously as though having made an error that a human might make. Some argue that this is entirely at the choice of the AI to decide whether to attempt and that doing so could either aid in the AI appearing to be human-like or might backfire on the AI by revealing that it is the AI and exploiting such a ploy by appearing to be dimwitted or human-like error-prone.

2.2.4 Element "Queries of the Turing Test"

The original establishment of the Turing Test did not specify the nature of the queries that the inquirer is supposed to ask of the human participant and the AI. Presumably, the inquirer should use their intellect to devise a sufficient series or set of questions that can achieve the end-goal of being able to ascertain whether the AI can be distinguished from the human participant. Furthermore, it might be reasonably assumed that the inquirer could devise new questions in real-time as needed, doing so in response to the answers of the AI or the human participant.

This kind of interactive dialogue would seem the more likely means to try and discern the intellectual prowess of the subjects.

Some have outlined the kinds of queries that might be used in a general intelligence Turing Testing. Nonetheless, there is no universally accepted set or specification of what the queries need to be.

Per word choice, herein the word "query" or "queries" is used, rather than words such as "questions" or the "inquiries," though those other phrasings are equally applicable and considered interchangeable for purposes herein.

In the overarching Turing Test, the queries are expected to cover all facets embodying general intelligence. For purposes of the Turing Test utilization in the context of this study, the queries are focused on the discipline of legal reasoning.

2.2.5 Element "Answers to the Turing Test"

The answers that are to be provided by the human participant and by the AI are presumed to be completely open-ended, meaning that their respective answers are whatever answers they wish to provide. It is then up the inquirer to decide whether the answers are appropriate and whether the answers are sensible or nonsensical, etc.

In the overarching Turing Test, the answers are expected to cover all facets embodying general intelligence. For purposes of the Turing Test utilization in the context of this study, the answers are presumed to be focused on the discipline of legal reasoning.

A longstanding question about legal reasoning is the degree to which law and legal reasoning involve and depend upon general intelligence, such that there might be little means of separating legal reasoning from general intelligence. In that sense, it could be asserted that the Turing Test in a legal context has no choice but to also involve the use of general intelligence, and therefore it is somewhat misleading to suggest that a Turing Test for legal reasoning is solely and exclusively only about the law and legal reasoning. This significant point is worthwhile to keep in mind.

2.2.6 Element "Rules of the Turing Test"

There are no established rules for the Turing Test, other than the general semblance of the inquirer opting to ask queries of the human participant and the AI, doing so in whatever manner the inquirer deems to do so. In other words, the inquirer does not need to alternate between the subjects, does not need to be balanced in asking questions, and so on. This is left entirely up to the discretion of the inquirer.

In theory, the inquirer could ask queries of only one of the subjects and opt to not ask any of the other. Furthermore, the inquirer could ask just one question and offer no other questions for the subjects. Since it would be a seeming undermining of the Turing Test for the inquirer to take such a stance, it has been proposed that there should be some explicitly stated rules associated with the Turing Test.

In the case of attempts at undertaking the Turing Test, there have been various rules sketched, though they have tended to be narrow and overly specific. For example, suppose a Turing Test is undertaken that stipulates the entire testing period will be five minutes in length. This does not seem a sufficiently long enough period to allow for a properly undertaken inquiry, and thus the resulting outcome would be specious or certainly suspect.

In the overarching Turing Test, rules would presumably be crafted aiming to cover all facets embodying general intelligence. For purposes of the Turing Test utilization in the context of this study, rules are presumed to be focused on covering the discipline of legal reasoning.

2.2.7 Element "Potential Observers"

In the original description of the Turing Test, there is no delineation of whether there might be observers involved in the Turing Test. Essentially, it is not a topic particularly brought up or considered. Subsequently, it has been envisioned that there would seem to be value in having observers, without which otherwise the nature of the Turing Test might be perceived as less viably undertaken and ultimately discounted.

Some assert that the inclusion of observers might impact the Turing Test and alter the results, somehow skewing the effort. Others point out that the observers could be kept astray of the matter and nonetheless still be able to observe the effort. If done properly, it can be argued that the inclusion of observers has no material effect on the Turing Test itself, while at the same time perhaps achieving an acceptance or acknowledgment of the result due to the allowance for having observers.

In the overarching Turing Test, observers would be principally anyone having an interest in general intelligence. For purposes of the Turing Test utilization in the context of this study, observers are presumed to be focused on having a particular interest in the discipline of legal reasoning.

2.2.8 Element "Conclusion Reached"

The primary outcome of the Turing Test consists of the inquirer declaring which of the subjects is the AI. If the inquirer correctly states which is the AI, presumably the AI has failed at being able to showcase the equivalence of human intelligence and somehow given itself away, thus, "failing" the Turing Test. If the inquirer is unable to state which is the AI, presumably the AI has been able to showcase the equivalence of human intelligence and thus "succeeded" in passing the Turing Test.

There are numerous qualms about this simplistic standpoint. Suppose for example that the inquirer merely flips a coin to ascertain which of the subjects is the AI. In that case, would the AI have "succeeded" if the coin toss failed to select the AI, and would the AI have "failed" if the coin toss perchance selected the AI? This certainly does not seem suitable. Another concern is that doing the Turing Test perhaps once, and then declaring a failure or success does not seem especially valid, and perhaps it ought to be done repeatedly until some level of repeated efforts provides a more substantive basis for rendering a result. In the overarching Turing Test, the conclusion reached would be whether the AI has apparently demonstrated general intelligence. For purposes of the Turing Test utilization in the context of this study, the conclusion reached is whether the AI has achieved sufficiency in the discipline of legal reasoning.

2.2.9 Element "Reverse Turing Test"

The traditional or conventional Turing Test has been described in these subsections. A variant known as the Reverse Turing Test has been identified in the literature and variously defined. One variant is that the Reverse Turing Test consists of the inquirer having to identify which of the subjects is the human, rather than which of the subjects is the AI. This of course does not appear to be demonstratively different than the conventional approach since by the act of identifying which is the AI, by default the assumption is that the other subject is indeed the human participant. Nonetheless, some assert that the focus on trying to identify the human participant rather than the AI is a notable difference and therefore merits its special attention as an approach to the Turing Test.

Another meaning for a Reverse Turing Test consists of the human participant attempting to masquerade as the AI. The basis for doing so is sometimes attributed to a software development technique called the Wizard of Oz, whereby a software developer pretends to be the computer and responds to human end-users, seeking to ferret out what kinds of interaction the human end-users are desirous of having, and then programming the computer system accordingly.

For purposes of the Turing Test utilization in the context of this study, the Reverse Turing Test is included as a form of completeness of coverage, without stipulating or assessing the value of the approach.

Section 3: Autonomous Levels of AI Legal Reasoning

In this section, a framework for the autonomous levels of AI Legal Reasoning is summarized and is based on the research described in detail in Eliot [20].

These autonomous levels will be portrayed in a grid that aligns with the Turing Test key elements identified in the prior section of this paper, and thus it is useful to first explain what each of the autonomous levels consists of.

The autonomous levels of AI Legal Reasoning are as follows:

Level 0: No Automation for AI Legal Reasoning

Level 1: Simple Assistance Automation for AI Legal Reasoning

Level 2: Advanced Assistance Automation for AI Legal Reasoning

Level 3: Semi-Autonomous Automation for AI Legal Reasoning

Level 4: Domain Autonomous for AI Legal Reasoning

Level 5: Fully Autonomous for AI Legal Reasoning

Level 6: Superhuman Autonomous for AI Legal Reasoning

See **Figure A-1** for an overview chart showcasing the autonomous levels of AI Legal Reasoning as via columns denoting each of the respective levels.

See **Figure A-2** for an overview chart similar to Figure A-1 which alternatively is indicative of the autonomous levels of AI Legal Reasoning via the rows as depicting the respective levels (this is simply a reformatting of Figure A-1, doing so to aid in illuminating this variant perspective, but does not introduce any new facets or alterations from the contents as already shown in Figure A-1).

3.1.1 Level 0: No Automation for AI Legal Reasoning

Level 0 is considered the no automation level. Legal reasoning is carried out via manual methods and principally occurs via paper-based methods.

This level is allowed some leeway in that the use of say a simple handheld calculator or perhaps the use of a fax machine could be allowed or included within this Level 0, though strictly speaking it could be said that any form whatsoever of automation is to be excluded from this level.

3.1.2 Level 1: Simple Assistance Automation for AI Legal Reasoning

Level 1 consists of simple assistance automation for AI legal reasoning.

Examples of this category encompassing simple automation would include the use of everyday computer-based word processing, the use of everyday computer-based spreadsheets, the access to online legal documents that are stored and retrieved electronically, and so on.

By-and-large, today's use of computers for legal activities is predominantly within Level 1. It is assumed and expected that over time, the pervasiveness of automation will continue to deepen and widen, and eventually lead to legal activities being supported and within Level 2, rather than Level 1.

3.1.3 Level 2: Advanced Assistance Automation for AI Legal Reasoning

Level 2 consists of advanced assistance automation for AI legal reasoning.

Examples of this notion encompassing advanced automation would include the use of query-style Natural Language Processing (NLP), Machine Learning (ML) for case predictions, and so on.

Gradually, over time, it is expected that computer-based systems for legal activities will increasingly make use of advanced automation. Law industry technology that was once at a Level 1 will likely be refined, upgraded, or expanded to include advanced capabilities, and thus be reclassified into Level 2.

3.1.4 Level 3: Semi-Autonomous Automation for AI Legal Reasoning

Level 3 consists of semi-autonomous automation for AI legal reasoning.

Examples of this notion encompassing semi-autonomous automation would include the use of Knowledge-Based Systems (KBS) for legal reasoning, the use of Machine Learning and Deep Learning (ML/DL) for legal reasoning, and so on.

Today, such automation tends to exist in research efforts or prototypes and pilot systems, along with some commercial legal technology that has been infusing these capabilities too.

3.1.5 Level 4: Domain Autonomous for AI Legal Reasoning

Level 4 consists of domain autonomous computer-based systems for AI legal reasoning.

This level reuses the conceptual notion of Operational Design Domains (ODDs) as utilized in the autonomous vehicles and self-driving cars levels of autonomy, though in this use case it is being applied to the legal domain [17] [18] [20].

Essentially, this entails any AI legal reasoning capacities that can operate autonomously, entirely so, but that is only able to do so in some limited or constrained legal domain.

3.1.6 Level 5: Fully Autonomous for AI Legal Reasoning

Level 5 consists of fully autonomous computer-based systems for AI legal reasoning.

In a sense, Level 5 is the superset of Level 4 in terms of encompassing all possible domains as per however so defined ultimately for Level 4. The only constraint, as it were, consists of the facet that the Level 4 and Level 5 are concerning human intelligence and the capacities thereof. This is an important emphasis due to attempting to distinguish Level 5 from Level 6 (as will be discussed in the next subsection)

It is conceivable that someday there might be a fully autonomous AI legal reasoning capability, one that encompasses all of the law in all foreseeable ways, though this is quite a tall order and remains quite aspirational without a clear cut path of how this might one day be achieved. Nonetheless, it seems to be within the extended realm of possibilities, which is worthwhile to mention in relative terms to Level 6.

3.1.7 Level 6: Superhuman Autonomous for AI Legal Reasoning

Level 6 consists of superhuman autonomous computer-based systems for AI legal reasoning.

In a sense, Level 6 is the entirety of Level 5 and adds something beyond that in a manner that is currently ill-defined and perhaps (some would argue) as yet unknowable. The notion is that AI might ultimately exceed human intelligence, rising to become superhuman, and if so, we do not yet have any viable indication of what that superhuman intelligence consists of and nor what kind of thinking it would somehow be able to undertake.

Whether a Level 6 is ever attainable is reliant upon whether superhuman AI is ever attainable, and thus, at this time, this stands as a placeholder for that which might never occur. In any case, having such a placeholder provides a semblance of completeness, doing so without necessarily legitimatizing that superhuman AI is going to be achieved or not. No such claim or dispute is undertaken within this framework.

Section 4: Turing Test Grid Integrating Autonomous Levels of AILR

4.1 Grid Indication of Levels of Autonomy (LoA) by Key Factors

In this section, the Turing Test key elements depicted in Section 2 are aligned into a grid that also contains the autonomous levels of AI Legal Reasoning which were described in Section 3.

Figure B-1 provides an overview chart depicting the rows as the respective LoA AILR levels and the columns denoting the Turing Test elements. A row-by-row explanatory narrative is provided in the subsections below.

Figure B-2 provides a similar overview chart of Figure B-1 but does so with the rows indicating the Turing Test key elements and the columns showcasing the AILR autonomous levels. This is simply an alternative perspective of Figure B-1 and does not introduce any new content or alterations from the contents depicted in Figure B-1. A row-by-row explanatory narrative is provided in the subsections below.

4.1.1 Level 0: No Automation for AI Legal Reasoning

As indicated in charts B-1 and B-2, Level 0 of the LoA AILR have an "n/a" (meaning not applicable) for each of the Turing Test key elements.

This designating of "n/a" is logically suitable for Level 0 since there is no autonomy associated with AILR at Level 0, therefore no relevancy in seeking to apply the Turing Test. Axiomatically, the Turing Test is inapplicable at Level 0. Any attempt to perform a Turing Test at Level 0 is inappropriate and unsuitable.

<u>Level 0</u>

- The Inquirer: **n/a**
- Human Participant: **n/a**
- AI-Based Legal Reasoner: **n/a**
- Queries of the Turing Test: **n/a**
- Answers to the Turing Test: **n/a**
- Rules of the Turing Test: **n/a**
- Potential Observers: **n/a**
- Conclusion Reached: **n/a**
- Reverse Turing Test: **n/a**

4.1.2 Level 1: Simple Assistance Automation for AI Legal Reasoning

As indicated in charts B-1 and B-2, Level 1 of the LoA AILR has an "n/a" (meaning not applicable) for each of the Turing Test key elements.

This designating of "n/a" is logically suitable for Level 1 since there is no autonomy associated with AILR at Level 1, therefore no relevancy in seeking to apply the Turing Test. Axiomatically, the Turing Test is inapplicable at Level 1. Any attempt to perform a Turing Test at Level 1 is inappropriate and unsuitable.

<u>Level 1</u>

- The Inquirer: **n/a**
- Human Participant: **n/a**
- AI-Based Legal Reasoner: **n/a**
- Queries of the Turing Test: **n/a**
- Answers to the Turing Test: **n/a**
- Rules of the Turing Test: **n/a**
- Potential Observers: **n/a**
- Conclusion Reached: **n/a**
- Reverse Turing Test: **n/a**

4.1.3 Level 2: Advanced Assistance Automation for AI Legal Reasoning

As indicated in charts B-1 and B-2, Level 2 of the LoA AILR has an "n/a" (meaning not applicable) for each of the Turing Test key elements.

This designating of "n/a" is logically suitable for Level 0 since there is no autonomy associated with AILR at Level 2, therefore no relevance in seeking to apply the Turing Test. Axiomatically, the Turing Test is inapplicable at Level 2. Any attempt to perform a Turing Test at Level 2 is inappropriate and unsuitable.

<u>Level 2</u>

- The Inquirer: **n/a**
- Human Participant: **n/a**
- AI-Based Legal Reasoner: **n/a**
- Queries of the Turing Test: **n/a**
- Answers to the Turing Test: **n/a**
- Rules of the Turing Test: **n/a**
- Potential Observers: **n/a**
- Conclusion Reached: **n/a**
- Reverse Turing Test: **n/a**

4.1.4 Level 3: Semi-Autonomous Automation for AI Legal Reasoning

As indicated in charts B-1 and B-2, Level 3 of the LoA AILR indicate several specific designations associated with the respective Turing Test elements.

Keep in mind that Level 3 is considered semi-autonomous, therefore situated partially in conventional automation and partially into autonomous capabilities. Since Level 3 is not defined as unqualified autonomy, there is no expectation that Level 3 AILR would be able to pass or succeed at the Turing Test. Nonetheless, it might be useful to administer the Turing Test as a means of gauging the extent of autonomous capabilities, along with being able to guide on what further advances might be needed to achieve Level 4 or higher.

For the inquirer, the preference is that an expert in legal reasoning would be utilized, rightfully so since the inquirer needs to be able to ask intelligent questions about the law, must be able to understand and assess the answers provided by the subjects participating, and must ultimately reach a conclusion about which is the human participant and which is the AI. The human participant should be an expert in the matters of legal reasoning being tested. The AI-based Legal Reasoner can consist of a minimal amount of AI legal reasoning capacity, having achieved a sufficient capacity to merit being categorized at Level 3.

The queries of the Turing Test can be minimal in terms of the depth of exploration of legal reasoning, and likewise, the answers can be similarly of a minimal nature. Since this is viewed as a looser variant of the Turing Test, the rules of the matter can be minimal. Observers could be of an open nature and the conclusion reached by the inquirer is expected to be no greater than rated as "Notable" if the AILR can respond in a manner such that the Turing Test is considered as a pass. A Reverse Turing Test might be useful as a means to explore how to best further the AILR toward higher achievement in Level 3 or toward attainment of Level 4 or higher.

<u>Level 3</u>

- The Inquirer: **Expert Preferred**
- Human Participant: **Expert**
- AI-Based Legal Reasoner: **Minimal**
- Queries of the Turing Test: **Minimal**
- Answers to the Turing Test: **Minimal**
- Rules of the Turing Test: **Minimal**
- Potential Observers: **Open**
- Conclusion Reached: **Limited As "Notable"**
- Reverse Turing Test: **Useful But Not Substantive**

4.1.5 Level 4: Domain Autonomous for AI Legal Reasoning

As indicated in charts B-1 and B-2, Level 4 of the LoA AILR indicate several specific designations associated with the respective Turing Test elements.

Level 4 is considered autonomous with respect to a given legal domain. Therefore, this is considered an opportunity for a full-scale Turing Test in AILR, though restricted to the domain so specified. There is no expectation that the AILR would be able to pass or succeed outside the domain stipulated.

For the inquirer, an expert in the identified domain of legal reasoning would be utilized, rightfully so since the inquirer needs to be able to ask intelligent questions about the law in that domain, must be able to understand and assess the answers provided by the subjects participating as it relates to the domain, and must ultimately reach a conclusion about which is the human participant, and which is the AI. The human participant should be an expert in the legal domain of legal reasoning being tested. The AI-based Legal Reasoner is to consist of a domain-specific AI legal reasoning capacity that fits the domain entailed, having achieved a sufficient capacity to merit being potentially categorized at Level 4.

The queries of the Turing Test should be bounded to the specific domain of legal reasoning, and likewise, the answers can be similarly bounded to the chosen domain. Since this is viewed as a full use of the Turing Test, the rules of the matter should be rigorously devised and applied. Observers would most likely be law specialists in the chosen domain and the conclusion reached by the inquirer is expected to be a domain-only pass if the AILR can respond in a manner such that the Turing Test is considered as succeeded. A Reverse Turing Test might be useful as a means to explore how to best further the AILR toward higher achievement in Level 4 or toward attainment of Level 5 or higher.

<u>**Level 4**</u>

- The Inquirer: **Expert in Domain**
- Human Participant: **Expert in Domain**
- AI-Based Legal Reasoner: **Domain Specific**
- Queries of the Turing Test: **Domain Specific**
- Answers to the Turing Test: **Domain Specific**
- Rules of the Turing Test: **Rigorous**
- Potential Observers: **Law Specialists**
- Conclusion Reached: **Domain-Only Pass in AILR**
- Reverse Turing Test: **Useful in Domain**

4.1.6 Level 5: Fully Autonomous for AI Legal Reasoning

As indicated in charts B-1 and B-2, Level 5 of the LoA AILR indicate several specific designations associated with the respective Turing Test elements.

Level 5 is considered autonomous with respect to all legal domains. Therefore, this is considered an opportunity for a full-scale Turing Test in AILR, being undertaken without any restrictions regarding the legal domains involved. The Turing Test should purposely seek to explore all legal domains since otherwise there would remain untested areas and any conclusion would be considered problematic.

For the inquirer, the likelihood is that one or more experts in the law would be utilized, rightfully so since an individual inquirer would seem unlikely to be able to encompass all legal domains, and the inquirer(s) need to be able to ask intelligent questions about the law in all legal domains, must be able to understand and assess the answers provided by the subjects participating as it relates to all legal domains, and must ultimately reach a conclusion about which is the human participant and which is the AI. The human participant might also consist of one or more experts due to the need to be able to respond across all legal domains and it seems unlikely that one individual could otherwise do so. The AI-based Legal Reasoner is to consist of an AI legal reasoning capacity that can be responsive across all legal domains, having achieved a sufficient capacity to merit being potentially categorized at Level 5.

The queries of the Turing Test should be bounded to the realm of law and require legal reasoning, and likewise, the answers are similarly bounded. Since this is viewed as a full use of the Turing Test, the rules of the matter should be rigorously devised and applied. Observers would most likely be law professionals across a variety of legal domains and the conclusion reached by the inquirer is expected to be a full pass if the AILR can respond in a manner such that the Turing Test is considered as succeeded. A Reverse Turing Test would likely be useful as a means to explore how to best further the AILR toward higher achievement in Level 5 or toward attainment of Level 6.

<u>**Level 5**</u>

- The Inquirer: **Multiple Experts**
- Human Participant: **Multiple Experts**
- AI-Based Legal Reasoner: **All Domains**
- Queries of the Turing Test: **All Domains**
- Answers to the Turing Test: **All Domains**
- Rules of the Turing Test: **Rigorous**
- Potential Observers: **Law Professionals**
- Conclusion Reached: **Full Pass in AILR**
- Reverse Turing Test: **Useful Overall**

4.1.7 Level 6: Superhuman Autonomous for AI Legal Reasoning

As indicated in charts B-1 and B-2, Level 6 of the LoA AILR indicate several specific designations associated with the respective Turing Test elements.

Level 6 is considered autonomous with respect to all legal domains. Therefore, this is considered an opportunity for a full-scale Turing Test in AILR, being undertaken without any restrictions regarding the legal domains involved. The Turing Test should purposely seek to explore all legal domains since otherwise there would remain untested areas and any conclusion would be considered problematic.

Level 6 poses a fundamental difficulty since it is as yet unknown as to what a superhuman capacity in the law might consist of, thus attempting to assess this capability via a Turing Test would seem challenging. Potentially, seemingly intractable legal questions that have stymied human legal reasoning might be utilized. Overall, it is unclear how those devising a test of an AI that is presumably at a heightened level of intellect could be suitably established since those creating the test are operating at a lower level of intellectual capacity. In any case, the Turing Test still might be viably applied and the nature of doing so is worthy of additional research, as mentioned in Section 5 of this paper.

For the inquirer, the likelihood is that one or more of the world's topmost experts in the law would be utilized, rightfully so since an individual inquirer would seem unlikely to be able to encompass all legal domains and since the attempt involves trying to challenge a superhuman AI capacity, and the inquirer(s) need to be able to ask hyper-intelligent questions about the law in all legal domains, must be able to understand and assess the answers provided by the subjects participating as it relates to all legal domains, and must ultimately reach a conclusion about which is the human participant and which is the AI.

The human participant might also consist of one or more of the world's topmost experts due to the need to be able to respond across all legal domains and it seems unlikely that one individual could otherwise do so.

The AI-based Legal Reasoner is to consist of an AI legal reasoning capacity that can be responsive across all legal domains, having achieved a sufficient capacity to merit being potentially categorized at Level 6 and considered as presumably superhuman in capability. The queries of the Turing Test should be bounded to the realm of law and require legal reasoning, and likewise, the answers are similarly bounded. Since this is viewed as a full use of the Turing Test, the rules of the matter should be rigorously devised and applied.

Observers would most likely be both those versed in the law and those non-law observers interested in the superhuman capacity overall, and the conclusion reached by the inquirer is expected to be an exemplary pass if the AILR can respond in a manner such that the Turing Test is considered as succeeded. A Reverse Turing Test would likely be useful as a means to explore how to best further the AILR toward higher achievement in Level 6.

Level 6

- The Inquirer: **Topmost Experts**
- Human Participant: **Topmost Experts**
- AI-Based Legal Reasoner: **Domain Plus**
- Queries of the Turing Test: **Domain Plus**
- Answers to the Turing Test: **Domain Plus**
- Rules of the Turing Test: **Rigorous**
- Potential Observers: **Law & Non-Law**
- Conclusion Reached: **Exemplary Pass in AILR**
- Reverse Turing Test: **Useful Overall**

4.2 Grid Indication of Turing Test Key Elements by Levels of Autonomy (LoA)

The next subsections showcase the Turing Test key factors as at-a-glance for each factor, listing the designations that have been postulated for each of the LoA AILR levels. Narrative discussion about these facets has already been covered in the prior Subsection 4.1 and thus it is not necessary to repeat it in this subsection (refer to the prior subsections as needed).

4.2.1 Turing Test "The Inquirer" by LoA

For a narrative discussion about the "The Inquirer" for each of the LoA AILR levels, see the preceding subsections. This list shown here provides a convenience of indication and is also portrayed on charts B-1 and B-2.

The Inquirer

- Level 0: **n/a**
- Level 1: **n/a**
- Level 2: **n/a**
- Level 3: **Expert Preferred**
- Level 4: **Expert in Domain**
- Level 5: **Multiple Experts**
- Level 6: **Topmost Experts**

4.2.2 Turing Test "Human Participant" by LoA

For a narrative discussion about the "Human Participant" for each of the LoA AILR levels, see the preceding subsections. This list shown here provides a convenience of indication and is also portrayed on charts B-1 and B-2.

<u>**Human Participant**</u>

- Level 0: **n/a**
- Level 1: **n/a**
- Level 2: **n/a**
- Level 3: **Expert**
- Level 4: **Expert in Domain**
- Level 5: **Multiple Experts**
- Level 6: **Topmost Experts**

4.2.3 Turing Test "AI-Based Legal Reasoner" LoA

For a narrative discussion about the "AI-Based Legal Reasoner" for each of the LoA AILR levels, see the preceding subsections. This list shown here provides a convenience of indication and is also portrayed on charts B-1 and B-2.

<u>**AI-Based Legal Reasoner**</u>

- Level 0: **n/a**
- Level 1: **n/a**
- Level 2: **n/a**
- Level 3: **Minimal**
- Level 4: **Domain Specific**
- Level 5: **All Domains**
- Level 6: **Domains Plus**

4.2.4 Turing Test "Queries of the Turing Test" by LoA

For a narrative discussion about the "Queries of the Turing Test" for each of the LoA AILR levels, see the preceding subsections. This list shown here provides a convenience of indication and is also portrayed on charts B-1 and B-2.

<u>Queries of the Turing Test</u>

- Level 0: **n/a**
- Level 1: **n/a**
- Level 2: **n/a**
- Level 3: **Minimal**
- Level 4: **Domain Specific**
- Level 5: **All Domains**
- Level 6: **Domain Plus**

4.2.5 Turing Test "Answers to the Turing Test" by LoA

For a narrative discussion about the "Answers to the Turing Test" for each of the LoA AILR levels, see the preceding subsections. This list shown here provides a convenience of indication and is also portrayed on charts B-1 and B-2.

<u>Answers to the Turing Test</u>

- Level 0: **n/a**
- Level 1: **n/a**
- Level 2: **n/a**
- Level 3: **Minimal**
- Level 4: **Domain Specific**
- Level 5: **All Domains**
- Level 6: **Domain Plus**

4.2.6 Turing Test "Rules of the Turing Test" by LoA

For a narrative discussion about the "Rules of the Turing Test" for each of the LoA AILR levels, see the preceding subsections. This list shown here provides the convenience of indication and is also portrayed on charts B-1 and B-2.

Rules of the Turing Test

- Level 0: **n/a**
- Level 1: **n/a**
- Level 2: **n/a**
- Level 3: **Minimal**
- Level 4: **Rigorous**
- Level 5: **Rigorous**
- Level 6: **Rigorous**

4.2.7 Turing Test "Potential Observers" LoA

For a narrative discussion about the "Potential Observers" for each of the LoA AILR levels, see the preceding subsections. This list shown here provides a convenience of indication and is also portrayed on charts B-1 and B-2.

Potential Observers

- Level 0: **n/a**
- Level 1: **n/a**
- Level 2: **n/a**
- Level 3: **Open**
- Level 4: **Law Specialists**
- Level 5: **Law Professionals**
- Level 6: **Law & Non-Law**

4.2.8 Turing Test "Conclusions Reached" by LoA

For a narrative discussion about the "Conclusions Reached" for each of the LoA AILR levels, see the preceding subsections. This list shown here provides a convenience of indication and is also portrayed on charts B-1 and B-2.

<u>**Conclusion Reached**</u>

- Level 0: **n/a**
- Level 1: **n/a**
- Level 2: **n/a**
- Level 3: **Limited As "Notable"**
- Level 4: **Domain-Only Pass in AILR**
- Level 5: **Full Pass in AILR**
- Level 6: **Exemplary Pass in AILR**

4.2.9 Turing Test "Reverse Turing Test" by LoA

For a narrative discussion about the "Reverse Turing Test" for each of the LoA AILR levels, see the preceding subsections. This list shown here provides a convenience of indication and is also portrayed on charts B-1 and B-2.

<u>**Reverse Turing Test**</u>

- Level 0: **n/a**
- Level 1: **n/a**
- Level 2: **n/a**
- Level 3: **Useful But Not Substantive**
- Level 4: **Useful in Domain**
- Level 5: **Useful Overall**
- Level 6: **Useful Overall**

Section 5: Additional Considerations and Future Research

The grid depicted in Figure B-1 and Figure B-2 is a strawman variant, meaning that the indications shown are an initial populating of the grid. Additional research is needed to explore the designations and ascertain whether the initial indications might be advisedly changed or possibly transformed into some other kind of designations, such as numeric scores or weights.

Another aspect of additional research involves the Turing Test key elements that are utilized in this strawman variant.

There are other ways to portray the elements, along with the possibility of adding elements or possibly opting to excise some of the elements from the grid. Research on such modifications is encouraged.

As a final point, there are potentially greater questions that arise from the grid, alluded to earlier in the discussion of the prior sections, entailing what actions would be taken if indeed AILR can achieve the autonomous levels of Level 4, Level 5, and Level 6. There remain many such open issues, each deserving of suitable attention.

This paper has proposed a variant of the Turing Test that is customized for specific use in the AILR realm, including depicting how this famous "gold standard" of AI fulfillment can be robustly applied across the autonomous levels of AI Legal Reasoning. Such an instrument can aid in addressing the open question underlying how we will know when AILR has achieved autonomous capacities.

References

1. Alarie, Benjamin (2016). "The Path of the Law: Toward Legal Singularity," May 27, 2016, SSRN, University of Toronto Faculty of Law and Vector Institute for Artificial Intelligence.

2. Aleven, Vincent (2003). "Using Background Knowledge in Case-Based Legal Reasoning: A Computational Model and an Intelligent Learning Environment," Artificial Intelligence.

3. Ashley, Kevin, and Karl Branting, Howard Margolis, and Cass Sunstein (2001). "Legal Reasoning and Artificial Intelligence: How Computers 'Think' Like Lawyers," Symposium: Legal Reasoning and Artificial Intelligence, University of Chicago Law School Roundtable.

4. Baker, Jamie (2018). "A Legal Research Odyssey: Artificial Intelligence as Disrupter," Law Library Journal.

5. Batsakis, Sotiris, and George Baryannis, Guido Governatori, Illias Tachmazidis, Grigoris Antoniou (2018). "Legal Representation and Reasoning in Practice: A Critical Comparison," Volume 313, Legal Knowledge and Information Systems.

6. Ben-Ari, Daniel and D., Frish, Y., Lazovski, A., Eldan, U., & Greenbaum, D. (2016). "Artificial Intelligence in the Practice of Law: An Analysis and Proof of Concept Experiment," Volume 23, Number 2, Richmond Journal of Law & Technology.

7. Bench-Capon, Trevor (2004). "AGATHA: Automation of the Construction of Theories in Case Law Domains," January 2004, Legal Knowledge and Information Systems Jurix 2004, Amsterdam.

8. Bench-Capon, Trevor and Givoanni Sartor (2003). "A Model of Legal Reasoning with Cases Incorporating Theories and Values," November 2013, Artificial Intelligence.

9. Breuker, Joost (1996). "A Functional Ontology of Law," October 1996, ResearchGate.

10. Buchanan, Bruce, and Thomas Headrick (1970). "Some Speculation about Artificial Intelligence and Legal Reasoning," Volume 23, Stanford Law Review.

11. Chagal-Feferkorn, Karni (2019). "Am I An Algorithm or a Product: When Products Liability Should Apply to Algorithmic Decision-Makers," Stanford Law & Policy Review.

12. Collingridge, David (1980). The Social Control of Technology. St. Martin's Press.

13. Douglas, William (1948). "The Dissent: A Safeguard of Democracy," Volume 32, Journal of the American Judicature Society.

14. Dung, P, and R. Kowalski, F. Toni (2006). "Dialectic Proof Procedures for Assumption-Based Admissible Argumentation," Artificial Intelligence.

15. Eliot, Lance (2016). AI Guardian Angels for Deep AI Trustworthiness. LBE Press Publishing.

16. Eliot, Lance (2020). "The Neglected Dualism of Artificial Moral Agency and Artificial Legal Reasoning in AI for Social Good." Harvard University, Harvard Center for Research on Computation and Society, AI for Social Good Conference, July 21, 2020.

17. Eliot, Lance (2020). AI and Legal Reasoning Essentials. LBE Press Publishing.

18. Eliot, Lance (2019). Artificial Intelligence and LegalTech Essentials. LBE Press Publishing.

19. Eliot, Lance (2020). "FutureLaw 2020 Showcases How Tech is Transforming The Law, Including the Impacts of AI," April 16, 2020, Forbes.

20. Eliot, Lance (2020). "An Ontological AI-and-Law Framework for the Autonomous Levels of AI Legal Reasoning," https://orcid.org/0000-0003-3081-1819, Cornell University arXiv.

21. Eliot, Lance (2018). "Turing Test for AI," January 30, 2018, AI Trends.

22. Eliot, Lance (2018). "Common Sense Reasoning and AI," April 10, 2018, AI Trends.

23. Eliot, Lance (2018). "Singularity and AI," July 10, 2018, AI Trends.

24. Eliot, Lance (2019). "Artificial Stupidity Could be the Crux to AI," December 8, 2019, Forbes.

25. Eliot, Lance (2020). "The Role of Human Judgement as a Presumed Integral Ingredient for Achieving True AI," March 9, 2020, Forbes.

26. Eliot, Lance (2020). "Strong AI Versus Weak AI Is Completely Misunderstood," July 15, 2020, Forbes.

27. Eliot, Lance (2020). "The Famous Turing Test Put In Reverse and Upside-Down," July 20, 2020, Forbes.

28. Galdon, Fernando, and Ashley Hall, Stephen Jia Wang (2020). "Designing Trust in Highly Automated Virtual Assistants: A Taxonomy of Levels of Autonomy," Artificial Intelligence in Industry 4.0: A Collection of Innovative Research Case-Studies.

29. Gardner, Anne (1987). Artificial Intelligence and Legal Reasoning. MIT Press.

30. Genesereth, Michael (2009). "Computational Law: The Cop in the Backseat," Stanford Center for Legal Informatics, Stanford University.

31. Ghosh, Mirna (2019). "Automation of Legal Reasoning and Decision Based on Ontologies," Normandie Universite.

32. Hage, Jaap (2000). "Dialectical Models in Artificial Intelligence and Law," Artificial Intelligence and Law.

33. Hage, Japp, and Ronald Leenes, Arno Lodder (1993). "Hard Cases: A Procedural Approach," Artificial Intelligence and Law.

34. Markou, Christopher, and Simon Deakin (2020). "Is Law Computable? From Rule of Law to Legal Singularity," May 4, 2020, SSRN, University of Cambridge Faculty of Law Research Paper.

35. McCarty, Thorne (1977). "Reflections on TAXMAN: An Experiment in Artificial Intelligence and Legal Reasoning," January 1977, Harvard Law Review.

36. McGinnis, John and Russell G. Pearce (2014). "The Great Disruption: How Machine Intelligence Will Transform the Role of Lawyers in the Delivery of Legal Services," Volume 82, Number 6, Fordham Law Review.

37. Mikhaylovskiy, N. (2020). "How Do You Test the Strength of AI?" September 2020, *International Conference on Artificial General Intelligence* (pp. 257-266).

38. Mnookin, Robert, and Lewis Kornhauser (1979). "Bargaining in the Shadow of the Law," Volume 88, Number 5, April 1979, The Yale Law Review.

39. Moor, J.H. (2003). The Turing Test. The Elusive Standard of Artificial Intelligence, Kluwer Academic Publishers.

40. Mowbray, Andrew and Philip Chung, Graham Greenleaf (2019). "Utilising AI in the Legal Assistance Sector," LegalAIIA Workshop, ICAIL, June 17, 2019, Montreal, Canada.

41. Neufeld, E., and Finnestad, S (2020). "In Defense of the Turing Test," *AI & Society*.

42. Powell, J. (2019). "Trust Me, I'm a Chatbot: How Artificial Intelligence in Health Care Fails the Turing Test," Volume 21, Number 10, Journal of Medical Internet Research.

43. Prakken, Henry, and Giovanni Sartor (2015). "Law and Logic: A Review from an Argumentation Perspective," Volume 227, Artificial Intelligence.

44. Reinbold, Patric (2020). "Taking Artificial Intelligence Beyond the Turing Test," Volume 20, Wisconsin Law Review.

45. Rissland, Edwina (1990). "Artificial Intelligence and Law: Stepping Stones to a Model of Legal Reasoning," Yale Law Journal.

46. SAE (2018). Taxonomy and Definitions for Terms Related to Driving Automation Systems for On-Road Motor Vehicles, J3016-201806, SAE International.

47. Saygin, A. P. and Cicekli, I., & Akman, V. (2000). "Turing Test: 50 Years Later," Volume 10, Number 4, Minds and Machines.

48. Sunstein, Cass (2001). "Of Artificial Intelligence and Legal Reasoning," University of Chicago Law School, Public Law and Legal Theory Working Papers.

49. Sunstein, Cass, and Kevin Ashley, Karl Branting, Howard Margolis (2001). "Legal Reasoning and Artificial Intelligence: How Computers 'Think' Like Lawyers," Symposium: Legal Reasoning and Artificial Intelligence, University of Chicago Law School Roundtable.

50. Surden, Harry (2014). "Machine Learning and Law," Washington Law Review.

51. Surden, Harry (2019). "Artificial Intelligence and Law: An Overview," Summer 2019, Georgia State University Law Review.

52. Turing, Alan (1950). "Computing Machinery and Intelligence," Volume 59, Number 236, Mind.

53. Valente, Andre, and Joost Breuker (1996). "A Functional Ontology of Law," Artificial Intelligence and Law.

54. Waltl, Bernhard, and Roland Vogl (2018). "Explainable Artificial Intelligence: The New Frontier in Legal Informatics," February 2018, Jusletter IT 22, Stanford Center for Legal Informatics, Stanford University.

55. Warwick, K., and Shah, H. (2016). "Can Machines Think? A Report on Turing Test Experiments at the Royal Society," Volume 28, Number 6, Journal of Experimental & Theoretical Artificial Intelligence.

56. Wolfman, Zack. ABA Model Definition of the Practice of Law, American Bar Association.

57. Yang, Guang, and James Cambias, Kevin Cleary, Eric Daimler, James Drake, Pierre Dupont, Nobuhiko Hata, Peter Kazanzides, Sylvain Martel, Rajni Patel, Veronica Santos, Russell Taylor (2017). "Medical Robots: Regulatory, Ethical, and Legal Considerations for Increasing Levels of Autonomy," March 15, 2017, Science Robotics.

Note: *For supplemental materials depicting the aspects discussed in this chapter, refer to Appendix B, which contains various augmented diagrams, charts, and additional related facets of relevance.*

CHAPTER 4
DUALISM OF MORAL AGENCY AND AI LEGAL REASONING

Abstract

A neglected dualism is occurring in AI for Social Good involving the lack of encompassing both the role of artificial moral agency and artificial legal reasoning in advanced AI systems. Efforts by AI researchers and AI developers have tended to focus on how to craft and embed artificial moral agents to guide moral decision making when an AI system is operating in the field but have not also focused on and coupled the use of artificial legal reasoning capabilities, which is equally necessary for robust moral and legal outcomes. This paper addresses this problematic neglect and offers insights to overcome a substantive prevailing weakness and vulnerability.

Section 1: Introduction

A key question in AI for Social Good is how to ensure that AI systems operating in the field are able to make needed and appropriate moral choices. As society becomes increasingly dependent on AI, there is a widening concern that AI systems might at times not conform to applicable moral norms.

By crafting and embedding Artificial Moral Agents, specialized components within an AI system, it is anticipated that a real-time capacity will enable the enactment and abidance of moral conventions [Cane, 2012; Huang, 2019; Misselhorn, 2019].

Even if Artificial Moral Agents can be suitably devised, there is a missing and crucial element that is currently being neglected, namely the dual role of morality and law. As pointed out by Shiell [1987], since at least the days of Plato there has been a struggle over the relationship between morality and law, and even still today debates about the nature and extent of how moral decisions intertwine with the law are persistent and contentious.

Overall, morality and law are generally viewed as inextricably bound to each other in some fashion and must be considered in concert, though their mutual interaction and dependencies are still an open-ended matter

As such, additional attention to Artificial Legal Reasoners (ALR) is needed, providing the other missing or underplayed element for achieving the requisite morality and law dualism. The inclusion of artificial legal reasoning provides the possibility of including a cooperating specialized ALR component within an AI system that offers a real-time capability for rendering legal-based decisions or awareness about the law [Eliot, 2019; Genesereth, 2009; Surden, 2019].

By considering the simultaneous use and deployment of components for both Artificial Moral Agent capabilities and Artificial Legal Reasoner capabilities, working in a coordinated and communicative manner, the moral agency of AI systems is likely to be more well-rounded and balanced by prevailing laws. This aspiration though is not as readily fulfilled as might seem at first glance since there are inherent tensions between morality and law, which will be further exemplified and revealed in a collaborative effort to have such automated agents work in conjunction with each other.

The remainder of this paper describes the possibilities and problems that will be encountered in seeking to achieve the proffered dualism.

In addition, insights about ways to cope with the consequent hurdles and difficulties are laid out as a research agenda for those pursuing the development of AI for Social Good.

Section 2: Dualism Tensions

As stated by Bickenbach [1989], "the relationship between morality and law is one of the more enduring problematics of jurisprudence." Those legal scholars in the domain of natural law argue that morality is the source of laws and serves as the binding power of laws. In contrast, scholars considered in the legal positivism domain are likely to contend that morality is categorically separate and distinct from law.

In a legal realism context, Kagan [1998] points out that morals and laws ultimately exhibit tensions between each other, and emphasizes that "the law may permit some particular act, even though that act is immoral; and the law may forbid an act, even though that act is morally permissible, or even morally required."

Morality is sometimes viewed as existing within the shadow of law [Mnookin and Kornhauser, 1979]. In that sense, a moral facet would be considered outside of the law and yet within reach of the law. Some view that morality is actually the halo of law, such as Regan [1987] indicating that law is imbued with moral sustenance, even if at times there might not be a moral obligation to abide by the law.

Consider a given body of moral tenets as represented by a designation M and a body of laws as represented by the use of a designation L. Envision these as circles or ovals for which there is a Venn diagram depicting them as overlapping, whereby the designator O represents their overlap:

$$O = M \cap L \quad (1)$$

Define M' and L' as follows:

$$M' = M - (M \cap L) \quad (2)$$
$$L' = L - (M \cap L) \quad (3)$$

If and only if M' is fully outside of the legal realm and not subject to the law, it will be assumed that any instance of an Artificial Moral Agent rendering such a moral choice within the scope of M' could ergo proceed unabated without any needed consultation with an Artificial Legal Reasoner.

Likewise, if and only if L' is fully outside of the moral realm and not subject to a moral underpinning, it will be assumed that any instance of an Artificial Legal Reasoner rendering such a legal indication could ergo proceed unabated without any needed consultation with an Artificial Moral Agent.

The O presents the key challenge for the dualistic nature of the two.

Divide O into those instances for which there is an agreement between the given M and L, which will be designated as A, and those instances for which there is disagreement which is to be designated as D:

$$O = A + D \quad (4)$$

In the case of A, the presumption is that since the M and L are in concordance on such instances, the Artificial Moral Agent and the Artificial Legal Reasoner have no conflict and thus either one can prevail in such a use case.

We are then left with the class D of instances, providing the essence of conflict that needs to be resolved or otherwise conveyed. Some form of automated conflict resolution will be required to contend with body D. In the study of law, there are considered "hard" cases that are less amenable to everyday legal reasoning [Hage et al, 1993].

Class D can be characterized as being composed of some combination of hard case instances, designated as D* and those that are non-hard, depicted as D° (do not conflate the notion of non-hard with a meaning of being easy or simple, since the non-hard cases can also pose quite arduous and complicated challenges).

For D then:

$$D = D^* + D^\circ \quad (5)$$

Algorithmically, an AI for Social Good system that makes use of an Artificial Moral Agent should correspondingly include an Artificial Legal Reasoner, and for which at any invoking of either one, the other should also be invoked, and the AI then would make a comparison of the results so rendered by each respectively.

For M', the AI proceeds with the result of the Artificial Moral Agent, and for the L' the AI proceeds with the result of the Artificial Legal Reasoner.

In the O, the AI can choose from either one in the instance of A, while for those that are D the AI would undertake a conflict resolution process (as discussed next). It is likely that the D^* will require an elaborate effort by the conflict resolution process, while the D° will be predominantly less protracted.

Section 3: Conflict Resolution

In this effort of the prescribed dualism, an a priori approach will need to be established for resolving the potential conflicts between the results tendered by the Artificial Moral Agent and those of the Artificial Legal Reasoner.

Undertaking a satisfactory conflict resolution of this sort is not straightforward, as this salient remark in The Law by Frederic Bastiat [1850] illuminates: "When law and morality contradict each other, the citizen has the cruel alternative of either losing his moral sense or losing his respect for the law."

An outline of the potential approaches to the morality and law conflicts in an AI for Social Good system is indicated next, numbering each approach as Cn, and for which the n is merely for reference purposes and not to suggest priority or sequence of which approach is valued over another.

3.1 Approach C1: Morality Prevails Over Law

In Hart [1961], morality is depicted as the ultimate standard for assessing human behavior and thus the law is considered second-best, namely that moral reasoning eclipses any legal reasoning.

As per Goparaju Ramachandra Rao [1980] in I Learn: "Whenever legality clashes with morality, legality should be opposed, and morality should be upheld."

In that case, for a conflict resolution approach labeled as C1, for those instances in the realm of class D, the M will always prevail, regardless of being either D° or D*.

This does not obviate the need for the use of an Artificial Legal Reasoner since there is still the class of L′ to be dealt with. It does though significantly reduce the run-time effort since anything other than L′ is transferred over to the Artificial Moral Agent to render a final decision.

3.2 Approach C2: Law Prevails Over Morality

In approach C2, the law is considered to prevail over the side of morality, and therefore any instances in class D are to be decided by the Artificial Legal Reasoner. This might be likened as a variant of the Rule of Law as exemplified by Albert Dicey's [1885] quote: "With us no man is above the law and every man, whatever be his rank or condition, is subject to the ordinary law of the realm and amenable to the jurisdiction of the ordinary tribunals." Thus, even if the Artificial Moral Agent has deemed that the instance is not morally aligned, nonetheless, the law shall prevail.

3.3 Approach C3: Determining Which Prevails

In approach C3, it is presumed that both the Artificial Moral Agent and the Artificial Legal Reasoner have a bona fide basis for why their respective rendered decisions are in conflict with each other and that the rules of C1 and C2 are not applicable.

Therefore, if a choice is to be made between the two, there must be some means to make such a choice.

Quite a number of algorithmic avenues could be utilized. Some are mentioned herein, each of which has tradeoffs and the particular class of AI for Social Good system will be a determiner in which such avenue is warranted. Also, this is by no means an exhaustive list and merely indicative of representative ways that conflicts might be resolved.

For example, there could be a weighting scheme that provides weights associated with rendered choices. This potentially introduces the use of uncertainty and probabilities into the Artificial Moral Agent and the Artificial Legal Reasoner, which is an advanced variant that some believe is needed in any case, regardless of this specific use for conflict resolution [Bench-Capon, 2020; Brandao et al, 2020].

Another approach would be to utilize an Arguing Machines methodology [Eliot, 2018; Fridman, 2017], consisting of the two components engaging in a dialogue or argument with each other, trying to convince the other that their choice ought to prevail on their own side of the matter. Whichever avenue is used, there are key considerations to be attended to. If the run-time execution of attempting to settle the open conflict is onerous, the impact of the conflict resolution can undermine the overarching actions of the AI for Social Good system. A delay in responsiveness might be more than simply aggravating or inconvenient since the AI system might be immersed in a real-time activity that entails life-or-death decisions of an extremely timely nature (such as in the case of autonomous systems, including self-driving cars [Eliot, 2016; Huang, 2019]).

A sense of AI self-awareness [Parasuraman et al, 2000] is required as part of the conflict resolution process, namely that the AI must be keeping tabs on the conflict resolution and have some means of ascertaining that either the process is taking too long for the matter at hand or that the process has potentially become indeterminate or intractable, and needs to be interrupted or halted [Eliot, 2017].

3.4 Approach C4: Neither Prevails

In approach C4, the question arises as to what the AI should do if the conflict between the Artificial Moral Agent and the Artificial Legal Reasoner cannot be otherwise resolved. Assume that C1 is not applicable, nor C2, and nor has C3 reached a resolution.

A final catchall that perhaps randomly picks between the two is conceivable, though likely unsatisfying in many respects, or apply a method that tries to assess whether the choice of one is somehow preferred over the other. Researchers such as Bench-Capon [2020] have identified options such as consequentialism might be used (the impacts of the activities chosen), or deontologically chosen (a worth associated with the act, irrespective of the consequences), or even a means abiding by Maslow's [Maslow, 1943] hierarchy of needs (a selection based on the option fulfilling the highest basic human need).

Another possibility is to seek a resolution from the enduser of the AI for Social Good system, including possibly offering an explanation associated with the impasse (using XAI, as described by Waltl and Vogl [2018]). Seeking such input from the end-user could be problematic in many ways, including allowing a selection preference with unintended consequences or other untoward possibilities and should carefully be assessed as to its utility [Freedman et al, 2020].

Section 4: Discussion

This paper provides insights into the neglected dualism of Artificial Moral Agents and Artificial Legal Reasoners and provides an indication as to the value of the moral-and-law dualism, along with offering ways to encompass that dualism. It is hoped that this study will spur additional research into an emerging area that is only yet being explored and will likely become increasingly crucial for the expanding and widespread adoption of AI for Social Good.

References

[Basitat, 1850] Frederic Basitat. The Law. Ludwig von Mises Institute, Auburn, Alabama, 1850.

[Bench-Capon, 2020] T.J.M. Bench-Capon. Ethical approaches and autonomous system. Artificial Intelligence, 281(3): 1-15, January 2020.

[Bickenbach, 1989] Jerome Bickenbach. Law and morality. Law and Philosophy, 3(3): 291-300, March 1989.

[Brandao et al, 2020] Martim Brandao, Marina Jirotka, Helena Webb, and Paul Luff. Fair navigation planning: A resource for characterizing and designing fairness in mobile robots. Artificial Intelligence, 282(1): 1-20, March 2020.

[Cane, 2012] Peter Cane. Morality, law and conflicting reasons for action. The Cambridge Law Journal, 71(1): 59- 85, March 2012.

[Dicey, 1885] Albert Dicey. Introduction to the Study of the Law of the Constitution. McMillan and Co., London, 1885.

[Eliot, 2016] Lance Eliot. AI Guardian Angels For Deep AI Trustworthiness. LBE Press Publishing, Los Angeles, California 2016.

[Eliot, 2017] Lance Eliot. Self-Aware AI. AI Trends, 2(8): 1-5, August 2017.

[Eliot, 2018] Lance Eliot. Probabilistic reasoning and AI. AI Trends, 3(2): 14-17, February 2018.

[Eliot, 2018] Lance Eliot. AI arguing machines. AI Trends, 3(11): 1-8, November 2018.

[Eliot, 2019] Lance Eliot. AI and Legal Reasoning Essentials. LBE Press Publishing, Los Angeles, California 2019.

[Freedman et al, 2020] Rachel Freedman, Jana Borg, Walter Sinnott-Armstrong, John Dickerson, and Vincent Conitzer. Adapting a kidney exchange algorithm to align with human values. Artificial Intelligence, 283(2): 1-14, March 2020.

[Fridman, 2017]. Lex Fridman, Li Ding, Benedikt Jenik, and Bryan Reimer. Arguing machines. Cornell University AI arXiv, 1710.04459, October 2017.

[Genesereth, 2009] Michael Genesereth. Computational law. Stanford Center for Legal Informatics, May 2019.

[Hage et al, 1993] Jaap Hage, Ronald Leenes, and Arno Lodder. Hard cases: A procedural approach. Artificial Intelligence and Law, 82(1): 52-67, February 1993.

[Huang, 2019] Bert Huang. Law's halo and the moral machine. Columbia Law Review, 119(7): 1811-1828, November 2019.

[Kagan, 1998] Shelly Kagan. The Limits of Morality. Oxford Scholarship Online, November 1998.

[Maslow, 1943] Abraham Maslow. A theory of human motivation. Psychological Review, 50(4): 370-396, April 1943.

[Misselhorn, 2019] Catrin Misselhorn. Artificial systems with moral capacities. Artificial Intelligence, 278(1): 1- 11, October 2019.

[Mnookin and Kornhauser, 1979] Robert Mnookin and Lewis Kornhauser. Bargaining in the shadow of law. The Yale Law Review, 88(5): 950-997, April 1979.

[Parasuraman et al, 2000] Raja Parasuraman, Thomas Sheridan, and Christopher Wickens. A model for types and levels of human interaction with automation. IEEE Transactions on Systems, Man, and Cybernetics, 30(3): 286-297, May 2000.

[Rao, 1980] Goparaju Ramachandra Rao. I Learn. Navjivan Trust, Ahmedabad, India, 1980.

[Regan, 1987] Donald Regan. Law's halo. Social Philosophy and Policy, 4(1): 15-30, April 1987.

[Shiell, 1987] Timothy Shiell. Making sense out of a necessary connection between law and morality. Public Affairs Quarterly, 1(3): 77-90, July 1987.

[Surden, 2019] Artificial Intelligence and the law: An overview. Georgia State University Law Review, 8(2): 41-57, August 2019.

[Waltl and Vogl, 2018] Bernhard Waltl and Roland Vogl. Increasing transparency in algorithmic decision-making with explainable AI. Datenschutz Datensich, 42(1): 613-617, October 2018.

CHAPTER 5

UNAUTHORIZED PRACTICE OF LAW (UPL) AND AI

Abstract

Advances in Artificial Intelligence (AI) and Machine Learning (ML) that are being applied to legal efforts have raised controversial questions about the existent restrictions imposed on the practice-of-law. Generally, the legal field has sought to define Authorized Practices of Law (APL) versus Unauthorized Practices of Law (UPL), though the boundaries are at times amorphous and some contend capricious and self-serving, rather than being devised holistically for the benefit of society all told. A missing ingredient in these arguments is the realization that impending legal profession disruptions due to AI can be more robustly discerned by examining the matter through the lens of a framework utilizing the autonomous levels of AI Legal Reasoning (AILR). This paper explores a newly derived instrumental grid depicting the key characteristics underlying APL and UPL as they apply to the AILR autonomous levels and offers key insights for the furtherance of these crucial practice-of-law debates.

Section 1: Background and Context

Advances in Artificial Intelligence (AI) and Machine Learning (ML) that are being applied to legal efforts have raised controversial questions about the existent restrictions imposed on the practice-of-law [1] [4] [31] [37].

Generally, the legal field has sought to define Authorized Practices of Law (APL) versus Unauthorized Practices of Law (UPL), though the boundaries are at times amorphous and some contend capricious and self-serving, rather than being devised holistically for the benefit of society all told [44] [47].

It is argued herein that a missing ingredient in these debates is the realization that impending legal profession disruptions due to AI can be more robustly discerned by examining the matter through the lens of a framework utilizing the autonomous levels of AI Legal Reasoning (AILR).

Such a grid is presented in this paper and discussed in several respects, including the basis for its formulation, the nature of its utility, and productive opportunities for further extension.

In this paper, five sections are used to cover the topic at hand:

- Section 1: Background and Context
- Section 2: Key Factors of the APL versus UPL
- Section 3: Autonomous Levels of AI Legal Reasoning
- Section 4: APL and UPL Grid Integrating Autonomous Levels of AILR
- Section 5: Additional Considerations and Future Research

In Section 1, an overall background on the matter of APL and UPL is provided. Section 2 then goes further in-depth and identifies what is asserted as key factors underlying APL and UPL. In Section 3, an overview is provided on the autonomous levels of AI Legal Reasoning, crucial to understanding Section 4, which provides a grid that aligns the APL/UPL key factors with the autonomous levels of AI Legal Reasoning. Section 5 is a discussion of additional considerations and also offers suggested avenues for future research on these matters.

1.3 Boundaries of APL and UPL

The legal profession has established and continues to maintain that there are Authorized Practices of Law and Unauthorized Practices of Law.

Questions regarding the scope and boundaries of APL versus UPL arise with some frequency and especially as technology has advanced, including for example issues surrounding online services such as LegalZoom that provide a claimed capability of producing legal documents by the act of filling in interactive questionnaires [47]. In short, some argue that this kind of service is tantamount to the practice of law and yet is not being performed by an attorney in the act of conducting those services, therefore, it should be considered as overtly unauthorized and deemed ergo unlawful (for legal analyses on these contentions, see for example Shipman [47], Gillers [31], McGinnis [38], and Barton [6]).

Matters such as the LegalZoom controversy remain unsettled and will likely increase in frequency and magnitude as Artificial Intelligence (AI) and especially Machine Learning (ML) are added into these computer-based systems that purport to provide legal services, often referred to as LegalTech [22] [23] [24]. As advances in LegalTech become boosted via AI and ML capabilities, the boundaries of whether those systems are APL or UPL will undoubtedly get further debated and fuel existent disputes over these issues.

One viewpoint on the LegalZoom type of offerings is that as long as such services are only providing static forms and not otherwise seemingly rendering legal advice, they can avoid falling into the unauthorized classification or UPL. As per Barton [6]: "UPL is prohibited in all fifty states. The definition of the 'practice of law' and the levels of enforcement differ from state to state, but at a minimum in no state may a nonlawyer appear in court on behalf of another party. Likewise, nonlawyers may not give 'legal advice.' State bars have long allowed the publication of 'forms books' despite the UPL strictures but have drawn the line at the provision of advice along with forms."

Note that a crucial cornerstone in such an argument entails the rendering or provisioning of legal advice.

Though that might seem like a straightforward restriction, attempts to definitively codify or stipulate exactly what constitutes legal advice has been generally problematic.

McClure [37] points out that "state law establishes the parameters of 'the practice of law,' these definitions vary from state to state, but generally, states require bar association admission before either an attorney or a layperson may engage in the practice of law." As such, the shift of attention goes toward whether someone is approved to grant legal advice, as opposed to focusing on what the nature of legal advice itself entails. Similarly, as pointed out further by McClure [37]: "The American Bar Association's Model Rule 5.5 prohibits a person not admitted to the bar association of a particular jurisdiction from practicing law in that specific jurisdiction. A person who is not admitted to the bar association may not represent to the public that he or she may practice law in that jurisdiction."

In essence, avoidance of defining the challenging constructs of "legal advice" is deftly undertaken by sidestepping over into the assertion that only bona fide attorneys can generate or produce legal advice. Thus, the practice of law is seen as that which attorneys do, instead of stating that it is a specified instantiation of legal counsel or legal reasoning involved. Shipman [47] emphasizes the disingenuously distorted logic that this portends in these matters: "It is ironic, given the zealous policing of unauthorized practice of law, that there is not a strong consensus for defining what the practice of law actually is. Comment 2 to Rule 5.5 in the *Model Rules* says that the definition of practice of law is jurisdiction specific and therefore a flexible construct."

This is not to suggest that being able to somehow articulate systematically and with measurable precision the practice-of-law and its constituent elements of legal reasoning can be readily achieved. In fact, it is generally deemed as problematic, resistant to specification, and persistently remains relatively non-standardized. As Shipman [47] aptly explains: "This amorphous standard makes sense given the fact that 'the boundaries of the practice of law are unclear and have been prone to vary over time and geography,' and also because the multifaceted nature of providing legal services makes it difficult to render an exhaustive list of everything the lawyer does in one definition."

In the next subsection, this discussion about these matters will address the various cited bases for why restricting the practice of law is ostensibly justified.

1.4 Restrictions on the Practice of Law

The oft-cited rationale for restricting the practice-of-law in terms of only allowing attorneys to undertake such privileges is that this appropriately protects the public and ensures that society is well-served when it comes to justice and the consumption of legal services [45] [51]. The posture taken is that if just anyone was allowed to assert that they were able to practice law, the layperson seeking legal advice might find themselves receiving specious legal advice or worse still outright untoward legal advisement. By keeping the provisioning of legal advice to those certified or authorized to do so, the assumption is that the public will more easily obtain such advice and be less likely to bear the foul fruits of insufficient or improper legal advice. Via a policing function by the legal profession itself, those that have been granted this duly decreed authorization to render legal advice will seemingly be countered and penalized if they violate this instituted capacity [41].

As will be articulated in a moment, besides the rendering of legal advice, there are several additional characteristics opined as essential to the rationale for an overall restriction related to dispensing of legal advice.

Besides seeking to control who can proffer legal advice, the asserted benefits of restricting the practice-of-law encompass other equally vital factors such as creating the venerated lawyer-client relationship and all of its afforded advantages. Per Shipman [47]: "There are many legitimate policy reasons for the restrictions against the unauthorized practice of law. These reasons include 'preserving and strengthening the lawyer-client relationship' and protecting 'the public from being advised and represented in legal matters by unqualified and undisciplined persons over whom the judicial department could exercise slight or no control.' The functioning of the legal system would not be possible without the privileges afforded to and obligations imposed on lawyers when they enter into a formal attorney-client relationship.

The formation of an attorney-client relationship subjects a lawyer to 'duties of care, loyalty, confidentiality, and communication, duties' enforceable by the client and through disciplinary sanctions."

Not everyone necessarily views these justifications as being unblemished or quite so pristine.

Some contend the legal profession has put in place rules that amount to a monopolistic effort and ought to be broken apart in an anti-trust manner [6] [31] [32]. Arguments are made that the primary purpose for the APL and UPL is to ensure the economic benefit of attorneys and the law industry and only incidentally exemplifies the nobler claims of seeking to provide a public good. Furthermore, there is the concern that these restrictions are stifling of new innovations, and merely reinforce that law should be practiced as it always has, attempting to keep out any disruption or transformations (this is generally known as the Collingridge [13] innovation conundrum).

Shipman [47] recaps some of these concerns as follows: "Despite the legitimate interests that unauthorized practice of law statutes protect, some critics have rebuked these rules for several reasons. One chief reason is that these rules inhibit innovation in the legal industry. Another major critique is that the bar's purpose in the promulgation of these rules has more to do with protecting lawyers' economic interests than with concerns for the public."

Indeed, the lack of clarity about what the practice of law embodies, and the amorphous notions of legal advice, might be construed as crucial to maintaining the status quo, accordingly stated further by Shipman [47]: "However, overly broad or vague definitions of the practice of law can be detrimental in that they allow lawyers to monopolize certain activities for their own gain and stifle the innovation of affordable alternatives in the world of legal services."

Some legal scholars such as Gillers [31] have examined how lawyers seem to make their own rules in terms of determining what the practice of law is allowed to be, for which might be interpreted as relatively self-serving, and that there ought to be a closer inspection of the rulemaking per se:

> "What is the responsibility of the profession itself when, through its various institutions and especially bar associations, it asks courts or (less often) lawmakers or agencies to adopt particular rules governing the conduct of lawyers? In other words, my subject is the professional responsibility of the legal profession itself, not the conduct of individual lawyers or the correctness of any particular rule. My purpose is to suggest how the work of devising the rules, not the content of a specific rule, might be improved."

Everything else being equal, the legal profession will presumably be able to continue to keep in place these restrictions, though added pressure will certainly arise due to the advent of AI and ML improvements in existing LegalTech. A key question asked by those in the legal profession is whether the AI advances in LegalTech can be kept at bay and repeatedly exhorted as an illegitimate means of rendering legal advice, despite the potential incremental AI Legal Reasoning (AILR) advances that will emerge [21] [24].

The seemingly easiest way to win that argument is by summarily indicating that the AI LegalTech is not an attorney, and as such, regardless of whether such systems can provide legal advice or not, they cannot be permitted to dispense legal counsel due to the rather axiomatic logic that such AI systems are not, in fact, a lawyer (i.e., overriding any need to examine and nor ascertain whether such AI systems can render proper and legitimate legal advice).

This circular kind of argument might not survive and per McGinnis et al [38] has these potential undermining facets:

> "The surest way for lawyers to retain the market power of old is to use bar regulation to delay and obstruct the use of machine intelligence. But bar regulation will generally be unavailing. First, lawyers will be able to use many machine-created products to make their own work more cost effective. Thus, using machine inputs can comply with bar regulation, while also creating competitive pressures by lowering costs and reducing the need for the aid of other lawyers. Second, even if unauthorized practice laws in the United States do not change to permit extensive

machine intelligence in the production of legal services, those laws will continue to prove ineffective in stemming the emergence of widespread machine lawyering and preserving lawyers' monopoly."

Overall, those points by McGinnis et al [38] suggest that AI LegalTech will potentially be incrementally embraced by attorneys as a vital legal advisement tool, and in so doing will spur AILR advancements more so. Thus, attempts to continue to keep these AI systems in the backend by the law profession overall might momentarily succeed in the nearer term, but those AI systems will be sought for their capabilities and likewise, the vendors will continue to push ahead avidly on advancing them. Presumably, at some future point, the encouragement and enablement on the backend will bring the matter to a head in that eventually those AILR systems might be considered sufficient enough to render legal advice per se, and therefore aim to be unshackled from a backend positioning-only and be repositioned to also encompass the frontend of legal services rendering.

Meanwhile, a second and simultaneous form of pressure might arise by global adoption of AI LegalTech for providing legal advice, doing so in locales that do not have the same restrictions of APL and UPL as does the United States. In this perspective, it is akin to the Genie being let out of the bottle, and some speculate that the prevailing approaches in the U.S. of denying that AI LegalTech can provide independent legal advice will be sorely tested by global adoptions.

In the next section, an in-depth examination of the key characteristics or factors used to shape the APL versus UPL debate is identified and explored.

Section 2: Key Factors of the APL versus UPL

Distilling the various characteristics or factors underlying the APL versus UPL debate provides a useful indication of the primary determiners involved.

These key factors will be used to then assess how they differ in terms of relevance and impact per a set of autonomous levels entailing AI Legal Reasoning, doing so to illuminate the salient facets of the ongoing dialogue over authorized versus unauthorized practice of law.

There are nine key factors identified, though realize that additional factors can be further gleaned from the myriad of elements utilized in ascertaining APL versus UPL. This core set of nine is evocative of the primary contentions and is sufficient for preparing and providing a grid that can be constructively employed for these discussions. Future research, which is mentioned in the final section of this paper, would be encouraged to consider adding additional key factors, along with subjecting the entire set of factors to an assessment mechanism to potentially rate and appropriately rank their respective significance.

2.1 Identified Key Factors

The primary key factors are depicted in a short-form description that is considered suitable for use in a grid and consist of keywords to represent each factor. The key factors consist of:

- Provides Legal Advice
- Asserts Practices Law
- Lawyer-Client Relationship
- Qualified in Law
- Incurs Duty of Care
- Legal Confidentiality
- Enforceable Prof Conduct
- Malpractice Susceptible
- Legal Liability

In the subsections, each key factor will be briefly explained and explored.

2.2 Details Underlying Key Factors

For each of the key factors, it is foundational to explain the nature and scope of the factor, doing so to ensure that each can be representative of its focused intent.

2.2.1 Provides Legal Advice

The short-form keywords of "Provides Legal Advice" refers to the aspect that ascertaining APL versus UPL involves whether or not there is legal advice that is being proffered. As per the ABA definition [54] of the practice of law and as to the nature of legal advice: "The 'practice of law' is the application of legal principles and judgment with regard to the circumstances or objectives of a person that require the knowledge and skill of a person trained in the law."

This legal advice or practice-of-law arises according to the ABA under these circumstances [54]: "A person is presumed to be practicing law when engaging in any of the following conduct on behalf of another: (1) Giving advice or counsel to persons as to their legal rights or responsibilities or to those of others; (2) Selecting, drafting, or completing legal documents or agreements that affect the legal rights of a person; (3) Representing a person before an adjudicative body, including, but not limited to, preparing or filing documents or conducting discovery; or (4) Negotiating legal rights or responsibilities on behalf of a person."

Presumably, if no legal advice is being rendered, there is no need to analyze whether there is an unauthorized or authorized practice-of-law taking place, simply due to the obvious aspect that there is a lack of legal advice being proffered. On the other hand, if legal advice is involved, potentially any legal advice, even the most infinitesimal, the question then can be dutifully asked about whether this is being done in an authorized versus unauthorized manner.

Whether there is some threshold required as to the significance or magnitude of the legal advice is an open question entailing ongoing research pursuits. For example, if someone makes an offhand remark that would seemingly fit within the scope of the ABA indication of "selecting, drafting, or completing legal documents or agreements that affect the legal rights of the person," does that offhand remark instantaneously invoke that legal advice is being given? Some assert that a kind of reasonableness test needs to be applied to ascertain whether the act has risen to a determinable limit.

2.2.2 Asserts Practices Law

The short-form keywords of "Asserts Practices Law" refer to the assertion or communicating that a capability of practicing law exists and that the giving of legal advice can be undertaken by the actor so stating the claimed capacity.

A pertinent ABA provision consists of Rule 7.1 [54]: "A lawyer shall not make a false or misleading communication about the lawyer or the lawyer's services. A communication is false or misleading if it contains a material misrepresentation of fact or law, or omits a fact necessary to make the statement considered as a whole not materially misleading."

Equally pertinent is the ABA Rule 5.5 [54]: "(a) A lawyer shall not practice law in a jurisdiction in violation of the regulation of the legal profession in that jurisdiction, or assist another in doing so. (b) A lawyer who is not admitted to practice in this jurisdiction shall not: (1) except as authorized by these Rules or other law, establish an office or other systematic and continuous presence in this jurisdiction for the practice of law; or (2) hold out to the public or otherwise represent that the lawyer is admitted to practice law in this jurisdiction."

2.2.3 Lawyer-Client Relationship

The short-form keywords of "Lawyer-Client Relationship" refers to the aspect that a special relationship is enacted between a lawyer and their client, offering various protections and legal obligations by the lawyer so bounded.

Per the ABA Rule 1.1 [54]: "A lawyer shall provide competent representation to a client. Competent representation requires the legal knowledge, skill, thoroughness and preparation reasonably necessary for the representation," and as stated in Rule 1.3 "A lawyer shall act with reasonable diligence and promptness in representing a client."

2.2.4 Qualified in Law

The short-form keywords of "Qualified in Law" refers to the requirement that the legal advisor is appropriately qualified in law.

Per the ABA [54], these are the expected licensing requirements to be an attorney and practice law: "Have a bachelor's degree or its equivalent. Complete three years at an ABA-accredited law school. Pass a state bar examination, which usually lasts for two or three days. The exam tests knowledge in selected areas of law. There are also required tests on professional ethics and responsibility. Pass a character and fitness review. Applicants for law licenses must be approved by a committee that investigates character and background. Take an oath, usually swearing to support the laws and the state and federal constitutions. Receive a license from the highest court in the state, usually the state supreme court."

2.2.5 Incurs Duty of Care

The short-form keywords of "Incurs Duty of Care" refers to the need for lawyers to act mindfully when performing their legal acts for clients, and the sufficiency of care is usually evaluated per the prevailing standards of professional competence in law and as applicable to the matter at hand.

As per the ABA indication of a lawyer's responsibilities [54]: "As a representative of clients, a lawyer performs various functions. As advisor, a lawyer provides a client with an informed understanding of the client's legal rights and obligations and explains their practical implications. As advocate, a lawyer zealously asserts the client's position under the rules of the adversary system. As negotiator, a lawyer seeks a result advantageous to the client but consistent with requirements of honest dealings with others. As an evaluator, a lawyer acts by examining a client's legal affairs and reporting about them to the client or to others."

2.2.6 Legal Confidentiality

The short-form keywords of "Legal Confidentiality" refers to the confidentiality formed as part of the lawyer-client relationship.

Per ABA Rule 1.6 [54]: "(a) A lawyer shall not reveal information relating to the representation of a client unless the client gives informed consent, the disclosure is impliedly authorized in order to carry out the representation or the disclosure is permitted by paragraph (b)." The aspects of permitted disclosure are stipulated in the Rule 1.6 portion "b" and include various conditions such as confidentiality may be usurped to prevent certain death or substantial bodily harm, to prevent a client from committing a crime or fraud, etc.

2.2.7 Enforceable Prof Conduct

The short-form keywords of "Enforceable Prof Conduct" refers to the aspect that there is an expectation of professional conduct by a lawyer in the practice of the law and that this requirement of conduct is enforceable such that if conduct falls below the requisite level then there are adverse consequences that can be imposed upon the attorney so violating the code of conduct.

As per the ABA stipulation [54]: "A lawyer's conduct should conform to the requirements of the law, both in professional service to clients and in the lawyer's business and personal affairs. A lawyer should use the law's procedures only for legitimate purposes and not to harass or intimidate others. A lawyer should demonstrate respect for the legal system and for those who serve it, including judges, other lawyers and public officials. While it is a lawyer's duty, when necessary, to challenge the rectitude of official action, it is also a lawyer's duty to uphold legal process."

2.2.8 Malpractice Susceptible

The short-form keywords of "Malpractice Susceptible" refers to a potential failing on the part of the legal advisor to render proper legal advice and to the degree that professional misconduct has occurred and caused harm to another person, making them susceptible to a malpractice claim. Per the ABA [54]: "Lawyers make mistakes. Sometimes those mistakes have consequences. Ultimately, a viable legal malpractice claim will turn on the facts of the case; but here are three basic things to consider in determining if an attorney's mistake justifies a legal malpractice lawsuit," which encompasses whether the attorney was negligent, whether the mistake caused damage, and whether the damages were significant.

2.2.9 Legal Liability

The short-form keywords of "Legal Liability" refers to a wide array of potential liability exposures for attorneys and oftentimes is bucketed into three major facets: (1) disciplinary or violation of legal professional ethics codes, (2) civil claims of liability including malpractice, and (3) criminal claims of liability in the duty of an attorney as an officer of the court and a presumed guardian of the legal system.

In the realm of civil claims of liability, malpractice is singled out in the list of the key factors as shown in the prior subsection. Beyond malpractice, it is customary to consider other acts of liability such as liability for breach of contract, liability for violation of regulatory statutes, and so on. Thus, the value of having a broader category of "Legal Liability" is to ensure that the narrower construing of malpractice would not inadvertently omit or overshadow other forms of legal liability.

2.3 Connecting Key Factors With AILR

This section has identified the APL/UPL key factors. The next section describes the autonomous levels of AI Legal Reasoning, providing sufficient context to then align together with the key factors and the LoA AILR in composing an instrumental assessment grid.

Section 3: Autonomous Levels of AI Legal Reasoning

In this section, a framework for the autonomous levels of AI Legal Reasoning is summarized and is based on the research described in detail in Eliot [25].

These autonomous levels will be portrayed in a grid that aligns with the APL/UPL key factors identified in the prior section of this paper, and thus it is useful to first explain what each of the autonomous levels consists of.

The autonomous levels of AI Legal Reasoning are as follows:

Level 0: No Automation for AI Legal Reasoning

Level 1: Simple Assistance Automation for AI Legal Reasoning

Level 2: Advanced Assistance Automation for AI Legal Reasoning

Level 3: Semi-Autonomous Automation for AI Legal Reasoning

Level 4: Domain Autonomous for AI Legal Reasoning

Level 5: Fully Autonomous for AI Legal Reasoning

Level 6: Superhuman Autonomous for AI Legal Reasoning

See **Figure A-1** for an overview chart showcasing the autonomous levels of AI Legal Reasoning as via columns denoting each of the respective levels.

See **Figure A-2** for an overview chart similar to Figure A-1 which alternatively is indicative of the autonomous levels of AI Legal Reasoning via the rows as depicting the respective levels (this is simply a reformatting of Figure A-1, doing so to aid in illuminating this variant perspective, but does not introduce any new facets or alterations from the contents as already shown in Figure A-1).

3.1.1 Level 0: No Automation for AI Legal Reasoning

Level 0 is considered the no automation level. Legal reasoning is carried out via manual methods and principally occurs via paper-based methods.

This level is allowed some leeway in that the use of say a simple handheld calculator or perhaps the use of a fax machine could be allowed or included within this Level 0, though strictly speaking it could be said that any form whatsoever of automation is to be excluded from this level.

3.1.2 Level 1: Simple Assistance Automation for AI Legal Reasoning

Level 1 consists of simple assistance automation for AILR.

Examples of this category encompassing simple automation would include the use of everyday computer-based word processing, the use of everyday computer-based spreadsheets, the access to online legal documents that are stored and retrieved electronically, and so on.

By-and-large, today's use of computers for legal activities is predominantly within Level 1. It is assumed and expected that over time, the pervasiveness of automation will continue to deepen and widen, and eventually lead to legal activities being supported and within Level 2, rather than Level 1.

3.1.3 Level 2: Advanced Assistance Automation for AI Legal Reasoning

Level 2 consists of advanced assistance automation for AI legal reasoning.

Examples of this notion encompassing advanced automation would include the use of query-style Natural Language Processing (NLP), Machine Learning (ML) for case predictions, and so on.

Gradually, over time, it is expected that computer-based systems for legal activities will increasingly make use of advanced automation. Law industry technology that was once at a Level 1 will likely be refined, upgraded, or expanded to include advanced capabilities, and thus be reclassified into Level 2.

3.1.4 Level 3: Semi-Autonomous Automation for AI Legal Reasoning

Level 3 consists of semi-autonomous automation for AI legal reasoning. Examples of this notion encompassing semi-autonomous automation would include the use of Knowledge-Based Systems (KBS) for legal reasoning, the use of Machine Learning and Deep Learning (ML/DL) for legal reasoning, and so on. Today, such automation tends to exist in research efforts or prototypes and pilot systems, along with some commercial legal technology that has been infusing these capabilities too.

3.1.5 Level 4: Domain Autonomous for AI Legal Reasoning

Level 4 consists of domain autonomous computer-based systems for AI legal reasoning.

This level reuses the conceptual notion of Operational Design Domains (ODDs) as utilized in the autonomous vehicles and self-driving cars levels of autonomy, though in this use case it is being applied to the legal domain [17] [18] [20].

Essentially, this entails any AI legal reasoning capacities that can operate autonomously, entirely so, but that is only able to do so in some limited or constrained legal domain.

3.1.6 Level 5: Fully Autonomous for AI Legal Reasoning

Level 5 consists of fully autonomous computer-based systems for AI legal reasoning.

In a sense, Level 5 is the superset of Level 4 in terms of encompassing all possible domains as per however so defined ultimately for Level 4. The only constraint, as it were, consists of the facet that the Level 4 and Level 5 are concerning human intelligence and the capacities thereof. This is an important emphasis due to attempting to distinguish Level 5 from Level 6 (as will be discussed in the next subsection). It is conceivable that someday there might be a fully autonomous AI legal reasoning capability, one that encompasses all of the law in all foreseeable ways, though this is quite a tall order and remains quite aspirational without a clear cut path of how this might one day be achieved. Nonetheless, it seems to be within the extended realm of possibilities, which is worthwhile to mention in relative terms to Level 6.

3.1.7 Level 6: Superhuman Autonomous for AI Legal Reasoning

Level 6 consists of superhuman autonomous computer-based systems for AI legal reasoning.

In a sense, Level 6 is the entirety of Level 5 and adds something beyond that in a manner that is currently ill-defined and perhaps (some would argue) as yet unknowable. The notion is that AI might ultimately exceed human intelligence, rising to become superhuman, and if so, we do not yet have any viable indication of what that superhuman intelligence consists of and nor what kind of thinking it would somehow be able to undertake.

Whether a Level 6 is ever attainable is reliant upon whether superhuman AI is ever attainable, and thus, at this time, this stands as a placeholder for that which might never occur. In any case, having such a placeholder provides a semblance of completeness, doing so without necessarily legitimatizing that superhuman AI is going to be achieved or not. No such claim or dispute is undertaken within this framework.

Section 4: APL and UPL Grid Integrating Autonomous Levels of AILR

4.1 Grid Indication of Levels of Autonomy (LoA) by Key Factors

In this section, the APL/UPL key factors depicted in Section 2 are aligned into a grid that also contains the autonomous levels of AI Legal Reasoning which were described in Section 3.

Figure B-1 provides an overview chart depicting the rows as the respective LoA AILR levels and the columns denoting the APL/UPL key factors. A row-by-row explanatory narrative is provided in the subsections below.

Figure B-2 provides a similar overview chart of Figure B-1 but does so with the rows indicating the APL/UPL key factors and the columns showcasing the APL/UPL key factors. This is simply an alternative perspective of Figure B-1 and does not introduce any new content or alterations from the contents depicted in Figure B-1. A row-by-row explanatory narrative is provided in the subsections below.

4.1.1 Level 0: No Automation for AI Legal Reasoning

As indicated in charts B-1 and B-2, Level 0 of the LoA AILR have an "n/a" (meaning "not applicable") for each of the APL/UPL key factors.

This designating of "n/a" seems applicable for Level 0 since there is considered no automation and no AILR autonomy involved at Level 0. As such, there is presumably no opportunity for any potential claim or contention that the automation or autonomy is providing legal advice, and likewise, it is not asserting that it is practicing law, it does not create a lawyer-client relationship, and so on.

Here then is Level 0:

<u>Level 0</u>

- Provides Legal Advice: **n/a**
- Asserts Practices Law: **n/a**
- Lawyer-Client Relationship: **n/a**
- Qualified in Law: **n/a**
- Incurs Duty of Care: **n/a**
- Legal Confidentiality: **n/a**
- Enforceable Prof Conduct: **n/a**
- Malpractice Susceptible: **n/a**
- Legal Liability: **n/a**

4.1.2 Level 1: Simple Assistance Automation for AI Legal Reasoning

As indicated in charts B-1 and B-2, Level 1 of the LoA AILR is designated as "no" for each of the APL/UPL key factors.

This designating of "no" seems applicable for Level 1 since the automation is considered a simple construct and does not embody any AI autonomous capabilities.

Note that though a vendor or developer of such simple legal technology might wish to claim that their system provides legal advice, and for which this is still an open question per the exemplar of LegalZoom discussed in Section 1, for the purposes herein, it is suggested that this is not the case at Level 1, but might be the case at Level 2 (see next subsection).

Here then is Level 1:

Level 1

- Provides Legal Advice: **No**
- Asserts Practices Law: **No**
- Lawyer-Client Relationship: **No**
- Qualified in Law: **No**
- Incurs Duty of Care: **No**
- Legal Confidentiality: **No**
- Enforceable Prof Conduct: **No**
- Malpractice Susceptible: **No**
- Legal Liability: **No**

4.1.3 Level 2: Advanced Assistance Automation for AI Legal Reasoning

As indicated in charts B-1 and B-2, the Level 2 of the LoA AILR is designated as "no" for the preponderance of the APL/UPL key factors, and has the designation of "maybe" for two of the factors, namely for "Provides Legal Advice" and for "Legal Liability."

This designating of "no" seems applicable for most of Level 2 since the automation does not embody any AI autonomous capabilities.

Despite the lack of AI autonomous capabilities, there is the gray area of whether the automation has entered into the realm of providing legal advice and thus the use of "maybe" as a designator.

Referring to the discussion of Section 1 about LegalZoom as an exemplar, there is still an open question of how far beyond the act of providing a form does it take for the threshold of dispensing legal advice to arise. If there is legal advice being proffered, it would seem logically consequential that an invocation of legal liability could potentially also be raised regarding the legal advice being so offered, and thus the use of "maybe" as a designator for the "Legal Liability" factor.

Here then is Level 2:

<u>**Level 2**</u>

- Provides Legal Advice: **Maybe**
- Asserts Practices Law: **No**
- Lawyer-Client Relationship: **No**
- Qualified in Law: **No**
- Incurs Duty of Care: **No**
- Legal Confidentiality: **No**
- Enforceable Prof Conduct: **No**
- Malpractice Susceptible: **No**
- Legal Liability: **Maybe**

4.1.4 Level 3: Semi-Autonomous Automation for AI Legal Reasoning

As indicated in charts B-1 and B-2, the Level 3 of the LoA AILR is designated as a mixture of "no" for many of the APL/UPL key factors, and has the designation of "yes," "minimal," and "likely" for three factors, respectively "Provides Legal Advice," "Qualified in Law," and "Legal Liability." This designating of "no" seems applicable for much of Level 3 since the automation is only partially embodying AI autonomous capabilities, considered as semi-autonomous. Due to the semi-autonomous nature, it could be argued that systems in Level 3 are providing legal advice, of which presumably do so they need to be qualified in law (at least to some minimal amount), and the provisioning of legal advice would seem to place such systems into the exposure of legal liability for doing so.

Here then is Level 3:

<u>**Level 3**</u>

- Provides Legal Advice: **Yes**
- Asserts Practices Law: **No**
- Lawyer-Client Relationship: **No**
- Qualified in Law: **Minimal**
- Incurs Duty of Care: **No**
- Legal Confidentiality: **No**
- Enforceable Prof Conduct: **No**
- Malpractice Susceptible: **No**
- Legal Liability: **Likely**

4.1.5 Level 4: Domain Autonomous for AI Legal Reasoning

As indicated in charts B-1 and B-2, the Level 4 of the LoA AILR is designated as a mixture of "likely" for many of the APL/UPL key factors, and has the designation of "yes" and "partial" for three factors, respectively "Asserts Practices Law," "Lawyer-Client Relationship," "Qualified in Law."

For purposes of nomenclature, the use of the word "partial" and the word "likely" are admittedly somewhat ill-defined and open to interpretation, which is intended for now as to the initial instantiation of this grid. As mentioned in Section 5, it is hoped and anticipated that further research will be undertaken to clarify and more discretely specify these designations.

In Level 4, a significant consideration is that the autonomy of the AILR arises only in selected domain or subdomain strata, thus, there is an inherent restriction or qualification involved. As will be indicated for Level 5 and Level 6, there are no such limits and therefore the use of designators such as "partial" or "likely" are no longer warranted in those levels.

Here then is Level 4:

<u>Level 4</u>

- Provides Legal Advice: **Yes**
- Asserts Practices Law: **Yes**
- Lawyer-Client Relationship: **Partial**
- Qualified in Law: **Partial**
- Incurs Duty of Care: **Likely**
- Legal Confidentiality: **Likely**
- Enforceable Prof Conduct: **Likely**
- Malpractice Susceptible: **Likely**
- Legal Liability: **Likely**

4.1.6 Level 5: Fully Autonomous for AI Legal Reasoning

As indicated in charts B-1 and B-2, Level 5 of the LoA AILR are designated as a series of "yes" designations for each of the APL/UPL key factors.

In brief, since the AI Legal Reasoning is considered fully versed at the Level 5, it would seem corresponding that there would be an expectation enveloping the AILR that it ought to comply with the same set of APL/UPL factors as established for human lawyers.

There are thorny questions that arise in this indication due to the unclear nature of whether the AILR itself can be held accountable and considered responsible per se, or whether this semblance of assignability is not extendable to AI systems, perhaps being borne instead by others such as those that have developed the AILR or fielded the AILR. These are ongoing and problematic questions, already being earnestly explored in the field of AI and the law, which will undoubtedly continue for quite some time ahead.

Here then is Level 5:

<u>**Level 5**</u>

- Provides Legal Advice: **Yes**
- Asserts Practices Law: **Yes**
- Lawyer-Client Relationship: **Yes**
- Qualified in Law: **Yes**
- Incurs Duty of Care: **Yes**
- Legal Confidentiality: **Yes**
- Enforceable Prof Conduct: **Yes**
- Malpractice Susceptible: **Yes**
- Legal Liability: **Yes**

4.1.7 Level 6: Superhuman Autonomous for AI Legal Reasoning

As indicated in charts B-1 and B-2, the Level 6 of the LoA AILR is designated as a series of "yes" designations for each of the APL/UPL key factors, and three indicating "yes plus," consisting of "Provides Legal Advice," "Asserts Practices Law," and "Qualified in Law."

The basis for providing a "yes plus" designation is that this Level 6 is the as-yet-known superhuman formulation of AI, and presumably, such AI would exceed the human capacity of lawyering. In that light, it seems prudent to suggest that the Level 6 can provide legal advice beyond that of humans, designated as "yes plus," and asserts the practice of law to a "yes plus" accordingly, and surpasses the human boundaries of being qualified for the law too.

Similar to the discussion given about the Level 5 aspect, mentioned in the prior subsection, since the AI Legal Reasoning is considered fully versed at the Level 6 (and even more so versed, at some superhuman capacity), it would seem corresponding that there would be an expectation enveloping the AILR that it ought to comply with the same set of APL/UPL factors as established for human lawyers.

As stated about Level 5, there are thorny questions that arise in this indication for Level 6 too, due to the unclear nature of whether the AILR itself can be held accountable and considered responsible per se, or whether this semblance of assignability is not extendable to AI systems, perhaps being borne instead by others such as those that have developed the AILR or fielded the AILR. These are ongoing and problematic questions, already being earnestly explored in the field of AI and the law, which will undoubtedly continue for quite some time ahead.

Here then is Level 6:

<u>Level 6</u>

- Provides Legal Advice: **Yes Plus**
- Asserts Practices Law: **Yes Plus**
- Lawyer-Client Relationship: **Yes**
- Qualified in Law: **Yes Plus**
- Incurs Duty of Care: **Yes**
- Legal Confidentiality: **Yes**
- Enforceable Prof Conduct: **Yes**
- Malpractice Susceptible: **Yes**
- Legal Liability: **Yes**

4.2 Grid Indication of APL/UPL Key Factors by Levels of Autonomy (LoA)

The next subsections showcase the APL/UPL key factors as at-a-glance for each factor, listing the designations that have been postulated for each of the LoA AILR levels.

Narrative discussion about these facets has already been covered in the prior Subsection 4.1 and thus it is not necessary to repeat it in this subsection (refer to the prior subsections as needed).

4.2.1 APL/UPL "Provides Legal Advice" by LoA

For a narrative discussion about the "Provides Legal Advice" for each of the LoA AILR levels, see the preceding subsections. This list shown here provides the convenience of indication and is also portrayed on charts B-1 and B-2.

<u>Provides Legal Advice</u>

- Level 0: **n/a**
- Level 1: **No**
- Level 2: **Maybe**
- Level 3: **Yes**
- Level 4: **Yes**
- Level 5: **Yes**
- Level 6: **Yes Plus**

4.2.2 APL/UPL "Asserts Practices Law" by LoA

For a narrative discussion about the "Asserts Practices Law" for each of the LoA AILR levels, see the preceding subsections. This list shown here provides the convenience of indication and is also portrayed on charts B-1 and B-2.

<u>Asserts Practices Law</u>

- Level 0: **n/a**
- Level 1: **No**
- Level 2: **No**
- Level 3: **No**
- Level 4: **Yes**
- Level 5: **Yes**
- Level 6: **Yes Plus**

4.2.3 APL/UPL "Lawyer-Client Relationship" LoA

For a narrative discussion about the "Lawyer-Client Relationship" for each of the LoA AILR levels, see the preceding subsections. This list shown here provides the convenience of indication and is also portrayed on charts B-1 and B-2.

<u>**Lawyer-Client Relationship**</u>

- Level 0: **n/a**
- Level 1: **No**
- Level 2: **No**
- Level 3: **No**
- Level 4: **Partial**
- Level 5: **Yes**
- Level 6: **Yes**

4.2.4 APL/UPL "Qualified in Law" by LoA

For a narrative discussion about the "Qualified in Law" for each of the LoA AILR levels, see the preceding subsections. This list shown here provides the convenience of indication and is also portrayed on charts B-1 and B-2.

<u>**Qualified in Law**</u>

- Level 0: **n/a**
- Level 1: **No**
- Level 2: **No**
- Level 3: **Minimal**
- Level 4: **Partial**
- Level 5: **Yes**
- Level 6: **Yes Plus**

4.2.5 APL/UPL "Incurs Duty of Care" by LoA

For a narrative discussion about the "Incurs Duty of Care" for each of the LoA AILR levels, see the preceding subsections. This list shown here provides the convenience of indication and is also portrayed on charts B-1 and B-2.

<u>**Incurs Duty of Care**</u>

- Level 0: **n/a**
- Level 1: **No**
- Level 2: **No**
- Level 3: **No**
- Level 4: **Likely**
- Level 5: **Yes**
- Level 6: **Yes**

4.2.6 APL/UPL "Legal Confidentiality" by LoA

For a narrative discussion about the "Legal Confidentiality" for each of the LoA AILR levels, see the preceding subsections. This list shown here provides the convenience of indication and is also portrayed on charts B-1 and B-2.

<u>**Legal Confidentiality**</u>

- Level 0: **n/a**
- Level 1: **No**
- Level 2: **No**
- Level 3: **No**
- Level 4: **Likely**
- Level 5: **Yes**
- Level 6: **Yes**

4.2.7 APL/UPL "Enforceable Prof Conduct" LoA

For a narrative discussion about the "Enforceable Prof Conduct" for each of the LoA AILR levels, see the preceding subsections. This list shown here provides the convenience of indication and is also portrayed on charts B-1 and B-2.

<u>**Enforceable Prof Conduct**</u>

- Level 0: **n/a**
- Level 1: **No**
- Level 2: **No**
- Level 3: **No**
- Level 4: **Likely**
- Level 5: **Yes**
- Level 6: **Yes**

4.2.8 APL/UPL "Malpractice Susceptible" by LoA

For a narrative discussion about the "Malpractice Susceptible" for each of the LoA AILR levels, see the preceding subsections. This list shown here provides the convenience of indication and is also portrayed on charts B-1 and B-2.

<u>**Malpractice Susceptible**</u>

- Level 0: **n/a**
- Level 1: **No**
- Level 2: **No**
- Level 3: **No**
- Level 4: **Likely**
- Level 5: **Yes**
- Level 6: **Yes**

4.2.9 APL/UPL "Legal Liability" by LoA

For a narrative discussion about the "Legal Liability" for each of the LoA AILR levels, see the preceding subsections. This list shown here provides the convenience of indication and is also portrayed on charts B-1 and B-2.

Legal Liability

- Level 0: **n/a**
- Level 1: **No**
- Level 2: **Maybe**
- Level 3: **Likely**
- Level 4: **Likely**
- Level 5: **Yes**
- Level 6: **Yes**

Section 5: Additional Considerations and Future Research

The grid depicted in Figure B-1 and Figure B-2 is a strawman variant, meaning that the indications shown are an initial populating of the grid.

Additional research is needed to explore the designations and ascertain whether the initial indications might be advisedly changed or possibly transformed into some other kind of designations, such as numeric scores or weights.

Another aspect of additional research involves the APL/UPL key factors that are utilized in this strawman variant. There are other ways to portray the factors, along with the possibility of adding factors or possibly opting to excise some of the factors from the grid. Research on such modifications is encouraged.

As a final point, there are potentially greater questions that arise from the grid, alluded to earlier in the discussion of the prior sections, entailing what actions would be taken if indeed AILR can achieve the autonomous levels of Level 4, Level 5, and Level 6. There remain many such open issues, each deserving of suitable attention.

The FTC observed that the practice-of-law is being buffeted and disrupted by a multitude of societal, economic, and technological changes, as stated in a 2016 memorandum [47]:

> "The legal services marketplace has experienced a number of changes in recent years. These trends include: client demands for more cost-effective and efficient services; unbundling of services and disaggregation of legal matters across multiple service providers; development of new billing models and law firm models; geographic expansion of law firms and other legal services providers; provision by non-law firms of certain services previously obtained exclusively from law firms; increased use of automation technologies; online matching, reviewing, and ranking of lawyers; and use of Internet, World Wide Web, and related computer technologies to deliver legal services. In particular, the increased use of computer, software, and online technologies has enabled non-lawyers to provide many services that historically were provided exclusively by lawyers and traditional law firms."

As pointed out in the FTC commentary, legal technologies are increasingly enabling non-lawyers to provide legal services that would normally be considered more so UPL then APL.

The next step would seem to be excising the need for a non-lawyer, making use of an autonomous AI Legal Reasoning system in place of any human-based assistance or intervention in delivering legal services and legal advice [51] [53].

That day has not yet arrived [5] [35], but the future appears to encompass such a possibility and it is worthwhile today to examine how the legal profession might need to inexorably adjust in the face of such a significant disruption.

This paper has provided and explored a newly derived instrumental grid depicting the key characteristics underlying APL and UPL as they apply to the AILR autonomous levels and has sought to provide key insights and spur informed discussions regarding the furtherance of crucial practice-of-law deliberations.

References

1. Alarie, Benjamin (2016). "The Path of the Law: Toward Legal Singularity," May 27, 2016, SSRN, University of Toronto Faculty of Law and Vector Institute for Artificial Intelligence.
2. Aleven, Vincent (2003). "Using Background Knowledge in Case-Based Legal Reasoning: A Computational Model and an Intelligent Learning Environment," Artificial Intelligence.
3. Ashley, Kevin (1991). "Reasoning with Cases and Hypotheticals in HYPO," Volume 34, International Journal of Man-Machine Studies.
4. Ashley, Kevin, and Karl Branting, Howard Margolis, and Cass Sunstein (2001). "Legal Reasoning and Artificial Intelligence: How Computers 'Think' Like Lawyers," Symposium: Legal Reasoning and Artificial Intelligence, University of Chicago Law School Roundtable.
5. Baker, Jamie (2018). "A Legal Research Odyssey: Artificial Intelligence as Disrupter," Law Library Journal.
6. Barton, Benjamin (2014). "The Lawyer's Monopoly: What Goes and What Stays." Volume 82, Number 6, Fordham Law.
7. Batsakis, Sotiris, and George Baryannis, Guido Governatori, Illias Tachmazidis, Grigoris Antoniou (2018). "Legal Representation and Reasoning in Practice: A Critical Comparison," Volume 313, Legal Knowledge and Info Sys.
8. Bench-Capon, Trevor (2004). "AGATHA: Automation of the Construction of Theories in Case Law Domains," January 2004, Legal Knowledge and Information Systems Jurix 2004.
9. Bench-Capon, Trevor and Givoanni Sartor (2003). "A Model of Legal Reasoning with Cases Incorporating Theories and

Values," November 2013, Artificial Intelligence.

10. Breuker, Joost (1996). "A Functional Ontology of Law," October 1996, ResearchGate.
11. Buchanan, Bruce, and Thomas Headrick (1970). "Some Speculation about Artificial Intelligence and Legal Reasoning," Volume 23, Stanford Law Review.
12. Chagal-Feferkorn, Karni (2019). "Am I An Algorithm or a Product: When Products Liability Should Apply to Algorithmic Decision-Makers," Stanford Law & Policy Rev.
13. Collingridge, David (1980). The Social Control of Technology. St. Martin's Press.
14. Douglas, William (1948). "The Dissent: A Safeguard of Democracy," Volume 32, Journal of the American Judicature Society.
15. Drucker, Peter (1963). "Managing for Business Effectiveness," May 1963, Harvard Business Review.
16. Dung, P, and R. Kowalski, F. Toni (2006). "Dialectic Proof Procedures for Assumption-Based Admissible Argumentation," Artificial Intelligence.
17. Eliot, Lance (2016). AI Guardian Angels for Deep AI Trustworthiness. LBE Press Publishing.
18. Eliot, Lance (2017). New Advances in AI Autonomous Driverless Self-Driving Cars. LBE Press Publishing.
19. Eliot, Lance (2018). "AI Arguing Machines," November 7, 2018, AI Trends.
20. Eliot, Lance (2019). "Explaining Level 4 and Level 5 of Self-Driving Cars," December 20, 2019, Forbes.
21. Eliot, Lance (2020). "The Neglected Dualism of Artificial Moral Agency and Artificial Legal Reasoning in AI for Social Good." Harvard University, Harvard Center for Research on Computation and Society, AI for Social Good Conference, July 21, 2020.
22. Eliot, Lance (2020). AI and Legal Reasoning Essentials. LBE Press Publishing.
23. Eliot, Lance (2019). Artificial Intelligence and LegalTech

Essentials. LBE Press Publishing.

24. Eliot, Lance (2020). "FutureLaw 2020 Showcases How Tech is Transforming The Law, Including the Impacts of AI," April 16, 2020, Forbes.
25. Eliot, Lance (2020). "An Ontological AI-and-Law Framework for the Autonomous Levels of AI Legal Reasoning," https://orcid.org/0000-0003-3081-1819, Cornell University arXiv.
26. Erdem, Esra, and Michael Gelfond, Nicola Leone (2016). "Applications of Answer Set Programming," AI Magazine.
27. Galdon, Fernando, and Ashley Hall, Stephen Jia Wang (2020). "Designing Trust in Highly Automated Virtual Assistants: A Taxonomy of Levels of Autonomy," Artificial Intelligence in Industry 4.0: A Collection of Innovative Research Case-Study.
28. Gardner, Anne (1987). Artificial Intelligence and Legal Reasoning. MIT Press.
29. Genesereth, Michael (2009). "Computational Law: The Cop in the Backseat," Stanford Center for Legal Informatics.
30. Ghosh, Mirna (2019). "Automation of Legal Reasoning and Decision Based on Ontologies," Normandie Universite.
31. Gillers, Stephen (2013). "How to Make Rules for Lawyers: The Professional Responsibility of the Legal Profession," Volume 40, Number 2, Pepperdine Law Review.
32. Hage, Jaap (2000). "Dialectical Models in Artificial Intelligence and Law," Artificial Intelligence and Law.
33. Hage, Japp, and Ronald Leenes, Arno Lodder (1993). "Hard Cases: A Procedural Approach," Artificial Intelligence and Law.
34. Katz, Daniel, and Michael Bommarito, Josh Blackman (2017). "A General Approach for Predicting the Behavior of the Supreme Court of the United States," April 12, 2017, PLOS ONE.
35. Markou, Christopher, and Simon Deakin (2020). "Is Law Computable? From Rule of Law to Legal Singularity," May 4, 2020, SSRN, University of Cambridge Faculty of Law Research Paper.

36. McCarty, Thorne (1977). "Reflections on TAXMAN: An Experiment in Artificial Intelligence and Legal Reasoning," January 1977, Harvard Law Review.

37. McClure, Emily (2017). "LegalZoom and Online Legal Service Providers: Is the Development and Sale of Interactive Questionnaires that Generate Legal Documents the Unauthorized Practice of Law?," Volume 105, Number 3, Kentucky Law Journal.

38. McGinnis, John and Russell G. Pearce (2014). "The Great Disruption: How Machine Intelligence Will Transform the Role of Lawyers in the Delivery of Legal Services," Volume 82, Number 6, Fordham Law Review.

39. Miller, George (1956). "The Magical Number Seven, Plus Or Minus Two: Some Limits On Our Capacity For Processing Information." Volume 63, Number 2, Psychological Review.

40. Mnookin, Robert, and Lewis Kornhauser (1979). "Bargaining in the Shadow of the Law," Volume 88, Number 5, April 1979, The Yale Law Review.

41. Mowbray, Andrew and Philip Chung, Graham Greenleaf (2019). "Utilising AI in the Legal Assistance Sector," LegalAIIA Workshop, ICAIL, June 17, 2019, Montreal, Canada.

42. Popple, James (1993). "SHYSTER: A Pragmatic Legal Expert System," Ph.D. Dissertation, Australian National University.

43. Prakken, Henry, and Giovanni Sartor (2015). "Law and Logic: A Review from an Argumentation Perspective," Volume 227, Artificial Intelligence.

44. Rissland, Edwina (1988). Artificial Intelligence and Legal Reasoning: A Discussion of the Field and Gardner's Book," Volume 9, AI Magazine.

45. Rissland, Edwina (1990). "Artificial Intelligence and Law: Stepping Stones to a Model of Legal Reasoning," Yale Law J.

46. SAE (2018). Taxonomy and Definitions for Terms Related to Driving Automation Systems for On-Road Motor Vehicles, J3016-201806, SAE International.

47. Shipman, Caroline (2019). "Unauthorized Practice of Law

Claims Against LegalZoom—Who Do These Lawsuits Protect, and is the Rule Outdated?" Volume 32, Number 9, The Georgetown Journal of Legal Ethics.

48. Sunstein, Cass (2001). "Of Artificial Intelligence and Legal Reasoning," University of Chicago Law School, Public Law and Legal Theory Working Papers.

49. Sunstein, Cass, and Kevin Ashley, Karl Branting, Howard Margolis (2001). "Legal Reasoning and Artificial Intelligence: How Computers 'Think' Like Lawyers," Symposium: Legal Reasoning and Artificial Intelligence, University of Chicago Law School Roundtable.

50. Surden, Harry (2014). "Machine Learning and Law," Washington Law Review.

51. Surden, Harry (2019). "Artificial Intelligence and Law: An Overview," Summer 2019, Georgia State University Law Review.

52. Valente, Andre, and Joost Breuker (1996). "A Functional Ontology of Law," Artificial Intelligence and Law.

53. Waltl, Bernhard, and Roland Vogl (2018). "Explainable Artificial Intelligence: The New Frontier in Legal Informatics," February 2018, Jusletter IT 22, Stanford Center for Legal Informatics, Stanford University.

54. Wolfman, Zack. ABA Model Definition of the Practice of Law, American Bar Association.

55. Yang, Guang, and James Cambias, Kevin Cleary, Eric Daimler, James Drake, Pierre Dupont, Nobuhiko Hata, Peter Kazanzides, Sylvain Martel, Rajni Patel, Veronica Santos, Russell Taylor (2017). "Medical Robots: Regulatory, Ethical, and Legal Considerations for Increasing Levels of Autonomy," March 15, 2017, Science Robotics

---

Note: *For supplemental materials depicting the aspects discussed in this chapter, refer to Appendix B, which contains various augmented diagrams, charts, and additional related facets of relevance.*

CHAPTER 6
MULTIDIMENSIONALITY OF AI LEGAL SINGULARITY

Abstract

Legal scholars have in the last several years embarked upon an ongoing discussion and debate over a potential Legal Singularity that might someday occur, involving a variant or law-domain offshoot leveraged from the Artificial Intelligence (AI) realm amid its many decades of deliberations about an overarching and generalized technological singularity (referred to classically as *The Singularity*). This paper examines the postulated Legal Singularity and proffers that such AI and Law cogitations can be enriched by these three facets addressed herein: (1) dovetail additionally salient considerations of *The Singularity* into the Legal Singularity, (2) make use of an in-depth and innovative multidimensional parametric analysis of the Legal Singularity as posited in this paper, and (3) align and unify the Legal Singularity with the Levels of Autonomy (LoA) associated with AI Legal Reasoning (AILR) as propounded in this paper

Section 1: Background of The Singularity

In section 1 of the paper, the topic of *The Singularity* is introduced and addressed. Doing so establishes the groundwork for section 2, covering a form of singularity that has come to be known as the Legal Singularity (LS), considered to be an offshoot or a domain-specific variant of the overarching *The Singularity*.

Section 3 indicates the Levels of Autonomy (LoA) of AI Legal Reasoning (AILR), which will be instrumental in the discussions undertaken in Section 4. Section 4 then provides an in-depth analysis of the Legal Singularity as it relates to the LoA of AI Legal Reasoning and lays out an important parametric analysis of the Legal Singularity. The final section, Section 5, covers additional considerations and future research.

This paper then consists of these five sections:

- Section 1: Background of The Singularity
- Section 2: Legal Singularity
- Section 3: Autonomous Levels of AI Legal Reasoning
- Section 4: Legal Singularity Multidimensionality, Alignment with LoA AILR
- Section 5: Additional Considerations and Future Research

Since the word "singularity" is used in at least two contexts within this paper, one context being an overarching or grandiose kind of singularity, typically referred to as *The Singularity*, and the other being a singularity specific to the field of law, known as the Legal Singularity, the convention in this paper will be that whenever referring to the Legal Singularity this will be done by stating "Legal Singularity" or by the abbreviation of "LS," while the larger *The Singularity* will be referred to as the "singularity" or "AI singularity" or "Technological singularity," and when desiring to especially emphasize such a reference it will be stated as *The Singularity* (such an emphasize is done solely for drawing attention to the matter and not due to suggesting any differences of meaning or connotation).

1.1 Understanding *The Singularity*

A longstanding discussion and debate in the field of Artificial Intelligence entails a controversy referred to as *The Singularity* [9] [14] [28] [39]. Sometimes also coined as the AI Singularity or the Technological Singularity, the concept underlying the matter is relatively ill-defined and has substantively varied in details of its meaning and substance over the now many years of its postulation (dating back to the 1950s).

Often first-traced to commentary by the famous mathematician and pioneering computer scientist John von Neumann, here is what researcher Ulman [58] in 1958 indicated had occurred in a conversation with Von Neumann: "One conversation centered on the ever-accelerating progress of technology and changes in the mode of human life, which gives the appearance of approaching some essential singularity in the history of the race beyond which human affairs, as we know them, could not continue."

Essentially, the sentiment at the time was that computers might eventually be able to achieve human intelligence, potentially even eclipsing human intelligence, and the result could be problematic for humanity. Of course, similar exhortations have been replete in science fiction, though typically proffered by imaginative writers with unsupported visions rather than by bona fide scientists that are making such speculations based on their assessment of the underlying technology and attempting to anticipate future outcomes. That's not to suggest that those scientists will necessarily be on par with predicting the future, and there are many documented instances of scientists that were wildly off-the-target and baseless in their prophesizing. In short, expertise in a subject matter is a worthwhile basis for providing meaningful predictions, nonetheless, that expertise can still be misguided or mistaken as to what the future might hold.

In 1965, Oxford researcher Irving John Good [36] published a cornerstone research paper that extended the singularity notion and tied the topic to the emergence of computers that might be considered as ultra-intelligent, commonly today referred to as aiming to be super-intelligent or super-human in capability. Rather than emphasizing the dangers associated with mankind developing an ultra-intelligent machine, Good [36] urged that the survival of humanity depended on being able to craft such a system and indeed ought to be done as soon as possible: "The survival of man depends on the early construction of an ultra-intelligent machine."

Here is Good's [36] definition associated with the capabilities envisaged:

> "Let an ultra-intelligent machine be defined as a machine that can far surpass all the intellectual activities of any man however clever. Since the design of machines is one of these intellectual activities, an ultra-intelligent machine could design even better machines; there would then unquestionably be an intelligence explosion, and the intelligence of man would be left far behind. Thus, the first ultra-intelligent machine is the last invention that man need ever make."

In this initial elucidation of the topic by Good, a key facet that has become inextricably woven into the singularity rubric is the speculative idea of an intelligence explosion. In short, if mankind can craft an AI system to some threshold of intelligence, it is presumed that the AI could then further progress, essentially on its own accord, by using its core base of intelligence to further produce more intelligence. No one as yet knows what this minimum threshold might be, and nor is there any viable means to anticipate how far the presumed intelligence explosion might proceed in terms of the upper limits of some unknown super-intelligence, raising the perennial question of how high is up, as it were.

Pursuing for the moment the somewhat tangential but relevant question concerning the notion of an intelligence explosion, let's consider the ramifications of such a phenomenon, if indeed possible (no one knows whether it is or not). Similar to questions that arose during the creation of the atom bomb, whereby scientists were somberly worried that the ignition and exploding of an atomic bomb might somehow catch hold and violently and rapidly spread across the globe in an unheralded conflagration, some assert that the same might happen in the case of an intelligence explosion. To wit, the intelligence being produced might magnify and expand, for which the result could be to have humans seem like mere ants in intelligence versus the super-intelligence spawned by AI. Again, some view this outcome as disastrous for humanity, possibly being enslaved by a super-intelligent AI, while others believe that mankind might be saved due to an artificial super-intelligence that could solve the gravest problems confronting the survivability of humans.

In his research, Good attempted to outline some of the overall features or elements that seemed at the time to potentially be required to achieve an AI super-intelligence. For example, he debated those theories of the period concerning a tremendous amount of parallelism that would be needed, a facet of modern-day computers that were not especially viable when Good [36] wrote his paper in the 1960s: "It cannot be regarded as entirely certain that an ultra-intelligent machine would need to be ultraparallel since the number of binary operations per second performed by the brain might be far greater than is necessary for a computer made of reliable components. Neurons are not fully reliable; for example, they do not all last a lifetime; yet the brain is extremely efficient. This efficiency must depend partly on 'redundancy' in the sense in which the term is used in information theory. A machine made of reliable components would have an advantage, and it seems just possible that ultraparallel working will not be essential. But there is a great waste in having only a small proportion of the components of a machine active at any one time."

At this time, there is still no definitive means to specify what the AI might be composed of that would lead to the singularity, and the work on these facets remains exploratory and speculative in nature. Furthermore, not everyone conceives of the singularity as necessarily requiring super-intelligence, and nor an intelligence explosion. Some proffer that the singularity might be considered as the reaching of human intelligence via AI, often referred to as Artificial General Intelligence (AGI). At that achievement alone, the singularity will have been achieved, some contend. Whether this then leads to a subsequent intelligence explosion, and some kind of super-intelligence, can be considered a separate aspect, for which the singularity then perhaps is essentially a furtherance or extension rather than an initial arrival per se.

Consider these variations:

a) Singularity is the achievement of AI such that the AI has attained human intelligence capabilities
b) Singularity is the eclipsing of human intelligence by AI and attaining a super-intelligence
c) Singularity is an intelligence explosion whereby AI generates or spawns further intelligence.

Arguments ensue as to which of those is the "singularity" and also whether they must be combined or co-existent to count as the singularity occurring. Perhaps "a" or arrival at human intelligence is mandatory for getting to "b," though others contend that it is possible that an AI decidedly less-than-human intelligence levels might percolate via "c" per an intelligence explosion and then nearly instantaneously exceed "a" and arrive at "b," thus never especially settling down at the mere capacity of human intelligence. Others argue that there is not anything feasibly beyond human intellectual capacities, regardless of how adept the AI might be, and as such the achievement of human intelligence is the capstone limit. In that case, the singularity would be solely about the "a" and not take into account the "b" and "c" postulates which are deemed as impossible and a false aspiration.

Additionally, some assert that a super-intelligence might be reached without any need for and indeed no occurrence at all of an intelligence explosion. In this claim, an intelligence explosion is unlikely, perhaps even impossible per se, and that the super-intelligence might arise is some other more "mundane" manner and not due to a speculative and seeming spectacular intelligence explosion. Variations of that theory are that an intelligence explosion might very well occur, but it will be more of a whimper than a bang, such that the explosion is not particularly explosive. Instead, envision that intelligence oozes or synergizes with other intelligence, doing so demurely, rather than in a highly combustive manner.

The variants consist of these possibilities (but not limited to) that might constitute *The Singularity*:

- "a" only
- "b" only
- "c" only
- "a" and "b" mandatory
- "b" and "c" mandatory
- "a" and "c" mandatory
- "a" and "b" and "c" mandatory
- Other

For purposes of this discussion, we relax the potential requirement that the singularity must have a super-intelligence and also that an intelligence explosion is required. Since the singularity is already a highly conceptualized theory, to begin with, it seems reasonable to accept the notion that if human intelligence is achieved via AI, this accomplishment by itself would present the same potentiality as would the super-intelligence and the intelligence explosion. In essence, wherein some believe that only a super-intelligence bodes for the outcomes of either goodness or badness for society, there is ample room to equally speculate that an AI of human intelligence capability could likewise give rise to magnitudes of goodness and badness for society. Keep in mind that such an AI would presumably be able to be replicated and shared all across the globe, giving a boost to its potential impacts, regardless that it might not be deemed as super-intelligent or was not borne from an intelligence explosion.

It is further conceivable that we might split the difference and find a middle ground of a singularity at phase one, consisting of reaching human intelligence, and then a phase two of singularity that involves super-intelligence. Some are not satisfied with this two-phased division and insist that the singularity can only occur if super-intelligence is achieved. This is somewhat a disingenuous contention though if there is no means to codify or specify what the super-intelligence consists of. Indeed, one of the ongoing disputes about the very notion of super-intelligence is that there is a paucity of substantive criteria to pin down the capacities that super-intelligence presumably guarantees, raising the question of how will we know that super-intelligence has been attained and that it is not an AI-based human level of intelligence that just so happens to seem super-intelligent from our perspective. Those that proffer the archetypal "I'll know it when I see it" retort are not especially contributory to these serious-minded deliberations.

The renowned book about AI Singularity by Ray Kurzweil [39] in 2006 has become a foundational treatise on the topic of *The Singularity* and wrestles comparably with many of the potential facets of what the singularity constitutes. Kurzweil directly tackles the numerous criticisms about the singularity, including instances of doubt expressed by the assumed limits on neural processing, the Church-Turing thesis, Searle's Chinese Room Argument, theism, holism, and the like.

After examining those numerous and varied critiques, Kurzweil [39] steadfastly asserts: "The Singularity, as we have discussed it in this book, does not achieve infinite levels of computation, memory, or any other measurable attribute. But it certainly achieves vast levels of all of these qualities, including intelligence. With the reverse engineering of the human brain, we will be able to apply the parallel, self-organizing, chaotic algorithms of human intelligence to enormously powerful computational substrates."

In that sense, it does not seem well-intentioned to debate in any preoccupied manner on the merits of AI Singularity as to whether a super-intelligence is attained, and nor whether there is an intelligence explosion, and instead concentrate on the overwhelming and overarching factor of AI embodiment of human-level intelligence, for which the potential outcomes are amplified when considering the presumed likelihood that this means that the AI could be readily replicated and distributed, doing so in a manner and form that heretofore of human intelligence could not be equally realized.

Kurzweil's book is provocatively titled as indicating that the singularity is near [39]. Others such as Walsh [61] offer a less optimistic timeline, indicating that the singularity is not only not near, it might not ever be near. Braga [9] suggests that despite whatever timing might be involved, the possibility of the singularity is surrounded by fallacies and that the debates about the singularity ought to be leveraged for considering how the dispute themselves gives rise to potential new opportunities in AI.

For speculations about the timing of the singularity, there are said to be potential "defeaters" that could undermine the postulated timelines. For example, many in the AI field are apt to offer that extraordinary and undefined AI breakthroughs have to occur if the singularity is going to be attained and that the timelines oft-stated are based on as-yet discovered technological innovations [58] [59]. Assumptions are made that technological progress on AI is going to proceed in some determinable fashion, and as long as that estimated path continues, the timing for the singularity remains on-target. Chalmers [14] offers this pronouncement about the role and nature of defeaters in this manner:

> "As for defeaters: I will stipulate that these are anything that prevents intelligent systems (human or artificial) from manifesting their capacities to create intelligent systems. Potential defeaters include disasters, disinclination, and active prevention. For example, a nuclear war might set back our technological capacity enormously, or we (or our successors) might decide that a singularity would be a bad thing and prevent research that could bring it about. I do not think considerations internal to artificial intelligence can exclude these possibilities, although we might argue on other grounds about how likely they are."

Another salient point frequently discussed about *The Singularity* involves the so-called Singularity Paradox. This is a presumed paradox that seems to undercut the doomsday scenarios that have been prophesied about the singularity. For example, one of the most famous doomsday indications involves the Paperclip Problem as described by Bostrom [8]. In this invented scenario, AI that has achieved singularity is asked by humanity to undertake the production of paperclips. The AI proceeds to do so, and takes this goal to an extreme, ultimately consuming all of the earth's production capacity to make paperclips. In the exceptionally sorrowful versions of the Paperclip Problem, the AI determines that humans are preventing the AI from maximizing the making of paperclips and thus does away with humans entirely. Though this might seem like a reasoned concern, Ympolskiy [65] explains why the Singularity Paradox is a worthwhile consideration to refute some of these doomsday manifestations: "Investigators concerned with the existential risks posed to humankind by the appearance of superintelligence often describe what we shall call a Singularity Paradox (SP) as their main reason for thinking that humanity might be in danger. Briefly, SP could be described as: 'Superintelligent machines are feared to be too dumb to possess commonsense.'"

In other words, why would it be that an AI that we have deemed as achieving super-intelligence be so dimwitted that it would fall into these simpleton mental traps?

As such, the doomsday scenarios ought to be eyed with a grain of salt, since they at times make assumptions in favor of what a super-intelligence might do, while simultaneously treating the super-intelligence as sub-par intelligence in what it might do.

In this section, *The Singularity* has been briefly expounded to showcase that it is a concept that has been in existence for a considerable while (at least seventy years or so), it is a topic of fluidity and multiple definitions, and that it posits quite serious and significant aspects about the future of AI and the future of humanity. We do not know that it will happen, and we do not know that it will <u>not</u> happen, and yet it is certainly worthwhile contemplating as it bodes for substantive impacts on society if it does indeed occur. Though some technologists are at times focused solely on the challenges and enthralling feat of developing AI to the point of *The Singularity*, there is a great deal of handwringing and concern among those of the AI community about the matter. This is noteworthy since there is often criticism of technologists that they fail to consider the Frankenstein-like potential outcomes of their work [36] [39], which does assuredly happen, yet the special case of *The Singularity* seems to have brought forth an awareness that pushing AI to such an extent requires consideration on what the results might portend.

Section 2: Legal Singularity

In this section, the conceptual underpinnings of a potential Legal Singularity are explored. This is undertaken by first examining what the Legal Singularity might consist of, and then identifying how the Legal Singularity leverages *The Singularity* and also what is either omitted or being added beyond the conventional scope of *The Singularity*.

2.1 Defining Legal Singularity

The research by Alarie [1] provides a cornerstone indication of what a Legal Singularity might constitute. In brief, he asserts that the expansion of today's Machine Learning capabilities entailing predictive and pattern matching facilities will grow stronger and be fed by masses of data about the law, doing so in an increasingly recursive fueled manner [1]:

"The first is that technological progress continues to generate more data. The second is that our methods for analyzing data continue to improve due to increases in computing power and better methods of machine learning."

This would seem to be a phenomenon that would gradually and inexorably evolve and emerge, rather than any kind of overnight or instantaneous type of intelligence explosion. Furthermore, there is nothing overtly indicative that the resulting AI would be of a super-intelligence capacity. It would seem to be computationally impressive and extensive, though not somehow extending beyond the scope of everyday human intelligence as we understand such intelligence to be. Indeed, Alarie makes explicit that *The Singularity* is a provocateur that led to the conceiving of a Legal Singularity, yet does not necessarily embrace the various keystones thereof: "The legal singularity is inspired by and different from the idea of the technological singularity popularized by the futurist Ray Kurzweil. The technological singularity refers to the stage when machines themselves become capable of building ever more capable and powerful machines, to the point of an intelligence explosion that exceeds human understanding or capacity to control (technological singularity is akin, then, to superintelligence)."

Ultimately, according to Alarie [1], the Legal Singularity will be achieved or arrived at and impacts to the law and the practice of law will be overwhelmingly demonstrative, once legal certainty is attained: "The legal singularity will arrive when the accumulation of massively more data and dramatically improved methods of inference make legal uncertainty obsolete. The legal singularity contemplates complete law."

This is a crucial demarcation about the nature of an envisioned Legal Singularity. There is a presumed and explicitly stated arrival point at which the Legal Singularity can apparently be said to have been attained, namely once legal certainty is achieved, or on the other side of the coin, once all legal uncertainty is eliminated.

An interesting and quite worth noting aspect of this as a measuring stick is that it perhaps can be utilized to escape the boundaries of necessarily assuming that Machine Learning and the accumulation of data are the required source for the Legal Singularity to be reached. In other words, if the Legal Singularity is principally defined as the attainment of pure legal certainty, we might then set aside how we got there, and be willing to consider other means by which that target of legal certainty could be attained. There is no need to cling per se to or be anchored to the assumption that it might be due to Machine Learning and the accumulation of data, and there might other explanations that give rise to the Legal Singularity (though the explanation of utilizing Machine Learning and the vast collection of data seems most convincing, today, given what we know about AI as of today).

In an overall sense, the Legal Singularity is defined as an outcome. The outcome is the state at which the law is entirely certain and there is no uncertainty remaining.

Various phrases have arisen to depict this potentiality, including:

- Complete law
- Seamless legal order
- Self-executing legal system
- Completely specified legal system
- Functionally complete law
- Etc.

Another corresponding set of elements underlying this conception of the Legal Singularity is that it will of necessity allow universal access and real-time access to the law, which Alarie explains as: "The legal singularity contemplates the elimination of legal uncertainty and the emergence of a seamless legal order, universally accessible in real-time. In the legal singularity, disputes over the legal significance of agreed facts will be rare. They may be disputes over facts, but the once found, the facts will map on to clear legal consequences. The law will be functionally complete."

And the Legal Singularity will be in existence within specific domains of the law, along with inevitably occurring in all areas of the law. Alarie uses tax law as an exemplar of a particular domain of law, from which we can generalize across all subdomains of law [1]: "I predict that coming decades will witness three gradual transitions as the legal singularity draws nearer: (1) improved dispute resolution and access to justice in tax law, primarily through the transition from our current reliance on standards (adjudicated *ex post*) to greater reliance on query-able systems of complex rules (knowable *ex ante*); (2) a transition to superior and increasingly more complete specifications of tax law (*i.e.*, a gradual transition from the complex, unwieldy, uncoordinated tax systems of today to tax systems that are massively complex and yet precisely and effectively distribute benefits and burdens); and, (3) with the realization of the legal singularity, a complete specification of tax law (and, indeed, all the other areas of law), which will thenceforth remain (more or less) in positive and normative equilibrium."

Two additional key facets seem to be given notable consideration. One is that the Legal Singularity will be beneficial to justice and provide a presumably better consequence for society concerning the law [1]: "Ultimately, I believe these developments will result in the "legal singularity" which results in a more or less positively and normatively stable legal system."

Meanwhile, a noted downside to the Legal Singularity will be that it would render the law as less scrutable, perhaps even inscrutable, and thus have correspondingly negative consequences [1]: "The apotheosis of the legal system will be extraordinarily complex and will be beyond the complete understanding of any person." This latter point of a lack of explainability or inability to undertake interpretation is sometimes referred to as a form of computational irreducibility, of which the law would be considered a type of black box in the instantiation of the Legal Singularity.

As a quick recap of the major elements of a postulated Legal Singularity:

- Outcome-based
- Posited on achieving absolute legal certainty
- Will occur gradually, subdomains at a time
- Will ultimately occur across all of law
- Leads to a more stable legal approach
- Law becomes "black box" inscrutable
- Arrival likely occurs via advances in AI and data
- Does not seem to require an intelligence explosion
- Does not seem to require super-intelligence
- Loosely inspired by *The Singularity*

Other researchers have sought to identify both strengths and weaknesses in the case being made for a Legal Singularity. Some view with significant doubt that a Legal Singularity would necessarily produce the anticipated benefits and might instead have substantive adverse consequences. Weber [63] for example postulates that there might be (at least) a twofold threat emerging from a Legal Singularity: (1) it would institutionalize existent biases of the legal system, (2) it would treat human rights as though people are merely atomized data points. Both of those adverse consequences could turn the populace away from embracing a Legal Singularity amid severe qualms about the overturning of the existent normative.

These points are worthwhile to further explore. Per Weber [63], he suggests that we envision an AI system in the future, called Singulatim, and for which it embodies the Legal Singularity. Consider what might happen with Singulatim. There is already today an increasing awareness that contemporary Machine Learning algorithms tend to carryover biases that are inherently in the data used to train the AI systems. If a dataset has been collected that was based on prior decisions containing racist biases, and the Machine Learning patterns to that data, the result is likely to be an AI system that then incorporates and utilizes those biases. There is no common-sense or reasoning by the AI about what the data contains.

Furthermore, the AI might have mathematically patterned to the data in an obscure and complex manner, making it nearly impossible to ferret out whether biases are now within the AI system. As stated by Weber: "The first [threat] is essentially critical: that the Singulatim software, in learning from how the legal system works, would institutionalize algorithmically the existing inequalities in the way the legal system treats its subjects."

In the matter of the second major threat of a Legal Singularity, Weber [63] emphasizes that since the AI does not have any cognition or human intelligence per se, and it is merely a Machine Learning algorithm that computationally is doing pattern matching, the result is that humans being subject to the laws are being reduced from being considered as sentient beings and instead be treated as data points in a computational machine [63] "The second threat, on the other hand, strikes even deeper at the rule of law. The problem here is not that the Singulatim software cements in place some extra-legal hierarchy; instead, the issue is that the basic terms of universal rights might cease to make sense in the face of an epistemological shift that allows the law to only see atomized data points where it used to see integral, individual legal subjects." This raises primary and legal core questions that can be formulated by what Weber [63] describes as strong-form theorists and weak-form theorists: "Simplifying only somewhat, strong-form theorists pose the question *Does the legal system protect against arbitrary government power and thereby promote liberty?*, while weak-form theorists ask *Does the legal system promote and maintain social order?*"

In essence, perhaps ironically, the Legal Singularity might usurp and gut or undermine the essence of our approach to law and justice: "In those circumstances, the formerly latent tension holding together the rule of law and the universality principle would explode, destroying any normative force the latter was thought to impart to the former. To adopt the terminology in which legal futurism is often celebrated, the tension, no longer suppressed, would then *disrupt* the very foundations of the rule of law."

These weaknesses underlying the Legal Singularity are subtly predicated on a key facet that otherwise might have seemed not quite so consequential in this discussion so far, namely that the Legal Singularity is portrayed as being shaped by the Machine Learning that we conceive of today. If we reinvigorate the Legal Singularity by bringing from *The Singularity* that there might be a richer embodiment of human intelligence in AI, possibly even a super-intelligence, presumably the twofold threat is no longer quite as emboldened. Here's why. Suppose that the Singulatim had the capacity of human intelligence and therefore might be able to detect and overcome the biases inherent in the underlying data of the law. Furthermore, the Singulatim in the case of the second threat would not necessarily be configuring the status of humans as data points per se, at least to the degree that if human intelligence was equivalence in the AI that there would be some representation beyond the simple data basis that computers today might be ascribed. In essence, the argument made about the Legal Singularity as being limited to ingratiating biases and treating people as mere numbers is predicated on the assumption that the Legal Singularity will be composed of Machine Learning as we make use of it today. By shifting toward a broader futuristic perspective, and an AI of a much greater capability, such an argument does not necessarily continue to hold (that's not to mean that the AI would assuredly obviate biases and nor that it would not treat people as atomized data, only that it opens the door to the possibility that those key facets might not necessarily occur).

As earlier mentioned, there is the Singularity Paradox, proffering the conundrum that some futurists at times are willing to ascribe to AI that it will be something of human intelligence or super-intelligence, and yet in the same context will portray or assume that the AI is to be dimwitted or fail to exhibit intelligence. In the conception of the Legal Singularity, by seemingly removing the capacity of reaching human intelligence (let alone super-intelligence), a Pandora's box of concerns is readily opened widely. It might seem that an easy solution would be to reinsert into the Legal Singularity that AI of human intelligence levels will be required, in which case the "easy and obvious" problems inherent in the Legal Singularity could be explained as overcome by the intrinsic intelligence of the AI involved.

This does not suggest that other problems will not ergo arise, only that the ones associated with any automation that is less than the level of human intelligence would typically contain.

Skeptics though tend to deride the requirement of achieving human intelligence (or better) in such matters. First, whether AI can achieve human intelligence (or better) remains an unanswered question and might never be achieved. Thus, if the Legal Singularity did rely upon the assumption that human intelligence (or better) was a necessity for Legal Singularity, it would put the Legal Singularity into the same murky waters as *The Singularity* as to whether this will arise and if ever so. Second, some have a distaste for employing what they consider a magical fix, as it were, consisting of the assumption that human intelligence in AI will be achieved (this is seen as a "insert miracle here" kind of predicate). The viewpoint is that any kind of future can be devised by simply relying upon an amorphous and yet to be proven achievement of human intelligence into a machine.

As an example of this kind of conundrum, it is relatively straightforward to pick apart the Legal Singularity in terms of its potential impacts by aiming at the already known limitations and shortcomings of today's automation including Machine Learning. In the research by Deakin and Markou [18] they point out that law is a social institution and the Legal Singularity would operate in a social vacuum since it is computationally based (as we know of it today): "But if mathematical logic cannot capture the 'situation-specific understanding' of legal reasoning and the complexity of the social world it exists in—at least to any extent congruent with how natural language categories cognize social referents and character of meaning—the hypothetical totalization of 'AI judges' implied by the legal singularity would instantiate a particular view of law: one in which legal judgments are essentially deterministic or probabilistic outputs, produced on the basis of static or unambiguous legal rules, in a societal vacuum. This would deny, or see as irrelevant, competing conceptions of law, in particular the idea that law is a social institution, involving socially constructed activities, relationships, and norms not easily translated into numerical functions. It would also turn a blind eye to the reality that legal decision making involves an exercise of power which is both material and, in Pierre Bourdieu's sense, 'symbolic '."

Overall, the Legal Singularity as conceptualized without some apparent semblance of human intelligence (or better) in the underlying AI is endlessly vulnerable to any number of shotgun or scattergun attacks as to being unable to rise above the limitations already known (and some likely yet to be surfaced) about contemporary versions of AI. This is not an attempt to have Legal Singularity switchover to embracing a more powerful semblance or sense of AI, and only pointing out the quagmire associated with a definition of Legal Singularity that resides dependent upon and impotent due to the assumption of today's AI mechanizations. To be fair, the original concept does provide a type of escape clause by emphasizing that the Machine Learning would be based on better methods than used today, which is a crucial point that seems to be at times lost or lessened in criticisms of the conception of Legal Singularity. In any case, as will be discussed in Section 4, one means to cope with this difficulty is to recast the Legal Singularity in terms of the autonomous levels of AI Legal Reasoning, providing a path toward conceiving of the Legal Singularity across a spectrum of what AI might become.

Section 3: Autonomous Levels of AI Legal Reasoning

In this section, a framework for the autonomous levels of AI Legal Reasoning is summarized and is based on the research described in detail in Eliot [25].

These autonomous levels will be portrayed in a grid that aligns with key elements of autonomy and as matched to AI Legal Reasoning. Providing this context will be useful to the later sections of this paper and will be utilized accordingly.

The autonomous levels of AI Legal Reasoning are as follows:
Level 0: No Automation for AI Legal Reasoning
Level 1: Simple Assistance Automation for AI Legal Reasoning
Level 2: Advanced Assistance Automation for AI Legal Reasoning
Level 3: Semi-Autonomous Automation for AI Legal Reasoning
Level 4: Domain Autonomous for AI Legal Reasoning
Level 5: Fully Autonomous for AI Legal Reasoning
Level 6: Superhuman Autonomous for AI Legal Reasoning

See **Figure A-1** for an overview chart showcasing the autonomous levels of AI Legal Reasoning as via columns denoting each of the respective levels.

See **Figure A-2** for an overview chart similar to Figure A-1 which alternatively is indicative of the autonomous levels of AI Legal Reasoning via the rows as depicting the respective levels (this is simply a reformatting of Figure A-1, doing so to aid in illuminating this variant perspective, but does not introduce any new facets or alterations from the contents as already shown in Figure A-1).

3.1.1 Level 0: No Automation for AI Legal Reasoning

Level 0 is considered the no automation level. Legal reasoning is carried out via manual methods and principally occurs via paper-based methods.

This level is allowed some leeway in that the use of say a simple handheld calculator or perhaps the use of a fax machine could be allowed or included within this Level 0, though strictly speaking it could be said that any form whatsoever of automation is to be excluded from this level.

3.1.2 Level 1: Simple Assistance Automation for AI Legal Reasoning

Level 1 consists of simple assistance automation for AI legal reasoning.

Examples of this category encompassing simple automation would include the use of everyday computer-based word processing, the use of everyday computer-based spreadsheets, the access to online legal documents that are stored and retrieved electronically, and so on.

By-and-large, today's use of computers for legal activities is predominantly within Level 1. It is assumed and expected that over time, the pervasiveness of automation will continue to deepen and widen, and eventually lead to legal activities being supported and within Level 2, rather than Level 1.

3.1.3 Level 2: Advanced Assistance Automation for AI Legal Reasoning

Level 2 consists of advanced assistance automation for AI legal reasoning.

Examples of this notion encompassing advanced automation would include the use of query-style Natural Language Processing (NLP), Machine Learning (ML) for case predictions, and so on.

Gradually, over time, it is expected that computer-based systems for legal activities will increasingly make use of advanced automation. Law industry technology that was once at a Level 1 will likely be refined, upgraded, or expanded to include advanced capabilities, and thus be reclassified into Level 2.

3.1.4 Level 3: Semi-Autonomous Automation for AI Legal Reasoning

Level 3 consists of semi-autonomous automation for AI legal reasoning.

Examples of this notion encompassing semi-autonomous automation would include the use of Knowledge-Based Systems (KBS) for legal reasoning, the use of Machine Learning and Deep Learning (ML/DL) for legal reasoning, and so on.

Today, such automation tends to exist in research efforts or prototypes and pilot systems, along with some commercial legal technology that has been infusing these capabilities too.

3.1.5 Level 4: Domain Autonomous for AI Legal Reasoning

Level 4 consists of domain autonomous computer-based systems for AI legal reasoning.

This level reuses the conceptual notion of Operational Design Domains (ODDs) as utilized in the autonomous vehicles and self-driving cars levels of autonomy, though in this use case it is being applied to the legal domain [17] [18] [20].

Essentially, this entails any AI legal reasoning capacities that can operate autonomously, entirely so, but that is only able to do so in some limited or constrained legal domain.

3.1.6 Level 5: Fully Autonomous for AI Legal Reasoning

Level 5 consists of fully autonomous computer-based systems for AI legal reasoning.

In a sense, Level 5 is the superset of Level 4 in terms of encompassing all possible domains as per however so defined ultimately for Level 4. The only constraint, as it were, consists of the facet that the Level 4 and Level 5 are concerning human intelligence and the capacities thereof. This is an important emphasis due to attempting to distinguish Level 5 from Level 6 (as will be discussed in the next subsection)

It is conceivable that someday there might be a fully autonomous AI legal reasoning capability, one that encompasses all of the law in all foreseeable ways, though this is quite a tall order and remains quite aspirational without a clear cut path of how this might one day be achieved. Nonetheless, it seems to be within the extended realm of possibilities, which is worthwhile to mention in relative terms to Level 6.

3.1.7 Level 6: Superhuman Autonomous for AI Legal Reasoning

Level 6 consists of superhuman autonomous computer-based systems for AI legal reasoning.

In a sense, Level 6 is the entirety of Level 5 and adds something beyond that in a manner that is currently ill-defined and perhaps (some would argue) as yet unknowable.

The notion is that AI might ultimately exceed human intelligence, rising to become superhuman, and if so, we do not yet have any viable indication of what that superhuman intelligence consists of and nor what kind of thinking it would somehow be able to undertake.

Whether a Level 6 is ever attainable is reliant upon whether superhuman AI is ever attainable, and thus, at this time, this stands as a placeholder for that which might never occur. In any case, having such a placeholder provides a semblance of completeness, doing so without necessarily legitimatizing that superhuman AI is going to be achieved or not. No such claim or dispute is undertaken within this framework.

Section 4: Legal Singularity Multidimensionality, Alignment with LoA AILR

This section combines the prior sections respective discussions about or pertaining to the Legal Singularity, doing so in two key ways: (a) Showcase how the Legal Singularity aligns with the autonomous levels of AI Legal Reasoning, and (b) Indicate the multidimensionality of the Legal Singularity by conducting a parametric analysis. This then provides the core contributions of this paper, and Section 5 then offers concluding remarks and recommendations for further research on these matters.

4.1 Legal Singularity and the LoA AILR

Existing indications about the Legal Singularity seem to imply that the Legal Singularity will potentially arise at a particular point in time. Another viewpoint would be to consider that the Legal Singularity will arise in a series of stages or phases.

As shown in **Figure B-1**, the autonomous levels for AI Legal Reasoning are presented, and included in the lower region of the chart is a projected depiction of the Legal Singularity. This overlay provides a convenient means of portraying the possibility that the Legal Singularity will gradually emerge and evolve over time.

At the levels less than 3, there is no expectation of the Legal Singularity and thus it is a grayed-out indication. Even though an argument could be made that during Level 1 and Level 2 there is some amount of groundwork being laid for the seeding and later growth of the Legal Singularity, this seems to be a pre-seeding effort and not especially noteworthy for highlighting for the overall anticipated inception of the Legal Singularity.

During Level 3, the Legal Singularity begins to take some palpable shape, doing so during the advanced AI efforts that consist primarily of prototypes and research-based activities of applying AI to the law. This tryout status will aid in ascertaining the viability of a Legal Singularity and likely to reveal the feasibility of a Legal Singularity occurring all told.

Assuming that the Legal Singularity is viable, there is a denoted Stage A that might occur during Level 4, and a Stage B that might occur during Level 5, and a Stage C that might occur during Level 6. This indication should not be interpreted as a signal or prophecy that the Legal Singularity will indeed happen, since that is not the purpose or intent of this chart, and instead the viewpoint is that if the Legal Singularity were to arise that it might do so in the staged manner presented in the chart.

At Level 4, the Legal Singularity would be taking hold at various subdomains of the law, such as a Legal Singularity in real estate law, family law, and so on.

At Level 5, the Legal Singularity would be across all subdomains of law and therefore encompass all of the law. At Level 6, the Legal Singularity would be akin to Level 5 in that it would encompass all of the law and have an added aspect that the AI would be superhuman or consist of super-intelligence. As already noted earlier in this paper, it is unknown as to what the superhuman or super-intelligence might consist of, and thus highly speculative to assert what this might achieve in the case of Legal Singularity. In any case, since some believe a superhuman capacity might someday exist in AI, the Level 6 accounts for that possibility and similarly, the Legal Singularity accounts for the possibility too via an indicated Stage C.

Overall, the Legal Singularity is aligned with the levels of autonomy (LoA) of the AI Legal Reasoning (AILR) in this manner:

- **Level 0: <*not noteworthy*>**
- **Level 1: <*not noteworthy*> (pre-seed)**
- **Level 2: <*not noteworthy*> (pre-seed)**
- **Level 3: Tryout (pre-stage)**
- **Level 4: Stage A**
- **Level 5: Stage B**
- **Level 6: Stage C**

4.2 Multidimensionality of Legal Singularity

Law research and the scholarly literature about the Legal Singularity have tended to *silently* encompass various dimensions underlying the Legal Singularity, meaning that those research efforts have not usually explicitly stated the dimensions being considered. It is contended here that those dimensions are in fact overtly identifiable and distinct, and of necessity should be explicitly stated. In essence, the dimensions have often been treated implicitly, serving as hidden assumptions, and not directly and purposely addressed per se.

This lack of overtly naming the dimensions can confound discussions about the Legal Singularity. For example, research examining the Legal Singularity might fail to name a dimension and make essential unstated assumptions about its nature impacting the Legal Singularity. This omission or hidden assumption renders the research less informative and can undermine progress on explicating the Legal Singularity more fully. Furthermore, trying to compare one research effort on Legal Singularity to another can become onerous and unnecessarily argumentative due to a lack of stated dimensions, including the underlying assumptions the research authors are each respectively making regarding each such dimension.

In reviewing the prior research on Legal Singularity, a dozen key dimensions have been identified. These are not all of the dimensions that might be conceived of, and merely a considered core set, though nonetheless provides a helpful starter and foundational means to further explore the multidimensionality.

Figure B-2 indicates the dozen identified dimensions. Those identified dimensions consist of:

- **Alignment of Legal Singularity**
- **Pace of Legal Singularity**
- **Capability of Legal Singularity**
- **Cornerstone of Legal Singularity**
- **Scope of Legal Singularity**
- **Legal Profession and Legal Singularity**
- **Social Outcome of Legal Singularity**
- **Justice and Legal Singularity**
- **Paradoxes of Legal Singularity**
- **Defeaters of Legal Singularity**
- **Explainability of Legal Singularity**
- **Control of Legal Singularity**

Each of these dimensions will be discussed in the next subsections.

Note that the dimensions are not numbered, which is done purposely, since there is some apprehension that if they were shown in a numbered list it might imply a sense of priority or ranking among the dimensions. It is intended that the dimensions are to be considered without any overall ranking or priority and that they are all equal as elements or parameters of the Legal Singularity. That being said, there is certainly the usefulness of considering whether some dimensions are "more equal than others" and could be considered having greater weight in the emergence of the Legal Singularity or perhaps when assessing the potential impacts of the Legal Singularity. Thus, additional research could indeed opt to proffer weights or rankings to the dimensions, but doing so in this paper would seem to possibly undermine the crucial premise and distract from the overarching concept that there are dimensions and that those dimensions are worthy of attention (no need to distract from that premise by also simultaneously trying to tackle a ranking dispute too).

Figure B-3 indicates the dimensions as shown in a range measurement chart.

Each of the dimensions can be assigned a measuring element, doing so to further amplify and make visible the assumptions underlying the utilization of the dimension when discussing the Legal Singularity as a concept and potential phenomena. In this chart of Figure B-3, a range portrayal is used, indicating some semblance of varying assumptions about the dimension. Do not misinterpret the chart by assuming that the ranges are somehow all equal or comparable, which they are most decidedly not. The ranges are dimension specific. Furthermore, the ranges and the dimensions are not shown in any particular order that would imply prioritization or ranking (as earlier so pointed out).

The intent of the Figure B-3 chart will become more evident when used as a means of comparing how different research on Legal Singularity has tended to characterize the Legal Singularity and can aid too in making explicit the implicit assumptions of those research efforts. This will be further discussed in the subsections of this section. Note too that there is nothing magical or dogmatic about the range indicators, such that additional research is likely to indicate other means of specifying the ranges and their utility in being measured and compared.

4.2.1 Alignment of Legal Singularity

Alignment of Legal Singularity generally refers to its timing with respect to *The Singularity*.

Some assert that the Legal Singularity will occur and perhaps can only occur upon or after *The Singularity* has happened, whilst others claim that the Legal Singularity can occur before *The Singularity* and indeed there is not any necessity that The Singularity needs to ever happen (concerning the occurrence of the Legal Singularity).

4.2.2 Pace of Legal Singularity

Pace of Legal Singularity generally refers to the speed at which the Legal Singularity will emerge or arise.

Some assert that the Legal Singularity will playout gradually, step by step, over an elongated time, while others indicate that as per many beliefs about *The Singularity* that there will be a sparked moment or instantaneous emergence rather than a gradual one.

4.2.3 Capability of Legal Singularity

Capability of Legal Singularity generally refers to the magnitude of intelligence requisite for the onset of the Legal Singularity.

Some assert that the Legal Singularity will be enabled by AI and Machine Learning that is either at the human level of intelligence or akin to human intelligence but perhaps less so in certain respects, while others believe that the Legal Singularity will require a superhuman or super-intelligence capacity by the AI.

4.2.4 Cornerstone of Legal Singularity

Cornerstone of Legal Singularity generally refers to the crucial component of certainty, considered a cornerstone upon which Legal Singularity is founded.

Some assert that Legal Singularity will only be considered as emerged when legal certainty is achieved as an absolute, thus presumably eliminating all legal uncertainty, while others believe that some amount of legal uncertainty can remain and yet nonetheless still have the achievement of Legal Singularity.

4.2.5 Scope of Legal Singularity

Scope of Legal Singularity generally refers to the aspect of how much of the law will be encompassed by the Legal Singularity.

Some assert that the Legal Singularity will entail all of the law, while others indicate it could be instead selected subdomains of the law, for which both viewpoints might be in agreement if it is said that this will evolve, though these views could be in disagreement if it is stated as a winner-take-all that the Legal Singularity only arises when all of the law has been included.

4.2.6 Legal Profession and Legal Singularity

Legal Profession and Legal Singularity generally refers to the notion that the Legal Singularity might dramatically impact the legal profession in terms of the need for and employment of human legal professionals.

Some assert that a Legal Singularity might be seen as an augmentation to the legal profession, thus to some degree still employing and requiring the use of human legal professionals, whilst others suggest that the legal profession might be "wiped out" entirely and be replaced by AI as part of a Legal Singularity emergence.

4.2.7 Social Outcome of Legal Singularity

Social Outcome of Legal Singularity generally refers to the societal result of a Legal Singularity.

Some assert that a Legal Singularity might cause the law to become a societally oppressive tool and produce a Dystopian future, whilst others believe that the Legal Singularity will provide a societally uplifting capacity that will lead to a Utopian style future.

4.2.8 Justice and Legal Singularity

Justice and Legal Singularity generally refers to the impacts that the Legal Singularity would have on the principles of justice, equity, and fairness.

Some assert that the Legal Singularity might lessen justice, reduce equity, and usurp fairness, while others argue that it could instead boost justice, increase equity, and provide greater assurance of fairness.

4.2.9 Paradoxes of Legal Singularity

Paradoxes of Legal Singularity generally refer to the same notion as Singularity Paradoxes of *The Singularity* (as explicated in the prior sections) but as applicable to the Legal Singularity.

Some assert that if the Legal Singularity can eliminate legal uncertainty that it ergo is implausible to attack Legal Singularity for other potential failings since it would presumably be as strong in those other respects, while others argue that there are potential weak spots nonetheless and other problematic aspects that are detectable and decidedly not paradoxical.

4.2.10 Defeaters of Legal Singularity

Defeaters of Legal Singularity generally refer to the same notion as Defeaters with respect to *The Singularity* (as explicated in prior sections) but as applicable to the Legal Singularity.

An overarching question often posed about *The Singularity* it is inevitable or whether mankind will explicitly ascertain whether it will happen; likewise, the Legal Singularity can be said to subject to the same conditions, namely that there might be a plethora of aspects that could either delay the Legal Singularity or render it never to arise, and for which might be led by those within the law industry or those outside of the legal profession.

4.2.11 Explainability of Legal Singularity

Explainability of Legal Singularity generally refers to the aspect of whether the law and the legal mechanizations thereof will be explainable in the emergence of the Legal Singularity.

Some assert that the Legal Singularity will end-up rendering the law as inscrutable, whilst others contend that the law might become more visible, more explainable, and better understood as a result of the Legal Singularity.

4.2.12 Control of Legal Singularity

Control of Legal Singularity generally refers to the amount of control of the Legal Singularity by mankind versus automation.

Some assert that the Legal Singularity could produce an automation-based form of legal justice that becomes detached from humanity and might end-up with essentially AI being in control, whilst others argue that the touch of mankind would remain firmly on the wheels of justice and be overseeing and able to fully control the legal automation or autonomy.

4.3 Examples of the Legal Singularity Dimensions Chart

To illuminate the utility of having the Legal Singularity dimensions explicitly arrayed, consider how the dimensionality chart can be productively utilized.

Figure B-4 shows an example of the Legal Singularity dimensional chart as marked for a scenario labeled simply as Example 1A.

Envision that a researcher has examined the Legal Singularity and offered various nuances and arguments in favor of or opposition to other prior research.

Likely, there are numerous base assumptions that the researcher has made about the Legal Singularity.

By using the Legal Singularity dimensional chart, we can make explicit the assumptions being made. As shown in Figure B-4, the research is essentially postulating that:

- Alignment of Legal Singularity: **Before AI Singularity**
- Pace of Legal Singularity: **Gradual**
- Capability of Legal Singularity: **Human Intelligence (minimal needed)**
- Cornerstone of Legal Singularity: **Absolute Legal Certainty**
- Scope of Legal Singularity: **Subdomains (leading toward all)**
- Legal Profession and Legal Singularity: **Augmentation**
- Social Outcome of Legal Singularity: **Dystopian and Utopian (mixed)**
- Justice and Legal Singularity: **More Equity & Fairness (tends toward)**

- Paradoxes of Legal Singularity: **Some**
- Defeaters of Legal Singularity: **Within Law**
- Explainability of Legal Singularity: **Inscrutable**
- Control of Legal Singularity: **By Mankind**

Some notable facets to keep in mind are that the ranges are not intended to be numerical, which some might desire, such as numbering each of the markers between the ranges. It is not intended that the chart would be used in such a fashion, and once again if done as such might distract from its overall utility. Likewise, it is essentially inappropriate to try and state that a range endpoint is a descriptor when the diamond marker is somewhere along the given spectrum. In that sense, even the above indicates that the pace of legal singularity is "Gradual" provides a somewhat misleading and flat indication of what the actual marking consisted of, which was primarily toward gradual but with some semblance of leaning slightly toward the instantaneous.

Figure B-5 is another example, labeled as Example 1B.

This example showcases a circumstance whereby the research being analyzed for its base assumption across each of the dimensions has tended toward the extremes of the ranges. If there was interest in comparing the research depicted by Example 1A with Example 1B, it would be relatively straightforward to then compare the two as based on the assumptions they each respectively are making about how the Legal Singularity is to be considered.

5.0 Additional Considerations and Future Research

There is a myriad of additional considerations that arise from this discussion about Legal Singularity and further research is amply warranted.

As an example of open topics, consider the aspect that Legal Singularity appears to be predicated principally on the singular dimension or parameter entailing legal certainty (or if so preferred, legal uncertainty). This focus on an individual dimension as the particular underpinning can be viewed as problematic for a variety of demonstrative reasons, as I will outline next.

Concerns about the certainty dimension include these facets:

- **Oversized Requirement for Purity of Certainty**. A purity assumption of attaining absolute legal certainty as a precondition for Legal Singularity is potentially an insurmountable hurdle since it presumably precludes any amount of legal uncertainty, even the most infinitesimal trace, and this seems a prohibitive directive that does not allow for the likely wavering or fluctuation of and between states of legal certainty and legal uncertainty. As such, apparently, as long as there is any semblance of legal uncertainty, Legal Singularity cannot be deemed as having been reached and nor maintained, and the question arises whether the complete expungement of legal uncertainty shall be feasible.

- **Assumption of Exclusively Deterministic Algorithms**. The manner of Machine Learning and AI that will produce the legal certainty seems to be based on a form of deterministic algorithms, exclusively, as though there is no inclusion of non-deterministic algorithms. There does not seem to be any corroborated basis in the defining of Legal Singularity to support such a claim or assertion of this presumed deterministic nature. As such, given that non-determinism is a seemingly strong potential in the case of AI and the law, and perhaps even a necessary ingredient, this realization then introduces probabilistic behavior, which in turn substantively undermines the tenet of requiring complete and steadfast legal certainty.

- **Progression Toward Legal Uncertainty Rather Than Legal Certainty.** Research by D'Amato [68] asserts that legal certainty is decreasing over time, thus legal uncertainty is rising, and that there is a fallacy among many legal scholars that falsely propagate a myth of legal certainty increasing over time. He suggests that the rules and principles of law tend to splinter and be generative over time and thus engenders legal uncertainty [68]:

"Legal certainty decreases over time. Rules and principles of law become more and more uncertain in content and in application because legal systems are biased in favor of unraveling those rules and principles." In his view, legal rules suffer from several maladies [68]: "When I argue that rules unravel over time, I mean that, using any of these extended definitions of the term, a 'rule' becomes increasingly vague, inapplicable, remote, ambiguous, or exception ridden." The Legal Singularity appears to presuppose that due to the (future) AI capacity of predictiveness, the law will become increasingly certain, but this raises at least two considerations. First, this might be a proverbial cart before the horse in that the AI is assumed as somehow leading to certainty and yet the law itself might be inexorably moving intrinsically toward uncertainty. Second, if one assumes that the advent of AI is going to reverse the tendency of the law going toward uncertainty, this needs some robust rationalizing as to why this would of necessity be the case (i.e., it might provide some impetus, but the argument seems to be made is that it will magnetically do so to the degree of achieving ultimate and complete legal certainty).

- **Doctrinaire Belief That Legal Certainty Is The Pinnacle.** On the surface, there is a comforting sense that eliminating all legal uncertainty is a highly desirable outcome and that achieving purity of legal certainty is a proper and crucial goal. But there seems to be more to the tradeoffs between legal certainty and the allowance for some amount of legal uncertainty than otherwise ordinarily meets the eye. As per D'Amato [68], he indicates that though legal certainty is generally and primarily the desirable goal, there is nonetheless still a basis for some value from legal uncertainty: "One may ask, however, whether uncertainty in the law is undesirable. Although I contend that it is, in some cases it might not be." Thus, if the Legal Singularity is the apex, and for which legal certainty underlies it, there would seem to be a need to substantiate how the solidity of legal certainty will overcome those instances for which legal uncertainty is viewed as a positive rather than a negative element.

- **Legal Certainty Is Only One Leg Of The Law Triad:** Focusing solely on legal certainty as the bedrock dimension for Legal Singularity would appear to defy the assertion that legal certainty is part of a triad of the law (which will be elucidated momentarily herein), and thus encompasses only one of three key principles of the law that need to be observed. By many legal scholars, it is generally suggested that the legal triad is akin to a three-legged stool, whereby each leg exists to keep the others in balance, and a stool with but one leg would be unbalanced. Consider this indication of Radbruch's legal precepts as depicted by Leawood [69]: "To complete the concept of law Radbruch uses three general precepts: purposiveness, justice, and legal certainty. Therefore, Radbruch defines law as 'the complex of general precepts for the living-together of human beings' whose ultimate idea is oriented toward justice or equality." In the legal certainty leg of the law, Leawood depicts Radbruch's views in this manner: "Radbruch's final precept is legal certainty. An important part of legal certainty is the justice it provides through, if nothing else, its predictability." This then indubitably supports the importance of legal certainty and bolsters its basis for being at the core of Legal Singularity, but Leawood points out that legal certainty is not an island unto itself: "Certainly, the conflict between legal certainty and justice or between legal certainty and purposiveness is easy to imagine. For example, legal certainty would demand that a law be upheld even though the result would be an unjust application of the law. Therefore, in most cases the content, form, and validity of the law are understood in terms of Radbruch's triad; three equally weighted principles that, while in tension and possibly in contradiction, are found together." In short, how does the envisioned Legal Singularity motivate the triad if the seemingly sole measure is to be based on legal certainty, and as such might lead to serious deficiencies in the other two, namely purposiveness and justice, by overemphasizing and potentially undercutting the tension and dynamics of the triad?

- **Legal Certainty Reliance Upon Legal Rules Versus Legal Principles.** The Legal Singularity would appear to suggest that the advent of AI and Machine Learning will enable encapsulation of legal rules, and in turn, this will lead to the attainment of legal certainty. Essentially, the assumption would appear to be that legal rules will ultimately and unerringly produce legal certainty. Some legal scholars have argued that there are circumstances whereby legal rules can lead to legal certainty, and yet there is also circumstance for which legal principles lead to legal certainty and legal rules do not. Per Braithwaite [67]: "This has been an attempt to develop a theory of legal certainty and to show that questions like whether presumptive positivism is a legal theory that should attract our allegiance depends on testing its empirical claims and assumptions about how rules work. The theory we have come to has three propositions: (1) When the type of action to be regulated is simple, stable and does not involve huge economic interests, rules tend to regulate with greater certainty than principles. (2) When the type of action to be regulated is complex, changing and involves large economic interests: (a) principles tend to regulate with greater certainty than rules; (b) binding principles backing non-binding rules tend to regulate with greater certainty than principles alone; (c) binding principles backing non-binding rules are more certain still if they are embedded in institutions of regulatory conversation that foster shared sensibilities." If the Legal Singularity is foundationally assuming that only legal rules will lead to the desired legal certainty, this would seem to overlook or omit the role of legal principles, but if legal principles are also to be included it raises the corresponding question of how legal certainty is to be attained and legal uncertainty to be eradicated.

These probing questions about the legal certainty dimension are vital to the crux of the Legal Singularity concept. From such questions, it is potentially the case that further refinement and adjustment of the Legal Singularity might be spurred. Additional dimensions might be considered for inclusion or at least for explicit acknowledgment and placement.

Asking these kinds of questions is not to be interpreted as a disparaging of the Legal Singularity and instead should be viewed as aiding the future exploration and maturation of the Legal Singularity concept.

This paper has closely examined the postulated Legal Singularity and proffered that such AI and Law cogitations can be enriched by the three facets addressed herein: (1) by dovetailing additionally salient considerations of *The Singularity* into the Legal Singularity, (2) by making use of the in-depth and innovative multidimensional parametric analysis of the Legal Singularity as posited in this paper, and (3) by aligning and unifying the Legal Singularity with the Levels of Autonomy (LoA) associated with AI Legal Reasoning (AILR) as propounded in this paper.

References

1. Alarie, Benjamin (2016). "The Path of the Law: Toward Legal Singularity," May 27, 2016, SSRN, University of Toronto Faculty of Law and Vector Institute for Artificial Intelligence.

2. Alarie, Benjamin, and Anthony Niblett, Albert Yoon (2017). "Regulation by Machine," Volume 24, Journal of Machine Learning Research.

3. Aleven, Vincent (2003). "Using Background Knowledge in Case-Based Legal Reasoning: A Computational Model and an Intelligent Learning Environment," Artificial Intelligence.

4. Ashley, Kevin, and Karl Branting, Howard Margolis, and Cass Sunstein (2001). "Legal Reasoning and Artificial Intelligence: How Computers 'Think' Like Lawyers," Symposium: Legal Reasoning and Artificial Intelligence, University of Chicago Law School Roundtable.

5. Baker, Jamie (2018). "A Legal Research Odyssey: Artificial Intelligence as Disrupter," Law Library Journal.

6. Ben-Ari, Daniel, and D., Frish, Y., Lazovski, A., Eldan, U., & Greenbaum, D. (2016). "Artificial Intelligence in the Practice of Law: An Analysis and Proof of Concept Experiment," Volume 23, Number 2, Richmond Journal of Law & Technology.

7. Bench-Capon, Trevor, and Givoanni Sartor (2003). "A Model of Legal Reasoning with Cases Incorporating Theories and Values," November 2013, Artificial Intelligence.

8. Bostrom, Nick (2012). "The Superintelligent Will: Motivation and Instrumental Rationality in Advanced Artificial Agents," Volume 22, Number 2, Minds and Machines.

9. Braga, Adriana, and Robert Logan (2019). "AI and the Singularity: A Fallacy or a Great Opportunity," Volume 10, Number 2, Information.

10. Buchanan, Bruce, and Thomas Headrick (1970). "Some Speculation about Artificial Intelligence and Legal Reasoning," Volume 23, Stanford Law Review.

11. Casey, Anthony, and Anthony Niblett (2016). "Self-Driving Laws," Volume 429, University of Toronto Law Journal.

12. Casey, Anthony, and Anthony Niblett (2017). "The Death of Rules and Standards," Volume 92, Indiana Law Journal.

13. Chagal-Feferkorn, Karni (2019). "Am I An Algorithm or a Product: When Products Liability Should Apply to Algorithmic Decision-Makers," Stanford Law & Policy Review.

14. Chalmers, David (2010). "The Singularity: A Philosophical Analysis," Volume 17, Journal of Consciousness Studies.

15. Chen, Daniel (2019). "Machine Learning and the Rule of Law," in Law as Data: Computation, Text, and The Future of Legal Analysis (Michael A. Livermore and Daniel N. Rockmore.

16. Coglianese, Cary, and David Lehr (2017). "Rulemaking by Robot: Administrative Decision Making in the Machine-Learning Era," Volume 105, Georgetown Law Journal.

17. Collingridge, David (1980). The Social Control of Technology. St. Martin's Press.

18. Deakin, Simon, and Christopher Markou (2020). "From Rule of Law to Legal Singularity," University of Cambridge Faculty of Law.

19. Douglas, William (1948). "The Dissent: A Safeguard of Democracy," Volume 32, Journal of the American Judicature Society.

20. Eliot, Lance (2016). AI Guardian Angels for Deep AI Trustworthiness. LBE Press Publishing.

21. Eliot, Lance (2020). "The Neglected Dualism of Artificial Moral Agency and Artificial Legal Reasoning in AI for Social Good." Harvard University, Harvard Center for Research on Computation and Society, AI for Social Good Conference, July 21, 2020.

22. Eliot, Lance (2020). AI and Legal Reasoning Essentials. LBE Press Publishing.

23. Eliot, Lance (2019). Artificial Intelligence and LegalTech Essentials. LBE Press Publishing.

24. Eliot, Lance (2020). "FutureLaw 2020 Showcases How Tech is Transforming The Law, Including the Impacts of AI," April 16, 2020, Forbes.

25. Eliot, Lance (2020). "An Ontological AI-and-Law Framework for the Autonomous Levels of AI Legal Reasoning," Cornell University arXiv. https://arxiv.org/abs/2008.07328

26. Eliot, Lance (2020). "Turing Test and the Practice of Law: The Role of Autonomous Levels of AI Legal Reasoning," Cornell University arXiv. https://arxiv.org/abs/2008.07743

27. Eliot, Lance (2018). "Common Sense Reasoning and AI," April 10, 2018, AI Trends.

28. Eliot, Lance (2018). "Singularity and AI," July 10, 2018, AI Trends.

29. Eliot, Lance (2019). "Artificial Stupidity Could be the Crux to AI," December 8, 2019, Forbes.

30. Eliot, Lance (2020). "The Role of Human Judgement as a Presumed Integral Ingredient for Achieving True AI," March 9, 2020, Forbes.

31. Eliot, Lance (2020). "Strong AI Versus Weak AI Is Completely Misunderstood," July 15, 2020, Forbes.

32. Eliot, Lance (2020). "The Famous Turing Test Put In Reverse and Upside-Down," July 20, 2020, Forbes.

33. Gardner, Anne (1987). Artificial Intelligence and Legal Reasoning. MIT Press.

34. Genesereth, Michael (2009). "Computational Law: The Cop in the Backseat," Stanford Center for Legal Informatics, Stanford University.

35. Goertzel, Ben (2007). "Human-level Artificial General Intelligence and the Possibility of a Technological Singularity," Volume 171, Artificial Intelligence.

36. Good, Irving (1965). "Speculations Concerning the First Ultraintelligent Machine," Volume 6, Advances in Computers.

37. Hage, Jaap (2000). "Dialectical Models in Artificial Intelligence and Law," Artificial Intelligence and Law.

38. Kaplow, Louis (1992). "Rules Versus Standards: An Economic Analysis," Volume 42, Duke Law Journal.

39. Kurzweil, Ray (2006). The Singularity is Near: When Humans Transcend Biology, Gerald Duckworth & Co.

40. Markou, Christopher, and Simon Deakin (2020). "Is Law Computable? From Rule of Law to Legal Singularity," May 4, 2020, SSRN, University of Cambridge Faculty of Law Research Paper.

41. McCarty, Thorne (1977). "Reflections on TAXMAN: An Experiment in Artificial Intelligence and Legal Reasoning," January 1977, Harvard Law Review.

42. McGinnis, John, and Russell G. Pearce (2014). "The Great Disruption: How Machine Intelligence Will Transform the Role of Lawyers in the Delivery of Legal Services," Volume 82, Number 6, Fordham Law Review.

43. McGinnis, John, and Steven Wasick (2015). "Law's Algorithm," Volume 66, Florida Law Review.

44. Mikhaylovskiy, N. (2020). "How Do You Test the Strength of AI?" September 2020, *International Conference on Artificial General Intelligence* (pp. 257-266).

45. Mnookin, Robert, and Lewis Kornhauser (1979). "Bargaining in the Shadow of the Law," Volume 88, Number 5, April 1979, The Yale Law Review.

46. Mowbray, Andrew, and Philip Chung, Graham Greenleaf (2019). "Utilising AI in the Legal Assistance Sector," LegalAIIA Workshop, ICAIL, June 17, 2019, Montreal, Canada.

47. Prakken, H., G. Sartor (2015). "Law and Logic: A Review from an Argumentation Perspective," V227, Artificial Intelligence.

48. Reinbold, Patric (2020). "Taking Artificial Intelligence Beyond the Turing Test," Volume 20, Wisconsin Law Review.
49. Remus, Dana, and Frank Levy, "Can Robots be Lawyers? Computers, Robots, and the Practice of Law," Volume 30, Georgetown Journal of Legal Ethics.
50. Rich, Michael (2016). "Machine Learning, Automated Suspicion Algorithms, and the Fourth Amendment," Volume 164, University of Pennsylvania Law Review.
51. Rissland, Edwina (1990). "Artificial Intelligence and Law: Stepping Stones to a Model of Legal Reasoning," Yale Law Journal.
52. SAE (2018). Taxonomy and Definitions for Terms Related to Driving Automation Systems for On-Road Motor Vehicles, J3016-201806, SAE International.
53. Sunstein, Cass (2001). "Of Artificial Intelligence and Legal Reasoning," University of Chicago Law School, Public Law and Legal Theory Working Papers.
54. Sunstein, Cass, and Kevin Ashley, Karl Branting, Howard Margolis (2001). "Legal Reasoning and Artificial Intelligence: How Computers 'Think' Like Lawyers," Symposium: Legal Reasoning and Artificial Intelligence, University of Chicago Law School Roundtable.
55. Surden, Harry (2014). "Machine Learning and Law," Washington Law Review.
56. Surden, Harry (2019). "Artificial Intelligence and Law: An Overview," Summer 2019, Georgia State University Law Review.
57. Turing, Alan (1950). "Computing Machinery and Intelligence," Volume 59, Number 236, Mind.
58. Ulam, Stanislaw (1958). "Tribute to John von Neumann," Volume 64, Number 3, Bulletin of the American Mathematical Society.
59. Upchurch, Martin (2018). "Robots and AI at Work: The Prospects for Singularity," Volume 33, Number 3, New Technology Work and Employment.

60. Volokh, Eugne (2019). "Chief Justice Robots," Volume 68, Duke Law Journal.

61. Walsh, Toby (2017). "The Singularity May Never Be Near," Volume 38, Number 3, AAAI AI Magazine.

62. Waltl, Bernhard, and Roland Vogl (2018). "Explainable Artificial Intelligence: The New Frontier in Legal Informatics," February 2018, Jusletter IT 22, Stanford Center for Legal Informatics, Stanford University.

63. Weber, Robert (2019). "Will the 'Legal Singularity' Hollow Out Law's Normative Core?" CSAS Working Paper 19-38, Antonin Scalia Law School, George Mason University, November 15, 2019.

64. Wolfram, Stephen (2018). "Computational Law, Symbolic Discourse, and the AI Constitution," in Data-Driven Law: Data Analytics and the New Legal Services (Edward J. Walters ed.).

65. Ympolskiy, Roman (2012). "What to Do with the Singularity Paradox?" in Philosophy and Theory of Artificial Intelligence, SAPERE.

66. Baldwin, Robort (1990). "Why Rules Don't Work," Volume 55, Number 3, The Modern Law Review.

67. Braithwaite, John (2002). "Rules and Principles: A Theory of Legal Certainty," V27, Australian Journal of Legal Philosophy.

68. D'Amato, Anthony (2010). "Legal Uncertainty," Northwestern University School of Law, Faculty Working Papers.

69. Leawoods, Heather (2000). "Gusta Radbruch: An Extraordinary Legal Philosopher," Washington University Journal of Law & Policy.

Note: *For supplemental materials depicting the aspects discussed in this chapter, refer to Appendix B, which contains various augmented diagrams, charts, and additional related facets of relevance.*

CHAPTER 7

PRINCIPLES OF JUSTICE AND AI LEGAL REASONING

Abstract

Efforts furthering the advancement of Artificial Intelligence (AI) will increasingly encompass AI Legal Reasoning (AILR) as a crucial element in the practice of law. It is argued in this research paper that the infusion of AI into existing and future legal activities and the judicial structure needs to be undertaken by mindfully observing an alignment with the core principles of justice. As such, the adoption of AI has a profound twofold possibility of either usurping the principles of justice, doing so in a Dystopian manner, and yet also capable to bolster the principles of justice, doing so in a Utopian way. By examining the principles of justice across the Levels of Autonomy (LoA) of AI Legal Reasoning, the case is made that there is an ongoing tension underlying the efforts to develop and deploy AI that can demonstrably determine the impacts and sway upon each core principle of justice and the collective set.

Section 1: Background and Principles of Justice

Efforts toward the advancement of Artificial Intelligence (AI) will increasingly encompass AI Legal Reasoning (AILR) as a crucial element in the practice of law [1] [7] [17] [31] [45].

It is argued in this research paper that the infusion of AI into existing and future legal activities and the judicial structure needs to be undertaken by mindfully observing an alignment with the core principles of justice.

This research paper examines the nature of the core principles of justice in Section 1. In Section 2, a framework for the Levels of Autonomy (LoA) of AI Legal Reasoning (AILR) is depicted. Then, in Section 3, the core principles of justice are aligned across the LoA AILR to showcase an anticipated evolution, along with identifying corresponding outcome facets. Section 4 provides additional considerations and proffers insights for conducting further research on these matters.

The sections in this paper are:

- Section 1: Background and Principles of Justice
- Section 2: Autonomous Levels of AI Legal Reasoning
- Section 3: Grids and Analyses of Justice Principles and LoA AILR
- Section 4: Additional Considerations and Future Research

One important assertion in this discussion is that a multi-faceted perspective should be undertaken when considering how AI will shape or reshape the instantiation of the principles of justice [7] [9] [29]. A commonly assumed false dichotomy is that the adoption of AI into the practice of law will be exclusively Dystopian or exclusively Utopian, meanwhile, it is argued herein that either possibility can arise, doing so amid each distinct principle of justice, additionally collectively so too, and that it is incumbent upon the developers and adopters of AI in the law to observe and be attune to which direction their efforts are converging [19] [38] [42].

As such, the adoption of AI has a profound twofold possibility of either usurping the principles of justice, doing so in a Dystopian manner, and yet also capable to bolster the principles of justice, doing so in a Utopian way. By examining the principles of justice across the Levels of Autonomy (LoA) of AI Legal Reasoning, the case is made that there is an ongoing tension underlying the efforts to develop AI that can determine how each core principle of justice will be swayed.

1.1 identifying the Principles of Justice

Research by Susskind [44] in his book entitled "Online Courts and the Future of Justice" lays out an extensively established foundation that justice can be generally cast as consisting of seven core principles. Based on those key principles, his primary focus in the book entails an expounded argument that the emergence of online courts will both preserve justice and enhance justice, doing so via the prudent utilization of virtual hearings, plus asynchronous online judging, etc. He notably forewarns that it is not a foregone conclusion that such benefits will arise and that it will require sensible, determined, and systemic multi-generational adaptations to reach those aspirational goals.

For this research paper, the same set of core principles of justice will be utilized. This makes sense to do so herein in that the groundwork supporting the contention that those principles are indeed a bona fide and sufficient set of core principles has already been robustly well-established and therefore can be readily leveraged in a building blocks fashion accordingly, effectively and efficiently so (rather than trying to reinvent the wheel, as it were).

The emphasis herein will be to apply the emergence of AI into the practice of law amidst the core principles of justice and thus is a separate and distinct usage and analysis associated with the principles of justice in comparison to the work by Susskind that focused on the rise of online courts. Note that Susskind also identifies the significant role that AI will undoubtedly ultimately play: "In contemplating the second generation of online courts, it would be hard to ignore the recent upsurge of interest in artificial intelligence (AI) for lawyers and judges." It is that same observation of the arising spark in attention toward AI in the practice of the law that this research paper dovetails into. Similar to Susskind's argument that online courts will not axiomatically enable the principles of justice, and indeed might deter or undermine them, the same case is made herein that AI will variously have such results upon the principles of justice and that no foregone conclusion can conclusively be otherwise decreed or assumed.

The seven indicated core principles of justice consist of:

- Substantive Justice
- Procedural Justice
- Open Justice
- Distributive Justice
- Proportionate Justice
- Enforceable Justice
- Sustainable Justice

Note that the seven principles are not numbered and nor otherwise indicated as being prioritized or ranked in any particular order. They are all equally crucial. Imagine a three-legged stool that falls apart when any of the legs is missing, though in this instance envisage a seven-legged apparatus. There are tradeoffs among the principles, and it is not easy to ensure that they are each given their full and earnestly needed equal attention. Keep in mind too that existing attempts at justice are not necessarily able to live up to the ideals of the stated principles, and thus today's form of justice is undeniably at times existent of numerous shortcomings, including being too costly, taking too long, being unintelligible for many that rely upon the law, etc.

This emphasizes that today's barometer of justice is not somehow already affixed at the topmost stance [23] [31] [41]. If it were, the addition or incorporation of innovation such as the integration of AI could be argued as potentially messing with perfection, but this is not the case per se.

AI offers a chance of improving the day-to-day incurring and delivery of justice. In that same vein, if AI is improperly or inappropriately integrated, the existing justice system could be degraded, dropping from the place upon which it currently resides [8] [43].

Each of the next subsections examines each of the respective core principles of justice.

1.1.1 Substantive Justice

Here is an overall definition of substantive justice:

Substantive Justice: *Decisions and outcomes should be considered fair and substantive, requiring judging to be based on the laws of the land and not by whim or other divines.*

Substantive justice is about fairness, and also about the predictability of the law and what it portends [44]: "It is only fair that we are judged in accordance with whatever legislation and case law require of us. It is important in our daily activities that the law is to a great extent certain and predictable. Justice requires that judges apply law as it is, rather than what they or others think it ought to be." Also, since it is presumably possible that laws might be inherently unjust in some absolute or relativist respect, an additional criteria is that the laws as enacted and intended should be intrinsically stitched with being just [44]: "We should also insist that our justice system delivers outcomes that are themselves *just*."

1.1.2 Procedural Justice

Here is an overall definition of procedural justice:

Procedural Justice: *The process needs to be equitable and honest, independent of biases, and proffer procedures that avert the incursion of defectiveness or inconsistencies.*

Procedural justice is about the process by which justice is adjudicated, and for which if the process is skewed or malformed it can undermine and diminish the attainment of justice [44]: "A decision is considered unjust because it was handled in a manner that was in some way defective and inequitable." Within the overarching realm of procedural justice, at least two cornerstones are consisting of formal justice and natural justice. The nature of formal justice is that there should be a consistency of like cases being handled in an equivalent manner [44]: "One aspect of this concept is referred to as 'formal justice,' which is often characterized by some such phrase as 'like cases should be treated alike.'"

For natural justice, it is key that a case be heard and that self-judging is to be averted [44]: "A second aspect of procedural justice is known as 'natural justice.' I am using this term in a technical sense, frequently captured in two Latin phrases: *audi alteram partem*, which requires that all litigants should be given the opportunity to state and defend their cases and *nemo index in causa sua*, which means that no-one should be a judge in his or her own case."

1.1.3 Open Justice

Here is an overall definition of open justice:

Open Justice: *Efforts of the courts must be transparent, open to scrutiny, accountable, and intelligible, avoiding secrecy as much as can be so reasonably achieved (realizing that at times national security, the welfare of minors, and the like can motivate some degrees of confidentiality).*

Open justice entails ensuring that processes and activities are made highly visible and shall not be unduly disguised or hidden [44]: "We object to court systems whose workings are held in private or cloaked in secrecy. We call loudly for demystification." Not all proceedings are necessarily prudent to be completely visible and therefore exceptions of an appropriate kind might need to be accounted for, but only to the extent as absolutely necessary since embracing transparency is the crux. An offshoot of the visibility aspect is that justice and all its mechanizations should be intelligible to those that are non-lawyers and thus likely unfamiliar with the nomenclature and complexities of the law [44]: "There are strong arguments in support of the view that open justice also requires any information and data findings about the courts, as well as the court proceedings themselves, to be understandable to non-lawyers."

1.1.4 Distributive Justice

Here is an overall definition of distributive justice:

Distributive Justice: *Each person must be given their legal due and afforded access to justice, thus driving a semblance of distributiveness to ensure that regardless of means that all can gain access.*

Distributive justice entails seeking to make access to justice feasible since otherwise, denial of access is essentially no different from an altogether lack of justice itself [44]: "Distributive justice requires that court service is accessible and intelligible to all; that access to legal and court services is a benefit that is evenly spread across society; that rights and duties are equably allocated; that the powerful and rich are subject to the same law as the less well-off and less powerful; and that the service is affordable by all regardless of their means."

1.1.5 Proportionate Justice

Here is an overall definition of proportionate justice:

Proportionate Justice: *Fairness ought to arise at scale, straightforward processes for straightforward issues, attempting to ensure that speediness occurs and aligns too with complexity, suitable proportionality based on the assertion that justice delayed is justice diluted.*

Proportionality is a less often enumerated component of justice and tends to be assumed as existent or deemed as unworthy of being an *essential* element of justice and can be perhaps cast as a secondary condition, but here it is viewed as equally vital as the other principles. In brief, the notion is that the energy or effort of achieving justice should be proportional to the nature or magnitude of the underlying dispute for which justice is being sought, thus [44]: "The principle of proportionality requires, first of all, that we should ensure that the cost of handling individual cases in our courts makes sense by reference to the nature and value of each dispute." And, regarding our revered adversarial approach [44]: "In a similar vein, although our system is adversarial, this should not mean that all disputes are conducted in a highly combative spirit. Unwarranted escalation of disputes, especially in smaller cases, should be discouraged."

1.1.6 Enforceable Justice

Here is an overall definition of enforceable justice:

Enforceable Justice: *Results need to have teeth and be seen as binding, enforcement as enabled via the coercive power of the state, correctly deprive money and property and liberty to ensure justice is served.*

Enforceable justice entails the need to ensure that justice must not be hollow, namely that if there was no means or mechanism to enforce or bind the ascertained results then there would be no consequent impact or effect per se of having sought justice. In a sense, justice would have no semblance of potency since it could not be otherwise implemented or compelled [44]: "The determination of judges are binding and can be enforced by the coercive power of the state." And without such implementations, there would seem little reason for society to avail themselves of relying upon the efforts of the judiciary: "Without enforceable justice, the law runs the risk of affording a rather weak set of protections."

1.1.7 Sustainable Justice

Here is an overall definition of sustainable justice:

Sustainable Justice: *Have a stable basis for the ongoing instantiation of justice, sufficient resources must be allocated to maintain and incur upkeep for continually improving the means of the courts to act, including being able to demonstrably scale to whatever volume of cases might be presented.*

Sustainable justice necessitates the somewhat abstract but very real notion that justice and all of its elements must be in existence; otherwise, if it is intermittent or known to be unreliably sustained then such justice cannot be depended upon [44]: "Courts should be safe havens; solid and reliable; anchors to which, in times of need, people and organizations can confidently tether themselves." As an aside, it can be asserted that the sustainability of justice also intertwines with the technological capabilities of those being served [44]: "It is also hard to conceive of a truly sustainable court system that is not technologically in tune with the communities that it serves."

Section 2: Autonomous Levels of AI Legal Reasoning

In this section, a framework for the autonomous levels of AI Legal Reasoning is summarized and is based on the research described in detail in Eliot [20].

These autonomous levels will be portrayed in a grid that aligns with key elements of autonomy and as matched to AI Legal Reasoning. Providing this context will be useful to the later sections of this paper and will be utilized accordingly.

The autonomous levels of AI Legal Reasoning are as follows:
Level 0: No Automation for AI Legal Reasoning
Level 1: Simple Assistance Automation for AI Legal Reasoning
Level 2: Advanced Assistance Automation for AILR
Level 3: Semi-Autonomous Automation for AI Legal Reasoning
Level 4: Domain Autonomous for AI Legal Reasoning
Level 5: Fully Autonomous for AI Legal Reasoning
Level 6: Superhuman Autonomous for AI Legal Reasoning

2.1 Details of the LoA AILR

See **Figure A-1** for an overview chart showcasing the autonomous levels of AI Legal Reasoning as via columns denoting each of the respective levels.

See **Figure A-2** for an overview chart similar to Figure A-1 which alternatively is indicative of the autonomous levels of AI Legal Reasoning via the rows as depicting the respective levels (this is simply a reformatting of Figure A-1, doing so to aid in illuminating this variant perspective, but does not introduce any new facets or alterations from the contents as already shown in Figure A-1).

2.1.1 Level 0: No Automation for AI Legal Reasoning

Level 0 is considered the no automation level. Legal reasoning is carried out via manual methods and principally occurs via paper-based methods.

This level is allowed some leeway in that the use of say a simple handheld calculator or perhaps the use of a fax machine could be allowed or included within this Level 0, though strictly speaking it could be said that any form whatsoever of automation is to be excluded from this level.

2.1.2 Level 1: Simple Assistance Automation for AI Legal Reasoning

Level 1 consists of simple assistance automation for AI legal reasoning.

Examples of this category encompassing simple automation would include the use of everyday computer-based word processing, the use of everyday computer-based spreadsheets, the access to online legal documents that are stored and retrieved electronically, and so on.

By-and-large, today's use of computers for legal activities is predominantly within Level 1. It is assumed and expected that over time, the pervasiveness of automation will continue to deepen and widen, and eventually lead to legal activities being supported and within Level 2, rather than Level 1.

2.1.3 Level 2: Advanced Assistance Automation for AI Legal Reasoning

Level 2 consists of advanced assistance automation for AI legal reasoning.

Examples of this notion encompassing advanced automation would include the use of query-style Natural Language Processing (NLP), Machine Learning (ML) for case predictions, and so on.

Gradually, over time, it is expected that computer-based systems for legal activities will increasingly make use of advanced automation. Law industry technology that was once at a Level 1 will likely be refined, upgraded, or expanded to include advanced capabilities, and thus be reclassified into Level 2.

2.1.4 Level 3: Semi-Autonomous Automation for AI Legal Reasoning

Level 3 consists of semi-autonomous automation for AI legal reasoning.

Examples of this notion encompassing semi-autonomous automation would include the use of Knowledge-Based Systems (KBS) for legal reasoning, the use of Machine Learning and Deep Learning (ML/DL) for legal reasoning, and so on.

Today, such automation tends to exist in research efforts or prototypes and pilot systems, along with some commercial legal technology that has been infusing these capabilities too.

2.1.5 Level 4: Domain Autonomous for AI Legal Reasoning

Level 4 consists of domain autonomous computer-based systems for AI legal reasoning.

This level reuses the conceptual notion of Operational Design Domains (ODDs) as utilized in the autonomous vehicles and self-driving cars levels of autonomy, though in this use case it is being applied to the legal domain [17] [18] [20].

Essentially, this entails any AI legal reasoning capacities that can operate autonomously, entirely so, but that is only able to do so in some limited or constrained legal domain.

2.1.6 Level 5: Fully Autonomous for AI Legal Reasoning

Level 5 consists of fully autonomous computer-based systems for AI legal reasoning. In a sense, Level 5 is the superset of Level 4 in terms of encompassing all possible domains as per however so defined ultimately for Level 4. The only constraint, as it were, consists of the facet that the Level 4 and Level 5 are concerning human intelligence and the capacities thereof. This is an important emphasis due to attempting to distinguish Level 5 from Level 6 (as will be discussed in the next subsection)

It is conceivable that someday there might be a fully autonomous AI legal reasoning capability, one that encompasses all of the law in all foreseeable ways, though this is quite a tall order and remains quite aspirational without a clear cut path of how this might one day be achieved. Nonetheless, it seems to be within the extended realm of possibilities, which is worthwhile to mention in relative terms to Level 6.

2.1.7 Level 6: Superhuman Autonomous for AI Legal Reasoning

Level 6 consists of superhuman autonomous computer-based systems for AI legal reasoning.

In a sense, Level 6 is the entirety of Level 5 and adds something beyond that in a manner that is currently ill-defined and perhaps (some would argue) as yet unknowable. The notion is that AI might ultimately exceed human intelligence, rising to become superhuman, and if so, we do not yet have any viable indication of what that superhuman intelligence consists of and nor what kind of thinking it would somehow be able to undertake.

Whether a Level 6 is ever attainable is reliant upon whether superhuman AI is ever attainable, and thus, at this time, this stands as a placeholder for that which might never occur. In any case, having such a placeholder provides a semblance of completeness, doing so without necessarily legitimatizing that superhuman AI is going to be achieved or not. No such claim or dispute is undertaken within this framework.

Section 3: Grids and Analyses of the Principles of Justice and LoA AILR

In this section, the autonomous levels of AI Legal Reasoning will be aligned with the principles of justice, forming a grid that is indicative of how AI might impact the principles and likewise how the principles can be utilized to drive the development and maturation of AI for the law.

As for nomenclature, the nature of impacts involving the LoA AILR on the principles of justice is abbreviated as LoA-principles, while the impacts of the principles of justice on the LoA AILR is denoted as principles-LoA.

3.1 Principles of Justice and the LoA AILR

As shown in **Figure B-1**, it is useful and informative to align the seven core principles of justice with the seven levels of autonomy of AI Legal Reasoning. An explanation of the grid and its significance is discussed next.

For Level 0, Level 1, and Level 2, the grid indicates that the alignment is considered as "Traditional" in the sense that since the level of automation is conventional at those levels of LoA this ergo suggests that any impacts on or of the principles of justice consist of what we already generally know and anticipate. Level 3 is the first turning point as it is considered the semi-autonomous LoA and thus is expressed as "Emerging," which means that the impacts will start to become notable about the autonomy that might then emerge or exist once the Level 4 and above are achieved. Level 4 is the AILR domain autonomous level and the impacts are denoted as Phase X, which is explained in subsequent charts. Level 5 is the AILR fully autonomous level and the impacts are denoted as Phase Y, which is explained in subsequent charts. Level 6 is the AILR superhuman autonomous level and the impacts are denoted as Phase Z, which is explained in subsequent charts.

In a recap of this grid:

Substantive Justice

- Level 0: Traditional
- Level 1: Traditional
- Level 2: Traditional
- Level 3: Emerging
- Level 4: Phase X Impacts
- Level 5: Phase Y Impacts
- Level 6: Phase Z Impacts

Procedural Justice

- Level 0: Traditional
- Level 1: Traditional
- Level 2: Traditional
- Level 3: Emerging
- Level 4: Phase X Impacts
- Level 5: Phase Y Impacts
- Level 6: Phase Z Impacts

Open Justice

- Level 0: Traditional
- Level 1: Traditional
- Level 2: Traditional
- Level 3: Emerging
- Level 4: Phase X Impacts
- Level 5: Phase Y Impacts
- Level 6: Phase Z Impacts

Distributive Justice

- Level 0: Traditional
- Level 1: Traditional
- Level 2: Traditional
- Level 3: Emerging
- Level 4: Phase X Impacts
- Level 5: Phase Y Impacts
- Level 6: Phase Z Impacts

Proportionate Justice

- Level 0: Traditional
- Level 1: Traditional
- Level 2: Traditional
- Level 3: Emerging
- Level 4: Phase X Impacts
- Level 5: Phase Y Impacts
- Level 6: Phase Z Impacts

Enforceable Justice

- Level 0: Traditional
- Level 1: Traditional
- Level 2: Traditional
- Level 3: Emerging
- Level 4: Phase X Impacts
- Level 5: Phase Y Impacts
- Level 6: Phase Z Impacts

Sustainable Justice

- Level 0: Traditional
- Level 1: Traditional
- Level 2: Traditional
- Level 3: Emerging
- Level 4: Phase X Impacts
- Level 5: Phase Y Impacts
- Level 6: Phase Z Impacts

Figure B-2 is akin to Figure B-1, illustrating the same grid but with the LoA along the rows and the core principles of justice indicated as the columns. This is not a new introduction of facets and instead merely a convenient means of representing the content in a flipped format for ease of reference and furtherance to the discussion.

In a recap of the grid:

Level 0: No Automation

- Substantive Justice: *Traditional*
- Procedural Justice: *Traditional*
- Open Justice: *Traditional*
- Distributive Justice: *Traditional*
- Proportionate Justice: *Traditional*
- Enforceable Justice: *Traditional*
- Sustainable Justice: *Traditional*

Level 1: Simple Assistance Automation

- Substantive Justice: *Traditional*
- Procedural Justice: *Traditional*
- Open Justice: *Traditional*
- Distributive Justice: *Traditional*
- Proportionate Justice: *Traditional*
- Enforceable Justice: *Traditional*
- Sustainable Justice: *Traditional*

Level 2: Advanced Assistance Automation

- Substantive Justice: *Traditional*
- Procedural Justice: *Traditional*
- Open Justice: *Traditional*
- Distributive Justice: *Traditional*
- Proportionate Justice: *Traditional*
- Enforceable Justice: *Traditional*
- Sustainable Justice: *Traditional*

Level 3: Semi-Autonomous Automation

- Substantive Justice: *Emerging*
- Procedural Justice: *Emerging*
- Open Justice: *Emerging*
- Distributive Justice: *Emerging*
- Proportionate Justice: *Emerging*
- Enforceable Justice: *Emerging*
- Sustainable Justice: *Emerging*

Level 4: AILR Domain Autonomous

- Substantive Justice: *Phase X Impacts*
- Procedural Justice: *Phase X Impacts*
- Open Justice: *Phase X Impacts*
- Distributive Justice: *Phase X Impacts*
- Proportionate Justice: *Phase X Impacts*
- Enforceable Justice: *Phase X Impacts*
- Sustainable Justice: *Phase X Impacts*

Level 5: AILR Fully Autonomous

- Substantive Justice: *Phase Y Impacts*
- Procedural Justice: *Phase Y Impacts*
- Open Justice: *Phase Y Impacts*
- Distributive Justice: *Phase Y Impacts*
- Proportionate Justice: *Phase Y Impacts*
- Enforceable Justice: *Phase Y Impacts*
- Sustainable Justice: *Phase Y Impacts*

Level 6: AILR Superhuman Autonomous

- Substantive Justice: *Phase Z Impacts*
- Procedural Justice: *Phase Z Impacts*
- Open Justice: *Phase Z Impacts*
- Distributive Justice: *Phase Z Impacts*
- Proportionate Justice: *Phase Z Impacts*
- Enforceable Justice: *Phase Z Impacts*
- Sustainable Justice: *Phase Z Impacts*

3.2 AI Infusion and Potential Outcomes

Shown in **Figure B-3** is an indication of the seven core principles of justice and the notable aspect that the AI infusion can be construed in a twofold manner, consisting of outcomes that give rise to Utopian results and also consisting of outcomes that give rise to Dystopian results.

These are not to be considered as mutually exclusive of each other, in the sense that the results can vary, both by the distinct principles of justice, each individually so, and also collectively across the entire set. It is postulated that the results will be differentiated across the LoA AILR in the sense that there is a measured difference between the Level 4, Level 5, and Level 6, thus each of those level distinctions is given a phasing, respectively indicated as Phase X, Phase Y, and Phase Z (as will be explained further in the next subsection).

Note that this is not a prescriptive indication and thus there is no suggestion, implication, or proclamation that there will be

Utopian results, nor that there will be Dystopian results, and that instead this is providing a means of being able to both *reactively* assess the results of AI infusion and can also be *proactively* used to drive the directional nature of an AI infusion into the law.

3.3 Phase X, Phase Y, Phase Z

Shown in **Figure B-4** is an indication of the seven core principles and the respective Phase X, Phase Y, and Phase Z indications. Within each Level, the respective phase showcases the possibility of a Utopian outcome and a Dystopian outcome, per each of the respective core principles of justice. Note that the wording is evocative of being more so or less of the characteristic stated, such as the word "fairer" to indicate that the outcome would potentially be heightened in fairness, while the word "unfairer" to indicate that the outcome would potentially be heightened in unfairness.

Phase X is designated as the impacts at Level 4 and consists of:

Phase X: Level 4
Substantive Justice
Utopian: Fairer Decisions (law domains)
Dystopian: Unfairer Decisions (law domains)

Phase X: Level 4
Procedural Justice
Utopian: Fairer Processes (law domains)
Dystopian: Unfairer Processes (law domains)

Phase X: Level 4
Open Justice
Utopian: Greater Transparency (law domains)
Dystopian: Lessened Transparency (law domains)

Phase X: Level 4
Distributive Justice
Utopian: Expanded Access (law domains)
Dystopian: Reduced Access (law domains)

Phase X: Level 4
Proportionate Justice
Utopian: More Balanced (law domains)
Dystopian: Less Balanced (law domains)

Phase X: Level 4
Enforceable Justice
Utopian: Better Enforcement (law domains)
Dystopian: Worse Enforcement (law domains)

Phase X: Level 4
Sustainable Justice
Utopian: Greater Stability (law domains)
Dystopian: Lessened Stability (law domains)

Phase Y is designated as the impacts at Level 5 and consists of:

Phase Y: Level 5
Substantive Justice
Utopian: Fairer Decisions (all of law)
Dystopian: Unfairer Decisions (all of law)

Phase Y: Level 5
Procedural Justice
Utopian: Fairer Processes (all of law)
Dystopian: Unfairer Processes (all of law)

Phase Y: Level 5
Open Justice
Utopian: Greater Transparency (all of law)
Dystopian: Lessened Transparency (all of law)
Phase Y: Level 5
Distributive Justice
Utopian: Expanded Access (all of law)
Dystopian: Reduced Access (all of law)
Phase Y: Level 5
Proportionate Justice
Utopian: More Balanced (all of law)
Dystopian: Less Balanced (all of law)

Phase Y: Level 5
Enforceable Justice
Utopian: Better Enforcement (all of law)
Dystopian: Worse Enforcement (all of law)

Phase Y: Level 5
Sustainable Justice
Utopian: Greater Stability (all of law)
Dystopian: Lessened Stability (all of law)

Phase Z is designated as the impacts at Level 6 and consists of:

Phase Z: Level 6
Substantive Justice
Utopian: Ultra-Fair Decisions
Dystopian: Ultra-Unfair Decisions

Phase Z: Level 6
Procedural Justice
Utopian: Ultra-Fair Processes
Dystopian: Ultra-Unfair Processes

Phase Z: Level 6
Open Justice
Utopian: Ultimate Transparency
Dystopian: Utmost Opaqueness

Phase Z: Level 6
Distributive Justice
Utopian: Totality of Access
Dystopian: Utter Denial of Access

Phase Z: Level 6
Proportionate Justice
Utopian: Perfectly Balanced
Dystopian: Wholly Unbalanced

Phase Z: Level 6
Enforceable Justice
Utopian: Idea Enforcement
Dystopian: Horrendous Enforcement

Phase Z: Level 6
Sustainable Justice
Utopian: Completely Sustainable
Dystopian: Entirely Unsustainable

3.4 Examples of Impacts Analysis

When considering how AI infusion will potentially impact justice, the grids can be substantively conducive in at least two ways: (a) conducting an impact analysis anew, and (b) used when evaluating an existing impact analysis that is being presented by a given research study.

For any such analyses, questions to be asked and appropriately addressed include:

- Which of the core principles of justice is being included?
- Which of the core principles of justice is not being included and how might that omission alter the otherwise predicted impacts?
- Is the tension and balancing among the core principles of justice being encompassed?
- At what level of AI autonomy is the focus being undertaken?
- To what degree and nature do the AI impact a specific principle of justice?
- How does the AI impact across the core set of principles?
- Is a predominantly Utopian perspective being assumed?
- Is a predominantly Dystopian perspective being assumed?
- Does the analysis consider the separate impact by core principle rather than as a monolith?
- Does the analysis consider the collective impacts encompassing the set of principles?
- And so on.

Suppose for example that a research study has asserted that AI will lead to fairer decisions by the justice system. Consider using the grids to examine and assess the conclusion reached by this exemplar.

As viewed within the context of the grids, this might be equated with an assertion that entails Substantive Justice (due to invoking the notion of fairness in decisions) and posits a Utopian leaning impact (due to avowing that decisions will be fairer, rather than just as fair or perhaps even turning toward unfair). If so, there should presumably be a rational or justification provided in the research study as to not only why the Utopian leaning is warranted as an outcome, but would also need to ascertain why the Dystopian is unlikely to occur in lieu of the Utopian claim.

Meanwhile, this still leaves unstated by the research study as to what level of AI is being assumed, such as whether this is at a level below the autonomous levels of Level 4, Level 5, or Level 6, or those respective levels. This exposes a weakness in the impacts being alleged since the magnitude and scope of the AI infusion is either omitted or otherwise not explicitly addressed. Furthermore, focusing on just one principle, in this example the Substantive Justice principle, entirely undercuts the dependency nature of the core principles among each other. If there are apparently going to be fairer decisions in the realm of Substantive Justice, this might come at the cost of perhaps unfairer processes (i.e., worsened Procedural Justice) or at the cost of less Open Justice (lessened transparency), and so on. By consulting the grid, it becomes readily feasible to directly seek to discover whether a research study has covered the range of principles of justice. By the happenstance or oversight of not considering the full range, it is conceivable that a presumed optimization at one principle could seemingly undercut the performance on one or more of the other principles.

These grids then provide a tool or model for the pursuit of research on the impacts of AI on the principles of justice and the impacts of the principles on the development and deployment of AI.

Section 4: Additional Considerations and Future Research

As earlier stated, efforts toward the advancement of Artificial Intelligence (AI) will increasingly encompass AI Legal Reasoning (AILR) as a crucial element in the practice of law. It has been argued in this research paper that the infusion of AI into existing and future legal activities and the judicial structure needs to be undertaken by mindfully observing an alignment with the core principles of justice. The adoption of AI has a profound twofold possibility of either usurping the principles of justice, doing so in a Dystopian manner, and yet also capable to bolster the principles of justice, doing so in a Utopian way.

Any research examining the principles of justice and AI must strive to be as complete and cohesive as feasible, for which the grids provided in this paper are a proffered tool(s) or model(s) to be so productively utilized. Future research for evolving these tools or models provided is highly recommended. This might consist of the following types of studies:

- Conduct case studies using the tools or models
- Analyze existing research studies using the tools or models
- Craft new research that encompasses the tools or models
- Propose extensions to the tools or models
- Other

By considering the principles of justice across the Levels of Autonomy (LoA) of AI Legal Reasoning, and then addressing the singular facets of each principle, along with the collective set, research in this realm will assuredly be more robust. Also, undertaking such analyses will allow for greater comparison of such research studies, readily revealing which assumptions are being made, including any omissions or oversights, and aid in bolstering the state of research on these matters.

References

1. Alarie, Benjamin (2016). "The Path of the Law: Toward Legal Singularity," May 27, 2016, SSRN, University of Toronto Faculty of Law and Vector Institute for Artificial Intelligence.

2. Alarie, Benjamin, and Anthony Niblett, Albert Yoon (2017). "Regulation by Machine," Volume 24, Journal of Machine Learning Research.

3. Ashley, Kevin, and Karl Branting, Howard Margolis, and Cass Sunstein (2001). "Legal Reasoning and Artificial Intelligence: How Computers 'Think' Like Lawyers," Symposium: Legal Reasoning and Artificial Intelligence, University of Chicago Law School Roundtable.

4. Baker, Jamie (2018). "A Legal Research Odyssey: Artificial Intelligence as Disrupter," Law Library Journal.

5. Ben-Ari, Daniel, and D., Frish, Y., Lazovski, A., Eldan, U., & Greenbaum, D. (2016). "Artificial Intelligence in the Practice of Law: An Analysis and Proof of Concept Experiment," Volume 23, Number 2, Richmond Journal of Law & Technology.

6. Bench-Capon, Trevor, and Givoanni Sartor (2003). "A Model of Legal Reasoning with Cases Incorporating Theories and Values," November 2013, Artificial Intelligence.

7. Buchanan, Bruce, and Thomas Headrick (1970). "Some Speculation about Artificial Intelligence and Legal Reasoning," Volume 23, Stanford Law Review.

8. Casey, Anthony, and Anthony Niblett (2016). "Self-Driving Laws," Volume 429, University of Toronto Law Journal.

9. Casey, Anthony, and Anthony Niblett (2017). "The Death of Rules and Standards," Volume 92, Indiana Law Journal.

10. Chagal-Feferkorn, Karni (2019). "Am I An Algorithm or a Product: When Products Liability Should Apply to Algorithmic Decision-Makers," Stanford Law & Policy Review.

11. Chen, Daniel (2019). "Machine Learning and the Rule of Law," in Law as Data: Computation, Text, and The Future of Legal Analysis (Michael A. Livermore and Daniel N. Rockmore eds.).

12. Coglianese, Cary, and David Lehr (2017). "Rulemaking by Robot: Administrative Decision Making in the Machine-Learning Era," Volume 105, Georgetown Law Journal.

13. Deakin, Simon, and Christopher Markou (2020). "From Rule of Law to Legal Singularity," University of Cambridge Faculty of Law.

14. Douglas, William (1948). "The Dissent: A Safeguard of Democracy," Volume 32, Journal of the American Judicature Society.

15. Eliot, Lance (2016). AI Guardian Angels for Deep AI Trustworthiness. LBE Press Publishing.

16. Eliot, Lance (2020). "The Neglected Dualism of Artificial Moral Agency and Artificial Legal Reasoning in AI for Social Good." Harvard University, Harvard Center for Research on Computation and Society, AI for Social Good Conference, July 21, 2020.

17. Eliot, Lance (2020). AI and Legal Reasoning Essentials. LBE Press Publishing.
18. Eliot, Lance (2019). Artificial Intelligence and LegalTech Essentials. LBE Press Publishing.
19. Eliot, Lance (2020). "FutureLaw 2020 Showcases How Tech is Transforming The Law, Including the Impacts of AI," April 16, 2020, Forbes.
20. Eliot, Lance (2020). "An Ontological AI-and-Law Framework for the Autonomous Levels of AI Legal Reasoning," Cornell University arXiv. https://arxiv.org/abs/2008.07328

21. Eliot, Lance (2020). "Turing Test and the Practice of Law: The Role of Autonomous Levels of AI Legal Reasoning," Cornell University arXiv. https://arxiv.org/abs/2008.07743

22. Eliot, Lance (2018). "Multidimensionality of the Legal Singularity: The Role of Autonomous Levels of AI Legal Reasoning," Cornell University arXiv. https://arxiv.org/abs/2008.10575

23. Eliot, Lance (2018). "Singularity and AI," July 10, 2018, AI Trends.

24. Eliot, Lance (2020). "The Role of Human Judgement as a Presumed Integral Ingredient for Achieving True AI," March 9, 2020, Forbes.

25. Gardner, Anne (1987). Artificial Intelligence and Legal Reasoning. MIT Press.

26. Genesereth, Michael (2009). "Computational Law: The Cop in the Backseat," Stanford Center for Legal Informatics, Stanford University.

27. Hage, Jaap (2000). "Dialectical Models in Artificial Intelligence and Law," Artificial Intelligence and Law.

28. Kaplow, Louis (1992). "Rules Versus Standards: An Economic Analysis," Volume 42, Duke Law Journal.

29. Markou, Christopher, and Simon Deakin (2020). "Is Law Computable? From Rule of Law to Legal Singularity," May 4, 2020, SSRN, University of Cambridge Faculty of Law Research Paper.

30. McCarty, Thorne (1977). "Reflections on TAXMAN: An Experiment in Artificial Intelligence and Legal Reasoning," January 1977, Harvard Law Review.

31. McGinnis, John, and Russell G. Pearce (2014). "The Great Disruption: How Machine Intelligence Will Transform the Role of Lawyers in the Delivery of Legal Services," Volume 82, Number 6, Fordham Law Review.

32. McGinnis, John, and Steven Wasick (2015). "Law's Algorithm," Volume 66, Florida Law Review.

33. Mnookin, Robert, and Lewis Kornhauser (1979). "Bargaining in the Shadow of the Law," Volume 88, Number 5, April 1979, The Yale Law Review.

34. Mowbray, Andrew, and Philip Chung, Graham Greenleaf (2019). "Utilising AI in the Legal Assistance Sector," LegalAIIA Workshop, ICAIL, June 17, 2019, Montreal, Canada.

35. Reinbold, Patric (2020). "Taking Artificial Intelligence Beyond the Turing Test," Volume 20, Wisconsin Law Review.

36. Remus, Dana, and Frank Levy, "Can Robots be Lawyers? Computers, Robots, and the Practice of Law," Volume 30, Georgetown Journal of Legal Ethics.

37. Rich, Michael (2016). "Machine Learning, Automated Suspicion Algorithms, and the Fourth Amendment," Volume 164, University of Pennsylvania Law Review.

38. Rissland, Edwina (1990). "Artificial Intelligence and Law: Stepping Stones to a Model of Legal Reasoning," Yale Law Journal.

39. SAE (2018). Taxonomy and Definitions for Terms Related to Driving Automation Systems for On-Road Motor Vehicles, J3016-201806, SAE International.

40. Sunstein, Cass (2001). "Of Artificial Intelligence and Legal Reasoning," University of Chicago Law School, Public Law and Legal Theory Working Papers.

41. Sunstein, Cass, and Kevin Ashley, Karl Branting, Howard Margolis (2001). "Legal Reasoning and Artificial Intelligence: How Computers 'Think' Like Lawyers," Symposium: Legal Reasoning and Artificial Intelligence, University of Chicago Law School Roundtable.
42. Surden, Harry (2014). "Machine Learning and Law," Washington Law Review.
43. Surden, Harry (2019). "Artificial Intelligence and Law: An Overview," Summer 2019, Georgia State University Law Review.
44. Susskind, Richard (2019). Online Courts and the Future of Justice. Oxford University Press.
45. Volokh, Eugne (2019). "Chief Justice Robots," Volume 68, Duke Law Journal.
46. Waltl, Bernhard, and Roland Vogl (2018). "Explainable Artificial Intelligence: The New Frontier in Legal Informatics," February 2018, Jusletter IT 22, Stanford Center for Legal Informatics, Stanford University.
47. Weber, Robert (2019). "Will the 'Legal Singularity' Hollow Out Law's Normative Core?" CSAS Working Paper 19-38, Antonin Scalia Law School, George Mason University, November 15, 2019.
48. Wolfram, Stephen (2018). "Computational Law, Symbolic Discourse, and the AI Constitution," in Data-Driven Law: Data Analytics and the New Legal Services (Edward J. Walters ed.).
49. Braithwaite, John (2002). "Rules and Principles: A Theory of Legal Certainty," Volume 27, Australian Journal of Legal Philosophy.
50. D'Amato, Anthony (2010). "Legal Uncertainty," Northwestern University School of Law, Faculty Working Papers

---

Note: *For supplemental materials depicting the aspects discussed in this chapter, refer to Appendix B, which contains various augmented diagrams, charts, and additional related facets of relevance.*

CHAPTER 8

AI-ENABLED LEGAL MICRO-DIRECTIVES

Abstract

Recent research by legal scholars suggests that the law might inevitably be transformed into legal micro-directives consisting of legal rules that are derived from legal standards or that are otherwise produced automatically or via the consequent derivations of legal goals and then propagated via automation for everyday use as readily accessible lawful directives throughout society. This paper examines and extends the legal micro-directives theories in three crucial respects: (1) By indicating that legal micro-directives are likely to be AI-enabled and evolve over time in scope and velocity across the autonomous levels of AI Legal Reasoning, (2) By exploring the tradeoffs between legal standards and legal rules as the imprinters of the micro-directives, and (3) By illuminating a set of brittleness exposures that can undermine legal micro-directives and proffering potential mitigating remedies to seek greater robustness in the instantiation and promulgation of such AI-powered lawful directives.

Section 1: Background on Legal Micro-Directives

Recent research by legal scholars advises that the law might inevitably be transformed into legal micro-directives consisting of legal rules that are derived from legal standards or that are otherwise produced automatically or via the consequent derivations of legal goals [8] [9] [28] [32].

These legal micro-directives would be propagated via automation for everyday use as readily accessible, lawful directives, throughout society. This paper examines and extends the legal micro-directives theories in three crucial respects:

(1) By indicating that legal micro-directives are likely to be AI-enabled and evolve over time in scope and velocity across the autonomous levels of AI Legal Reasoning [20] [22],

(2) By exploring the tradeoffs between legal standards and legal rules as the imprinters of the micro-directives, and

(3) By illuminating a set of brittleness exposures that can undermine legal micro-directives and proffering potential mitigating remedies to seek greater robustness in the instantiation and promulgation of such AI-enabled lawful directives.

In Section 1 of this paper, the topic of legal micro-directives is introduced and addressed. Doing so establishes the groundwork for the subsequent sections. Section 2 introduces the Levels of Autonomy (LoA) of AI Legal Reasoning (AILR), which is instrumental in the discussions undertaken in Section 3. Section 3 provides an indication of the AI-enablement of legal micro-directives, along with exploring the tradeoffs of legal rules versus legal standards, and the brittleness facets thereof. The final section, Section 4, covers additional considerations and recommendations for future research.

This paper then consists of these four sections:

- Section 1: Background on Legal Micro-Directives
- Section 2: Autonomous Levels of AI Legal Reasoning
- Section 3: Legal Micro-Directives and AI Enablement
- Section 4: Additional Considerations and Future Research

1.1 Legal Micro-Directives

In the research literature about the law, there has been a longstanding philosophical dialogue about the nature of legal standards and legal rules as two keystone elements of the law [2] [25] [26] [28].

The general view is that legal standards are typically indicative of broad strokes about the delineation of lawful behavior while legal rules are more tightly specified. Legal standards are considered open to interpretation and flexible, thus able to encompass a wide variety of acts and activities that would be assessed as lawful, but do so at the potential peril or downside that loose interpretation can lead to unlawful efforts that seemingly were feasible within the scope implied. Legal rules on the other hand are generally considered of a specific nature, being more pinpoint descriptive and reducing interpretive uncertainty about what the law portends [37] [42] [49].

Casey and Niblett [09] indicate this about legal standards and legal rules: "Rules are precise and ex ante in nature. Rules indicate to an individual whether certain behavior will violate or comply with the law. When a rule is enacted, effort must be undertaken by lawmakers to give full and precise content to the law before the individuals act. Standards, on the other hand, are imprecise when they are enacted. The exact content of the law comes after an individual acts, as judges and other adjudicators determine whether the individual's specific behavior in a particular context violates the standard."

Furthermore, with respect to uncertainty, they indicate [09]: "Uncertainty about the content of a law is greater with standards than with simple rules. When regulated by a simple rule, an individual will more likely know whether her behavior is allowed or prohibited. When regulated by a standard, on the other hand, the individual does not know how any particular judge with wide discretion will apply the standard to the facts. She may not know what behavior a judge will consider reasonable."

To readily depict this difference between legal standards and legal rules, a frequently provided example is the use case of automobile driving and laws related to driving that are legal standards versus driving-related legal rules. Per McGinnis and Wasick [32]:

> "The prototypical example of a rule-based law is a speed limit that holds that a driver must drive at sixty-five miles per hour or less. In contrast, a standard 'requires the judge both to discover the facts of a particular situation and to assess them in terms of the

purposes or social values embodied in the standard.' A standards-based speed limit, for example, would hold that a driver must drive at a 'reasonable' speed."

Per the work of Kaplow, as summarized and recounted in [32], legal rules would tend toward presumably greater conformity to the law: "If actors are able to inform themselves as to the consequences of the law beforehand, they are more likely to act in accordance with the law. Under a system of rule-based law, the legal norm is stated before an individual has the opportunity to act, giving them the chance to inform themselves about the law and act accordingly. In a standards-based law, the individual does not know the exact outlines of the law until it is given content by the court. This lack of information would result in less conformity with the law."

With the emergence of computer-based automation that is increasingly becoming ubiquitous throughout society, a relatively new concept or theory has been ventured in the realm of the law that has been coined as the use of legal micro-directives.

Essentially, a legal micro-directive is a legal rule that is made available via automation so that society can be made aware of the legal rule in a real-time and anyplace manner. Casey and Niblett [08] define micro-directives in this way: "Ultimately, law will exist in a catalogue of precisely tailored directives, specifying exactly what is permissible in every unique situation. In this world, when a citizen faces a legal decision, she is informed of exactly how to comply with every relevant law before she acts. The citizen does not have to weigh the reasonableness of her actions nor does she have to search for the content of a law. She follows a simple directive that is optimized for her situation. We call these refined laws 'micro-directives.' These micro-directives will be largely automated." From a lawmaker's perspective, these legal micro-directives are characterized as a new form of law [08]: "The lawmaker's decision between rules and standards will become unnecessary. A new form of law – the micro-directive – will emerge. The micro-directive provides ex ante behavioral prescriptions finely tailored to every possible scenario."

Returning to the example of automobile driving, consider this scenario about the use of legal micro-directives [08]: "To see how the mechanism might work, consider the regulation of traffic speed. In a world of rules and standards, a legislature hoping to optimize safety and travel time could enact a rule (a sixty miles-per-hour speed limit) or a standard ("drive reasonably"). With microdirectives, however, the law looks quite different. The legislature merely states its goal. Machines then design the law as a vast catalog of context-specific rules to optimize that goal. From this catalog, a specific microdirective is selected and communicated to a particular driver (perhaps on a dashboard display) as a precise speed for the specific conditions she faces. For example, a microdirective might provide a speed limit of 51.2 miles per hour for a particular driver with twelve years of experience on a rainy Tuesday at 3:27 p.m. The legislation remains constant, but the microdirective updates as quickly as conditions change."

At first glance, the adoption of legal micro-directives might seem a mere technological advancement and thus otherwise not be especially significant regarding the nature of the law and its ramifications. According to Casey and Niblett [09], they foresee that legal micro-directives could have a potent and enduring impact on law in many vital ways: "First, it will change the broad institutional balance of power in our political and legal system. Second, it may change the development and substantive content of legislative policy. Third, it will transform the practice and training of law. Fourth, it will have moral and ethical consequences for individual citizens, altering their day-to-day decision-making process and changing their relationship with lawmakers and government."

In that impactful sense, it is worthwhile therefore to provide additional attention to the nature and scope of legal micro-directives.

One core element consists of the notion that the legal micro-directives can be readily changed, doing so at a velocity unlike that of today's laws, and furthermore that the legal micro-directives will be better targeted [09]: "The technological changes will allow the law to be more precise, better calibrated, more flexible, more consistent, and less biased."

Likening this to the emergence of autonomous vehicles and self-driving cars, it is said that law will become *self-driving* (borrowing the phrase but not intending to somehow be commingled with autonomous vehicles per se) [09]: "If the state of the world changes, or if the objective of the law is changed, the vast array of micro-directives will instantly update. These laws will be better calibrated, more precise, and more consistent. The law will become, for all intents and purposes, 'self-driving.'"

If one conceives of the legal micro-directives as a variant of the notion of a legal rule, this implies that legal micro-directives will inherit the same advantages of legal rules as stated earlier in comparing the legal standards difficulty versus the benefits of legal rules [32]: "This difficulty is a problem both *ex ante* and *ex post*. *Ex ante*, an actor subject to a law wants to understand what actions the law requires, so that he may avoid liability. Instead of simply looking up a statute, as in the case of a rule, an actor subject to a standard would need to try and collect the relevant case law to determine the outlines of the standard and how it applies to him. *Ex post*, an actor subject to a standard would have to go through the same process to determine the likelihood of success at trial. At trial, the judge has the additional burden of determining the proper application of the standard to the particular facts of the case."

And thus, the benefits of using legal rules [32]: "If actors are able to inform themselves as to the consequences of the law beforehand, they are more likely to act in accordance with the law. Under a system of rule-based law, the legal norm is stated before an individual has the opportunity to act, giving them the chance to inform themselves about the law and act accordingly. In a standards-based law, the individual does not know the exact outlines of the law until it is given content by the court. This lack of information would result in less conformity with the law."

Some assert that micro-directives might entirely replace legal standards and legal rules, while others opine that there will still be legal standards, perhaps depicted as legal goals, out of which legal rules will be derived, and then out of which legal micro-directives are specified and promulgated.

In that latter perspective, lawmakers would continue to work at a legal standards or legal goals vantage point, and then be able to automatically have legal rules and legal micro-directives spawned from those legal standards. Those that advocate the contrary posture that all legal standards and legal rules will be eliminated and replaced entirely by micro-directives are apt to argue that there should not be any gaps per se between legal standards and the resultant legal micro-directives, while those that assert the continuing importance of legal standards are apt to suggest that lawmakers would not be readily able to produce law at a legal micro-directive level, and would be more amenable to establishing legal standards or legal goals that would then generate appropriately aligned legal micro-directives.

Open-ended questions about legal micro-directives include whether these legal micro-directives would necessarily be ascertained by humans or might be determined or generated via some form of AI Legal Reasoning (AILR) system or by other automated means [20] [22].

In the work by McGinnis and Wasick [32], they use the phrase "dynamic rules" defined as: "Dynamic rules are rules that automatically change without intervention by the rule giver according to changes in future conditions that the rule itself comprehensively and accurately fixes. As computation increases, it becomes easier to add complex conditions, both because these conditions can be continually monitored and because the application of the new rule can be more readily calculated."

The changes in the legal *dynamic rules* could be tied to data changes [32]: "Dynamic rules are rules that are tied directly to real world empirical data, so that they automatically update as the data to which they are tied changes. Dynamic rules can therefore increase the ability of rules to adapt to continuously changing circumstances rather than await another legislative decision to adapt." An example given to highlight how dynamic rules might function includes the realm of tax brackets [32]:

> "There are several examples of dynamic rules that are currently in effect, many with very successful results. For instance, the Economic Recovery Tax Act of 1981 indexed tax brackets to

inflation. Before this change, taxpayers experienced 'bracket creep' when inflation pushed them into higher tax brackets while their purchasing power remained the same.281 This led to a period during the 1970s when tax brackets had to be frequently changed by Congress in order to keep pace with inflation. By indexing brackets, Congress eliminated the need to revisit tax policy solely due to the inevitable increase of inflation."

Given the tremendous volume of potential legal dynamic rules or legal micro-directives that could end up being produced, it seems unlikely that lawmakers could cope with or manage laws at that granular of a level, and thus would need to be able to continue lawmaking at a higher level [32]: "In theory, rules could also be changed by legislatures or regulatory bodies in response to new information. In practice, however, rules tend to be sticky even in the face of changing circumstances that should modify them. Legislatures tend to be reactive to crises and thus may not update rules continuously as new information becomes available. The legislatures' crowded agendas often make it difficult to find time to update rules."

At the mid-level and granular level of the law, automation potentially consisting of AILR could be the spawning mechanism for legal rules and legal micro-directives, meanwhile, human lawmakers would continue their efforts at higher-levels of lawmaking [09]: "Human policy makers will still play a crucial role. Just as self-driving cars will determine the safest and fastest route to a destination selected by humans, self-driving laws will determine the optimal way to achieve a policy objective chosen by humans. Even though the micro-directives are automated and update in real time, human lawmakers will be required to set the broad objectives of the law."

There are potential downsides to the advent of legal micro-directives, including dystopian possibilities of automation that is restrictive beyond what was intended [08]:

"A far more dystopian vision is one where lawmakers turn microdirectives into physical restraints on behavior. Rather than commanding which action should be taken, the individual is restrained from undertaking actions that do not comply with the law. Instead of simply telling the doctor that surgery is not the wisest course of action and that performing surgery will constitute negligence, imagine now that the medical technology required to perform the surgery is automatically switched off, denying the doctor the possibility of performing the surgery."

All told, the upside potential for legal micro-directives in light of the potential adverse consequences of the adoption of legal micro-directives, merits additional research [08]: "The consequences relating to morality, privacy, and autonomy should be addressed before micro-directives arrive."

The next section of this paper introduces the autonomous levels of AI Legal Reasoning, doing so to then aid Section 3 that explores how legal micro-directives might vary across the levels of autonomy. Section 3 also covers more introspection of the legal rules versus legal standards facets and examines how legal micro-directives might be entailed via a macroscopic process flow indication. Also, the potential for brittleness in the use of legal micro-directives is identified, including potential mitigations or remedies that might be leveraged.

Section 2: Autonomous Levels of AI Legal Reasoning

In this section, a framework for the autonomous levels of AI Legal Reasoning is summarized and is based on the research described in detail in Eliot [20]. These autonomous levels will be portrayed in a grid that aligns with key elements of autonomy and as matched to AI Legal Reasoning. Providing this context will be useful to the later sections of this paper and will be utilized accordingly.

The autonomous levels of AI Legal Reasoning are as follows:
Level 0: No Automation for AI Legal Reasoning
Level 1: Simple Assistance Automation for AI Legal Reasoning
Level 2: Advanced Assistance Automation for AI Legal Reasoning
Level 3: Semi-Autonomous Automation for AI Legal Reasoning
Level 4: Domain Autonomous for AI Legal Reasoning
Level 5: Fully Autonomous for AI Legal Reasoning
Level 6: Superhuman Autonomous for AI Legal Reasoning

2.1 Details of the LoA AILR

See **Figure A-1** for an overview chart showcasing the autonomous levels of AI Legal Reasoning as via columns denoting each of the respective levels.

See **Figure A-2** for an overview chart similar to Figure A-1 which alternatively is indicative of the autonomous levels of AI Legal Reasoning via the rows as depicting the respective levels (this is simply a reformatting of Figure A-1, doing so to aid in illuminating this variant perspective, but does not introduce any new facets or alterations from the contents as already shown in Figure A-1).

2.1.1 Level 0: No Automation for AI Legal Reasoning

Level 0 is considered the no automation level. Legal reasoning is carried out via manual methods and principally occurs via paper-based methods.

This level is allowed some leeway in that the use of say a simple handheld calculator or perhaps the use of a fax machine could be allowed or included within this Level 0, though strictly speaking it could be said that any form whatsoever of automation is to be excluded from this level.

2.1.2 Level 1: Simple Assistance Automation for AI Legal Reasoning

Level 1 consists of simple assistance automation for AI legal reasoning.

Examples of this category encompassing simple automation would include the use of everyday computer-based word processing, the use of everyday computer-based spreadsheets, the access to online legal documents that are stored and retrieved electronically, and so on.

By-and-large, today's use of computers for legal activities is predominantly within Level 1.

It is assumed and expected that over time, the pervasiveness of automation will continue to deepen and widen, and eventually lead to legal activities being supported and within Level 2, rather than Level 1.

2.1.3 Level 2: Advanced Assistance Automation for AI Legal Reasoning

Level 2 consists of advanced assistance automation for AI legal reasoning.

Examples of this notion encompassing advanced automation would include the use of query-style Natural Language Processing (NLP), Machine Learning (ML) for case predictions, and so on.

Gradually, over time, it is expected that computer-based systems for legal activities will increasingly make use of advanced automation. Law industry technology that was once at a Level 1 will likely be refined, upgraded, or expanded to include advanced capabilities, and thus be reclassified into Level 2.

2.1.4 Level 3: Semi-Autonomous Automation for AI Legal Reasoning

Level 3 consists of semi-autonomous automation for AI legal reasoning.

Examples of this notion encompassing semi-autonomous automation would include the use of Knowledge-Based Systems (KBS) for legal reasoning, the use of Machine Learning and Deep Learning (ML/DL) for legal reasoning, and so on.

Today, such automation tends to exist in research efforts or prototypes and pilot systems, along with some commercial legal technology that has been infusing these capabilities too.

2.1.5 Level 4: Domain Autonomous for AI Legal Reasoning

Level 4 consists of domain autonomous computer-based systems for AI legal reasoning.

This level reuses the conceptual notion of Operational Design Domains (ODDs) as utilized in the autonomous vehicles and self-driving cars levels of autonomy, though in this use case it is being applied to the legal domain [17] [18] [20].

Essentially, this entails any AI legal reasoning capacities that can operate autonomously, entirely so, but that is only able to do so in some limited or constrained legal domain.

2.1.6 Level 5: Fully Autonomous for AI Legal Reasoning

Level 5 consists of fully autonomous computer-based systems for AI legal reasoning.

In a sense, Level 5 is the superset of Level 4 in terms of encompassing all possible domains as per however so defined ultimately for Level 4. The only constraint, as it were, consists of the facet that the Level 4 and Level 5 are concerning human intelligence and the capacities thereof. This is an important emphasis due to attempting to distinguish Level 5 from Level 6 (as will be discussed in the next subsection)

It is conceivable that someday there might be a fully autonomous AI legal reasoning capability, one that encompasses all of the law in all foreseeable ways, though this is quite a tall order and remains quite aspirational without a clear cut path of how this might one day be achieved. Nonetheless, it seems to be within the extended realm of possibilities, which is worthwhile to mention in relative terms to Level 6.

2.1.7 Level 6: Superhuman Autonomous for AI Legal Reasoning

Level 6 consists of superhuman autonomous computer-based systems for AI legal reasoning.

In a sense, Level 6 is the entirety of Level 5 and adds something beyond that in a manner that is currently ill-defined and perhaps (some would argue) as yet unknowable. The notion is that AI might ultimately exceed human intelligence, rising to become superhuman, and if so, we do not yet have any viable indication of what that superhuman intelligence consists of and nor what kind of thinking it would somehow be able to undertake.

Whether a Level 6 is ever attainable is reliant upon whether superhuman AI is ever attainable, and thus, at this time, this stands as a placeholder for that which might never occur. In any case, having such a placeholder provides a semblance of completeness, doing so without necessarily legitimatizing that superhuman AI is going to be achieved or not. No such claim or dispute is undertaken within this framework.

Section 3: Legal Micro-Directives and AI Enablement

In this section, the advent of legal micro-directives is explored in several respects. First, the role of AI as an enabler in the advancement and utility of legal micro-directives is discussed. This discussion includes an indication of the alignment of the evolution of legal micro-directives across the autonomous levels of AI Legal Reasoning. Second, the tradeoffs involved in legal rules versus legal standards are addressed. As part of that analysis, a process flow is proffered on the relationship between legal rules and legal standards as to their deriving the instantiation and promulgation of legal micro-directives. Third, a core set of potential brittleness facets of legal micro-directives is identified.

Also, those brittleness concerns are then sought to be overcome via recommended mitigation or remedies, aiming to arrive at a more robust approach to the adoption and use of legal micro-directives.

A series of figures are included in the discussions to aid in illustrating the matters addressed.

3.1 Legal Micro-Directives and LoA AILR

As shown in **Figure B-1**, it is useful to align the evolution of legal micro-directives with the autonomous levels of AI Legal Reasoning. AI has the potential to aid in bolstering and strengthening the adoption of legal micro-directives, such that as AI Legal Reasoning improves over time the capabilities can be leveraged toward the creation, derivation, refinement, and application of legal micro-directives.

For each of the levels of autonomy of AI Legal Reasoning, the impacts upon legal micro-directives will be distinctive. A keyword phrasing is used in Figure B-1 to indicate these impacts and consists of:

LoA AILR – Legal Micro-Directives
Level 0: *n/a*
Level 1: *Impractical*
Level 2: *Incubatory*
Level 3: *Infancy*
Level 4: *Narrow*
Level 5: *Wide*
Level 6: *Consummate*

In brief, at Level 0, which consists of no automation for AI Legal Reasoning, the applicability to legal micro-directives is considered not applicable ("n/a"), simply due to the by-definition that there is no AI involved at this level. At Level 1, simple assistance automation, the characterization is indicated as "Impractical" since the AI is abundantly unrefined and unable to offer any substantive practical capacity to the legal micro-directive advent. At Level 2, advanced assistance automation, the characterization is indicated as "Incubatory" since the AI at this level can modestly assist in legal micro-directives but is considered quite preliminary in doing so.

At Level 3, the first substantive impact of AI Legal Reasoning comes to work, and this is characterized by the keyword of "Infancy," denoting that the AI is initially being used as a demonstrative enabler for legal micro-directives.

Maturing at Level 4, the AI Legal Reasoning is now substantively augmenting the legal micro-directives, yet does so only within particular legal domains, thus this is characterized as being "Narrow" in its impact. Upon Level 5, encompassing all legal domains, the AI Legal Reasoning has now infused across all legal micro-directives and characterized as now being "Wide" in its scope and velocity. Finally, at Level 6, the superhuman AI Legal Reasoning, the advent of micro-directives would be considered "Consummate," though keep in mind that Level 6 is a speculative notion and it is not clear as to what the superhuman capacity would bring forth.

To reiterate and clarify, these depictions are not prescriptive and do not intend to predict what will happen, and instead are a form of taxonomy to depict and describe what might happen and provide an ontological means to understand such phenomena if it should so arise.

3.2 Quadrants of Legal Rules Versus Legal Standards

As shown in **Figure B-2**, a four-square set of quadrants is indicative of the tradeoffs of legal rules versus legal standards. Along the rows are the two states or conditions consisting of Legal Rules and the No Legal Rules status. Along the columns are the two states or conditions consisting of Legal Standards and the No Legal Standards status. In combination, there are then four distinct possibilities as represented in the four-square quadrants.

In this case, the quadrants are characterized in this manner:

Four-square Quadrant of Legal Rules versus Legal Standards

- Legal Rules: Legal Standards
  Lawful (via stasis)
- No Legal Rules: No Legal Standards
  Lawlessness (a vacuum)
- Legal Rules: No Legal Standards
  Infinite Conundrum
- Legal Standards: No Legal Rules
  Vagueness Quandary

In brief, the next subsections consider each of the respective use cases.

3.2.1 Legal Rules: Legal Standards – *Lawful (via stasis)*

In this use case, when there are Legal Rules and Legal Standards, the presumption is that this will lead to a state of being lawful, at least concerning guiding as to what is considered lawful behavior. To provide a semblance of a legal direction, the Legal Rules and Legal Standards should be aligned or harmonized, otherwise, there is a potential for confounding of legal micro-directives that attempt to convey what is intrinsically misaligned. To be clear, if there is no overlap or intersection of some Legal Standard and some Legal Rule, this implies that there would <u>not</u> be a misalignment per se, since there is no semblance of alignment inherently involved. Overall, for the lawful facet to be sustainable the Legal Rules and Legal Standards need to maintain some form of stasis.

3.2.2 No Legal Rules: No Legal Standards – *Lawlessness (a vacuum)*

In this use case, when there are No Legal Rules and No Legal Standards, the presumption is that this will lead to a state of being lawless since there is a vacuum as to what the legal rules are and what the legal standards are. Behavior is apparently allowed to free-range and does so without any guidance as to what is considered legally abiding. In this instance, the legal micro-directives would consist of an empty set.

3.2.3 Legal Rules: No Legal Standards – *Infinite Conundrum*

In this use case, when there are Legal Rules and No Legal Standards, the presumption is that this is potentially viable though raises the question of what the legal rules are predicated upon. In theory, overarching legal standards are the cornerstone for the formulation and cohesion of legal rules, without which the legal rules might seem arbitrary and seemingly absent of any overall pattern.

In addition, legal rules without any corresponding legal standards can produce the so-called infinite conundrum. Namely, the number of legal rules might become massive, doing so to a degree that they potentially seem random and haphazard, lacking a structure or basis, and could stretch seemingly endlessly. The resultant legal micro-directives would potentially be perceived as a never-ending set that has little or no rationale or underlying constituency.

3.2.4 Legal Standards: No Legal Rules – *Vagueness Quandary*

In this use case, when there are Legal Standards and No Legal Rules, the presumption is that this is potentially viable though raises the difficulty of vagueness about appropriate and inappropriate behaviors. Legal standards provide an overarching semblance of legal behavior and yet allow for leeway and flexibility, but within that latitude also rests the possibility of inappropriate behaviors and thus without definitive legal rules to provide guidance it is potentially the matter that behaviors will flaunt standards and egress into what is ultimately ascertained as a lawless activity.

3.3 Macroscopic Process Flow of Legal Micro-Directives

As shown in **Figure B-3** and **Figure B-4**, it is useful to consider a macroscopic process flow that might underly the advent of legal micro-directives.

In Figure B-3, starting with the assumption that Legal Micro-Directives will flow from Legal Goals, there is a topmost process involving the creation of new legal goals. There is a baseline of existing legal goals that are utilized in the effort of new legal goals formulation. Once a new legal goal has been proposed, a legal micro-directives generator is invoked. There is next a reconciling of the generated legal micro-directives with the existing set of legal micro-directives, and a looping back to the formulation of Legal Goals is undertaken to contend with any legal micro-directives unable to be reconciled. After the reconciling has been accomplished, the promulgation of the legal micro-directives can be performed.

Figure B-4 is similar to Figure B-3, though this variant indicates the use of Legal Standards and Legal Rules, rather than the alternative proposition of Legal Goals and the elimination of Legal Standards and Legal Rules.

In Figure B-4, starting with the assumption that Legal Rules will flow from Legal Standards, there is a topmost process involving the creation of new legal standards. There is a baseline of existing standards that are utilized in the effort of new standards formulation. Once a new legal standard has been proposed, a legal rules generator is invoked, along with producing the legal micro-directives that are being postulated. There must be a reconciling of the Legal Rules, such that a comparison is made with the existing set of Legal Rules, and as needed a loop back to the formulation of Legal Standards is undertaken. After the reconciling has been accomplished, the promulgation of the legal micro-directives can be performed.

This is a macroscopic process flow and at a high-level does not encompass the variety of additional checks-and-balances and other facets that would be utilized for a more detailed delineation of the processes and sub-processes involved.

3.4 G.R.A.P.H.S. AI Enablement of Legal Micro-Directives

As shown in **Figure B-5**, AI enablement of Legal Micro-Directives consists of at least the following key AILR activities, denoted with an acronym of G.R.A.P.H.S. for convenience of reference:

- **Generate Legal Micro-Directives**
- **Reconcile Legal Micro-Directives**
- **Approve Legal Micro-Directives**
- **Promulgate Legal Micro-Directives**
- **Host Legal Micro-Directives**
- **Suspend Legal Micro-Directives**

Each of these AI activities is increasingly capable at each of the respective AILR Levels of Autonomy as discussed in the prior section of this paper.

Per the macroscopic process flow indicated in the prior subsection, the AILR would to some degree (per the respective LoA's) be able to generate legal micro-directives, be able to reconcile legal micro-directives, be able to approve legal micro-directives, be able to promulgate legal micro-directives, and in addition be a hosting component that would be able to serve out legal micro-directives on an authenticated basis (as covered in the next subsection), and be able to suspend legal micro-directives (when so needed). Since the legal micro-directives would be considered a somewhat sacrosanct societal law renderer, the AI involved in the G.R.A.P.H.S. would need to be of the highest order of security, integrity, consistency, resiliency, etc.

In essence, the AI is tantamount to being the law giver, as it were, though presumably the Legal Goals or Legal Standards are the cornerstone that is the basis for the laws; nonetheless any semblance of AI system instabilities such as AI system corruption, disruption, or other maladies or malfunctions would indubitably undermine the collective belief in the bona fide legality of the micro-directives and thus wholly undermine the legal underpinnings of the legal micro-directives structure and philosophical foundation.

3.5 Brittleness of Legal Micro-Directives And Potential Remedies

As shown in **Figure B-6**, various brittleness effects can undermine the utility of legal micro-directives. This necessitates a consideration of the brittleness that can appear, along with how to mitigate or remedy these aspects, doing so to attempt at achieving a more robust advent of legal micro-directives.

The brittleness effects are listed as:

- Ripple effect
- Amalgamation effect
- Off-guard effect
- Propagation effect
- Wariness effect
- Conflicts effect
- Spoofing effect

In brief, each is described as:

Ripple effect: *Changes in Legal Standards or Legal Goals can produce a cavalcade of Legal Rules or Legal Micro-Directives changes, creating a massive ripple effect or torrent that is overwhelming and confounding*

Amalgamation effect: *Existing Legal Rules or Legal Micro-Directives become embedded fabric in societal activities; new Legal Rules or Legal Micro-Directives are disruptive to abiding with and costly or arduous to inure*

Off-guard effect: *Caught off-guard by the unexpected appearance of new Legal Rules or Legal Micro-Directives, lack of notification and forewarning and potentially inappropriate notice to the nature of the lawful matters involved*

Propagation effect: *Receiving of new Legal Rules or Legal Micro-Directives might encounter propagation delays, those seeking to heed are not provided a timely awareness, meanwhile still operating under the presumption of the validness of the prior set*

Wariness effect: *Wariness toward new Legal Rules or Legal Micro-Directives if all Legal Rules or Legal Micro-Directives seem to be unstable and rapidly modified/revoked/suspended*

Conflicts effect: *Multiple Legal Rules or Legal Micro-Directives that intrinsically conflict with each other*

Spoofing effect: *Spoofing to make illegitimate Legal Rules or Legal Micro-Directives seem as official*

The overarching emphasis is that these and additional brittleness facets that could be identified are all potential limitations, constraints, or outright threats to the veracity of the deployment and acceptance of Legal Micro-Directives and could therefore weaken or entirely undermine the adoption of Legal Micro-Directives. A concerted effort will be need to ensure that the manner of automation used for the enactment and enablement of the Legal Micro-Directives is able to address and mitigate or remedy these challenges.

For example, potential means of remedying or mitigating these delineated adverse effects consist of:

- Ripple effect: ***Reconciliation***
- Amalgamation effect: ***Disentanglement***
- Off-guard effect: ***Notification***
- Propagation effect: ***Attestation***
- Wariness effect: ***Stabilization***
- Conflicts effect: ***Harmonization***
- Spoofing effect: ***Authentication***

Details underlying each of these effects and their respective proposed remedies are described in Eliot [16] [17] [21].

Section 4: Additional Considerations and Future Research

As earlier indicated, research by various legal scholars has advocated that the law might inevitably be transformed into legal micro-directives consisting of legal rules that are derived from legal standards. These legal rules are envisioned as being propagated via automation for everyday use as readily accessible lawful legal directives throughout society.

This paper has examined and sought to extend the legal micro-directives theories in three crucial respects: (1) By indicating that legal micro-directives are likely to be AI-enabled and evolve over time in scope and velocity across the autonomous levels of AI Legal Reasoning, (2) By exploring the tradeoffs between legal standards and legal rules as the imprinters of the micro-directives, and (3) By illuminating a set of brittleness exposures that can undermine legal micro-directives and proffering potential mitigating remedies to seek greater robustness in the instantiation and promulgation of such AI-enabled lawful directives.

Future research is needed to explore in greater detail the manner and means by which AI-enablement will occur, along with the potential for adverse consequences, including as conveyed the possibility of brittleness that could undermine the efficacy of legal micro-directives.

Additional research on the proposed mitigations or remedies of the legal micro-directive brittleness is also needed. If legal micro-directives are to be productively adopted, the full gamut of legal, economic, societal, and technological ramifications need to be sufficiently examined.

References

1. Alarie, Benjamin (2016). "The Path of the Law: Toward Legal Singularity," May 27, 2016, SSRN, University of Toronto Faculty of Law and Vector Institute for Artificial Intelligence.

2. Alarie, Benjamin, and Anthony Niblett, Albert Yoon (2017). "Regulation by Machine," Volume 24, Journal of Machine Learning Research.

3. Ashley, Kevin, and Karl Branting, Howard Margolis, and Cass Sunstein (2001). "Legal Reasoning and Artificial Intelligence: How Computers 'Think' Like Lawyers," Symposium: Legal Reasoning and Artificial Intelligence, University of Chicago Law School Roundtable.

4. Baker, Jamie (2018). "A Legal Research Odyssey: Artificial Intelligence as Disrupter," Law Library Journal.

5. Ben-Ari, Daniel, and D., Frish, Y., Lazovski, A., Eldan, U., & Greenbaum, D. (2016). "Artificial Intelligence in the Practice of Law: An Analysis and Proof of Concept Experiment," Volume 23, Number 2, Richmond Journal of Law & Technology.

6. Bench-Capon, Trevor, and Givoanni Sartor (2003). "A Model of Legal Reasoning with Cases Incorporating Theories and Values," November 2013, Artificial Intelligence.

7. Buchanan, Bruce, and Thomas Headrick (1970). "Some Speculation about Artificial Intelligence and Legal Reasoning," Volume 23, Stanford Law Review.

8. Casey, Anthony, and Anthony Niblett (2016). "Self-Driving Laws," Volume 429, University of Toronto Law Journal.

9. Casey, Anthony, and Anthony Niblett (2017). "The Death of Rules and Standards," Volume 92, Indiana Law Journal.

10. Chagal-Feferkorn, Karni (2019). "Am I An Algorithm or a Product: When Products Liability Should Apply to Algorithmic Decision-Makers," Stanford Law & Policy Review.

11. Chen, Daniel (2019). "Machine Learning and the Rule of Law," in Law as Data: Computation, Text, and The Future of Legal Analysis (Michael A. Livermore and Daniel N. Rockmore eds.).

12. Coglianese, Cary, and David Lehr (2017). "Rulemaking by Robot: Administrative Decision Making in the Machine-Learning Era," Volume 105, Georgetown Law Journal.

13. Deakin, Simon, and Christopher Markou (2020). "From Rule of Law to Legal Singularity," University of Cambridge Faculty of Law.

14. Douglas, William (1948). "The Dissent: A Safeguard of Democracy," Volume 32, Journal of the American Judicature Society.

15. Eliot, Lance (2016). AI Guardian Angels for Deep AI Trustworthiness. LBE Press Publishing.

16. Eliot, Lance (2020). "The Neglected Dualism of Artificial Moral Agency and Artificial Legal Reasoning in AI for Social Good." Harvard University, Harvard Center for Research on Computation and Society, AI for Social Good Conference, July 21, 2020.

17. Eliot, Lance (2020). AI and Legal Reasoning Essentials. LBE Press Publishing.

18. Eliot, Lance (2019). Artificial Intelligence and LegalTech Essentials. LBE Press Publishing.

19. Eliot, Lance (2020). "FutureLaw 2020 Showcases How Tech is Transforming The Law, Including the Impacts of AI," April 16, 2020, Forbes.

20. Eliot, Lance (2020). "An Ontological AI-and-Law Framework for the Autonomous Levels of AI Legal Reasoning," Cornell University arXiv. https://arxiv.org/abs/2008.07328

21. Eliot, Lance (2020). "Turing Test and the Practice of Law: The Role of Autonomous Levels of AI Legal Reasoning," Cornell University arXiv. https://arxiv.org/abs/2008.07743

22. Eliot, Lance (2018). "Multidimensionality of the Legal Singularity: The Role of Autonomous Levels of AI Legal Reasoning," Cornell University arXiv. https://arxiv.org/abs/2008.10575

23. Eliot, Lance (2018). "Singularity and AI," July 10, 2018, AI Trends.

24. Eliot, Lance (2020). "The Role of Human Judgement as a Presumed Integral Ingredient for Achieving True AI," March 9, 2020, Forbes.

25. Gardner, Anne (1987). Artificial Intelligence and Legal Reasoning. MIT Press.

26. Genesereth, Michael (2009). "Computational Law: The Cop in the Backseat," Stanford Center for Legal Informatics, Stanford University.

27. Hage, Jaap (2000). "Dialectical Models in Artificial Intelligence and Law," Artificial Intelligence and Law.

28. Kaplow, Louis (1992). "Rules Versus Standards: An Economic Analysis," Volume 42, Duke Law Journal.

29. Markou, Christopher, and Simon Deakin (2020). "Is Law Computable? From Rule of Law to Legal Singularity," May 4, 2020, SSRN, University Cambridge Faculty of Law Research.
30. McCarty, Thorne (1977). "Reflections on TAXMAN: An Experiment in Artificial Intelligence and Legal Reasoning," January 1977, Harvard Law Review.
31. McGinnis, John, and Russell G. Pearce (2014). "The Great Disruption: How Machine Intelligence Will Transform the Role of Lawyers in the Delivery of Legal Services," Volume 82, Number 6, Fordham Law Review.
32. McGinnis, John, and Steven Wasick (2015). "Law's Algorithm," Volume 66, Florida Law Review.
33. Mnookin, Robert, and Lewis Kornhauser (1979). "Bargaining in the Shadow of the Law," Volume 88, Number 5, April 1979, The Yale Law Review.
34. Mowbray, Andrew, and Philip Chung, Graham Greenleaf (2019). "Utilising AI in the Legal Assistance Sector," LegalAIIA Workshop, ICAIL, June 17, 2019, Montreal, Canada.
35. Reinbold, Patric (2020). "Taking Artificial Intelligence Beyond the Turing Test," Volume 20, Wisconsin Law Review.
36. Remus, Dana, and Frank Levy, "Can Robots be Lawyers? Computers, Robots, and the Practice of Law," Volume 30, Georgetown Journal of Legal Ethics.
37. Rich, Michael (2016). "Machine Learning, Automated Suspicion Algorithms, and the Fourth Amendment," Volume 164, University of Pennsylvania Law Review.
38. Rissland, Edwina (1990). "Artificial Intelligence and Law: Stepping Stones to a Model of Legal Reasoning," Yale Law J.
39. SAE (2018). Taxonomy and Definitions for Terms Related to Driving Automation Systems for On-Road Motor Vehicles, J3016-201806, SAE International.
40. Sunstein, Cass (2001). "Of Artificial Intelligence and Legal Reasoning," University of Chicago Law School, Public Law and Legal Theory Working Papers.
41. Sunstein, Cass, and Kevin Ashley, Karl Branting, Howard Margolis (2001). "Legal Reasoning and Artificial Intelligence:

How Computers 'Think' Like Lawyers," Symposium: Legal Reasoning and Artificial Intelligence, University of Chicago Law School Roundtable.

42. Surden, Harry (2014). "Machine Learning and Law," Washington Law Review.
43. Surden, Harry (2019). "Artificial Intelligence and Law: An Overview," Summer 2019, Georgia State University Law Review.
44. Susskind, Richard (2019). Online Courts and the Future of Justice. Oxford University Press.
45. Volokh, Eugne (2019). "Chief Justice Robots," Volume 68, Duke Law Journal.
46. Waltl, Bernhard, and Roland Vogl (2018). "Explainable Artificial Intelligence: The New Frontier in Legal Informatics," February 2018, Jusletter IT 22, Stanford Center for Legal Informatics, Stanford University.
47. Weber, Robert (2019). "Will the 'Legal Singularity' Hollow Out Law's Normative Core?" CSAS Working Paper 19-38, Antonin Scalia Law School, George Mason University, November 15, 2019.
48. Wolfram, Stephen (2018). "Computational Law, Symbolic Discourse, and the AI Constitution," in Data-Driven Law: Data Analytics and the New Legal Services (Edward J. Walters ed.).
49. Braithwaite, John (2002). "Rules and Principles: A Theory of Legal Certainty," Volume 27, Australian Journal of Legal Philosophy.
50. D'Amato, Anthony (2010). "Legal Uncertainty," Northwestern University School of Law, Faculty Working Papers.

Note: *For supplemental materials depicting the aspects discussed in this chapter, refer to Appendix B, which contains various augmented diagrams, charts, and additional related facets of relevance.*

CHAPTER 9

AI LEGAL SENTIMENT ANALYSIS AND OPINION MINING

Abstract

An expanding field of substantive interest for the theory of the law and the practice-of-law entails Legal Sentiment Analysis and Opinion Mining (LSAOM), consisting of two often intertwined phenomena and actions underlying legal discussions and narratives: (1) Sentiment Analysis (SA) for the detection of expressed or implied sentiment about a legal matter within the context of a legal milieu, and (2) Opinion Mining (OM) for the identification and illumination of explicit or implicit opinion accompaniments immersed within legal discourse. Efforts to undertake LSAOM have historically been performed by human hand and cognition, and only thinly aided in more recent times by the use of computer-based approaches. Advances in Artificial Intelligence (AI) involving especially Natural Language Processing (NLP) and Machine Learning (ML) are increasingly bolstering how automation can systematically perform either or both of Sentiment Analysis and Opinion Mining, all of which is being inexorably carried over into engagement within a legal context for improving LSAOM capabilities. This research paper examines the evolving infusion of AI into Legal Sentiment Analysis and Opinion Mining and proposes an alignment with the Levels of Autonomy (LoA) of AI Legal Reasoning (AILR), plus provides additional insights regarding AI LSAOM in its mechanizations and potential impact to the study of law and the practicing of law.

Section 1: Background on Legal Sentiment Analysis and Opinion Mining

In Section 1 of this paper, the literature on Legal Sentiment Analysis and Opinion Mining (LSAOM) is introduced and addressed. Doing so establishes the groundwork for the subsequent sections. Section 2 introduces the Levels of Autonomy (LoA) of AI Legal Reasoning (AILR), which is instrumental in the discussions undertaken in Section 3. Section 3 provides an indication of the field of Legal Sentiment Analysis and Opinion Mining as applied to the LoA AILR, along with other vital facets. Section 4 provides various additional research implications and anticipated impacts upon salient practice-of-law considerations.

This paper then consists of these four sections:

- Section 1: Background on Legal Sentiment Analysis and Opinion Mining
- Section 2: Levels of Autonomy (LOA) of AI Legal Reasoning (AILR)
- Section 3: LSAOM and LoA AILR
- Section 4: Additional Considerations and Future Research

1.1 Overview of Legal Sentiment Analysis and Opinion Mining

An expanding field of substantive interest for the theory of the law and the practice-of-law entails Legal Sentiment Analysis and Opinion Mining (LSAOM), based to a great extent on research and studies of judicial behaviors such as those of jurors, and likewise the expressions of judges [48] [53] [77] [82].

Legal Sentiment Analysis and Opinion Mining can be applied to essentially any legal-related actors involved in the legal process and does not need to be limited to judges or jurors, being able to encompass other participants such as lawyers, paralegals, expert witnesses, and the like [17] [41] [75] [79].

Generically, Sentiment Analysis (SA) is a discipline that brings together a mixture of linguistics, human and social behaviors, psychology, cognitive science, and other fields to try and ascertain the sentiment expressed during some discourse. As stated by Babu and Rawther [5]: "Sentiment Analysis is the process of analyzing the sentiments and emotions of various people in various situations."

Legal Sentiment Analysis is SA that has been particularly tuned or customized to legal discourse and the legal realm.

More formally:

Legal Sentiment Analysis entails the detection of expressed or implied sentiment about a legal matter within the context of a legal milieu.

Another area of attention involves Opinion Mining (OM), which is also a generic form of analysis that can be applied to a legal-specific context. Per the work of Hemmation and Sohrabi [45]: "Opinion mining is considered as a subfield of natural language processing, information retrieval, and text mining. Opinion mining is the process of extracting human thoughts and perceptions from unstructured texts."

Legal Opinion Mining is OM that has been particularly tuned or customized to legal discourse and the legal realm.

More formally:

Legal Opinion Mining (OM) entails the identification and illumination of explicit or implicit opinion accompaniments immersed within legal discourse.

Likened somewhat to reading the tea leaves, as it were, the use of Sentiment Analysis in a legal context can aid in gauging the attitudes and feelings of those involved in legal discourse. Likewise, Opinion Mining can be useful in attempting to discern the nature of an opinion that is being expressed. Also, in the case of OM, there is often a keen interest in determining whether the expressed opinion appears to be fact-based or might be construed as non-factually based (this is further elucidated in Section 3).

1.2 Separability of Legal SA and Legal OM

In this paper, Legal Sentiment Analysis and Legal Opinion Mining are considered as separate and distinct from each other, as they are construed to be independent constructs, able to operate, or be utilized of each upon their own accord.

Imagine for discussion sake the extreme, whereby Legal Sentiment Analysis solely focuses on the emotional or feelings characterizations, while Legal Opinion Mining focuses solely on the identification of opinions. This is certainly viable and productive. Both though are admittedly and intentionally apt to be used in conjunction, at the same time and potentially each informing the other, in order to do a more substantive job of their respective tasks. An opinion might very well be wrapped within an aura of emotion and feelings. And, alternatively, emotion or feelings might be emoted via the expression of an opinion. There is a type of duality that can readily and often frequently arises between undertaking a Sentiment Analysis and that of an Opinion Mining effort.

But this does not render them inseparable and nor distinctly undistinguishable of each other.

The reason to provide such an emphasis on this matter of being either one-and-the-same or being separable is due to the conventional manner in which SA and OM are treated in (especially) the AI literature. For example, as stated in [38]: "Sentiment analysis, also known as opinion mining (OM), is defined as figuring out the public attitude of individuals toward distinct topics and news." Note that SA and OM are portrayed as synonymous rather than as differing.

Another example of this commingling includes this indication in [63]: "Sentiment analysis and opinion mining is an area that has experienced considerable growth over the last decade. This area of research attempts to determine the feelings, opinions, emotions, among other things, of people on something or someone.

To do this, natural language techniques and machine learning algorithms are used." In this example, the two are not as explicitly declared as synonymous, and instead are treated as though effectively they are the same, albeit also proffering that they are perhaps named differently. The usage here, in this paper, for clarification, assumes that (at least) Legal Sentiment Analysis and the reference to Legal Opinion Mining are each distinctive of each other, and though they are oftentimes joined at the hip, as it were, they are nonetheless still each a separate form of analysis and have different results or aims of what they seek to produce. The emphasis on the *legal incarnations* of SA and OM allows, perhaps, for the generic SA and generic OM to be considered as merged or inextricably intertwined (as per the dominance in the AI literature thereof).

One other related facet that partially explains why SA and OM are so closely coupled in the AI literature is due to the incorporation of in-common AI techniques and technologies. In that sense, since the underlying architecture or technological ecosystem is of the same ilk, it is easiest to then blend together that SA and OM are the same. The view here is that despite the possibility of the alike system underpinnings, they are still separable.

1.3 **Legal SA and Legal OM: Notable Exemplar**

As a vivid and classic demonstration of the use of sentiment and opinion in a legal context, many American attorneys are likely aware of the famous *Tribute to a Dog*, a matter that arose in a court case from the U.S. courts in the 1870s that is often taught or cited in law schools even still today. This is worthwhile to briefly explore herein, showcasing how sentiment and opinion are at times employed in a legal context.

Here are the particulars of the *Tribute to a Dog* matter. In the case of *Burden v. Hornsby*, a case tried in Pettis County of Missouri on September 23, 1870, attorney George Graham Vest represented Charles Burden in a case against a sheep farmer named Leonidas Hornsby, accused of killing "Old Drum," a local hunting dog owned by Burden, the dog having been killed on October 18, 1869 while on Hornsby's farm.

Purportedly, Hornsby had beforehand vowed to kill any dog that wandered onto his farm, which subsequently "Old Drum" owned by Charles Burden came onto the farm, and the dog was shot to death by Hornsby. There seems to be little dispute over these facts of the case. Burden sued Hornsby for $150 in damages as to the killing of "Old Drum" (this was the maximum monetary penalty allowed by local law at the time).

During the trial, Vest boastfully vowed outside of court that he would "win the case or apologize to every dog in Missouri," and did indeed ultimately prevail, though the jury awarded just $50 rather than the sought for $150. The case was subsequently appealed and eventually landed at the Missouri Supreme Court, where Vest also prevailed.

Over time, the case and Vest became rather famous for his closing argument in the original trial, gaining fame not especially due to his handling of the case per se but because of his closing remarks. The renown of the closing argument is known for explicitly not having made any reference to the case specifics, nor citing any testimony or evidence presented and served seemingly wholly as a eulogy or tribute about the deceased dog (which, for purposes herein in this paper, showcase the potential significance of the use of sentiment, and the use of opinion, respectively).

The homage has become famously known as the *Tribute to a Dog*.

Here is the closing argument made by Vest (source: https://www.historyplace.com/speeches/vest.htm): "The best friend a man has in the world may turn against him and become his enemy. His son or daughter that he has reared with loving care may prove ungrateful. Those who are nearest and dearest to us, those whom we trust with our happiness and our good name may become traitors to their faith. The money that a man has, he may lose. It flies away from him, perhaps when he needs it most. A man's reputation may be sacrificed in a moment of ill-considered action. The people who are prone to fall on their knees to do us honor when success is with us, may be the first to throw the stone of malice when failure settles its cloud upon our heads."

"The one absolutely unselfish friend that man can have in this selfish world, the one that never deserts him, the one that never proves ungrateful or treacherous is his dog. A man's dog stands by him in prosperity and in poverty, in health and in sickness. He will sleep on the cold ground, where the wintry winds blow and the snow drives fiercely, if only he may be near his master's side. He will kiss the hand that has no food to offer. He will lick the wounds and sores that come in encounters with the roughness of the world. He guards the sleep of his pauper master as if he were a prince. When all other friends desert, he remains. When riches take wings, and reputation falls to pieces, he is as constant in his love as the sun in its journey through the heavens."

"If fortune drives the master forth, an outcast in the world, friendless and homeless, the faithful dog asks no higher privilege than that of accompanying him, to guard him against danger, to fight against his enemies. And when the last scene of all comes, and death takes his master in its embrace and his body is laid away in the cold ground, no matter if all other friends pursue their way, there by the graveside will the noble dog be found, his head between his paws, his eyes sad, but open in alert watchfulness, faithful and true even in death."

This closing argument has been used as a case study in the use of legal rhetoric and its impact, for which the layers of sentiment and opinion are readily detectible.

1.4 Computer-based Aided LSAOM

Efforts to undertake Legal Sentiment Analysis and Legal Opinion Mining have historically been performed by humans, doing so upon inspecting or observing fellow humans, including their real-time behavior, their recorded behavior via video or audio recordings, and their written words via printed or online narratives. An attorney for example might study the efforts of their opponent at trial to try and discern how they are using opinion or sentiment, potentially countering or objecting at an advantageous opportunity to do so, or detected to then seek to deflate the efforts of the opposing counsel. Experts at social psychology might be employed to examine jurors or judges and seek to interpret their sentiments and opinions.

Upon the advent of computers, attempts to make use of computational methods to conduct Legal SA and Legal OM have been thinly aided by the use of computer-based approaches. Simplistic uses of computers can be used to do wordcounts and attempt to ascertain embedded sentiments and opinions, while more complex approaches make use of statistical models. Besides analyzing the written word, voice detection and translation software can also be used, along with the use of facial images captured by cameras and the analysis of the video.

Advances in Artificial Intelligence (AI) involving especially Natural Language Processing (NLP) and Machine Learning (ML) are increasingly bolstering how automation can systematically perform either or both of Sentiment Analysis and Opinion Mining, all of which is being inexorably carried over into engagement within a legal context for improving LSAOM capabilities.

For example, Wyner and Moens [82] make use of a specialized context-free grammar technique to employ NLP for the LSAOM of legal cases: "This paper describes recent approaches using text-mining to automatically profile and extract arguments from legal cases. We outline some of the background context and motivations. We then turn to consider issues related to the construction and composition of corpora of legal cases. We show how a Context-Free Grammar can be used to extract arguments, and how ontologies and Natural Language Processing can identify complex information such as case factors and participant roles. Together the results bring us closer to automatic identification of legal arguments."

In the work by Liu and Chen [55], a two-phased approach of feature extraction from precedents is used to classify judgments per Sentiment Analysis and Opinion Mining:

> "Factual scenario analysis of a judgment is critical to judges during sentencing. With the increasing number of legal cases, professionals typically endure heavy workloads on a daily basis. Although a few previous studies have applied information technology to legal cases, according to our research, no prior studies have predicted a pending judgment

> using legal documents. In this article, we introduce an innovative solution to predict relevant rulings. The proposed approach employs text mining methods to extract features from precedents and applies a text classifier to automatically classify judgments according to sentiment analysis. This approach can assist legal experts or litigants in predicting possible judgments. Experimental results from a judgment data set reveal that our approach is a satisfactory method for judgment classification."

The gradual advent of legal e-Discovery has also further spurred progress in LSAOM, including as described in this work by Joshi and Deshpande [51]: "e-Discovery Review is a type of legal service that aims at finding relevant electronically stored information (ESI) in a legal case. This requires manual reviewing of large number of documents by legal analysts, thus involving huge costs. In this paper, we investigate the use of IT, specifically text mining techniques, for improving the efficiency and quality of the e-discovery review service. We employ near duplicate detection and automatic classification techniques that can be used to create coherent groups of documents."

Machine Learning advances and the utilization of Deep Learning via large-scale Artificial Neural Networks (ANN) has also sparked LSAOM, such as this research involving the analysis of legal judgments for criminal cases [18]:

> "Text mining has become an effective tool for analyzing text documents in automated ways. Conceptually, clustering, classification and searching of legal documents to identify patterns in law corpora are of key interest since it aids law experts and police officers in their analyses. In this paper, we develop a document classification, clustering and search methodology based on neural network technology that helps law enforcement department to manage criminal written judgments more efficiently. In order to maintain a manageable number of independent Chinese keywords, we use term extraction scheme to select top-*n* keywords with the highest frequency as inputs of the Back-Propagation Network (BPN), and select seven criminal categories as target

> outputs of it. Related legal documents are automatically trained and tested by pre-trained neural network models. In addition, we use Self Organizing Map (SOM) method to cluster criminal written judgments. The research shows that automatic classification and clustering modules classify and cluster legal documents with a very high accuracy. Finally, the search module which uses the previous results helps users find relevant written judgments of criminal cases."

An interesting variant of LSAOM comes to play when considering the use of legal vocabulary for the general public, as typified by this effort utilizing a three-phase prediction (TPP) algorithm [54]: "Applying text mining techniques to legal issues has been an emerging research topic in recent years. Although a few previous studies focused on assisting professionals in the retrieval of related legal documents, to our knowledge, no previous studies could provide relevant statutes to the general public using problem statements. In this work, we design a text mining based method, the three-phase prediction (TPP) algorithm, which allows the general public to use everyday vocabulary to describe their problems and find pertinent statutes for their cases. The experimental results indicate that our approach can help the general public, who are not familiar with professional legal terms, to acquire relevant statutes more accurately and effectively."

Again, as a gentle reminder, realize that as pointed out in Subsection 1.2., within the AI field, generic SA and generic OM are typically treated as one and the same, in the sense that there is no distinction made between that which is sentiment and that which is opinion. They are oftentimes construed as synonymous and interchangeably used in the AI literature. It is argued herein that within the field of law, there is a bona fide case to be made to consider SA and OM to be distinct in their scope, nature, and focus. Thus, Legal Sentiment Analysis is construed herein as per the definition given earlier in this subsection, and Legal Opinion Mining is construed herein as per the definition given earlier in this subsection.

Beyond a legal context, Sentiment Analysis and Opinion Mining have advanced due to interest in analyzing visual social media, going beyond the written word to examine visual content too [85]:

"Social media sentiment analysis (also known as opinion mining) which aims to extract people's opinions, attitudes and emotions from social networks has become a research hotspot. Conventional sentiment analysis concentrates primarily on the textual content. However, multimedia sentiment analysis has begun to receive attention since visual content such as images and videos is becoming a new medium for self-expression in social networks. In order to provide a reference for the researchers in this active area, we give an overview of this topic and describe the algorithms of sentiment analysis and opinion mining for social multimedia. Having conducted a brief review on textual sentiment analysis for social media, we present a comprehensive survey of visual sentiment analysis on the basis of a thorough investigation of the existing literature." This same attention to visual elements is likewise entering into the LSAOM realm.

In seeking to discern Legal Opinion Mining, and to some degree Legal Sentiment Analysis, the study by Conrad and Schilder examined legal blogs that were posted online [20]: "We perform a survey into the scope and utility of opinion mining in legal Weblogs (a.k.a. blawgs). The number of 'blogs' in the legal domain is growing at a rapid pace and many potential applications for opinion detection and monitoring are arising as a result. We summarize current approaches to opinion mining before describing different categories of blawgs and their potential impact on the law and the legal profession. In addition to educating the community on recent developments in the legal blog space, we also conduct some introductory opinion mining trials. We first construct a Weblog test collection containing blog entries that discuss legal search tools. We subsequently examine the performance of a language modeling approach deployed for both subjectivity analysis (i.e., is the text subjective or objective?) and polarity analysis (i.e., is the text affirmative or negative towards its subject?). This work may thus help establish early baselines for these core opinion mining tasks."

Related to the topic of online and social media, those such advances have equally stimulated advancement in generic SA and generic OM, and for which then can be carried into LSAOM. Perhaps the most popular focus of social media for undertaking SA and OM consists of examining tweets, such as this study [5]:

"Understanding the behavior of people or a particular user using his comments or tweets in various social media is an advancement of the Sentiment Analysis. Sentiment Analysis or Opinion Mining is used to understand the overall sentiments present in the data collected from various social media. The people have more exposure to the outside world due to the existence of the Internet and Various Social Medias like Twitter, Facebook, Instagram, etc. where they will be sharing their thoughts. Cheap and fast communication has made social media more valuable among the public. Social Media data can be used for various scientific and commercial applications. The combination of Sentiment Analysis and Behavior Analysis made the extraction of needed or useful data more easy and simple for various applications which include character analyzing, Depression Testing etc. Moreover, the behavior analysis will be done based on the text and emoticon sentiment score obtained during the analysis."

Similar kinds of studies have examined the reviews of products, as posted online at sites including Amazon, Facebook, etc., as developed in this study on using SA and OM techniques and technologies [49]: "Sentiment Analysis and Opinion Mining is a most popular field to analyze and find out insights from text data from various sources like Facebook, Twitter, and Amazon, etc. It plays a vital role in enabling the businesses to work actively on improving the business strategy and gain an in-depth insight of the buyer's feedback about their product. It involves computational study of behavior of an individual in terms of his buying interest and then mining his opinions about a company's business entity. This entity can be visualized as an event, individual, blog post or product experience. In this paper, Dataset has taken from Amazon which contains reviews of Camera, Laptops, Mobile phones, tablets, TVs, video surveillance. After preprocessing we applied machine learning algorithms to classify reviews that are positive or negative. This paper concludes that, Machine Learning Techniques gives best results to classify the Products Reviews. Naïve Bayes got accuracy 98.17% and Support Vector machine got accuracy 93.54% for Camera Reviews."

As will be addressed in Section 3, this research paper examines the evolving infusion of AI into Legal Sentiment Analysis and Opinion Mining and proposes an alignment with the Levels of Autonomy (LoA) of AI Legal Reasoning (AILR), plus provides additional insights regarding AI LSAOM in its mechanizations and potential impact to the study of law and the practicing of law.

1.5 Conventional Legal Contexts for LSAOM

Aristotle philosophized that the law should be free of passion [48].

There is much focus in the theory of law and the practice of law to presumably excise emotion from the nature of law and the practice of law, such that the law is aimed to be entirely objective, free of subjectivity, dispassionate, and carried by the strength of logic and legal argument [41]. Though this might be a desired arrangement, the reality is that the law and the practice of law are intimately bound into human behavior and therefore subject to human sentiment and to human opinion [79] (both "vacuous" opinion, as it were, if non-factual opinion could be so labeled, and fact-based opinion or ostensibly substantiated opinion).

One of the most visible arenas involving the interest in performing LSAOM consists of jury selection. There is a desire to detect so-called emotional loyalties of jurors, tipping their hands as to their presumed likely proclivities while possibly serving on a jury, as explained by Gobin [41]: "Scientific or Systematic Jury Selection (SJS) originated during the Vietnam War Era and remains targeted by the scientific community as a practice more artistic than factual. But while the motives of the procedure and its status as a recognized science are still controversial, a close examination of its methods provides insight into the hidden pathways of emotional assumption relied upon by jury selectors. Jury consultants who practice SJS usually focus on certain strategic markers: demographic classification, behavioral responses, and psychological attributes. On the surface, these categories create a very satisfying array of options."

And, further by [41]: "Jury instructions–such as those in capital penalty phases, which warn jurors that they 'must not be swayed by mere sentiment, conjecture, sympathy, passion, prejudice, public opinion or public feeling,' urge jurors to abandon any emotional loyalties that they had disclosed in voir dire, and to deliver a verdict they believe to be their impartial best. When jurors are selected through a procedure littered with emotional analysis, however, is it then reasonable to expect an impartial verdict from those selected using a partial process? In other words, can a juror who has been selected based on predictions of his or her emotional responses subsequently be placed in a courtroom and enter judgments devoid of those emotions?"

Walker and Shapiro discuss the overall psychology that permeates trials and thusly embodies a cauldron of sentiment and opinion, notwithstanding efforts to keep such "subjective" emulsions at bay [79]: "Despite skepticism that psychologists were mind readers and could manipulate people, coupled with concern over attorneys and even mental health professionals that might overstep their bounds, the area of trial consultation and jury selection has become an important area of forensic psychology. Much of the research and development in this area stems from social psychology, and methods such as public opinion polls, focus groups, mock trials, and analogue jury studies are used to accomplish the goals of, preparing witnesses for their statements and selecting (or, rather, deselecting) jurors in the *voir dire*, or the process by which juries are chosen for a trial. Forensic psychologists serving as trial consultants also use research to assist the attorney in trial strategies such as decisions on which pieces of evidence to emphasize, how to arrange evidence in terms of order of presentation, preparation of opening and closing statements, and determining when and if a change of venue is necessary in order to obtain a fair trial for clients, among other tasks."

Judges are also subject to sentiment and opinion, and the psychology of trial judging showcases the significant impacts therein [77]:

> "Trial court judges play a crucial role in the administration of justice for both criminal and civil matters.

> Although psychologists have studied juries for many decades, they have given relatively little attention to judges. Recent writings, however, suggest increasing interest in the psychology of judicial decision making. This essay reviews several selected topics where judicial discretion appears to be influenced by psychological dispositions, but cautions that a mature psychology of judging field will need to consider the influence of the bureaucratic court setting in which judges are embedded, their legal training, and the constraints of legal precedent."

It might be assumed that judges would be able to readily overcome sentiment, and yet some studies have indicated that even when directly informed to exclude biasing material, they appeared (along with jurors) to nonetheless not be able to logically and "objectively" do so [53]: "Reviews the presumptions and the differential treatment accorded American judges and jurors by the civil procedure system. An experiment was conducted in which 88 judges and 104 jurors were exposed to potentially biasing material with respect to a civil trial vignette. Judges and jurors randomly received 1 of 3 versions of a product liability case: no exposure to biasing material, exposure with a judicial decision to exclude the material, and exposure with a judicial decision to admit the material. Ss were asked to indicate (1) whether they would find the defendant liable or not liable and (2) their level of confidence in their decisions. Results suggest that judges and jurors may be similarly influenced by such exposure, regardless of whether the biasing material was ruled admissible or inadmissible."

Importantly, rather than taking a blind eye toward the inclusion of sentiment, some argue that it is better to put the sentiment upfront, perhaps even asserting that the embodiment of emotions and feeling by judges can be considered an element for rendering good legal judgments [48]: "There has been an explosion of emotion research in which emotions are no longer seen in opposition to reason. Instead, emotions are increasingly appreciated as being indispensable in cognitive processes because they comprise sets of perceptions and evaluations that enable judgment. Emotions are no longer set aside as mere obstacles to good judgment. At the same time, it is a well-known fact that emotions often prevent people from judging carefully."

And continuing [48]: "The question is raised, for example, whether it is desirable for judges to express their emotions and what the right way would be for them to do so. Questions like this introduce new arguments into the ongoing debate in legal philosophy about legal positivism: about its rationalist ideal of the dispassionate judge who merely applies rules."

1.6 Hierarchical Nature of LSAOM

A topic that will be addressed in Section 3 and for which is worthwhile to first introduce in Section 1 consists of the granularity associated with undertaking LSAOM.

It is important to consider the granularity at which a Legal Sentiment Analysis might be undertaken, and likewise at which a Legal Opinion Mining might be undertaken.

Use the *Tribute of a Dog* as a vehicle for exploring the granularity facets of LSAOM. One could examine perhaps the first sentence: "The best friend a man has in the world may turn against him and become his enemy." When the sentence was uttered by Vest, presumably a SA could be done as to his tonality and manner in which he expressed the sentence. From an OM perspective, the sentence could be examined for its essence of opinion expressed, and whether it appeared to be fact-based or non-factually based.

Certainly, we might though desire to inspect the entire initial paragraph, rather than merely the first sentence. Or, we might wish to examine the entire closing argument.

Any of these could be a proper or appropriate granularity at which to undertake an LSAOM or could be inappropriate and produce a false or misleading conclusion arising from the SA and the OM derivations, and thus the application of LSAOM has to be weighed with respect to its value and utility for what amount of granularity it is being applied.

As indicated by Do et al [22]:

"A current research focus for sentiment analysis is the improvement of granularity at aspect level, representing two distinct aims: aspect extraction and sentiment classification of product reviews and sentiment classification of target-dependent tweets. *Deep learning* approaches have emerged as a prospect for achieving these aims with their ability to capture both syntactic and semantic features of text without requirements for high-level feature engineering, as is the case in earlier methods."

Similarly, in the work by Gamal et al [38]:

"SA is categorized into three main levels—the aspect or feature level (AL), the sentence level (SL) and the document level (DL). The AL refers to classify the sentiments that are expressed on various features or aspects of an entity. In the SL, the fundamental concern is to pick whether each sentence infers a positive, negative or neutral opinion. In the DL, the basic concern is to classify whether the whole opinion in a document implies a positive or negative sentiment. The SL and DL analyses are insufficient to precisely monitor what people accept and reject. This research focuses on the document level of sentiment analysis."

Overall, those advancing the theory of law in the realm of LSAOM, and those practicing law by the leveraging of LSAOM, need to be fully aware of the granularity facets, likely of a hierarchical and at times circular nature in any particular legal case or legal contextual application (this is further discussed in Section 3).

Section 2: Levels of Autonomy (LOA) of AI Legal Reasoning (AILR)

In this section, a framework for the autonomous levels of AI Legal Reasoning is summarized and is based on the research described in detail in Eliot [28] [29] [30] [31] [32] [33] [34] [35] [36]. These autonomous levels will be portrayed in a grid that aligns with key elements of autonomy and as matched to AI Legal Reasoning.

The autonomous levels of AI Legal Reasoning are as follows:
Level 0: No Automation for AI Legal Reasoning
Level 1: Simple Assistance Automation for AI Legal Reasoning
Level 2: Advanced Assistance Automation for AILR
Level 3: Semi-Autonomous Automation for AI Legal Reasoning
Level 4: Domain Autonomous for AI Legal Reasoning
Level 5: Fully Autonomous for AI Legal Reasoning
Level 6: Superhuman Autonomous for AI Legal Reasoning

2.1 Details of the LoA AILR

See **Figure A-1** for an overview chart showcasing the autonomous levels of AI Legal Reasoning as via columns denoting each of the respective levels.

See **Figure A-2** for an overview chart similar to Figure A-1 which alternatively is indicative of the autonomous levels of AI Legal Reasoning via the rows as depicting the respective levels (this is simply a reformatting of Figure A-1, doing so to aid in illuminating this variant perspective, but does not introduce any new facets or alterations from the contents as already shown in Figure A-1).

2.1.1 Level 0: No Automation for AI Legal Reasoning

Level 0 is considered the no automation level. Legal reasoning is carried out via manual methods and principally occurs via paper-based methods.

This level is allowed some leeway in that the use of say a simple handheld calculator or perhaps the use of a fax machine could be allowed or included within this Level 0, though strictly speaking it could be said that any form whatsoever of automation is to be excluded from this level.

2.1.2 Level 1: Simple Assistance Automation for AI Legal Reasoning

Level 1 consists of simple assistance automation for AI legal reasoning.

Examples of this category encompassing simple automation would include the use of everyday computer-based word processing, the use of everyday computer-based spreadsheets, the access to online legal documents that are stored and retrieved electronically, and so on.

By-and-large, today's use of computers for legal activities is predominantly within Level 1. It is assumed and expected that over time, the pervasiveness of automation will continue to deepen and widen, and eventually lead to legal activities being supported and within Level 2, rather than Level 1.

2.1.3 Level 2: Advanced Assistance Automation for AI Legal Reasoning

Level 2 consists of advanced assistance automation for AI legal reasoning.

Examples of this notion encompassing advanced automation would include the use of query-style Natural Language Processing (NLP), Machine Learning (ML) for case predictions, and so on.

Gradually, over time, it is expected that computer-based systems for legal activities will increasingly make use of advanced automation. Law industry technology that was once at a Level 1 will likely be refined, upgraded, or expanded to include advanced capabilities, and thus be reclassified into Level 2.

2.1.4 Level 3: Semi-Autonomous Automation for AI Legal Reasoning

Level 3 consists of semi-autonomous automation for AI legal reasoning. Examples of this notion encompassing semi-autonomous automation would include the use of Knowledge-Based Systems (KBS) for legal reasoning, the use of Machine Learning and Deep Learning (ML/DL) for legal reasoning, and so on.

Today, such automation tends to exist in research efforts or prototypes and pilot systems, along with some commercial legal technology that has been infusing these capabilities too.

2.1.5 Level 4: Domain Autonomous for AI Legal Reasoning

Level 4 consists of domain autonomous computer-based systems for AI legal reasoning.

This level reuses the conceptual notion of Operational Design Domains (ODDs) as utilized in the autonomous vehicles and self-driving cars levels of autonomy, though in this use case it is being applied to the legal domain [24] [25] [26] [27]. Essentially, this entails any AI legal reasoning capacities that can operate autonomously, entirely so, but that is only able to do so in some limited or constrained legal domain.

2.1.6 Level 5: Fully Autonomous for AI Legal Reasoning

Level 5 consists of fully autonomous computer-based systems for AI legal reasoning.

In a sense, Level 5 is the superset of Level 4 in terms of encompassing all possible domains as per however so defined ultimately for Level 4. The only constraint, as it were, consists of the facet that the Level 4 and Level 5 are concerning human intelligence and the capacities thereof. This is an important emphasis due to attempting to distinguish Level 5 from Level 6 (as will be discussed in the next subsection)

It is conceivable that someday there might be a fully autonomous AI legal reasoning capability, one that encompasses all of the law in all foreseeable ways, though this is quite a tall order and remains quite aspirational without a clear cut path of how this might one day be achieved. Nonetheless, it seems to be within the extended realm of possibilities, which is worthwhile to mention in relative terms to Level 6.

2.1.7 Level 6: Superhuman Autonomous for AI Legal Reasoning

Level 6 consists of superhuman autonomous computer-based systems for AI legal reasoning.

In a sense, Level 6 is the entirety of Level 5 and adds something beyond that in a manner that is currently ill-defined and perhaps (some would argue) as yet unknowable. The notion is that AI might ultimately exceed human intelligence, rising to become superhuman, and if so, we do not yet have any viable indication of what that superhuman intelligence consists of and nor what kind of thinking it would somehow be able to undertake.

Whether a Level 6 is ever attainable is reliant upon whether superhuman AI is ever attainable, and thus, at this time, this stands as a placeholder for that which might never occur. In any case, having such a placeholder provides a semblance of completeness, doing so without necessarily legitimatizing that superhuman AI is going to be achieved or not. No such claim or dispute is undertaken within this framework.

Section 3: LSAOM and LoA AILR

In this Section 3, various aspects of Legal Sentiment Analysis and Opinion Mining (LSAOM) will be identified and discussed with respect to AI Legal Reasoning (AILR). A series of diagrams and illustrations are included to aid in depicting the points being made. In addition, the material draws upon the background and LSAOM research literature indicated in Section 1 and combines with the material outlined in Section 2 on the Levels of Autonomy (LoA) of AI Legal Reasoning.

3.1 LSAOM Aligned with LoA AILR

The nature and capabilities of Legal Sentiment Analysis and Opinion Mining will vary across the Levels of Autonomy for AI Legal Reasoning.

Though it is argued in this paper that legal-oriented SA and legal-oriented OM are two distinct facets, which are often intertwined but not necessarily so, and for which they are most decidedly not considered as synonymous with each other, they nonetheless can be treated as two akin capacities that will likely advance and mature correspondingly in the same overarching manner, over time and amidst the advent of AILR levels of autonomy.

Refer to **Figure B-1**.

As indicated, Legal Sentiment Analysis and Opinion Mining becomes increasingly more sophisticated and advanced as the AI Legal Reasoning increases in capability. To aid in typifying the differences between each of the Levels in terms of the incremental advancement of LSAOM, the following phrasing is used:

- Level 0: **n/a**
- Level 1: **Rudimentary Detection**
- Level 2: **Complex Detection**
- Level 3: **Symbolic Intertwined**
- Level 4: **Domain Perceptive**
- Level 5: **Holistic Perceptive**
- Level 6: **Pansophic Perceptive**

Briefly, each of the levels of LSAOM is described next.

At Level 0, there is an indication of "n/a" at Level 0 since there is no AI capability at Level 0 (the *No Automation* level of the LoA).

At Level 1, the LoA is *Simple Assistance Automation* and this can be used to undertake Legal Sentiment Analysis and Opinion Mining though it is rated or categorized as being rudimentary and making use of relatively simplistic calculative models and formulas. Thus, this is coined as "Rudimentary Detection."

At Level 2, the LoA is *Advanced Assistance Automation* and the LSAOM is coined as "Complex Detection," which is indicative of Legal Sentiment Analysis and Opinion Mining being performed in a more advanced manner than at Level 1.

This consists of complex statistical methods such as those techniques mentioned in Section 1 of this paper. To date, most of the research and practical use of Legal Sentiment Analysis and Opinion Mining has been within Level 2. Future efforts are aiming at Level 3 and above.

At Level 3, the LoA is *Semi-Autonomous Automation* and the LSAOM is coined as "Symbolic Intermixed," which can undertake Legal Sentiment Analysis and Opinion Mining at an even more advanced capacity than at Level 2. Recall, in Level 2, the focus tended to be on traditional numerical formulations for LSAOM, albeit sophisticated in the use of statistical models. In Level 3, the symbolic capability is added and fostered, including at times acting in a hybrid mode with the conventional numerical and statistical models. Generally, the work at Level 3 to-date has primarily been experimental, making use of exploratory prototypes or pilot efforts.

At Level 4, the LoA is *AILR Domain Autonomous* and the LSAOM coined as "Domain Perceptive," meaning that this can be used to perform Legal Sentiment Analysis and Opinion Mining within particular specialties of domains or subdomains of the legal field, but does not necessarily cut across the various domains and is not intended to be able to do so. The capacity is done in a highly advanced manner, incorporating the Level 3 capabilities, along with exceeding those levels and providing a more fluent and capable perceptive means.

At Level 5, the LoA is *AILR Fully Autonomous,* and the LSAOM coined as "Holistic Perceptive," meaning that the use of Legal Sentiment Analysis and Opinion Mining can go across all domains and subdomains of the legal field. The capacity is done in a highly advanced manner, incorporating the Level 4 capabilities, along with exceeding those levels and providing a more fluent and capable perceptive means.

At Level 6, the LoA is *AILR Superhuman Autonomous*, which as a reminder from Section 2 is not a capability that exists and might not exist, though it is included as a provision in case such a capability is ever achieved. The LSAOM at this level is considered "Pansophic Perceptive" and would encapsulate the Level 5 capabilities, and then go beyond that would use the AI superhuman capacity.

3.2 Framework of Legal Sentiment Analysis and Opinion Mining

Based on the discussion in Section 1, it is useful to consider the overarching nature of the approaches utilized in ascertaining Legal Sentiment Analysis and Opinion Mining and provide a framework for establishing the elements involved.

Refer to **Figure B-2**.

The framework indicates that LSAOM consists of two facets that are often intertwined, though can be distinctively articulated as they proffer differing scope, nature, and focus. Sentiment Analysis (SA) is utilized for the detection of expressed or implied sentiment about a legal matter within the context of a legal milieu, while Opinion Mining (OM) is utilized for the identification and illumination of explicit or implicit opinion accompaniments immersed within legal discourse.

For the Legal Sentiment Analysis, three major elements are consisting of: (1) SA Visual, (2) SA Oral, and (3) SA Written. The SA Visual is typically aimed at facial recognition for sentiment detection, but other visual indications can be encompassed, such as body language, posturing, etc. SA Oral entails discourse that is orally expressed rather than in writing. Within SA Oral, there is the tonality that is examined to aid in ascertaining the sentiment expression, along with the words spoken as part of a legal narrative. SA Written entails discourse that consists of written narrative.

For the Legal Opinion Mining, there are two major elements: (1) OM Oral, and (2) OM Written. Underlying each of these two elements is the vital aspect of detecting whether an expressed or implied opinion is seemingly facts-based or whether it is non-factual based.

Refer next to **Figure B-3**.

Customarily, the use of Legal Sentiment Analysis and Opinion Mining entails examining human utterances and expressions. This might consist of the sentiment and/or opinions of a judge, of a jury member, of an attorney, and so on.

In the future, in addition to the use of LSAOM on human utterances and expressions, it is anticipated that the LSAOM will be applied to AI utterances and expressions. This might seem farfetched at this time, and yet the future might indeed involve AI systems that will be providing legal arguments and undertaking legal discourses, which today is rudimentary and minimal at best by any existent AILIR.

Consider the four-square grid in **Figure B-4**.

As shown in Figure B-4, consider a four-square grid that presents some notable nuances between the Legal Sentiment Analysis and the Legal Opinion Mining capabilities.

On the vertical axis are the two capacities, Legal Sentiment Analysis, and Legal Opinion Mining, respectively. Along the horizontal axis is time as divided into real-time versus offline.

Generally, the primary use of Legal Sentiment Analysis occurs when analyzing in real-time the facial and voice aspects of a person speaking (or, an AI system speaking). This can be undertaken to gauge a "now expressing" detection of sentiment. Legal Sentiment Analysis can also be used in an offline mode, such as analyzing an audio or video recording, or for examining a written narrative.

Generally, the primary use of Legal Opinion Mining occurs when analyzing an offline transcript of written words (this could be in an audio or video format and transformed into a written word format). This is utilized to ascertain explicitly or implicitly expressed opinions, along with whether they are fact-based or non-factual based (as within the context of the provided narrative being used as the scope of the analysis). Legal Opinion Mining can also be used in real-time settings, though this is a usually less impactful manner.

In practice, the Legal Sentiment Analysis might not be able to ascertain any semblance of sentiment expressed. Thus, Legal Sentiment Analysis can consist of two polarity states, SA SD1 (detected) and SA SD0 (not detected).

Likewise, in Legal Opinion Mining, an opinion might not be detected (coding of OM OD0), or might be detected and be factual based (coding of OM OD1-FB) or non-factual based (coding of OM OD1-NFB).

Next, refer to **Figure B-5**.

Earlier in this subsection, it was mentioned that the LSAOM can be applied to AI utterances and expressions, seeking to detect sentiments and opinions as exhibited by an AI system. This does not suggest that the AI is sentient, and leaves aside the question about the potential of AI becoming sentient. In short, an AI system could present a legal argument or legal discourse that embodies sentiment and opinion, doing so without any need per se of somehow having reached sentience. This possibility can occur by a certain kind of happenstance in how the AI has been set up and been designed.

In a somewhat similar vein, the LSAOM capabilities can be used to generate sentiments and opinions, doing so by an AI "reverse" generating approach. Thus, the point being that the same capacity of detection can also potentially be "reversed" into becoming generators.

Refer to **Figure B-6**.

Another important facet of Legal Sentiment Analysis and Opinion Mining is the locus of granularity.

A semblance of sentiment can be sought at a macro-level. Also, sentiment can be sought at a micro-level, and also at a sub-micro-level, and so on. These can be distinctive at each such level or can be rolled-up or rolled-down. Similarly, detection of opinion can be sought at a macro-level. In addition, an opinion can be sought at a micro-level, and also at a sub-micro-level, and so on. These can be distinctive at each such level or can be rolled-up or rolled-down. This is an important facet of LSAOM, namely that it is unlikely that any given SA or any given OM will be upon a monolith that exhibits one and only one such sentiment or opinion. Instead, the greater likelihood is that sentiment will differ at various levels of expression and opinion will differ at various levels of expression.

Section 4: Additional Considerations and Future Research

As earlier indicated, efforts to undertake Legal Sentiment Analysis and Opinion Mining have historically been performed by human hand and cognition, and only thinly aided in more recent times by the use of computer-based approaches. Advances in Artificial Intelligence (AI) involving especially Natural Language Processing (NLP) and Machine Learning (ML) are increasingly bolstering how automation can systematically perform either or both of Sentiment Analysis and Opinion Mining, all of which is being inexorably carried over into engagement within a legal context for improving LSAOM capabilities. This research paper has examined the evolving infusion of AI into Legal Sentiment Analysis and Opinion Mining and proposed alignment with the Levels of Autonomy (LoA) of AI Legal Reasoning (AILR), plus provided additional insights regarding AI LSAOM in its mechanizations and potential impact to the study of law and the practicing of law.

Artificial Intelligence (AI) based approaches have been increasingly utilized and will undoubtedly have a pronounced impact on how LSAOM is performed and its use in the practice of law, which will inevitably also have an impact upon theories of the law.

Future research is needed to explore in greater detail the manner and means by which AI-enablement will occur in the law along with the potential for both positive and adverse consequences due to LSAOM. Autonomous AILR is likely to materially impact the effort, theory, and practice of Legal Sentiment Analysis and Opinion Mining, including as a minimum playing a notable or possibly even pivotal role in such advancements.

References

1. Alarie, Benjamin, and Anthony Niblett, Albert Yoon (2017). "Regulation by Machine," Volume 24, Journal of Machine Learning Research.

2. Ashley, Kevin, and Karl Branting, Howard Margolis, and Cass Sunstein (2001). "Legal Reasoning and Artificial Intelligence: How Computers 'Think' Like Lawyers," Symposium: Legal Reasoning and Artificial Intelligence, University of Chicago Law School Roundtable.

3. Ashley, Kevin, and Stefanie Bruninghaus (2009). "Automatically Classifying Case Texts and Predicting Outcomes," Volume 17, Number 2, Artificial Intelligence and Law.

4. Atkinson, Katie, and Trevor Bench-Capon, Danushka Bollegala (2020). "Explanation in AI and Law: Past, Present, and Future," Artificial Intelligence.

5. Babu, Nirmal, and Fabeela Rawther (2019). "User Behavior Analysis On Social Media Data Using Sentiment Analysis Or Opinion Mining, Volume 6, Number 6, International Research Journal of Engineering and Technology.

6. Baker, Jamie (2018). "A Legal Research Odyssey: Artificial Intelligence as Disrupter," Law Library Journal.

7. Baum, Lawrence (2009). The Puzzle of Judicial Behavior. University of Michigan Press.

8. Ben-Ari, Daniel, and D., Frish, Y., Lazovski, A., Eldan, U., & Greenbaum, D. (2016). "Artificial Intelligence in the Practice of Law: An Analysis and Proof of Concept Experiment," Volume 23, Number 2, Richmond Journal of Law & Technology.

9. Bench-Capon, and Givoanni Sartor (2003). "A Model of Legal Reasoning with Cases Incorporating Theories and Values," November 2013, Artificial Intelligence.

10. Bose, Rajesh, and Raktim Dey, Sandip Roy (2018). "Analyzing Political Sentiment Using Twitter Data," Volume 107, Smart Innovation, Systems, and Technologies.

11. Braithwaite, John (2002). "Rules and Principles: A Theory of Legal Certainty," Volume 27, Australian Journal of Legal Philosophy.
12. Buchanan, Bruce, and Thomas Headrick (1970). "Some Speculation about Artificial Intelligence and Legal Reasoning," Volume 23, Stanford Law Review.

13. Casey, Anthony, and Anthony Niblett (2016). "Self-Driving Laws," Volume 429, University of Toronto Law Journal.

14. Chagal-Feferkorn, Karni (2019). "Am I An Algorithm or a Product: When Products Liability Should Apply to Algorithmic Decision-Makers," Stanford Law & Policy Review.

15. Chen, C., and Jeffery Chi (2010). "Use Text Mining Approach To Generate The Draft Of Indictment For Prosecutor," Association for Information Systems 14th Pacific Asia Conference on Information Systems.

16. Chen, Daniel (2019). "Machine Learning and the Rule of Law," in Law as Data: Computation, Text, and The Future of Legal Analysis (Michael A. Livermore and Daniel N. Rockmore eds.).

17. Chen, Y., and Y. Liu, W. Ho (2013). "A Text Mining Approach To Assist The General Public In The Retrieval Of Legal Documents," Volume 64, Number 2, Journal of the American Society for Information Science and Technology.

18. Chou, S. (2010). "Text Mining Technique for Chinese Written Judgment of Criminal Case," IEEE Intelligence and Security Informatics Conference, India.

19. Coglianese, Cary, and David Lehr (2017). "Rulemaking by Robot: Administrative Decision Making in the Machine-Learning Era," Volume 105, Georgetown Law Journal.

20. Conrad, J., and F. Schilder (2007). "Opinion Mining In Legal Blogs," Proceedings of the ICAIL 11th International Conference on Artificial Intelligence and Law.

21. D'Amato, Anthony (2010). "Legal Realism Explains Nothing," Working Paper Number 84, Northwestern University School of Law.

22. Do, Hai, and PWC Prasad, Angelika Maag, Abeer Alsadoon (2019). "Deep Learning for Aspect-Based Sentiment Analysis: A Comparative Review," Volume 118, Expert Systems with Application.

23. Dung, Phan (1993). "On the Acceptability of Arguments and its Fundamental Role in Nonmonotonic Reasoning and Logic Programming," Proceedings of the 13th International Joint Conference on Artificial Intelligence.

24. Eliot, Lance (2016). AI Guardian Angels for Deep AI Trustworthiness. LBE Press Publishing.

25. Eliot, Lance (2020). "The Neglected Dualism of Artificial Moral Agency and Artificial Legal Reasoning in AI for Social Good." Harvard University, Harvard Center for Research on Computation and Society, AI for Social Good Conference, July 21, 2020.

26. Eliot, Lance (2020). AI and Legal Reasoning Essentials. LBE Press Publishing.

27. Eliot, Lance (2019). Artificial Intelligence and LegalTech Essentials. LBE Press Publishing.

28. Eliot, Lance (2020). "The Next Era of American Law Amid The Advent of Autonomous AI Legal Reasoning," Cornell University arXiv. https://arxiv.org/abs/2009.11647

29. Eliot, Lance (2020). "An Ontological AI-and-Law Framework for the Autonomous Levels of AI Legal Reasoning," Cornell University arXiv. https://arxiv.org/abs/2008.07328

30. Eliot, Lance (2020). "Turing Test and the Practice of Law: The Role of Autonomous Levels of AI Legal Reasoning," Cornell University arXiv. https://arxiv.org/abs/2008.07743

31. Eliot, Lance (2020). "Multidimensionality of the Legal Singularity: The Role of Autonomous Levels of AI Legal Reasoning," Cornell University arXiv. https://arxiv.org/abs/2008.10575

32. Eliot, Lance (2020). "Authorized and Unauthorized Practices of Law: The Role of Autonomous Levels of AI Legal Reasoning," Cornell University arXiv. https://arxiv.org/abs/2008.09507

33. Eliot, Lance (2020). "An Impact Model of AI on the Principles of Justice," Cornell University arXiv. https://arxiv.org/abs/2008.12615

34. Eliot, Lance (2020). "Robustness and Overcoming Brittleness of AI-Enabled Legal Micro-Directives," Cornell University arXiv. https://arxiv.org/abs/2009.02243

35. Eliot, Lance (2020). "AI and Legal Argumentation," Cornell University arXiv. https://arxiv.org/abs/2009.11180

36. Eliot, Lance (2020). "Legal Judgment Prediction (LJP) Amid the Advent of Autonomous AI Legal Reasoning," Cornell University arXiv. htttps://arxiv.org/abs/2009.14620

37. Feteris, Eveline, and Harm Kloosterhuis (2009). "The Analysis and Evaluation of Legal Argumentation: Approaches from Legal Theory and Argumentation Theory," Volume 16, Studies in Logic, Grammar and Rhetoric.

38. Gamal, Donia, and Marco Alfonse, El-Sayed M. El-Horbaty, Abdel-Badeeh M. Salem (2018). "A Comparative Study On Opinion Mining Algorithms Of Social Media Statuses," IEEE Proceedings of the Eighth International Conference on Intelligent Computing and Information Systems.

39. Gardner, Anne (1987). Artificial Intelligence and Legal Reasoning. MIT Press.

40. Genesereth, Michael (2009). "Computational Law: The Cop in the Backseat," Stanford Center for Legal Informatics, Stanford University.

41. Gobin, A. (2019). "Mind Reader: How Emotions Taint Jury Selection," University of Central Florida Department of Legal Studies.

42. Hage, Jaap (2000). "Dialectical Models in Artificial Intelligence and Law," Artificial Intelligence and Law.

43. Hall, Mark, and Ronald Wright (2006). "Systematic Content Analysis of Judicial Opinions," Volume 96, Issue 1, California Law Review.

44. Harbert, T. (2013). "The Law Machine," Volume 50, Issue 11, IEEE Spectrum.

45. Hemmation, Fatemeh, and Mohammad Sohrabi (2019). "A Survey On Classification Techniques For Opinion Mining And Sentiment Analysis," Volume 52, Artificial Intelligence Review.

46. Holmes, Oliver Wendell (1897). "The Path of the Law," Harvard Law Review.

47. Huhn, Wilson (2003). "The Stages of Legal Reasoning: Formalism, Analogy, and Realism," Volume 48, Villanova Law Review.

48. Huppes-Cluysenaer, Liesbeth, and Nuno M.M.S Coelho (2018). "The Debate About Emotion in Law and Politics," In" Aristotle on Emotions in Law and Politics.

49. Jagdale, Rajkumar, and Vishal Shirsat, Sachin Deshmukh (2018). "Sentiment Analysis On Product Reviews Using Machine Learning Techniques," Volume 768, Advances in Intelligent Systems and Computing.

50. Jasti, Sireesha, and Tummala Mahalkshmi (2018). "A Review On Sentiment Analysis Of Opinion Mining," Volume 768, Advances in Intelligent Systems and Computing.

51. Joshi, S., and P. Deshpande, T. Hampp (2011). "Improving The Efficiency Of Legal E-Discovery Services Using Test Mining Techniques," IEEE Proceedings of the 2011 Annual SRII Global Conference.

52. Kaplow, Louis (1992). "Rules Versus Standards: An Economic Analysis," Volume 42, Duke Law Journal.

53. Landsman, S., and R.F. Rakos (1994). "A Preliminary Inquiry Into The Effect Of Potentially Biasing Information On Judges And Jurors In Civil Litigation," Volume 12, Behavioral Sciences and the Law.

54. Liu, Y., and Yen-Liang Chen, W. Ho (2015). "Predicting Associated Statutes for Legal Problems," Volume 51, Number 1, Inform Process Management.

55. Liu, Yi-Hung, and Yen-Liang Chen (2017). "A Two-Phase Sentiment Analysis Approach For Judgment Prediction," Journal of Information Science.

56. Llewellyn, Karl (1950). "Remarks on the Theory of Appellate Decision and the Rules or Canons About How Statutes Are to Be Construed," Volume 3, Number 4, Vanderbilt Law Review.

57. MacCormick, Neil (1978). Legal Reasoning and Legal Theory.

58. McCarty, L. (1995)." An implementation of Eisner v. Macomber," Proceedings of the 5th International Conference on Artificial Intelligence and Law.

59. McCarty, Thorne (1977). "Reflections on TAXMAN: An Experiment in Artificial Intelligence and Legal Reasoning," January 1977, Harvard Law Review.

60. McGinnis, John, and Russell G. Pearce (2014). "The Great Disruption: How Machine Intelligence Will Transform the Role of Lawyers in the Delivery of Legal Services," Volume 82, Number 6, Fordham Law Review.

61. McGinnis, John, and Steven Wasick (2015). "Law's Algorithm," Volume 66, Florida Law Review.

62. Mnookin, Robert, and Lewis Kornhauser (1979). "Bargaining in the Shadow of the Law," Volume 88, Number 5, April 1979, The Yale Law Review.

63. Norambuena, Brian, and Fuentes Lettura, Meneses Villegas (2019). "Sentiment Analysis And Opinion Mining Applied To Scientific Paper Reviews," Volume 23, Number 1, Intelligent Data Analysis.

64. Prakken, Henry (1995). "From Logic to Dialectics in Legal Argument," Proceedings of the 5th International Conference on Artificial Intelligence and Law.

65. Reinbold, Patric (2020). "Taking Artificial Intelligence Beyond the Turing Test," Volume 20, Wisconsin Law Review.

66. Remus, Dana, and Frank Levy, "Can Robots be Lawyers? Computers, Robots, and the Practice of Law," Volume 30, Georgetown Journal of Legal Ethics.

67. Rich, Michael (2016). "Machine Learning, Automated Suspicion Algorithms, and the Fourth Amendment," Volume 164, University of Pennsylvania Law Review.

68. Rissland, Edwina (1990). "Artificial Intelligence and Law: Stepping Stones to a Model of Legal Reasoning," Yale Law Journal.

69. SAE (2018). Taxonomy and Definitions for Terms Related to Driving Automation Systems for On-Road Motor Vehicles, J3016-201806, SAE International.

70. Sunstein, Cass (2001). "Of Artificial Intelligence and Legal Reasoning," University of Chicago Law School, Working Papers.

71. Sunstein, Cass, and Kevin Ashley, Karl Branting, Howard Margolis (2001). "Legal Reasoning and Artificial Intelligence: How Computers 'Think' Like Lawyers," Symposium: Legal Reasoning and Artificial Intelligence, University of Chicago Law School Roundtable.

72. Surden, Harry (2014). "Machine Learning and Law," Washington Law Review.

73. Surden, Harry (2019). "Artificial Intelligence and Law: An Overview," Summer 2019, Georgia State University Law Review.

74. Susskind, Richard (2019). Online Courts and the Future of Justice. Oxford University Press.

75. Terris, Callie K. (2016). "Jury Bias: Myth and Reality," Volume 3, Politics Summer Fellows.

76. Verheij, B. (2001). "Legal Decision Making as Dialectical Theory Construction with Argumentation Schemes," Proceedings of the 8th International Conference of Artificial Intelligence and Law.

77. Vidmar, Neil (2011). "The Psychology of Trial Judging," Volume 20, Current Directions in Psychological Science.
78. Volokh, Eugne (2019). "Chief Justice Robots," Volume 68, Duke Law Journal.
79. Walker, L.E., and D. Shapiro, S. Akl (2020). "Jury Selection and Psychology of the Trial," Introduction to Forensic Psychology. Springer.
80. Waltl, Bernhard, and Roland Vogl (2018). "Explainable Artificial Intelligence: The New Frontier in Legal Informatics," February 2018, Jusletter IT 22, Stanford Center for Legal Informatics, Stanford University.
81. Wolfram, Stephen (2018). "Computational Law, Symbolic Discourse, and the AI Constitution," in Data-Driven Law: Data Analytics and the New Legal Services (Edward J. Walters ed.).
82. Wyner, A, and R. Mochales-Palau, M. Moens (2010). "Approaches To Text Mining Arguments From Legal Cases. Lecture Notes in Computer Science.
83. Xu, Nuo, and Pinghui Wang, Long Chen, Li Pan, Xiaoyan Wang, Junzhou Zhao (2020). "Distinguish Confusing Law Articles for Legal Judgment Prediction," Proceedings of the 58th Annual Meeting of the Association for Computational Linguistics.
84. Zhong, Haoxi, and Zhipeng Guo, Cunchao Tu, Chaojun Xiao, Zhiyuan Liu, Maosong Sun (2017). "Legal Judgment Prediction via Topological Learning," Proceedings of the 2018 Conference on Empirical Methods in Natural Language Processing.
85. Zuhe, Li (2019). "A Survey On Sentiment Analysis And Opinion Mining For Social Multimedia," Volume 78, Multimedia Tools and Applications

---

Note: *For supplemental materials depicting the aspects discussed in this chapter, refer to Appendix B, which contains various augmented diagrams, charts, and additional related facets of relevance.*

CHAPTER 10

ANTICIPATING THE FOURTH ERA OF THE LAW

Abstract

Legal scholars have postulated that there have been three eras of American law to-date, consisting in chronological order of the initial Age of Discovery, the Age of Faith, and then the Age of Anxiety. An open question that has received erudite attention in legal studies is what the next era, the fourth era, might consist of, and for which various proposals exist including examples such as the Age of Consent, the Age of Information, etc. There is no consensus in the literature as yet on what the fourth era is, and nor whether the fourth era has already begun or will instead emerge in the future. This paper examines the potential era-elucidating impacts amid the advent of autonomous Artificial Intelligence Legal Reasoning (AILR), entailing whether such AILR will be an element of a fourth era or a driver of a fourth, fifth, or perhaps the sixth era of American law. Also, a set of meta-characteristics about the means of identifying a legal era changeover are introduced, along with an innovative discussion of the role entailing legal formalism versus legal realism in the emergence of the American law eras.

Section 1: Background on Eras of American Law

In Section 1 of this paper, the eras of American law are introduced and addressed. Doing so establishes the groundwork for the subsequent sections. Section 2 introduces the Levels of Autonomy (LoA) of AI Legal Reasoning (AILR), which is instrumental in the discussions undertaken in Section 3. Section 3 provides an indication of the eras of American law as it applies to the LoA AILR. Section 4 provides various additional considerations and recommendations.

This paper then consists of these four sections:

- Section 1: Background on Eras of American Law
- Section 2: Autonomous Levels of AI Legal Reasoning
- Section 3: Next Eras and Autonomous AI Legal Reasoning
- Section 4: Additional Considerations and Future Research

1.2 Three Eras of American Law

The history of American law has been extensively studied and analyzed (see for example [29] [34] [60]). In the 1970s, legal scholar Grant Gilmore [32] proposed that the history of American law could be stratified into three distinct eras.

The first era was coined as the *Age of Discovery* and occurred from the 1800s until the Civil War, during which there was an initial formulation of a legal edifice for America. This was based to a great extent on the reuse of English common law, inexorably being shorn into a stylized and substantive instantiation that would become uniquely American law.

The second era lasted from the Civil War until WWI and was named as the *Age of Faith*. During this era, there was a purported attempt to perceive and shape the law as a form of rigorous science, out of which there were presumably legal truths that could axiomatically be discovered and derived. It was said to be a time when one ought to have utter faith that the law was right and just since it was essentially scientifically provable as such.

The third era arose following WWI and is referred to as the *Age of Anxiety*, and, when Gilmore wrote about these eras, he indicated that the Age of Anxiety was still underway. The anxiety being spurred as a realization that the faith in legal truths was mislaid and could no longer adequately serve as a foundational structure for understanding and maturation of the field of law.

As will be later discussed in this paper, there have been subsequent suggestions that we are either now in a fourth era or perhaps on the verge of such [7] [44], and thus it could be that we are already past the third era and into the fourth era. On the other hand, there does not appear to be any preponderance of agreement or consensus in the legal literature that a fourth era is indeed already taking place. Ergo, for purposes of this discussion herein, we assume that we are still in the third era and that the nature, timing, and impacts of a fourth era are not as yet collectively ascertained and nor cast into stone, as it were.

It is instructive to take a somewhat closer look at the considered prevailing three eras, doing so via the analyses and interpretations that have been made by legal scholars subsequent to Gilmore's groundbreaking book. On a related note, it can be said that the book was groundbreaking, though it is also notable to emphasize that Gilmore's work was based on the earlier efforts of Llewellyn [39]. Thus, it is significant and appropriate to saliently point out that Gilmore too indicates that his articulation of the three eras was based on the earlier work of Karl Llewellyn (from his respective book of 1960). Throughout the discussion herein, the primary reference for the three eras is based on Gilmore, though at the same time it is rightfully noteworthy to point out the earlier work by Llewellyn.

Consider the analysis by Webster [59] concerning Gilmore's eras. Per Webster: "The initial Age of Discovery, lasting from the early nineteenth century to the Civil War, is said to have been a golden age, likened perhaps somewhat excessively-to the period of late sixteenth century English theater or late eighteenth century Viennese music. It was an age when a society's best minds (for no particular reason) naturally gravitated towards a particular endeavor: the creation of an American legal system."

Especially well-known historical figures and legal jurists such as John Marshall, Joseph Story, and Lemuel Shaw are representative of this first era.

The second era was prompted by a slew of factors, as Webster [59] states: "As is often the case, golden ages flourish briefly and then disappear as new political, social, and economic realities overtake them. Such was the case with American law at about the time of the Civil War. The fluidity, innovation and imagination which had created the new system of American law were replaced by a far more formalistic system emphasizing stability, certainty, and predictability."

This shift towards greater formalism has been depicted as an assumption that the law could be cast as a type of science and therefore embody the corresponding rigors, as per Webster [59], some believed that the law was "capable of being synthesized or reduced to basic truths or principles which, like laws of physics or chemistry, could be used as the criteria for legal decision-making." This has been coined as the era of faith, meaning having a kind of righteousness faith in the law and believing without reservation that it was only a matter of scientifically discovering and codifying irrefutable and immutable laws.

Bobbitt [7] points out that the "Age of Faith lasted from the Civil War through World War I, and was notable for the Olympian status it accorded law and its demigods, including Christopher Columbus Langdell and Oliver Wendell Holmes, Jr. Langdell believed that law was a science from which scientific truths could be derived, and even the skeptical Holmes, according to Gilmore, refined and judicialized Langdellianism." Webster equally points out that the law as science was replaced or desired to be replaced with an indication that law is a social science. There is some ongoing debate about whether the third era is therefore a complete rejection and departure of the second era, or perhaps a refinement, demonstrably so, and a shift toward a greater realism about the law.

This is how Gilmore expresses the semblance of the third era [32]:

"As lawyers we will do well to be on our guard against any suggestion that, through law, our society can be reformed, purified or saved. The function of law, in a society like our own, is altogether more modest and less apocalyptic. It is to provide a mechanism for the settlement of disputes in the light of broadly conceived principles on whose soundness, it must be assumed, there is a general consensus among us. If the assumption is wrong, if there is no consensus, then we are headed for war, civil strife, and revolution, and the orderly administration of justice will become an irrelevant, nostalgic whimsy until the social fabric has been stitched together again and a new consensus has emerged."

Subsequent to Gilmore's book there have been extensive and ongoing deliberations about the naming used to reflect the three eras.

As pointed out by Webster [59]: "His book runs the risk of being criticized for affixing catchwords to time periods for which other and perhaps better names have already been given-liberalism, activism, and progressivism are just a few." In whatever manner the eras might be so coined, there seems little doubt about the importance of pointing out the eras per se and engaging in an overarching discussion about the evolution of America law, per Bobbitt [7]: "Gilmore's lectures satisfied and mesmerized their audience, and they were soon fashioned into a book, also titled *The Ages of American Law*, which became a foundational text for introducing law students to American legal studies."

In brief, the three eras as postulated seem to have become relatively accepted by the legal literature. Undoubtedly, arguments can be made as to whether these are the "right" eras and that perhaps the American law timeline period can be sliced in a different fashion. For example, suppose there have been ten eras, brandishing this notion as a provocative point of conjecture, or that there has only been one era and it has lasted since the beginnings of American law. Such provocateur outside-the-box considerations are not in the scope of this paper and it is taken at face value that there have been three eras and those three eras are reasonably stated and depicted by Gilmore and others that have similarly allied with the generally accepted stratification.

1.1 Important Influence of Legal Realism

Another notable perspective on the three eras is that they are all interconnected by an at-times hidden underlying variable. The postulated crux of the three eras has to do with the philosophical milieu known as legal formalism, which, in short, legal formalism can be defined as [20]: "A theory that legal rules stand separate from other social and political institutions. According to this theory, once lawmakers produce rules, judges apply them to the facts of a case without regard to social interests and public policy." In contrast, there is legal realism, defined as [20]: "A theory that all law derives from prevailing social interests and public policy. According to this theory, judges consider not only abstract rules, but also social interests and public policy when deciding a case."

In the prevailing implications of the three eras, the first era was a mild form of legal formalism but that was grappling with establishing the new American law and thus only modestly embraced such formalism precepts, while the second era was a dramatic extension and gravitation toward legal formalism, and then the third era a kind of retreat from legal formalism in place of alternatively embracing legal realism.

Per Webster [59]: "Had those early legal figures instead adopted a formalistic approach to the problem of creating a new law for America, they would have sought to adopt the far more static and fixed principles of English common law and the English legal system. To an extent, of course, this happened. But for reasons relating, in part, to political and social hostility towards the utilization of an English system, English common law and, more importantly, the English approach to law were not simply imported to these shores without question. Because those early lawyers were not formalists, an innovative, creative and uniquely American system arose." And, as already cited in the prior subsection [59], the second era was a flourishing of legal formalism: "The fluidity, innovation and imagination which had created the new system of American law were replaced by a far more formalistic system emphasizing stability, certainty, and predictability."

And then, the third era, as described accordingly by Bobbitt [7]: "After that came the Age of Anxiety, Gilmore's own era, an Age when legal realism gnawed through the core assumptions of the Age of Faith and the nation groped unsuccessfully for new creeds to replace them."

The legal profession and legal scholars continue to debate the merits of legal formalism versus legal realism. Perhaps one of the most infamous euphemisms about the law is that supposedly a good lawyer knows the law, while a great lawyer knows the judge. In this paper, we do not address this at times acrimonious discourse and simply acknowledge that these matters are still being examined and assessed by ongoing legal research. In any case, if one is seeking a measure or barometer toward identifying the pattern underlying the eras, it could be reasonably argued that the degree of legal formalism has been crucial if not a predominant factor at play. This will be further explored in Section 3.

The next section of this paper introduces the autonomous levels of AI Legal Reasoning, doing so to then aid Section 3. Section 3 explores how the eras of American law and the elucidations of the fourth era can be explored in light of the autonomous levels of AI Legal Reasoning. Section 4 provides some conclusionary remarks and also an indication of recommended future research.

Section 2: Autonomous Levels of AI Legal Reasoning

In this section, a framework for the autonomous levels of AI Legal Reasoning is summarized and is based on the research described in detail in Eliot [20].

These autonomous levels will be portrayed in a grid that aligns with key elements of autonomy and as matched to AI Legal Reasoning. Providing this context will be useful to the later sections of this paper and will be utilized accordingly.

The autonomous levels of AI Legal Reasoning are as follows:
Level 0: No Automation for AI Legal Reasoning
Level 1: Simple Assistance Automation for AI Legal Reasoning
Level 2: Advanced Assistance Automation for AI Legal Reasoning
Level 3: Semi-Autonomous Automation for AI Legal Reasoning
Level 4: Domain Autonomous for AI Legal Reasoning
Level 5: Fully Autonomous for AI Legal Reasoning
Level 6: Superhuman Autonomous for AI Legal Reasoning

2.1 Details of the LoA AILR

See **Figure A-1** for an overview chart showcasing the autonomous levels of AI Legal Reasoning as via columns denoting each of the respective levels.

See **Figure A-2** for an overview chart similar to Figure A-1 which alternatively is indicative of the autonomous levels of AI Legal Reasoning via the rows as depicting the respective levels (this is simply a reformatting of Figure A-1, doing so to aid in illuminating this variant perspective, but does not introduce any new facets or alterations from the contents as already shown in Figure A-1).

2.1.1 Level 0: No Automation for AI Legal Reasoning

Level 0 is considered the no automation level. Legal reasoning is carried out via manual methods and principally occurs via paper-based methods.

This level is allowed some leeway in that the use of say a simple handheld calculator or perhaps the use of a fax machine could be allowed or included within this Level 0, though strictly speaking it could be said that any form whatsoever of automation is to be excluded from this level.

2.1.2 Level 1: Simple Assistance Automation for AI Legal Reasoning

Level 1 consists of simple assistance automation for AI legal reasoning.

Examples of this category encompassing simple automation would include the use of everyday computer-based word processing, the use of everyday computer-based spreadsheets, the access to online legal documents that are stored and retrieved electronically, and so on.

By-and-large, today's use of computers for legal activities is predominantly within Level 1. It is assumed and expected that over time, the pervasiveness of automation will continue to deepen and widen, and eventually lead to legal activities being supported and within Level 2, rather than Level 1.

2.1.3 Level 2: Advanced Assistance Automation for AI Legal Reasoning

Level 2 consists of advanced assistance automation for AI legal reasoning.

Examples of this notion encompassing advanced automation would include the use of query-style Natural Language Processing (NLP), Machine Learning (ML) for case predictions, and so on.

Gradually, over time, it is expected that computer-based systems for legal activities will increasingly make use of advanced automation. Law industry technology that was once at a Level 1 will likely be refined, upgraded, or expanded to include advanced capabilities, and thus be reclassified into Level 2.

2.1.4 Level 3: Semi-Autonomous Automation for AI Legal Reasoning

Level 3 consists of semi-autonomous automation for AI legal reasoning.

Examples of this notion encompassing semi-autonomous automation would include the use of Knowledge-Based Systems (KBS) for legal reasoning, the use of Machine Learning and Deep Learning (ML/DL) for legal reasoning, and so on.

Today, such automation tends to exist in research efforts or prototypes and pilot systems, along with some commercial legal technology that has been infusing these capabilities too.

2.1.5 Level 4: Domain Autonomous for AI Legal Reasoning

Level 4 consists of domain autonomous computer-based systems for AI legal reasoning.

This level reuses the conceptual notion of Operational Design Domains (ODDs) as utilized in the autonomous vehicles and self-driving cars levels of autonomy, though in this use case it is being applied to the legal domain [15] [17] [18]. Essentially, this entails any AI legal reasoning capacities that can operate autonomously, entirely so, but that is only able to do so in some limited or constrained legal domain.

2.1.6 Level 5: Fully Autonomous for AI Legal Reasoning

Level 5 consists of fully autonomous computer-based systems for AI legal reasoning.

In a sense, Level 5 is the superset of Level 4 in terms of encompassing all possible domains as per however so defined ultimately for Level 4. The only constraint, as it were, consists of the facet that the Level 4 and Level 5 are concerning human intelligence and the capacities thereof. This is an important emphasis due to attempting to distinguish Level 5 from Level 6 (as will be discussed in the next subsection)

It is conceivable that someday there might be a fully autonomous AI legal reasoning capability, one that encompasses all of the law in all foreseeable ways, though this is quite a tall order and remains quite aspirational without a clear cut path of how this might one day be achieved. Nonetheless, it seems to be within the extended realm of possibilities, which is worthwhile to mention in relative terms to Level 6.

2.1.7 Level 6: Superhuman Autonomous for AI Legal Reasoning

Level 6 consists of superhuman autonomous computer-based systems for AI legal reasoning.

In a sense, Level 6 is the entirety of Level 5 and adds something beyond that in a manner that is currently ill-defined and perhaps (some would argue) as yet unknowable. The notion is that AI might ultimately exceed human intelligence, rising to become superhuman, and if so, we do not yet have any viable indication of what that superhuman intelligence consists of and nor what kind of thinking it would somehow be able to undertake.

Whether a Level 6 is ever attainable is reliant upon whether superhuman AI is ever attainable, and thus, at this time, this stands as a placeholder for that which might never occur. In any case, having such a placeholder provides a semblance of completeness, doing so without necessarily legitimatizing that superhuman AI is going to be achieved or not. No such claim or dispute is undertaken within this framework.

Section 3: Next Eras and Autonomous AI Legal Reasoning

As outlined in Section 1, make the assumption that there are three eras of American law and that they have been appropriately and indubitably identified and correctly typified.

See **Figure B-1** for a visual illustration of the three eras.

The logical questions that naturally flow from those three presumed eras consists of:

- What will be the fourth era?
- When will the fourth era begin (or has it already)?
- What is the basis for asserting there will be a fourth era?
- How will the fourth era be differentiated from the prior eras?
- To what degree does legal formalism partake in a fourth era?
- And so on.

There have been various proffered proposals about a fourth era. None of the postulated fourth eras has seemed to gain traction, as yet. This would appear to leave open for the time being the possibility of considering the nature and significance of a fourth era. Presumably, we are either not in a fourth era, or we might be in a fourth era and are generally unaware that we are.

For those that might believe it folly or valueless to speculate about a fourth era, this kind of matter is actually of both a notable theoretical and practical significance. By being able to anticipate the fourth era, we might collectively as a society and especially within the legal field be able to prepare accordingly for what is to come, along with the added potential of shaping or altering course if the emergent fourth era seems untoward or otherwise undesirable. For legal practitioners, knowing what the fourth era constitutes could aid significantly in their training and attention, and be a crucial harbinger of what the practice of law is coming to possibly become.

Consider two especially noted propositions for the possible fourth era, which are respectively known as the Age of Consent [7] and the other referred to as the Age of Information [44]. Both were proposed at approximately the same time and of relatively recent note (doing so around the year 2015). A proposed fourth era coined as the Age of Consent was postulated by Bobbitt [7]: "As we enter the Age of Consent, the era of a new, already emerging constitutional order that puts the maximization of individual choice at the pinnacle of public policy, it would be well to appreciate the structuring role for choice that American law has always provided. Far from obviating the need for our consciences, our laws structure a necessary role for them. That highly structured role is reflected in representative government (rather than plebiscites), in the composition of juries (rather than mobs, even when they form over the Internet rather than outside a jail), in the belief in liberal education (rather than indoctrination), in the responsibility of judges and lawyers to shape as well as defend the Constitution that gives them unique power. Those structures will be strictly scrutinized in this era, as they should be. How else will these habits find defenders unless they are convinced, after rigorous examination, that this way of structuring choice is worthy of defense?"

Another proposed fourth era is called the Age of Information, postulated by McGinnis and Wasick [44]: "Today we inhabit the Age of Information and this age is creating a new synthesis for the structure of law. If the Age of Faith required formalism to regulate the legal world, the Age of Information, like the Age of Anxiety, accepts that many factors may influence the law. But the Age of Information, like the Age of Faith, has greater confidence in creating legal clarity. Both the Age of Information and the Age of Faith have their gods of legal order, but if the god of the Age of Faith was formalism, today's god is computable realism. The rise of computable standards and dynamic rules will be this age's contribution to legal expression."

See **Figure B-2** for a visual illustration indicative of the fourth eras postulated.

An intriguing and potentially co-existent matter entails the advent of autonomous AI Legal Reasoning (AILR), as outlined generally in the prior section of this paper. Consider whether the emergence of autonomous AILR will be an element of the fourth era, or whether it is conceivable that autonomous AILR would be more than merely an ingredient and essentially constitute the namesake of a fourth era.

In the Age of Information, there is ample indication of the importance of AI in the law and how it will be a considered element. The Age of Consent does not directly tie the role of AI and the law into its depiction, though it is possible to discern underlying aspects that could be construed within the framework indicated. An additional argument to be made is that perhaps, if we are already in a fourth era, it could be that the rise of autonomous AILR might be a noteworthy contributor to the fourth era and ultimately be the forerunner or instigator of a fifth era.

See **Figure B-3** for a visual illustration of these possibilities.

Aligning the Section 2 indication of the levels of autonomy for AI Legal Reasoning, it is instructive to consider the impacts per each of the levels thereof.

See **Figure B-4** for an indication of the LoA AILR with the added indication accordingly.

In brief, the levels and the alignment to the eras consist of:

- Level 0: In Eras 1, 2, 3+
- Level 1: In Eras 3, (4+)
- Level 2: In Eras 3, (4+)
- Level 3: In Eras 3, {4+)
- Level 4: Shape Eras 4 or 5
- Level 5: Define Eras 4 or 5
- Level 6: Be Eras 5 or 6

Here is an overview explanation associated with these stated possibilities.

At Level 0, the lack of computer-based automation was certainly the case during the first era, and during the second era too. During the third era, there are still ongoing examples of the lack of computer-based automation being utilized. It is presumably the case that the law will always be amenable to the nonuse of automation, thus the indication of "3+" meaning from the third era onward. An outstretched case can be made that there will be a future era during which computer-based automation will be so pervasive and so crucial that the law cannot exist or be undertaken without it, but this seems an outlier consideration at this time.

At Level 1, the advent of simple computer-based automation emerged in the third era and continues to this day. Presumably, this will continue into the fourth era and beyond. It would though seem that Level 1 is substantively lacking in the sense that it would not drive or materially spark a shift into a fourth era and thus the "(4+)" is used to indicate as such.

At Level 2, the advent of advanced computer-based automation also emerged in the third era and continues to this day. Presumably, this will continue into the fourth era and beyond. It would though seem that Level 2 is substantively lacking in the sense that it would not drive or materially spark a shift into a fourth era and thus the "(4+)" is used to indicate as such.

At Level 3, the advent of semi-autonomous AILR automation is gradually appearing in the prevailing third era and continues to this day. Presumably, this will continue into the fourth era and beyond. It would though seem that Level 3 is substantively lacking in the sense that it would not drive or materially spark a shift into a fourth era, despite whatever otherwise innovative prototypes or tryouts are launched, and thus the "(4+)" is used to indicate as such.

If Level 4 can be achieved, this would seem to be a notable basis for shaping or possibly even instigating the next era, whether it be the fourth era or a fifth era.

If Level 5 can be achieved, this would seem to be of such a transformative facet that it would dramatically define a fourth or fifth era.

If Level 6 can be achieved, this would be an even more momentous transformative facet, perhaps driving a fifth or sixth era.

3.1 Meta-Characteristics of Eras

This subsection introduces a strawman set of meta-characteristics that might be used to aid in delineating and identify the eras.

These five core facets are proffered:

- Distinctive
- Substantive
- Observable
- Paradigmatic
- Explainable

See **Figure B-5** for a visual illustration of these core facets.

Consider a brief explanation for each of the meta-characteristics, covering each of the key foundations for the application of each one:

- Distinctiveness entails that an era, regardless of sequence and whether already existent or still inexistent, showcases boundaries that can be distinctly identified, allowing us to realize that the era exists. Without distinctiveness, an alleged era would be indistinguishable presumably from the prior era, being no more than a blur or presumed extension of that era, and therefore could not demonstrably and verifiably be claimed as an era.

- Substantive refers to the era being of a convincing magnitude and substance to warrant the era moniker. If a proposed era was distinctive but without sufficient import or degree, it would be readily arguable whether it truly standalone as an era or might be a momentary aberration in the existing prevailing era.

- Observable refers to the era being detectible, such that if there is no means to discern that the era exists, it would be presumably imaginary and thusly suspect to being counted as real or notable.

- Paradigmatic refers to the aspect that an era would presumably need to fit within the paradigm associated with what eras are contended to be composed of. This is not to suggest that an era might breakaway from the existent paradigm, which certainly could be the case, though generally it is assumed that the collectively accepted paradigm is sufficient (obviously, a new paradigm is always worthy of consideration).

- Finally, it is suggested that an era would need to be explainable, which involves being able to provide a rationale and explication of why an era is thought to exist. This is not an especially necessary condition, since it is conceivable that an era exists and has resisted being naturally explained, but nonetheless it can be argued that without a sufficient explanation for the era it is unlikely to gain consensus for acknowledging its existence and substance.

The meta-characteristics are not numbered since to do so might imply prioritization or ranking. They are each of their own merit. In addition, they are a collective set, without which any individual one would be less capable and certainly lacking in robustness to indicate the entire arch or form of an era.

3.2 Legal Formalism As Era Triggering Mechanism

In this subsection, further discussion about the role of legal formalism is undertaken.

As mentioned in Section 1, there are assertions that legal formalism is at the underpinning of the three eras. See **Figure B-6** for a visual illustration of the legal formalism underpinning facets.

Consider this proffered explanation of the legal formalism underlaying role in the eras matters:

- It has been speculated that legal formalism began with an initial and yet somewhat distracted driving force in the making of Era 1, and thus on a spectrum of legal formalism ranging from none to some maximal amount, there is an arrow shown in Figure B-6 for Era 1 indicating this forward movement in the direction towards greater adoption of legal formalism during the first era.

- In the second era, it has been speculated in the literature that legal formalism took an even greater dominance, and thus in Figure B-6 for Era 2 there is an additional arrow further extending the legal formalism on the spectrum provided.
- For the third era, it has been speculated that legal formalism encountered retreatment, giving way to legal realism. As such, the arrow of legal formalism for Era 3 in Figure B-6 is shown beneath the earlier two and indicative of a lessening on the legal formalism spectrum.

- Regarding a fourth era, if the breakpoints or triggering mechanism that demarks the eras is indeed the legal formalism factor, presumably a divergent rise or lessening of legal formalism might be an earmark for the fourth era. This is not to assert that legal formalism is a cause-and-effect of the eras, which it might be, or it might be an indicator that correlates thereto, and thus this should be interpreted cautiously. In any case, if there was a substantive boost to legal formalism, perhaps this would be a sign or signal of a revival and might necessitate ascertaining whether a new era has emerged (see Figure B-6, Era 4). Likewise, if there was a substantive lessening of legal formalism, perhaps this would be a sign or signal of the obviating of legal formalism and might necessitate ascertaining whether a new era has emerged (see Figure B-6, Era 4).

Note that this depiction is merely an invigorating means to conceptualize the American law era shifts, and not intended to be a prescriptive or otherwise determinative indicator regarding the eras.

Section 4: Additional Considerations and Future Research

As earlier indicated, legal scholars have postulated that three eras of American law have occurred to-date, consisting in chronological order of the initial Age of Discovery, the Age of Faith, and then the Age of Anxiety. Though there appears to be substantive consensus and acceptance of the three eras, there is the possibility that some other means of stratifying the history of American law could provide a new set of eras.

In any case, assuming that the three eras are the prevailing viewpoint, the open question of what is the fourth era remains available for ongoing discussion and debate. There is no consensus in the literature as yet on what the fourth era is, and nor whether the fourth era has already begun or will instead emerge in the future.

This paper has examined the potential impacts due to the advent of autonomous Artificial Intelligence Legal Reasoning (AILR) on the question of the next era, including whether such AILR will be an element of a fourth era or a driver of a fourth, fifth, or perhaps sixth era of American law.

Also, a set of meta-characteristics about the means of identifying a legal era changeover have been introduced, along with an innovative discussion of the role entailing legal formalism versus legal realism in the emergence of the American law eras.

Future research is needed to explore in greater detail the manner and means by which AI-enablement will occur in the law along with the potential for both positive and adverse consequences. Autonomous AILR is likely to materially impact the eras of American law, including as a minimum playing a notable or potentially pivotal role in the next era(s), and having the possibility of shaping and instigating future eras altogether.

References

1. Alarie, Benjamin, and Anthony Niblett, Albert Yoon (2017). "Regulation by Machine," Volume 24, Journal of Machine Learning Research.

2. Ashley, Kevin, and Karl Branting, Howard Margolis, and Cass Sunstein (2001). "Legal Reasoning and Artificial Intelligence: How Computers 'Think' Like Lawyers," Symposium: Legal Reasoning and Artificial Intelligence, University of Chicago Law School Roundtable.
3. Atkinson, Katie, and Pietro Baroni, Massimiliano Giacomin, Anthony Hunter, Henry Prakken, Chris Reed, Guillermo Simari, Matthias Thimm, Serena Villata (2017). "Toward Artificial Argumentation," AAAI AI Magazine.

4. Baker, Jamie (2018). "A Legal Research Odyssey: Artificial Intelligence as Disrupter," Law Library Journal.

5. Ben-Ari, Daniel, and D., Frish, Y., Lazovski, A., Eldan, U., & Greenbaum, D. (2016). "Artificial Intelligence in the Practice of Law: An Analysis and Proof of Concept Experiment," Volume 23, Number 2, Richmond Journal of Law & Technology.

6. Bench-Capon, and Givoanni Sartor (2003). "A Model of Legal Reasoning with Cases Incorporating Theories and Values," November 2013, Artificial Intelligence.

7. Bobbitt, Philip (2014). "The Age of Consent," Volume 123, Number 7, The Yale Law Journal.

8. Braithwaite, John (2002). "Rules and Principles: A Theory of Legal Certainty," Volume 27, Australian Journal of Legal Philosophy.

9. Buchanan, Bruce, and Thomas Headrick (1970). "Some Speculation about Artificial Intelligence and Legal Reasoning," Volume 23, Stanford Law Review.

10. Casey, Anthony, and Anthony Niblett (2016). "Self-Driving Laws," Volume 429, University of Toronto Law Journal.

11. Chagal-Feferkorn, Karni (2019). "Am I An Algorithm or a Product: When Products Liability Should Apply to Algorithmic Decision-Makers," Stanford Law & Policy Review.

12. Chen, Daniel (2019). "Machine Learning and the Rule of Law," in Law as Data: Computation, Text, and The Future of Legal Analysis (Michael A. Livermore and Daniel N. Rockmore eds.).

13. Coglianese, Cary, and David Lehr (2017). "Rulemaking by Robot: Administrative Decision Making in the Machine-Learning Era," Volume 105, Georgetown Law Journal.

14. Dung, Phan (1993). "On the Acceptability of Arguments and its Fundamental Role in Nonmonotonic Reasoning and Logic Programming," Proceedings of the 13th International Joint Conference on Artificial Intelligence.

15. Eliot, Lance (2016). AI Guardian Angels for Deep AI Trustworthiness. LBE Press Publishing.

16. Eliot, Lance (2020). "The Neglected Dualism of Artificial Moral Agency and Artificial Legal Reasoning in AI for Social Good." Harvard University, Harvard Center for Research on Computation and Society, AI for Social Good Conference, July 21, 2020.

17. Eliot, Lance (2020). AI and Legal Reasoning Essentials. LBE Press Publishing.

18. Eliot, Lance (2019). Artificial Intelligence and LegalTech Essentials. LBE Press Publishing.

19. Eliot, Lance (2020). "FutureLaw 2020 Showcases How Tech is Transforming The Law, Including the Impacts of AI," April 16, 2020, Forbes.

20. Eliot, Lance (2020). "An Ontological AI-and-Law Framework for the Autonomous Levels of AI Legal Reasoning," Cornell University arXiv. https://arxiv.org/abs/2008.07328

21. Eliot, Lance (2020). "Turing Test and the Practice of Law: The Role of Autonomous Levels of AI Legal Reasoning," Cornell University arXiv. https://arxiv.org/abs/2008.07743

22. Eliot, Lance (2020). "Multidimensionality of the Legal Singularity: The Role of Autonomous Levels of AI Legal Reasoning," Cornell University arXiv. https://arxiv.org/abs/2008.10575

23. Eliot, Lance (2020). "Authorized and Unauthorized Practices of Law: The Role of Autonomous Levels of AI Legal Reasoning," Cornell University arXiv. https://arxiv.org/abs/2008.09507

24. Eliot, Lance (2020). "An Impact Model of AI on the Principles of Justice: Encompassing the Autonomous Levels of AI Legal Reasoning," Cornell University arXiv. https://arxiv.org/abs/2008.12615
25. Eliot, Lance (2020). "Robustness and Overcoming Brittleness of AI-Enabled Legal Micro-Directives," Cornell University arXiv. https://arxiv.org/abs/2009.02243
26. Eliot, Lance (2018). "Singularity and AI," July 10, 2018, AI Trends.
27. Feteris E.T. (1999) MacCormick's Theory of the Justification of Legal Decisions. In: Fundamentals of Legal Argumentation. Argumentation Library, vol 1. Springer, Dordrecht.
28. Feteris, Eveline, and Harm Kloosterhuis (2009). "The Analysis and Evaluation of Legal Argumentation: Approaches from Legal Theory and Argumentation Theory," Volume 16, Studies in Logic, Grammar and Rhetoric.
29. Friedman, Lawrence (2019). A History of American Law, 4th ed. Oxford University Press.
30. Gardner, Anne (1987). Artificial Intelligence and Legal Reasoning. MIT Press.
31. Genesereth, Michael (2009). "Computational Law: The Cop in the Backseat," Stanford Center for Legal Informatics, Stanford University.
32. Gilmore, Grant (1977). The Ages of American Law. Yale University Press.
33. Hage, Jaap (2000). "Dialectical Models in Artificial Intelligence and Law," Artificial Intelligence and Law.
34. Hall, Kermit, and William Wiecek, Paul Finkelman (1996). American Legal History: Cases and Materials, 2nd ed. Oxford University Press.
35. Huhn, Wilson (2000). "Teaching Legal Analysis Using a Pluralistic Model of Law," Volume 36, Number 3, Gonzaga Law Review.
36. Huhn, Wilson (2003). "The Stages of Legal Reasoning: Formalism, Analogy, and Realism," V48, Villanova Law R.
37. Kaplow, Louis (1992). "Rules Versus Standards: An Economic Analysis," Volume 42, Duke Law Journal.

38. Llewellyn, Karl (1950). "Remarks on the Theory of Appellate Decision and the Rules or Canons About How Statutes Are to Be Construed," Volume 3, Number 4, Vanderbilt Law Review.
39. Llewellyn, Karl (1960). The Common Law Tradition: Deciding Appeals. Quid Pro Books.
40. MacCormick, Neil (1978). Legal Reasoning and Legal Theory.
41. Markou, Christopher, and Simon Deakin (2020). "Is Law Computable? From Rule of Law to Legal Singularity," May 4, 2020, SSRN, University of Cambridge Faculty of Law Research Paper.
42. McCarty, Thorne (1977). "Reflections on TAXMAN: An Experiment in Artificial Intelligence and Legal Reasoning," January 1977, Harvard Law Review.
43. McGinnis, John, and Russell G. Pearce (2014). "The Great Disruption: How Machine Intelligence Will Transform the Role of Lawyers in the Delivery of Legal Services," Volume 82, Number 6, Fordham Law Review.
44. McGinnis, John, and Steven Wasick (2015). "Law's Algorithm," Volume 66, Florida Law Review.
45. Mnookin, Robert, and Lewis Kornhauser (1979). "Bargaining in the Shadow of the Law," Volume 88, Number 5, April 1979, The Yale Law Review.
46. Prakken, Henry (1995). "From Logic to Dialectics in Legal Argument," Proceedings of the 5th International Conference on Artificial Intelligence and Law.
47. Reinbold, Patric (2020). "Taking Artificial Intelligence Beyond the Turing Test," Volume 20, Wisconsin Law Review.
48. Remus, Dana, and Frank Levy, "Can Robots be Lawyers? Computers, Robots, and the Practice of Law," Volume 30, Georgetown Journal of Legal Ethics.
49. Rich, Michael (2016). "Machine Learning, Automated Suspicion Algorithms, and the Fourth Amendment," Volume 164, University of Pennsylvania Law Review.
50. Rissland, Edwina (1990). "Artificial Intelligence and Law: Stepping Stones to a Model of Legal Reasoning," Yale Law J.

51. SAE (2018). Taxonomy and Definitions for Terms Related to Driving Automation Systems for On-Road Motor Vehicles, J3016-201806, SAE International.
52. Sunstein, Cass (2001). "Of Artificial Intelligence and Legal Reasoning," University of Chicago Law School, WP.
53. Sunstein, Cass, and Kevin Ashley, Karl Branting, Howard Margolis (2001). "Legal Reasoning and Artificial Intelligence: How Computers 'Think' Like Lawyers," Symposium: Legal Reasoning and Artificial Intelligence, University of Chicago.
54. Surden, Harry (2014). "Machine Learning and Law," Washington Law Review.
55. Surden, Harry (2019). "Artificial Intelligence and Law: An Overview," Summer 2019, Georgia State U. Law Review.
56. Susskind, Richard (2019). Online Courts and the Future of Justice. Oxford University Press.
57. Volokh, Eugne (2019). "Chief Justice Robots," Volume 68, Duke Law Journal.
58. Waltl, Bernhard, and Roland Vogl (2018). "Explainable Artificial Intelligence: The New Frontier in Legal Informatics," February 2018, Jusletter IT 22, Stanford Center for Legal Informatics, Stanford University.
59. Webster, David (1978). "The Ages of American Law," Volume 27, Issue 2. DePaul Law Review.
60. White, Edward (2016). Law in American History. Oxford University Press
61. Wolfram, Stephen (2018). "Computational Law, Symbolic Discourse, and the AI Constitution," in Data-Driven Law: Data Analytics and the New Legal Services (Edward J. Walters ed.)

Note: *For supplemental materials depicting the aspects discussed in this chapter, refer to Appendix B, which contains various augmented diagrams, charts, and additional related facets of relevance.*

CHAPTER 11

LEGAL JUDGMENT PREDICTION (LJP) AND AI

Abstract

Legal Judgment Prediction (LJP) is a longstanding and open topic in the theory and practice-of-law. Predicting the nature and outcomes of judicial matters is abundantly warranted, keenly sought, and vigorously pursued by those within the legal industry and also by society as a whole. The tenuous act of generating judicially laden predictions has been limited in utility and exactitude, requiring further advancement. Various methods and techniques to predict legal cases and judicial actions have emerged over time, especially arising via the advent of computer-based modeling. There has been a wide range of approaches attempted, including simple calculative methods to highly sophisticated and complex statistical models. Artificial Intelligence (AI) based approaches have also been increasingly utilized. In this paper, a review of the literature encompassing Legal Judgment Prediction is undertaken, along with innovatively proposing that the advent of AI Legal Reasoning (AILR) will have a pronounced impact on how LJP is performed and its predictive accuracy. Legal Judgment Prediction is particularly examined using the Levels of Autonomy (LoA) of AI Legal Reasoning, plus, other considerations are explored including LJP probabilistic tendencies, biases handling, actor predictors, transparency, judicial reliance, legal case outcomes, and other crucial elements entailing the overarching legal judicial milieu.

Section 1: Background on Legal Judgment Prediction

In Section 1 of this paper, the literature on Legal Judgment Prediction is introduced and addressed. Doing so establishes the groundwork for the subsequent sections. Section 2 introduces the Levels of Autonomy (LoA) of AI Legal Reasoning (AILR), which is instrumental in the discussions undertaken in Section 3. Section 3 provides an indication of the field of Legal Judgment Prediction as applied to the LoA AILR, along with other vital facets. Section 4 provides various additional research implications and anticipated impacts upon salient practice-of-law considerations.

This paper then consists of these four sections:

- Section 1: Background on Legal Judgment Prediction
- Section 2: Autonomous Levels of AI Legal Reasoning
- Section 3: Legal Judgment Prediction and AI Legal Reasoning
- Section 4: Additional Considerations and Future Research

1.3 Overview of Legal Judgment Prediction

Trying to make predictions about judicial matters is an ongoing and longstanding preoccupation that continues to be an open issue in both the theory of the law and the practice of the law [9] [44] [76] [91]. Making predictions about judicial aspects has been difficult and remains unresolved as to how to best or optimally derive such predictions [62] [78]. The advent of computers furthered the effort of making judicial predictions by providing a means of readily undertaking mathematical calculations and computations to aid in rendering predictions. Gradually, as hardware has become faster and less costly, and as software has become more advanced, the use of a myriad of sophisticated statistical techniques and models have also been employed for predicting judicial aspects [51] [54] [55] [77]. Included amongst these computer-based efforts has been the use of Artificial Intelligence (AI) capabilities, such as the use of Natural Language Processing (NLP), Machine Learning (ML), Knowledge-Based Systems (KBS), and the similar AI-enabled technologies and innovations [2] [4] [5] [52] [53] [85].

The focus of making judicial predictions is often referred to as Legal Judgment Prediction (LJP).

For example, Zhong et al [92] describe LJP in this manner: "Legal Judgment Prediction (LJP) aims to predict the judgment result based on the facts of a case and becomes a promising application of artificial intelligence techniques in the legal field. In real-world scenarios, legal judgment usually consists of multiple subtasks, such as the decisions of applicable law articles, charges, fines, and the term of penalty." And, similarly, this indication of the meaning of Legal Judgment Prediction by Xu et al [91]: "Legal judgment prediction (LJP) aims to predict a case's judgment results, such as applicable law articles, charges, and terms of penalty, based on its fact description."

There have been alternative interpretations of the scope associated with the phraseology of *Legal Judgment Prediction.*

Some indicate or infer that the phrasing is akin to a solely outcome-oriented viewpoint, while others use LJP in a wider meaning as encompassing any semblance of judicial decision making. Thus, the moniker could be interpreted as "Legal Outcome Prediction" or it could be viewed as Legal Decision-Making Prediction," a decidedly different connotation. The difference is that in the former case the focus and scope consist of predominantly aiming to predict the judicial result or judicial outcome, only, and doing so without any attention to any intermediary judicial elements, while in the latter case the predictive interest is widely attuned to any form of judicial decision making rather than uniquely an outcomes-based aim.

For purposes of this paper, the latter formulation is taken as the meaning of Legal Judgment Prediction and used in the context of being able to widely predict all manner of judicial judgments, wherein "judgment" does not refer to solely a final decision or outcome but to the presence and use of judicial choices and decision making, for which can occur throughout at any point during a legal case lifecycle and in other judicial contexts too. That being said, it can be acknowledged that this widened option provides a more arduous hurdle for the effort to craft predictive models and render apt predictions.

Meanwhile, to be clear, the former interpretation would be considered a subset of the wider definition, and therefore there is nothing somehow inconsistent with the narrower focus (it is consistent in the sense that it provides ample attention to a specialization or narrow subset within the larger set of considerations).

To some, the desire or need to make predictions about judicial matters is patently obvious and straightforward, suggesting that there ought not to be any debate about the intrinsic value in finding ways to make such predictions. The logical argument can be readily made that prediction is part-and-parcel of most everything undertaken in the practice of law, including making predictions about how a legal case will fare, how a judge will decide a legal matter, etc. As succinctly stated by Martin et al [62]: "Legal academics, too, possess expertise that should enable them to forecast legal events with some accuracy. After all, the everyday practice of law requires lawyers to predict court decisions in order to advise clients or determine litigation strategies." This points out that if the practice of law is greatly in need of being able to make judicial predictions, the theory of law and scholars of law would presumably be desirous of aiding in that quest as a means of furthering the underlying matters of law as a body of knowledge and a discipline of academic study.

In short, there does not appear to be an overarching objection per se to the notion of seeking to make judicial predictions and aiming to improve and enhance the capability to make such predictions. That being said, there are concerns expressed about how the act of making judicial predictions can adversely impact the rendering of judicial matters, perhaps telegraphing beforehand choices that then become chosen merely because they were predicted to occur (a self-fulfilling prophecy phenomenon), or that otherwise influence or shape those judicial judgments that have been subject to prediction [19]. Also, there are a wide array of ethical questions that arise, such as whether sophisticated and AI-based LJP models might only be available to those that can afford such mechanizations, therefore arming those that can afford such accouterments while leaving those that cannot afford them a less powerful position of legal armament [20].

These societal and legal ramifications are certainly noteworthy, though they are not the specific purview of this paper, nonetheless, those qualms about the potential adverse consequences of LJP are urged herein as worthy of ongoing research and attention (as mentioned in Section 4).

On a related note, here is a somewhat curt but revealing indication of how the self-fulfilling prophecy could work its way into efforts to undertake Legal Judgement Prediction [20]: "To take a fanciful example that proves the point, suppose an attorney in arguing to a court states that a team of his investigators has been observing the presiding judge every morning. The judge walks out of his downtown apartment and stops for a quick breakfast either at McDonald's or at Dunkin' Donuts. On McDonald's days his decisions favor the plaintiff 84 percent of the time. On Dunkin' days, his decisions favor the defendant 90 percent of the time. The attorney then argues that since he is representing the plaintiff, and since the judge this morning breakfasted at McDonald's, sound principles of statistical sociology require the judge to decide the case in favor of his client."

1.4 SCOTUS As Judicial Predictions Aim

One area of Legal Judgment Prediction that has received extensive attention entails making predictions about the Supreme Court of the United States (SCOTUS), logically so, due to fact that the Supreme Court and its several Justices are serving as the highest court in the land and the pinnacle at which laws can arrive for adjudication within the judicial system of the United States.

One of the earliest depicted quantitative analyses involving SCOTUS decision predictions was described by Kort in 1957 [54]:

> "This study represents an attempt to apply quantitative methods to the prediction of human events that generally have been regarded as highly uncertain, namely, decisions by the Supreme Court of the United States. The study is designed to demonstrate that, in at least one area of judicial review, it is possible to take some decided cases, to identify factual elements that influenced the decisions, to derive numerical values for these

> elements by using a formula, and then to predict correctly the decisions of the remaining cases in the area specified. The analysis will be made independently of what the Court said by way of reasoning in these cases; it will rely only on the factual elements which have been emphasized by the justices in their opinions and on their votes to affirm or set aside convictions. Changes in Court personnel made no decisive difference in the pattern of judicial action in this area; so the analysis will not need to take into account the fact that twenty-five different justices have occupied the nine seats on the Court during the period covered, *i.e.*, the past quarter century."

Next, Lawlor et al [56] in the early 1960s described how computers were being used to predict SCOTUS decisions, and offered in their paper an indication of specific application to right-to-counsel cases. Keep in mind that computers in that era were relatively slow and less capable than today's computers, and costlier to leverage, yet pointedly were already beginning to be used for LJP efforts. As stated by Grunbaum et al [41] in that same 1960's time period: "Predictions of the outcome of litigation by statistical methods is a relatively new and controversial field of study made possible by computers."

It would seem that almost immediately upon leveraging computers for undertaking Legal Judgment Prediction that debates over the appropriate or best means to construct such predictive models or calculations came to the forefront. For example, Grunbaum et al [41] shared insights into whether the unit of prediction should be the SCOTUS overall outcome or decision, or whether the focal point should be on the Supreme Court Justices per se, and examined numerous studies at that time, reaching this conclusion: "They show that individual Justices, rather than the Court as a whole, should be used as the unit of prediction." Debate and lack of agreement over the "best" unit of prediction for LJP continue to this day, remaining unsettled and undeniably a still unresolved question.

Beyond the question of the unit of prediction, there was also effort involved in trying to ascertain which model or statistical approach might be better suited for Legal Judgment Prediction. Nagel in 1963 proffered this [68]:

> "This article illustrates and systematically compares three methods for quantitatively predicting case outcomes. The three methods are correlation, regression, and discriminant analysis, all of which involve standard social science research techniques." The focus was about SCOTUS [68]: "The cases used to illustrate the methods consist of 149 civil liberties cases decided by the United States Supreme Court from 1956 through 1960."

The predictor variables of interest by Nagel in the 1963 paper were [68]: "All three methods rely on the relationship between case outcomes and various predictor variables. In this article, the outcome to be predicted is whether a given civil liberties case will be decided in the direction of narrowing civil liberties or in the direction of broadening civil liberties." And, as indicative of that time period, punch cards were used to feed the data into the statistical programs being used [68]: "To use a computer program for regression or discriminant analysis, one punched card per case is needed unless the number of variables necessitates the use of more. Certain columns on each card should be set aside for each variable. Thus, if hole 1 is punched on column 12 of the card corresponding to case 23, this punch might indicate that a certain variable was present."

During the 1980s, SCOTUS predictive models became more pronounced in both being predictive and potentially being explanatory as to judicial behavior and judgment. This is illustrated via Segal [77]: "The overwhelming consensus of Fourth Amendment scholars is that the Supreme Court's sea and seizure cases are a mess. This article proposes that the confusion arises from the manner in which the cases were studied, not from the decisions themselves. A legal model with variables that include the prior justification of the search, the nature of the intrusion, and a few mitigating circumstance used to explain the Court's decisions on the reasonableness of a given search or seizure. The parameters are estimated through probit. The results show that the search and seizure cases are much more ordered than had commonly been believed. Virtually all of the estimates are as expected. Additionally, the Court is shown to act favorably toward the federal government than toward the states. Preliminary analysis suggests the model has predictive as well as explanatory value."

In more recent times, the SCOTUS predictive models have gradually advanced beyond one-dimensional versions and become multi-dimensional. This is highlighted by the work of Lauderdale and Clark [55]: "One-dimensional spatial models have come to inform much theorizing and research on the U.S. Supreme Court. However, we argue that judicial preferences vary considerably across areas of the law, and that limitations in our ability to measure those preferences have constrained the set of questions scholars pursue. We introduce a new approach, which makes use of information about substantive similarity among cases, to estimate judicial preferences that vary across substantive legal issues and over time. We show that a model allowing preferences to vary over substantive issues as well as over time is a significantly better predictor of judicial behavior than one that only allows preferences to vary over time. We find that judicial preferences are not reducible to simple left-right ideology and, as a consequence, there is substantial variation in the identity of the median justice across areas of the law during all periods of the modern court. These results suggest a need to reconsider empirical and theoretical research that hinges on the existence of a single pivotal median justice."

There has also been keen interest in exploring the use of classification trees as a means to aid in bolstering the Legal Judgment Prediction capacity, once again using SCOTUS as an aim for making judicial predictions, per Kastellec [51]: "A key question in the quantitative study of legal rules and judicial decision making is the structure of the relationship between case facts and case outcomes. Legal doctrine and legal rules are general attempts to define this relationship. This article summarizes and utilizes a statistical method relatively unexplored in political science and legal scholarship—classification trees—that offers a flexible way to study legal doctrine. I argue that this method, while not replacing traditional statistical tools for studying judicial decisions, can better capture many aspects of the relationship between case facts and case outcomes. To illustrate the method's advantages, I conduct classification tree analyses of search and seizure cases decided by the U.S. Supreme Court and confession cases decided by the courts of appeals. These analyses illustrate the ability of classification trees to increase our understanding of legal rules and legal doctrine."

This brings us to the latest variants of studying and attempting to predict SCOTUS, including the work by Katz et al [52]. Making use of an AI-like technique consisting of time-evolving random forest classifiers, here is the nature of their Legal Judgment Prediction efforts: "Building on developments in machine learning and prior work in the science of judicial prediction, we construct a model designed to predict the behavior of the Supreme Court of the United States in a generalized, out-of-sample context. To do so, we develop a time-evolving random forest classifier that leverages unique feature engineering to predict more than 240,000 justice votes and 28,000 cases outcomes over nearly two centuries (1816-2015). Using only data available prior to decision, our model outperforms null (baseline) models at both the justice and case level under both parametric and non-parametric tests. Over nearly two centuries, we achieve 70.2% accuracy at the case outcome level and 71.9% at the justice vote level. More recently, over the past century, we outperform an in-sample optimized null model by nearly 5%. Our performance is consistent with, and improves on the general level of prediction demonstrated by prior work; however, our model is distinctive because it can be applied out-of-sample to the entire past and future of the Court, not a single term. Our results represent an important advance for the science of quantitative legal prediction and portend a range of other potential applications."

Part of the impetus for the approach used by Katz et al was stated as due to faltering or weaknesses in prior works of Legal Judgment Prediction, namely containing these faults or limitations [52]: "Despite the multitude of pundits and vast human effort devoted to the task, the quality of the resulting predictions and the underlying models supporting most forecasts is unclear. Not only are these models not backtested historically, but many are difficult to formalize or reproduce at all. When models are formalized, they are typically assessed ex post to infer causes, rather than used ex ante to predict future cases."

This raises an important point about the assumed underlying principle about much of the Legal Judgment Prediction capacities, pointedly that the primary means of making a prediction is often lacking in being reproducible and that one-instance exemplars do little to showcase true predictive power.

In addition, the facet that reliance upon prior data can be detrimental over-reliance [52]: 'Court outcomes are potentially influenced by a variety of dynamics, including public opinion, inter-branch conflict, both changing membership and shifting views of the Justices, and judicial norms and procedures. The classic adage 'past performance does not necessarily predict future results' is very much applicable."

Besides ultimately comparing the predictions of LJP to the actual outcomes, another avenue of gauging the efficacy of LJP models involves the use of legal experts that are asked to make predictions too, as indicated in Martin et al [62]: "Employing two different methods, we attempted to predict the outcome of every case pending before the Supreme Court during its October 2002 term and compared those predictions to the actual decisions. One method used a statistical forecasting model based on information derived from past Supreme Court decisions. The other captured the expert judgments of legal academics and professionals. Using these two distinct methods allows us to test their predictive power not only against actual Court outcomes, but also against each other."

As to the rationale for utilizing both statistical modeling and the polling of legal experts, the basis is depicted this way [62]: "The critical difference between the two methods of prediction lies not in the law/politics dichotomy, but in the nature of the inputs used to generate predictions. The statistical model looked at only a handful of case characteristics, each of them gross features easily observable without specialized training. The legal experts, by contrast, could use particularized knowledge, such as the specific facts of the case or statements by individual justices in similar cases. The statistical model also differed from the experts in explicitly taking into account every case decided by this natural court prior to the 2002 term. No individual could have such comprehensive knowledge of the Court's output for the last eight terms, and so the experts necessarily relied on fewer (albeit more detailed) observations of past Court behavior. Not surprisingly, these different decision-making processes often resulted in divergent predictions in particular cases."

Arising from the advent of online access and the widespread Internet, some assert that Legal Judgment Prediction can be or should be more than the running of computer-based programs, incorporating the opinions and predictions of human experts about judicial matters, and even going so far as including a larger audience of human predictors via the use of a modern-day crowdsourcing approach [52]: "Future research will seek to find the optimal blend of experts, crowds, and algorithms as some ensemble of these three streams of intelligence likely will produce the best performing model for a wide class of prediction problems."

1.5 AI and Legal Judgment Prediction

As earlier indicated, AI has increasingly been utilized for Legal Judgment Prediction, as illustrated via some of the SCOTUS prediction studies mentioned in Section 1.2. Enlarging the viewpoint beyond SCOTUS, AI is being used in numerous ways for a variety of judicial milieu. For example, in the work by Aletras et al [2], the use of NLP and ML was employed for predicting legal cases of the European Court of Human Rights: "Recent advances in Natural Language Processing and Machine Learning provide us with the tools to build predictive models that can be used to unveil patterns driving judicial decisions. This can be useful, for both lawyers and judges, as an assisting tool to rapidly identify cases and extract patterns which lead to certain decisions. This paper presents the first systematic study on predicting the outcome of cases tried by the European Court of Human Rights based solely on textual content. We formulate a binary classification task where the input of our classifiers is the textual content extracted from a case and the target output is the actual judgment as to whether there has been a violation of an article of the convention of human rights. Textual information is represented using contiguous word sequences, i.e., N-grams, and topics. Our models can predict the court's decisions with a strong accuracy (79% on average). Our empirical analysis indicates that the formal facts of a case are the most important predictive factor. This is consistent with the theory of legal realism suggesting that judicial decision-making is significantly affected by the stimulus of the facts. We also observe that the topical content of a case is another important feature in this classification task and explore this relationship by conducting a qualitative analysis."

An important point in these studies includes the facet that there are judicial factors at play, along with the need to consider so-called non-legal factors that nonetheless impact the predictive capacity for Legal Judgment Predictions [2]: "These results could be understood as providing some evidence for judicial decision-making approaches according to which judges are primarily responsive to non-legal, rather than to legal, reasons when they decide appellate cases."

When stated bluntly, one viewpoint is that the justices themselves are not merely some form of automata that render legal rulings in a logically and purely mathematically systematic way, instead of as indicated by Grunbaum [40]: "And lastly . . . maybe it should be firstly . .. judges have personalities. They have prejudices and stomach aches and pride and stalled cars and inspirations and hangovers and far visions and sore feet. All judges try, and most succeed in reducing the impact of 'gastronomical jurisprudence,' but few reduce its effect to zero. For after all judges are. . . thanks be to Heaven . . . human. They are not computers controlled by always knowable inputs. Neither are they scientists indifferently imposing inexorable rules. They are only humans, judging only humans, hopefully themselves in turn to be similarly judged."

Per the discussion in Section 1.1, Legal Judgment Prediction can be viewed in a larger context than the sole focus of judicial outcomes, and for which an example of AI used to predict billings or legal fee charges for a given legal case indicates this wide interpretation [59]: "The charge prediction task is to determine appropriate charges for a given case, which is helpful for legal assistant systems where the user input is fact description. We argue that relevant law articles play an important role in this task, and therefore propose an attention-based neural network method to jointly model the charge prediction task and the relevant article extraction task in a unified framework. The experimental results show that, besides providing legal basis, the relevant articles can also clearly improve the charge prediction results, and our full model can effectively predict appropriate charges for cases with different expression styles."

This particular study also raises the point that the source materials used for making Legal Judgment Predictions do not necessarily need to be only legal documents or artifacts, and could very well be potentially "non-legal" materials too, such as news related elements [59]: "By experimenting on news data, we show that, although trained on judgment documents, our model also has reasonable generalization ability on fact descriptions written by non-legal professionals. While promising, our model still cannot explicitly handle multidefendant cases, and there is also a clear gap between our model and the upper bound improvement that relevant articles can achieve."

One concern raised about the use of AI and in particular Machine Learning is that the data used as input is oftentimes required to be pre-labeled, tending to entail manual and labor-intensive efforts to get the data into suitable categorization for use by the ML models. This point is raised by Xu et al [91]: "Existing approaches for legal judgment prediction (LJP) are mainly divided into three categories. In early times, works usually focus on analyzing existing legal cases in specific scenarios with mathematical and statistical algorithms. However, these methods are limited to small datasets with few labels. Later, a number of machine learning-based methods were developed to solve the problem of LJP, which almost combine some manually designed features with a linear classifier to improve the performance of case classification. The shortcoming is that these methods rely heavily on manual features, which suffer from the generalization problem. In recent years, researchers tend to exploit neural networks to solve LJP tasks."

The work by Xu et al [91] proposes an innovative means to cope with these issues: "To solve the confusing charges issue, we propose an end-to-end framework, i.e., Law Article Distillation based Attention Network (LADAN). LADAN uses the difference among similar law articles to attentively extract features from law cases' fact descriptions, which is more effective in distinguishing confusing law articles, and improve the performance of LJP."

And as further elaborated [91]: "For an input law case, we learn both macro- and microlevel features. Macro-level features are used for predicting which community includes the applicable law articles. Micro-level features are attentively extracted by the attention vector of the selected community for distinguishing confusing law articles within the same community."

Extending the notion of looking beyond the outcome itself, and thus considering intermediary states of a legal case, the work by Keown [53] provides a methodical means of using a state-of-the-case series of pinpoints or junctures as part of the mathematical modeling for Legal Judgment Prediction, as described this way: "The fact pattern underlying a judicial decision comprises issues that may be classified either as (1) evidence and argument supporting the position of plaintiff denoted by the symbol P, or (2) evidence and argument supporting that of defendant denoted by D. In law, of course, who is plaintiff and who is defendant may depend on which party wins the race to the courthouse, rather than on the nature of the dispute involved."

Furthermore, this [53]: "In civil cases, plaintiff wins his case if the trier of fact, sometimes a judge and sometimes a jury, finds a preponderance of the evidence in his favor. Considering D and P as conflicting factors in a judicial process enjoying a suitably discontinuous behavior, one arrives by means of the Zeemanian process at: Hypothesis I. The standard model of the judicial process is a cusp catastrophe with plaintiffs evidence and argument denoted by P and defendant's evidence and argument denoted by D as conflicting factors determining the outcome." And then emphases the states in time facets [53]: "As intended, these terms indicate that, with certain exceptions to be discussed below, the state of the case is (defined by a point on the behavior manifold that indicates a victory either for plaintiff or for defendant at any given time). If the state of the case is represented by a point on judgment for plaintiff, then it tends to remain there, while if it is represented by a point on judgment for the defendant then by stable equilibrium it tends to remain there. A state of the case in which the outcome is uncertain corresponds to a point on the cross-hatched surface representing a situation of unstable equilibrium. Introduction of evidence and argument soon displaces the state to judgment for plaintiff or judgment for defendant."

Much of the literature on Legal Judgment Prediction tends to suggest that it is insufficient to make a prediction as though being out-of-the-blue or by some divine means, and argues at times quite vigorously that being able to sensibly or reasonably explain how the prediction was derived is perhaps as important as the prediction itself. Consider the points made by Ashley and Bruninghaus [4] in their efforts to construct their Issue-Based Prediction (IBP) approach: "Computerized algorithms for predicting the outcomes of legal problems can extract and present information from particular databases of cases to guide the legal analysis of new problems. They can have practical value despite the limitations that make reliance on predictions risky for other real-world purposes such as estimating settlement values. An algorithm's ability to generate reasonable legal arguments also is important. In this article, computerized prediction algorithms are compared not only in terms of accuracy, but also in terms of their ability to explain predictions and to integrate predictions and arguments. Our approach, the Issue-Based Prediction algorithm, is a program that tests hypotheses about how issues in a new case will be decided. It attempts to explain away counterexamples inconsistent with a hypothesis, while apprising users of the counterexamples and making explanatory arguments based on them."

As a further extension of this explanatory notion, the IBP was enhanced as SMILE+IBP, as described in [5]:

> "Work on a computer program called SMILE + IBP (SMart Index Learner Plus Issue-Based Prediction) bridges case-based reasoning and extracting information from texts. The program addresses a technologically challenging task that is also very relevant from a legal viewpoint: to extract information from textual descriptions of the facts of decided cases and apply that information to predict the outcomes of new cases. The program attempts to automatically classify textual descriptions of the facts of legal problems in terms of Factors, a set of classification concepts that capture stereotypical fact patterns that effect the strength of a legal claim, here trade secret misappropriation. Using these classifications, the program can evaluate and explain predictions about a problem's outcome given a database of

previously classified cases. This paper provides an extended example illustrating both functions, prediction by IBP and text classification by SMILE, and reports empirical evaluations of each. While IBP's results are quite strong, and SMILE's much weaker, SMILE + IBP still has some success predicting and explaining the outcomes of case scenarios input as texts. It marks the first time to our knowledge that a program can reason automatically about legal case texts."

As also mentioned in Section 1.1, not everyone necessarily concurs that making judicial predictions is appropriate, regardless of how it is undertaken, which recently came to the fore when France banned certain aspects of publishing judge analytics in 2019, as indicated in [84]: "France has banned the publication of judge analytics, and breaking this law carries up to five years in prison. The new Article 33 of the Justice Reform Act reads: 'No personally identifiable data concerning judges or court clerks may be subject to any reuse with the purpose or result of evaluating, analyzing or predicting their actual or supposed professional practices. The violation of this law shall be punished by the measures outlined in articles 226-18, 226-24, and 226-31 of the penal code, without prejudice of the measures and sanctions provided for under the law 78-17 of 6 January 1978 concerning data processing, files and freedoms,' as translated by Rebecca Loescher, a professor of French at St. Edward's University at the Angers, France campus. The law appears to apply to anyone—individuals, researchers, technology companies."

Returning to the point about aiming solely at the outcome of a legal case, it is perhaps confounding to consider exactly what is considered the outcome if there is a possibility that a case might be appealed. In other words, when referring to an outcome, does the outcome imply the true final outcome after all appeals have been exhausted and potentially a final court has ruled or does outcome refer to the initial ruling or judgment about a legal case. Per Atkinson et al [7]: "The point is that the outcome of a case is often not clear: in any serious legal dispute there are opposing arguments, and very often opinions differ as to who has the better of it. Decisions are reversed on appeal, and may be reversed again at the highest level of appeal."

And, once again, theory dovetails into the Legal Judgment Prediction realm and as embodied perhaps in AI efforts as depicted by McCarty [63]: "Using a variety of schemes to represent different kinds of argument (such as Argument from Expert Opinion, Argument from Negative Consequences, Argument from Rules, etc.) was introduced into AI and Law. Argumentation schemes can be seen as a generalisation of the rules of inference." In fact, there is an argument to be made that predictions should be based upon and potentially preceded with a strong theory construction about the law [7]: "Some researchers have argued that reasoning with legal cases should be seen as a process of theory construction, following the ideas of McCarty. The idea is to construct a theory which will explain the past cases and determine an outcome for the current case."

This also potentially recognizes the multitude of subtasks within a legal case and the potential for modeling those subtasks as part of the outcome-focused predictions, utilizing a Directed Acyclic Graph approach [92]: "While most existing works only focus on a specific subtask of judgment prediction and ignore the dependencies among subtasks, we formalize the dependencies among subtasks as a Directed Acyclic Graph (DAG) and propose a topological multi-task learning framework, TOPJUDGE, which incorporates multiple subtasks and DAG dependencies into judgment prediction. We conduct experiments on several real-world large-scale datasets of criminal cases in the civil law system. Experimental results show that our model achieves consistent and significant improvements over baselines on all judgment prediction tasks."

As indicative of the legal case lifecycle and the role of Legal Judgment Prediction, consider these types of questions that are customarily asked about a legal case [78]: "Usually, the process of prediction starts with one or more questions. Whether to take a case in hand or not? Whether to settle the case outside or take it to the court? Will the settlement amount be worth it? What are the chances of winning the case? These are some of the questions that involve predicting the outcome of a case and the legal practitioners have to deal with, on a regular basis. These questions represent the importance of outcome prediction in case selection, making settlement decisions, and various aspects of legal processes."

Consider too that there are judicial per se factors and then there are extra-judicial factors to be encompassed when performing LJP [78]: "Considering the fact that judges are human beings, this approach assumes that judges may be ideologically inclined towards some side in various issues, have their own perception and other biases, and various other social and political factors that affect their judgment such as mental resources of a judge and decision of lower court. Hence, descriptors considered for predicting outcomes are extra-judicial factors that may generate or represent human bias. Examples of these factors are votes of other justices, justice gender, case origin, petitioner type, respondent type, the ideological direction of the court, etc."

Besides conventional numeric coding of judicial factors, there is also a linguistic approach that can be utilized for Legal Judgment Prediction, as indicated in [78]: "Another approach considers the linguistic features of legal judgments for predicting outcomes. Ngo tried to predict outcomes on a database of 2019 Dutch legal cases according to their linguistic features. Some of the considered features were word count and frequency of different types of pronouns. In, the authors replaced case-specific names and instances by their role and used propositional patterns for predicting trade secret cases."

For those seeking to establish law as a form of science, one that would adhere to rigorous principles of nature and be readily described via formulas and the means of science, and thus presumably be more readily predicted and predictable, Noonan offers this thought in his 1961 work about the law [69]: "Other sciences may be more easily circumscribed. Their subject matter is defined by the Baconian purpose for which they are normally pursued: the prediction and control of the properties of a particular kind of physical matter. It would appear that a similar ambition to achieve prediction and control 'like a science' may have animated such Austinian offshoots as Legal Realism."

1.6 Theories of Law and LJP

Embroiled within Legal Judgment Prediction is the role of underlying theories about the law.

In particular, there has been much focus on the emergence of legal realism versus legal formalism, and thus this carries over inevitably into the predictive realm too [2]: "Without going into details with respect to a particularly complicated debate that is out of the scope of this paper, we may here simplify by observing that since the beginning of the 20th century, there has been a major contention between two opposing ways of making sense of judicial decision-making: legal formalism and legal realism. Very roughly, legal formalists have provided a *legal model* of judicial decision-making, claiming that the law is rationally determinate: judges either decide cases deductively, by subsuming facts under formal legal rules or use more complex legal reasoning than deduction whenever legal rules are insufficient to warrant a particular outcome. On the other hand, legal realists have criticized formalist models, insisting that judges primarily decide appellate cases by responding to the stimulus of the facts of the case, rather than on the basis of legal rules or doctrine, which are in many occasions rationally indeterminate."

Seeking to encompass these underlying tensions of legal theories, a study by Hall and Wright utilized content analysis, whose roots can be said to epistemologically be in the legal realism realm, as described in [44]: "To provide methodological guidance, we survey the questions that legal scholars have tried to answer through content analysis, and use that experience to generalize about the strengths and weaknesses of the technique compared with conventional interpretive legal methods. The epistemological roots of content analysis lie in legal realism. Any question that a lawyer might ask about what courts say or do can be studied more objectively using one of the four distinct components of content analysis: 1) replicable selection of cases; 2) objective coding of cases; 3) counting case contents for descriptive purposes; or 4) statistical analysis of case coding."

The researchers point out that there are noted objections to such an approach [44]:

> "Each of these components contributes something of unique epistemological value to legal research, yet at each of these four stages, some legal scholars have objected to the

> technique. The most effective response is to recognize that content analysis does not occupy the same epistemological ground as conventional legal scholarship. Instead, each method renders different kinds of insights that complement each other, so that, together, the two approaches to understanding caselaw are more powerful that either alone. Content analysis is best used when each decision should receive equal weight, that is, when it is appropriate to regard the content of opinions as generic data."

The argument for content analysis is further made [44]: "Scholars have found that it is especially useful in studies that question or debunk conventional legal wisdom. Content analysis also holds promise in the study of the connections between judicial opinions and other parts of the social, political, or economic landscape. The strongest application is when the subject of study is simply the behavior of judges in writing opinions or deciding cases. Then, content analysis combines the analytical skills of the lawyer with the power of science that comes from articulated and replicable methods."

As earlier emphasized in Section 1.1, there can be problematic issues underlying the approaches used for Legal Judgment Prediction, including this aspect highlighted about the use of content analysis [44]: "However, analyzing the cause-and-effect relationship between the outcome of cases and the legally relevant factors presented by judges to justify their decisions raises a serious circularity problem. Therefore, content analysis is not an especially good tool for helping lawyers to predict the outcome of cases based on real-world facts. This article also provides guidance on the best practices for using this research method. We identify techniques that meet standards of social science rigor and account for the practical needs of legal researchers. These techniques include methods for case sampling, coder training, reliability testing, and statistical analysis."

1.7 Holmes And The Path Of The Law

It would seem that any in-depth discussion about prediction and the law, which entails any notable theoretical semblance, would be inclined or perhaps obligated to address the now-classic "prediction theory of the law" as commonly prompted by the work of Oliver Wendell Holmes in his 1897 "The Path of the Law" work [40]. For those not familiar with the premise, Holmes could be construed as arguing that law is to its essence a form of a prediction.

This is worthwhile for elucidation and detailed consideration in these matters on Legal Judgment Prediction.

A singular quote of Holmes has been promulgated time and again over the years, of which there is a multitude of interpretations about the purported meaning, that quote being this one [40]: 'The prophecies of what the courts will do in fact, and nothing more pretentious, are what I mean by the law."

Before examining the myriad of interpretations, it is instructive to consider the overall context of what else Holmes indicated and how his famous article arrived at that particular statement or sentiment.

First, Holmes indicates that law is weighed in the minds of the public as to the amount of governmental force that can be applied to ensure that the law itself is abided by, such that [40]: "People want to know under what circumstances and how far they will run the risk of coming against what is so much stronger than themselves, and hence it becomes a business to find out when this danger is to be feared. The object of our study, then, is prediction, the prediction of the incidence of the public force through the instrumentality of the courts."

In that frame of thinking, laws can be considered prophecies or predictions about how the ax, as it were, might fall upon someone [40]:

> "The means of the study are a body of reports, of treatises, and of statutes, in this country and in England, extending back for six hundred years, and now increasing annually by hundreds. In these sibylline leaves are gathered the scattered prophecies of the past upon the cases in which

> the axe will fall. These are what properly have been called the oracles of the law. Far the most important and pretty nearly the whole meaning of every new effort of legal thought is to make these prophecies more precise, and to generalize them into a thoroughly connected system."

To reiterate then, in Holmes own words, the law is a prediction of what can befall those that possibly avert the law [40]: "But, as I shall try to show, a legal duty so called is nothing but a prediction that if a man does or omits certain things he will be made to suffer in this or that way by judgment of the court; and so of a legal right." And to add emphasis, he states: "I wish, if I can, to lay down some first principles for the study of this body of dogma or systematized prediction which we call the law, for men who want to use it as the instrument of their business to enable them to prophesy in their turn, and, as bearing upon the study, I wish to point out an ideal which as yet our law has not attained."

This then leads to the famous line, which is shown herein in the context of both the preceding background and the entire passage of which the line occurs (it is the last sentence here) [40]: "Take the fundamental question, What constitutes the law? You will find some text writers telling you that it is something different from what is decided by the courts of Massachusetts or England, that it is a system of reason, that it is a deduction from principles of ethics or admitted axioms or what not, which may or may not coincide with the decisions. But if we take the view of our friend the bad man we shall find that he does not care two straws for the axioms or deductions, but that he does want to know what the Massachusetts or English courts are likely to do in fact. I am much of this mind. The prophecies of what the courts will do in fact, and nothing more pretentious, are what I mean by the law."

As an aside, some object to the characterization of "bad man" or "bad men" to which the law is apparently aimed (in today's terminology it would be bad people, which is likely what Holmes had intended), and per Hart, the pointed question is asked [46]:

"Why should not law be equally if not more concerned with the 'puzzled man' or 'ignorant man' who is willing to do what is required, if only he can be told what it is? Or with the 'man who wishes to arrange his affairs' if only he can be told how to do it?" This aside is not addressed in this paper herein and merely noted as one of various criticisms or analyses that have been made of Holmes's statements and philosophy about the law.

Continuing, what is perhaps equally crucial in the viewpoint expressed by Holmes is that it is not merely the words of the law that are crucial, but also and perhaps as much so (or more) the operationalizing of the law too [40]: "You see how the vague circumference of the notion of {legal} duty shrinks and at the same time grows more precise when we wash it with cynical acid and expel everything except the object of our study, the operations of the law."

As a point that has become commonly cited about the law presumably (possibly) not being amenable to logic, and perhaps not amenable to mathematical modeling and computations that might attempt to embody or utilize it for predictive purposes, here's what Holmes stated [40]: "So in the broadest sense it is true that the law is a logical development, like everything else. The danger of which I speak is not the admission that the principles governing other phenomena also govern the law, but the notion that a given system, ours, for instance, can be worked out like mathematics from some general axioms of conduct.

Furthermore, the law can turn on a dime, one might assert, and presumably undercut the notion of the past being used to predict the future [40]: "Such matters really are battle grounds where the means do not exist for the determinations that shall be good for all time, and where the decision can do no more than embody the preference of a given body in a given time and place. We do not realize how large a part of our law is open to reconsideration upon a slight change in the habit of the public mind. No concrete proposition is self-evident, no matter how ready we may be to accept it, not even Mr. Herbert Spencer's 'Every man has a right to do what he wills, provided he interferes not with a like right on the part of his neighbors.'"

There is though a role, an important one, in applying overarching statistics and economic postulates to the prediction of the predictions: "The rational study of law is still to a large extent the study of history. History must be a part of the study, because without it we cannot know the precise scope of rules which it is our business to know. It is a part of the rational study, because it is the first step toward an enlightened skepticism, that is, towards a deliberate reconsideration of the worth of those rules. When you get the dragon out of his cave on to the plain and in the daylight, you can count his teeth and claws, and see just what is his strength. But to get him out is only the first step. The next is either to kill him, or to tame him and make him a useful animal. For the rational study of the law the blackletter man may be the man of the present, but the man of the future is the man of statistics and the master of economics. It is revolting to have no better reason for a rule of law than that so it was laid down in the time of Henry IV. It is still more revolting if the grounds upon which it was laid down have vanished long since, and the rule simply persists from blind imitation of the past." Along with this point too [40]: "The statistics of the relative increase of crime in crowded places like large cities, where example has the greatest chance to work, and in less populated parts, where the contagion spreads more slowly, have been used with great force in favor of the latter view. But there is weighty authority for the belief that, however this may be, 'not the nature of the crime, but the dangerousness of the criminal, constitutes the only reasonable legal criterion to guide the inevitable social reaction against the criminal.'"

Out of this array of vital considerations about the law has become an assertion that these points can arrive at a contention that the courts and judges are ultimately the true determiners of what the law is.

Rather than being in the role of law-applier, which in theory the courts and judges are supposed to be focused and limited to thereof, it has been interpreted that Holmes was arguing that the courts and the judges are instead the lawmakers, in lieu of the legislature that was presumed to be the lawmakers. This is argued under the assertion that the courts and the judges are the final arbiters of the meaning of the law, along with the applying of the forces that Holmes argued are the basis for why the laws are seen as having teeth and thus the foundational face for the public to consider when abiding by the laws.

If a law is a predictor of the potential force to be applied, but the courts and the judges can sway that "law" in whatever manner so desired, the law itself no longer is as meaningful as is the judgment that the courts and judges will make, regardless potentially of what the law otherwise seemingly appears to signify. Thus, this leads to the logical conclusion that the focus for Legal Judgment Prediction should not be to the law itself, being a mere secondary or surrogate at best, but instead to the courts and judges as to their judgments (and potential whims, some would argue). As described by D'Amato [20]: "The judge who finds it more interesting to invent new law rather than restate the old is stealthily undermining public confidence in the rule of law and narrowing the ambit of personal freedom. He is acting as a legislator, not a judge—a legislator of the worst sort, who enacts new law and holds it against innocent people who were dutifully complying with the old law. If the judge in addition believes that he embodies the law, he is saying that, if the public wants to understand the law, they should study him. For in the end he has no theory of law. He cannot explain what the law is; he can only say that law is what he does—but he does not say that it is a shortcoming on his part that he cannot explain what the law is. Instead it is a failing on the law's part!"

Indeed, this active role of lawmaking can be construed as a form of reverse legislation [20]: "A judge who invents a rule and applies it retroactively to conduct that has already occurred seems to be engaging in a kind of reverse legislation. If in doing so the judge changes the law retroactively, then indeed it would be reverse-perverse legislation-penalizing a party for failure to obey a rule that the judge has just invented. But if the judge just finds the law as it existed when the facts of the case arose, then the judge is not making new law but only taking a picture of the old—the same picture the litigants could have taken when their case arose."

Returning to the Holmes remark about the law as a prophecy, subsequent to Holmes points becoming popularized, many interpreted that this meant that lawyers are essentially like weather predictors [20]:

> "After hearing Holmes speak, the scholars and practitioners in the audience undoubtedly understood him to be comparing a lawyer with other public predictors of events

> such as weather forecasters. This particular comparison has become the standard interpretation of Holmes's prediction theory. Thus a lawyer predicts judicial decisions (which constitute the law), and the meteorologist predicts tomorrow's weather."

Per D'Amato [20], this opened a can of worms amid the legal profession: "It may be warranted to say that legal realism was a disastrous setback for American law. It seemed to justify as an uncontestable fact of empiricism that judges may make all kinds of decisions based upon a wide range of factors: emotions, prejudices (unless they amount to a conflict of interest), party affiliation, rewarding campaign contributors, facile study of the law, liking or disliking the attorneys arguing a case, mere whim, and other bells and whistles. Law-school curriculums are then skewed to prepare students to argue successfully before judges who may only care minimally about what the law says." Leading to this rather stark conclusion about the path of lawyers in the law [20]: "Better yet, once he becomes a judge, he will not have to pay much attention to what the lawyers say about the law (any more than he did in the classroom). For the 'law' will be whatever he proclaims it to be."

In considering the role of uncertainty, which naturally flows from the topic of making predictions (this will be future explored in Section 3), it is insightful to consider that if the law is predicated on the courts and the ruling of judges, the public then would presumably be keenly focused on the present probability of the predicted outcome of the court and the judges, more so than the law per se [20]: "In short, it is the present probability of what the court will do that is of great interest to the bad man rather than the future fact of what the court will decide because by then it will be too late to influence the bad man's decision in the present."

As a vivid illustration of this point about assessing the present probability of a future predicted event, D'Amato offers this illustration [20]:

> "To this Holmes may have added that all decisions, not just those with legal consequences, are based on probabilities.

For example, a jaywalker decides to cross the street. He figures that his chances of reaching the other side are 99.99% He has allowed 0.01% for the possibility that he will stumble halfway through and be run over by a passing car. On top of that calculation he must also consider the probability of being arrested for jaywalking—an arrest that would defeat his purpose of crossing the street in between the traffic signals. He looks around and does not see a police officer. Nevertheless, he has to allocate some degree of probability that a police officer may be standing behind a truck parked on the other side of the street. Thus his probability of successfully jaywalking reduces from 99.99% to, say, 97%. This probability may or may not lead him to decide to jaywalk. There may be other factors that enter into his decision. Every one of those factors can be measured as a numerical probability. His decision whether or not to jaywalk, just like every other decision he makes or will ever make, is based on the summation of all the relevant probabilities of which he is aware at the time he makes his decision."

In short, this aptly sums up the viewpoint about the role of prediction and the law [20]:

"We cannot know exactly what the law is right now when we want to factor it into our decision whether to act or not to act, but we can assign a numerical prediction in the present to what a court will later decide and treat the prediction as the law."

This discussion about Holmes perhaps makes abundantly clear that the act of prediction and the role of Legal Judgment Prediction have merit, substantially so, and presumably can be said to be at the core of the law, including both the theory of the law and the practice of the law.

For those that at times suggest that Legal Judgment Prediction only needs to consider the courts and the judges, omitting entirely the law itself, under the guise that the law will be whatever the courts say it to be, this seems somewhat misguided as a rule of thumb.

The law still is nonetheless the essence of what is relied upon, and for which the courts and the judges will presumably emanate from, and thus acting as though for LJP purposes that the laws are unworthy of inclusion seems an extreme and relatively imprudent posture. In that same view, perhaps, taking the extreme of only relying upon the laws as written would seem to be missing the boat, as it were, neglecting to take into account the role and impact of the decisions made by the courts and the judges. All told, attempting to portray the law and the courts/judges as somehow mutually exclusive when undertaking LJP seems exceedingly ill-advised.

In any case, the Holmes exploration has also highlighted the importance of realizing that predictions via Legal Judgment Prediction are not to be cast as imbuing absolute certainty and that there needs to be the realization and infusion of probabilities in order to consider the predictions of proper value and utility.

Section 2: Autonomous Levels of AI Legal Reasoning

In this section, a framework for the autonomous levels of AI Legal Reasoning is summarized and is based on the research described in detail in Eliot [27] [28] [29] [30] [31] [32].

These autonomous levels will be portrayed in a grid that aligns with key elements of autonomy and as matched to AI Legal Reasoning. Providing this context will be useful to the later sections of this paper and will be utilized accordingly.

The autonomous levels of AI Legal Reasoning are as follows:
Level 0: No Automation for AI Legal Reasoning
Level 1: Simple Assistance Automation for AI Legal Reasoning
Level 2: Advanced Assistance Automation for AILR
Level 3: Semi-Autonomous Automation for AI Legal Reasoning
Level 4: Domain Autonomous for AI Legal Reasoning
Level 5: Fully Autonomous for AI Legal Reasoning
Level 6: Superhuman Autonomous for AI Legal Reasoning

2.1 Details of the LoA AILR

See **Figure A-1** for an overview chart showcasing the autonomous levels of AI Legal Reasoning as via columns denoting each of the respective levels.

See **Figure A-2** for an overview chart similar to Figure A-1 which alternatively is indicative of the autonomous levels of AI Legal Reasoning via the rows as depicting the respective levels (this is simply a reformatting of Figure A-1, doing so to aid in illuminating this variant perspective, but does not introduce any new facets or alterations from the contents as already shown in Figure A-1).

2.1.1 Level 0: No Automation for AI Legal Reasoning

Level 0 is considered the no automation level. Legal reasoning is carried out via manual methods and principally occurs via paper-based methods.

This level is allowed some leeway in that the use of say a simple handheld calculator or perhaps the use of a fax machine could be allowed or included within this Level 0, though strictly speaking it could be said that any form whatsoever of automation is to be excluded from this level.

2.1.2 Level 1: Simple Assistance Automation for AI Legal Reasoning

Level 1 consists of simple assistance automation for AI legal reasoning.

Examples of this category encompassing simple automation would include the use of everyday computer-based word processing, the use of everyday computer-based spreadsheets, the access to online legal documents that are stored and retrieved electronically, and so on.

By-and-large, today's use of computers for legal activities is predominantly within Level 1. It is assumed and expected that over time, the pervasiveness of automation will continue to deepen and widen, and eventually lead to legal activities being supported and within Level 2, rather than Level 1.

2.1.3 Level 2: Advanced Assistance Automation for AI Legal Reasoning

Level 2 consists of advanced assistance automation for AI legal reasoning.

Examples of this notion encompassing advanced automation would include the use of query-style Natural Language Processing (NLP), Machine Learning (ML) for case predictions, and so on.

Gradually, over time, it is expected that computer-based systems for legal activities will increasingly make use of advanced automation. Law industry technology that was once at a Level 1 will likely be refined, upgraded, or expanded to include advanced capabilities, and thus be reclassified into Level 2.

2.1.4 Level 3: Semi-Autonomous Automation for AI Legal Reasoning

Level 3 consists of semi-autonomous automation for AI legal reasoning.

Examples of this notion encompassing semi-autonomous automation would include the use of Knowledge-Based Systems (KBS) for legal reasoning, the use of Machine Learning and Deep Learning (ML/DL) for legal reasoning, and so on.

Today, such automation tends to exist in research efforts or prototypes and pilot systems, along with some commercial legal technology that has been infusing these capabilities too.

2.1.5 Level 4: Domain Autonomous for AI Legal Reasoning

Level 4 consists of domain autonomous computer-based systems for AI legal reasoning.

This level reuses the conceptual notion of Operational Design Domains (ODDs) as utilized in the autonomous vehicles and self-driving cars levels of autonomy, though in this use case it is being applied to the legal domain [22] [23] [24]. Essentially, this entails any AI legal reasoning capacities that can operate autonomously, entirely so, but that is only able to do so in some limited or constrained legal domain.

2.1.6 Level 5: Fully Autonomous for AI Legal Reasoning

Level 5 consists of fully autonomous computer-based systems for AI legal reasoning.

In a sense, Level 5 is the superset of Level 4 in terms of encompassing all possible domains as per however so defined ultimately for Level 4. The only constraint, as it were, consists of the facet that the Level 4 and Level 5 are concerning human intelligence and the capacities thereof. This is an important emphasis due to attempting to distinguish Level 5 from Level 6 (as will be discussed in the next subsection)

It is conceivable that someday there might be a fully autonomous AI legal reasoning capability, one that encompasses all of the law in all foreseeable ways, though this is quite a tall order and remains quite aspirational without a clear cut path of how this might one day be achieved. Nonetheless, it seems to be within the extended realm of possibilities, which is worthwhile to mention in relative terms to Level 6.

2.1.7 Level 6: Superhuman Autonomous for AI Legal Reasoning

Level 6 consists of superhuman autonomous computer-based systems for AI legal reasoning.

In a sense, Level 6 is the entirety of Level 5 and adds something beyond that in a manner that is currently ill-defined and perhaps (some would argue) as yet unknowable. The notion is that AI might ultimately exceed human intelligence, rising to become superhuman, and if so, we do not yet have any viable indication of what that superhuman intelligence consists of and nor what kind of thinking it would somehow be able to undertake.

Whether a Level 6 is ever attainable is reliant upon whether superhuman AI is ever attainable, and thus, at this time, this stands as a placeholder for that which might never occur. In any case, having such a placeholder provides a semblance of completeness, doing so without necessarily legitimatizing that superhuman AI is going to be achieved or not. No such claim or dispute is undertaken within this framework.

Section 3: Legal Judgement Prediction and AI Legal Reasoning

In this Section 3, various aspects of Legal Judgment Prediction (LJP) will be identified and discussed with respect to AI Legal Reasoning (AILR). A series of diagrams and illustrations are included to aid in depicting the points being made. In addition, the material draws upon the background and LJP research literature indicated in Section 1 and combines with the material outlined in Section 2 on the Levels of Autonomy (LoA) of AI Legal Reasoning.

3.1 LJP and LoA AILR

The nature and capabilities of Legal Judgment Prediction will vary across the Levels of Autonomy for AI Legal Reasoning.

Refer to **Figure B-1**.

As indicated, the Legal Judgment Prediction becomes increasingly more sophisticated and advanced as the AI Legal Reasoning increases in capability. To aid in typifying the differences between each of the Levels in terms of the incremental advancement of LJP, the following phrasing is used:

- Level 0: **n/a**
- Level 1: **Rudimentary Calculative**
- Level 2: **Complex Statistical**
- Level 3: **Symbolic Intertwined**
- Level 4: **Domain Predictive**
- Level 5: **Holistic Predictive**
- Level 6: **Pansophic Predictive**

Briefly, each of the levels is described next.

At Level 0, there is an indication of "n/a" at Level 0 since there is no AI capability at Level 0 (the *No Automation* level of the LoA).

At Level 1, the LoA is *Simple Assistance Automation* and this can be used to undertake Legal Judgment Prediction though it is rated or categorized as being rudimentary and making use of relatively simplistic calculative models and formulas. Thus, this is coined as "Rudimentary Calculative."

At Level 2, the LoA is *Advanced Assistance Automation* and the LJP is coined as "Complex Statistical," which is indicative of Legal Judgment Prediction being performed in a more advanced manner than at Level 1. This consists of complex statistical methods such as those techniques mentioned in Section 1 of this paper. To date, most of the research and practical use of Legal Judgment Prediction has been within Level 2. Future efforts are aiming at Level 3 and above.

At Level 3, the LoA is *Semi-Autonomous Automation* and the LJP is coined as "Symbolic Intermixed," which can undertake Legal Judgment Prediction at an even more advanced capacity than at Level 2. Recall, in Level 2, the focus tended to be on traditional numerical formulations for LJP, albeit sophisticated in the use of statistical models. In Level 3, the symbolic capability is added and fostered, including at times acting in a hybrid mode with the conventional numerical and statistical models. Generally, the work at Level 3 to-date has primarily been experimental, making use of exploratory prototypes or pilot efforts.

At Level 4, the LoA is *AILR Domain Autonomous* and coined as "Domain Predictive," meaning that this can be used to perform Legal Judgment Predictions within particular specialties of domains or subdomains of the legal field, but does not necessarily cut across the various domains and is not intended to be able to do so. The predictive capacity is done in a highly advanced manner, incorporating the Level 3 capabilities, along with exceeding those levels and providing a more fluent and capable predictive means.

At Level 5, the LoA is *AILR Fully Autonomous* and coined as "Holistic Predictive," meaning that the use of Legal Judgment Predictions can go across all domains and subdomains of the legal field. The predictive capacity is done in a highly advanced manner, incorporating the Level 4 capabilities, along with exceeding those levels and providing a more fluent and capable predictive means.

At Level 6, the LoA is *AILR Superhuman Autonomous*, which as a reminder from Section 2 is not a capability that exists and might not exist, though it is included as a provision in case such a capability is ever achieved. In any case, the Legal Judgment Prediction at this level is considered "Pansophic Predictive" and would encapsulate the Level 5 capabilities, and then go beyond that in a manner that would leverage the AI superhuman capacity.

3.2 Legal Judgment Prediction: Approaches Utilized

Based on the discussion in Section 1, it is useful to consider the overarching nature of the approaches utilized in ascertaining Legal Judgment Prediction efforts.

Refer to **Figure B-2**.

As indicated, within the overall legal milieu there are the laws and the courts, of which there are then legal outcomes that are derived and produced. Presumably, the laws are made by lawmakers, while the courts consist of judges in the role of law-appliers (see Section 1 for further explanation about these matters).

For any given specific legal case, the goal of Legal Judgment Prediction is ostensibly to predict the legal outcome of that particular legal case.

The predictive approach typically uses as key factors:

- Case-Specific Legal Factors
- Judge-Specific Legal Factors
- Exogenous Factors
- Other

In the case-specific legal factors, the data or information collected, assessed, and used for making the outcome prediction is often quantified numerically. As per the discussion in Section 1, this might include codifying the factors into binary numeric values, stratified ranges, and so on. Also, there are linguistic bases for conducting the predictive efforts, involving examining the linguistical nuances and nature of the case. There is also the symbolic understanding approach that attempts to go beyond the traditional numeric or quantified approaches and seemingly include some form of comprehension toward the symbolic nature of the elements involved to make predictions.

Per the points made in Section 3, the judge-specific factors can also be included in the effort to undertake Legal Judgment Predictions. These can be categorized into two major sets, consisting of judicial oriented factors (such as the prior rulings of the judge) and extra-judicial oriented factors (e.g., what the judge ate for breakfast, which is an oft used exemplar).

Exogenous factors consist of elements that are beyond those of the case-specific and judge-specific, such as considering societal matters, socio-economic aspects, and the like.

Consider next some variants and additional considerations about the various factors and their usage. As indicated in **Figure B-3**, for those that argue that judges are apt to be "lawmakers" rather than solely acting as law-appliers, it would imply that the judge-specific factors become even more predominant and crucial than otherwise might be the case.

To further illustrate this perspective about Legal Judgment Prediction, consider the illustrations shown in **Figure B-4**.

All else being equal, it might be the case that the focus of the Legal Judgment Prediction would be based primarily on the laws themselves and less so than the courts, assuming that the courts are considered as consisting of law-appliers rather than as lawmakers. For the viewpoint that the courts and judges are actually working in a lawmaking capacity, presumably, the focus of Legal Judgment Prediction would center on the judges, more so than the laws themselves.

3.3 Four-Square Grid of Judicial Role

The discussion in Section 3.2 can be further extended.

Refer to **Figure B-5**.

This depicts a grid consisting of four quadrants.

Along the horizontal axis, there are two ways of interpreting the role of the judiciary, either as strictly law-appliers or as lawmakers. On the vertical axis, there are two ways shown that the law itself might be construed, either consisting of resolute law (as devised by legislative lawmakers) or as a kind of legal scaffolding (meaning that the law is malleable and porous).

The two horizontal and two vertical indications allow for a four-square quadrant representation and thus the grid as depicted.

In theory, the notion of judges as strictly being law-appliers can be mated with the notion of a resolute law facet, and thus the upper left quadrant that is labeled as V1 and indicated as "The Conventional Assumption." This square consists of the perspective that the courts and judges act to operationalize the law, rather than to make law per se.

Considered a more contemporary view is the square labeled as V2, in the lower right quadrant of the grid. This is the veritable "law is what the courts say it is" positioning, consisting of the judges as lawmakers and the law being perceived or acted upon as though it is malleable and porous.

This leaves two additional squares of the quadrant.

The lower left of the grid consists of the judges as lawmakers which is mated with the resolute law notion. As stated, this generally creates an inherent conflict, due to the possibility of essentially having two cooks in the kitchen, as it were.

Finally, the upper right grid indicates the judges as strictly law-appliers when mated with the law as scaffolding. It can be argued that this creates the possibility of a legal void in the law. Inevitably, there are likely pressures that would come to bear as to seeking to close or narrow the void. The intrinsic tension is whether the courts and judges are the appropriate void fillers, or whether the lawmakers of the legislative are the appropriate void fillers, or some combination thereof.

3.4 Legal Case Lifecycle Aspects

An important aspect of Legal Judgment Prediction consists of the legal case timeline and the stage at which a prediction is being rendered and the target stage of the prediction.

Much of the research described in Section 1 was generally based on the assumption that a prediction is to be rendered at the start of a case and the target is the outcome of the case. This though is somewhat amorphous and ill-specified and can be reconsidered more comprehensively by considering the full lifecycle of a legal case.

Refer to **Figure B-6**.

Consider these key junctures in a legal case:

- Pre-Case
- Case Start
- Case Underway
- Case Outcome (initial)
- Case Appeal #1
- Case Appeal #N
- Case Outcome (final)

It could be that before a legal case even gets started, there is interest in undertaking a Legal Judgment Prediction, thus it would be considered as occurring at a pre-case juncture of the legal case lifecycle. This differs by definition from making a prediction once a case has already started, and also implies that there is likely more known about the case once it has started versus when it is in a pre-case mode.

In terms of predicting the outcome of the legal case, it could be that the prediction is aimed at the initial outcome of the case, and for which the case might continue under appeal, gradually and ultimately coming to a final outcome. Thus, it can be ambiguous to refer to a case outcome without clarifying which such outcome the prediction is aiming to derive.

Refer next to **Figure B-7**.

It is often assumed that the start of the case is the prediction deriving juncture, and the target of the prediction is the legal case outcome. Though this is likely a popular choice of the junctures, it is not necessarily the only manner of choice available. In short, at any juncture in the legal case lifecycle, a Legal Judgment Prediction might be rendered.

Thus, a legal case might already be underway and there is interest in predicting the initial case outcome.

Note that this points out too that a target aim can be an intermediate state of the legal case and not solely the end state of the legal case.

For the convenience of reference, Figure B-7 indicates each of the primary junctures as "Jx" whereby the "x" is indicative of a simple numbering of the junctures. This is not meant to be definitive and merely showcases that a numbering scheme can be used to label the stages or phases of a legal case throughout its lifecycle. A legal case could be subdivided into any number Z of junctures (rather than the seven indicated in this example), and thus at any juncture, a prediction can seek to be rendered for some Z+y number of junctures ahead in the lifecycle.

Presumably, the tighter the range between the juncture of the prediction and the juncture of the target stage, the more accurate the prediction can be, assuming all else is equal therein, and likewise that the further along the case is in the lifecycle and thus the higher at which the juncture Z is utilized as a point at which to render a prediction the more accurate the prediction can be, all else being equal.

As mentioned in Section 4 about future research, these postulations about the points at which Legal Judgment Prediction is rendered and targeted are deserving of further research and empirical study.

3.5 Aims of the Prediction Targeting

Much of the research literature depicted in Section 1 has been varied as to what the nature of the legal case outcome is to consist of.

In other words, it could be that the outcome is solely about whether the case has been ruled in favor or opposition. And though that is obviously a vital element for an outcome, it is not the only such element, and thus it is useful to consider the other elements that might also be considered as prediction targets.

Refer to **Figure B-8**.

As indicated, the legal case outcome can consist of a variety of aspects, including but limited to:

- Prevailing Party
- Mistrial
- Settlement
- Case Dropped
- Verdict
- Penalty
- Etc.

The use of Legal Judgment Prediction can consist of aiming at only one of those such outcomes, or more than one, and/or a combination of those potential outcomes. Research on the nature of LJP can better be utilized by clarifying what the outcome(s) are that are being targeted and also the differences, if any, in how to undertake LJP depending upon the outcome(s) being targeted (this is a recommendation also made in Section 4 on further research).

There are additional targets to be considered.

One is the legal case rationale, which consists of why the outcome was ascertained, or at least a predicted rationale (whether it was the true basis is another question altogether, of course).

Legal Judgment Prediction can also be called upon to predict the legal case costs, the legal case effort, the legal case rationale, and so on.

And, as mentioned in Section 3.4, keep in mind that these predictive matters can occur at any given juncture Z of the legal case lifecycle and be targeting some Z+y juncture, and does not suggest that it is always and only at the start and nor always and only targeting the final state.

3.6 LJP And Basket Or Bundling of Legal Cases

Generally, most of the research literature indicated in Section 1 has primarily focused on using Legal Judgment Prediction for taking a specific legal case and predicting the outcome of that specific case.

Legal Judgment Prediction can also be utilized in a basket or bundling manner.

Refer to **Figure B-9**.

As shown, a set of legal cases might be clumped together in a basket of legal cases, or considered a bundle of legal cases, and as a set be used to predict a legal outcome that is anticipated to be the singular outcome applicable to each member of the set.

Thus, there is one singular outcome, and for which it applies presumably to each of the legal cases of the devised set.

Doing this kind of basket or bundling has its own complexities and facets, thus, it is worthwhile to highlight that this is another form in which Legal Judgment Prediction can be utilized, and ergo can be studied as a variant thereof.

3.7 Additional Crucial Facets

To further aid in identifying facets that are crucial to the maturity of Legal Judgement Prediction, consider the elements indicated in **Figure B-10**.

The elements shown include:

- Transparency
- Actor Predictors
- Biases Handling
- Probabilistic Tendencies

Consider each of these elements.

- Transparency.

In brief, one consideration involves the transparency involved in a Legal Judgment Prediction. The method used for the LJP might be available for inspection and fully transparent, or it might be a Black Box that is considered opaque. Another facet is whether the LJP can explain how it worked, or whether it might be inscrutable or lacking in being able to be interpreted.

- Actor Predictors

In brief, the question arises as to how the Legal Judgment Prediction will be carried out. This can consist of a human-only based prediction, an AI-only based prediction, or a human and AI jointly undertaken prediction.

- Biases Handling

In brief, there are many aspects to be addressed regarding the potential for biases being an ingredient within a Legal Judgment Prediction. There can be hidden biases, which can distort or alter the nature of the prediction and the predictive capacity. There can be explicitly noted biases, which then need to be considered in light of the predictions rendered. Various bias correction methods and approaches can be utilized. And so on.

- Probabilistic Tendencies

Much of the research literature as depicted in Section 1 does not especially bring forth the aspect that the prediction is undoubtedly one of a probabilistic nature. In a sense, without explicitly mentioning the certainty or uncertainty of a prediction, the default tends to imply that the certainty is complete, though this is rarely the likely case. As such, it is vital to acknowledge and recognize the uncertainties involved and then indicate what those consist of, along with how the certainty can be impacted by the methods used in the course of the Legal Judgment Prediction.

3.8 AILR and LJP Impact

An important consideration worth exploring is the over-time judicial reliance upon human judicial judgment versus AILR capabilities.

Refer to **Figure B-11.**

A graph is portrayed that consists of the magnitude of judicial reliance on the Y-axis (ranging from low to high), while time is exhibited on the X-axis. Time is indicated as beginning at t-0 and proceeding forward in time, of which there are two especially salient points in time marked, consisting of time t-r and time t-u, explained momentarily.

A dashed line representing the reliance upon human judicial judgment is shown as starting at the high position on the Y-axis and then proceeding in a sloping downward motion over-time, inexorably proceeding toward the lower ends of reliance.

Meanwhile, a second line is shown as starting at the origin point of zero, proceeding on an upward slope over-time, and indicative of the AILR capabilities that will presumably increase over time and thus it is assumed there will be an increasing reliance upon the AILR for participating in or providing judicial judgment.

Note that the graph is not drawn to scale and is intended merely as an overall gauge or macroscopic illustration of the issues being discussed herein.

At some point in time, designated as t-r, the reliance upon AILR begins to exceed the reliance upon human judicial judgment (so postulated). It is not a foregone conclusion that this will necessarily occur and purely indicated as worthwhile for discussion. Likewise, it is not necessarily the case that the rising AILR reliance necessitates a reducing reliance on human judicial judgment, though this is the postulated theory that oft is argued about the gradual advance of AILR. After passing the crossover, there is a Zone S, into which it is possible that the problematic aspects of performing Legal Judgment Prediction might wane, due to the facet that the AILR is becoming dominant in the reliance upon rendering judicial decisions and (if one assumes) the AILR will be explicative and thus presumably transparent. This transparency would suggest that predicting what the AILR is going to judicial proffer is much more predictable and straightforward (though, not necessarily the case if the AILR has been allowed to become opaque or otherwise closed in its inner workings).

The line representing the reliance upon human judicial judgment does not touch the X-axis as it is unknown as to whether there would ever be a point at which all human judicial judgment would be no longer utilized such that only AILR was utilized (this is a classic open debate).

Section 4: Additional Considerations and Future Research

As earlier indicated, Legal Judgment Prediction (LJP) is a longstanding and open issue in the theory and practice-of-law. Predicting the nature and outcomes of judicial matters is important. Intrinsically, generating judicially laden predictions has been limited in utility and exactitude, as illustrated via the literature review of Section 1. Though various methods and techniques to predict legal cases and judicial actions have emerged over time, especially arising via the advent of computer-based modeling, including simple calculative methods to highly sophisticated and complex statistical models, much still needs to be done to improve LJP.

Artificial Intelligence (AI) based approaches have been increasingly utilized and will undoubtedly have a pronounced impact on how LJP is performed and its predictive accuracy. Per Section 3, Legal Judgment Prediction can holistically be understood by using the Levels of Autonomy (LoA) of AI Legal Reasoning, plus, other considerations are further to be advanced, including LJP probabilistic tendencies, biases handling, actor predictors, transparency, judicial reliance, legal case outcomes, and other crucial elements entailing the overarching legal judicial milieu. Future research is needed to explore in greater detail the manner and means by which AI-enablement will occur in the law along with the potential for both positive and adverse consequences in LJP. Autonomous AILR is likely to materially impact the effort, theory, and practice of Legal Judgment Prediction, including as a minimum playing a notable or possibly even pivotal role in such advancements.

References

1. Alarie, Benjamin, and Anthony Niblett, Albert Yoon (2017). "Regulation by Machine," V24, Journal of Machine Learning.

2. Aletras, Nikolaos, and Dimitrios Tsarapatsanis, Daniel Preoţiuc-Pietro, and Vasileios Lampos. 2016. Predicting judicial decisions of the european court of human rights: A natural language processing perspective. PeerJ Computer Science, 2:e93.

3. Ashley, Kevin, and Karl Branting, Howard Margolis, and Cass Sunstein (2001). "Legal Reasoning and Artificial Intelligence: How Computers 'Think' Like Lawyers," Symposium: Legal Reasoning and Artificial Intelligence, University of Chicago Law School Roundtable.

4. Ashley, Kevin and Stefanie Bruninghaus (2006). "Computer Models for Legal Prediction," Volume 46, Number 3, Jurimetrics.

5. Ashley, Kevin and Stefanie Bruninghaus (2009). "Automatically Classifying Case Texts and Predicting Outcomes," Volume 17, Number 2, Artificial Intelligence Law.

6. Atkinson, Katie, and Pietro Baroni, Massimiliano Giacomin, Anthony Hunter, Henry Prakken, Chris Reed, Guillermo Simari, Matthias Thimm, Serena Villata (2017). "Toward Artificial Argumentation," AAAI AI Magazine.

7. Atkinson, Katie, and Trevor Bench-Capon, Danushka Bollegala (2020). "Explanation in AI and Law: Past, Present, and Future," Artificial Intelligence.

8. Baker, Jamie (2018). "A Legal Research Odyssey: Artificial Intelligence as Disrupter," Law Library Journal.

9. Baum, Lawrence (2009). The Puzzle of Judicial Behavior. University of Michigan Press.

10. Ben-Ari, Daniel, and D., Frish, Y., Lazovski, A., Eldan, U., & Greenbaum, D. (2016). "Artificial Intelligence in the Practice of Law: An Analysis and Proof of Concept Experiment," Volume 23, Number 2, Richmond Journal of Law & Tech.

11. Bench-Capon, and Givoanni Sartor (2003). "A Model of Legal Reasoning with Cases Incorporating Theories and Values," November 2013, Artificial Intelligence.

12. Bobbitt, Philip (2014). "The Age of Consent," Volume 123, Number 7, The Yale Law Journal.

13. Braithwaite, John (2002). "Rules and Principles: A Theory of Legal Certainty," Volume 27, Australian Journal of Legal Philosophy.

14. Buchanan, Bruce, and Thomas Headrick (1970). "Some Speculation about Artificial Intelligence and Legal Reasoning," Volume 23, Stanford Law Review.

15. Casey, Anthony, and Anthony Niblett (2016). "Self-Driving Laws," Volume 429, University of Toronto Law Journal.

16. Chagal-Feferkorn, Karni (2019). "Am I An Algorithm or a Product: When Products Liability Should Apply to Algorithmic Decision-Makers," Stanford Law & Policy Review.

17. Chen, Daniel (2019). "Machine Learning and the Rule of Law," in Law as Data: Computation, Text, and The Future of Legal Analysis (Michael A. Livermore and Daniel N. Rockmore.

18. Coglianese, Cary, and David Lehr (2017). "Rulemaking by Robot: Administrative Decision Making in the Machine-Learning Era," Volume 105, Georgetown Law Journal.

19. D'Amato, Anthony (2008). "A New (and Better) Interpretation of Holmes's Prediction Theory of Law," Working Paper Number 163, Northwestern University School of Law.

20. D'Amato, Anthony (2010). "Legal Realism Explains Nothing," Working Paper Number 84, Northwestern U. School of Law.

21. Dung, Phan (1993). "On the Acceptability of Arguments and its Fundamental Role in Nonmonotonic Reasoning and Logic Programming," Proceedings of the 13th International Joint Conference on Artificial Intelligence.

22. Eliot, Lance (2016). AI Guardian Angels for Deep AI Trustworthiness. LBE Press Publishing.

23. Eliot, Lance (2020). "The Neglected Dualism of Artificial Moral Agency and Artificial Legal Reasoning in AI for Social Good." Harvard University, Harvard Center for Research on Computation and Society, AI for Social Good Conference, July 21, 2020.

24. Eliot, Lance (2020). AI and Legal Reasoning Essentials. LBE Press Publishing.

25. Eliot, Lance (2019). Artificial Intelligence and LegalTech Essentials. LBE Press Publishing.

26. Eliot, Lance (2020). "The Next Era of American Law Amid The Advent of Autonomous AI Legal Reasoning," Cornell University arXiv. https://arxiv.org/abs/2009.11647

27. Eliot, Lance (2020). "An Ontological AI-and-Law Framework for the Autonomous Levels of AI Legal Reasoning," Cornell University arXiv. https://arxiv.org/abs/2008.07328

28. Eliot, Lance (2020). "Turing Test and the Practice of Law: The Role of Autonomous Levels of AI Legal Reasoning," Cornell University arXiv. https://arxiv.org/abs/2008.07743

29. Eliot, Lance (2020). "Multidimensionality of the Legal Singularity: The Role of Autonomous Levels of AI Legal Reasoning," Cornell University arXiv. https://arxiv.org/abs/2008.10575

30. Eliot, Lance (2020). "Authorized and Unauthorized Practices of Law: The Role of Autonomous Levels of AI Legal Reasoning," Cornell University arXiv. https://arxiv.org/abs/2008.09507

31. Eliot, Lance (2020). "An Impact Model of AI on the Principles of Justice," Cornell University arXiv. https://arxiv.org/abs/2008.12615

32. Eliot, Lance (2020). "Robustness and Overcoming Brittleness of AI-Enabled Legal Micro-Directives," Cornell University arXiv. https://arxiv.org/abs/2009.02243

33. Eliot, Lance (2020). "AI and Legal Argumentation," Cornell University arXiv. https://arxiv.org/abs/2009.11180

34. Feteris E.T. (1999) MacCormick's Theory of the Justification of Legal Decisions. In: Fundamentals of Legal Argumentation. Argumentation Library, vol 1. Springer, Dordrecht.

35. Feteris, Eveline, and Harm Kloosterhuis (2009). "The Analysis and Evaluation of Legal Argumentation: Approaches from Legal Theory and Argumentation Theory," Volume 16, Studies in Logic, Grammar and Rhetoric.

36. Friedman, Lawrence (2019). A History of American Law, 4th ed. Oxford University Press.

37. Gardner, Anne (1987). Artificial Intelligence and Legal Reasoning. MIT Press.

38. Genesereth, Michael (2009). "Computational Law: The Cop in the Backseat," Stanford Center for Legal Informatics, Stanford University.

39. Gilmore, Grant (1977). The Ages of American Law. Yale University Press.

40. Grunbaum, Werner (1971). "Response – Werner F. Grunbaum," Volume 1971, Issue 2, Washington University Law Review.

41. Grunbaum, Werner and Albert Newhouse (1965). "Quantitative Analysis of Judicial Decisions: Some Problems in Prediction. Volume 201, Number 3, Houston Law Review.

42. Hage, Jaap (2000). "Dialectical Models in Artificial Intelligence and Law," Artificial Intelligence and Law.

43. Hall, Kermit, and William Wiecek, Paul Finkelman (1996). American Legal History: Cases and Materials, 2nd ed. Oxford University Press.

44. Hall, Mark, and Ronald Wright (2006). "Systematic Content Analysis of Judicial Opinions," Volume 96, Issue 1, California Law Review.

45. Harbert, T. (2013). "The Law Machine," Volume 50, Issue 11, IEEE Spectrum.

46. Hart, H (1961). The Concept of Law. Oxford University Press.

47. Holmes, Oliver Wendell (1897). "The Path of the Law," Harvard Law Review.

48. Huhn, Wilson (2000). "Teaching Legal Analysis Using a Pluralistic Model of Law," Volume 36, Number 3, Gonzaga Law Review.

49. Huhn, Wilson (2003). "The Stages of Legal Reasoning: Formalism, Analogy, and Realism," Volume 48, Villanova Law Review.

50. Kaplow, Louis (1992). "Rules Versus Standards: An Economic Analysis," Volume 42, Duke Law Journal.

51. Kastellec, Jonathan (2010). "The Statistical Analysis of Judicial Decisions and Legal Rules with Classification Trees," Volume 7, Number 2, Journal of Empirical Legal Studies.

52. Katz, Daniel, and Michael Bommarito, Josh Blackman (2017). "A General Approach for Predicting the Behavior of the Supreme Court of the United States," Volume 12, Number 4, Plos One.

53. Keown, R. (1980). "Mathematical Models for Legal Prediction," Volume 2, Issue 1, Computer/Law Journal.

54. Kort, F. (1957). "Predicting Supreme Court Decisions Mathematically: A Quantitative Analysis of the "Right to Counsel" Cases," Volume 51, Number 1, American Political Science Review.

55. Lauderdale, Benjamin, and Tom Clark (2012). "The Supreme Court's Many Median Justices," Volume 106, Number 4, American Political Science Review.

56. Lawlor, Reed (1963). "What Computers Can Do: Analysis and Prediction of Judicial Decisions," Volume 49, Number 4, American Bar Association Journal.

57. Llewellyn, Karl (1950). "Remarks on the Theory of Appellate Decision and the Rules or Canons About How Statutes Are to Be Construed," Volume 3, Number 4, Vanderbilt Law Review.

58. Llewellyn, Karl (1960). The Common Law Tradition: Deciding Appeals. Quid Pro Books.

59. Luo, Bingfeng, and Yansong Feng, Jianbo Xu, Xiang Zhang, Dongyan Zhao (2017). "Learning to Predict Charges for Criminal Cases with Legal Basis," arXiv preprint arXiv:1707.09168.

60. MacCormick, Neil (1978). Legal Reasoning and Legal Theory.

61. Markou, Christopher, and Simon Deakin (2020). "Is Law Computable? From Rule of Law to Legal Singularity," May 4, 2020, SSRN, University of Cambridge Faculty of Law Research Paper.

62. Martin, Andrew, and Kevin Quinn, Theodore Ruger, Pauline Kim (2004). "Competing Approaches to Predicting Supreme Court Decision Making," Perspectives on Politics.

63. McCarty, L. (1995)." An implementation of Eisner v. Macomber," Proceedings of the 5th International Conference on Artificial Intelligence and Law.

64. McCarty, Thorne (1977). "Reflections on TAXMAN: An Experiment in Artificial Intelligence and Legal Reasoning," January 1977, Harvard Law Review.

65. McGinnis, John, and Russell G. Pearce (2014). "The Great Disruption: How Machine Intelligence Will Transform the Role of Lawyers in the Delivery of Legal Services," Volume 82, Number 6, Fordham Law Review.

66. McGinnis, John, and Steven Wasick (2015). "Law's Algorithm," Volume 66, Florida Law Review.

67. Mnookin, Robert, and Lewis Kornhauser (1979). "Bargaining in the Shadow of the Law," Volume 88, Number 5, April 1979, The Yale Law Review.

68. Nagel, Stuart (1963). "Applying Correlation Analysis to Case Prediction," Volume 42, Texas Law Review.

69. Noonan, John (1961). "Review of Hart's Book 'The Concept of Law'," Volume 7, Issue 1, The American Journal of Jurisprudence.

70. Prakken, Henry (1995). "From Logic to Dialectics in Legal Argument," Proceedings of the 5th International Conference on Artificial Intelligence and Law.

71. Reinbold, Patric (2020). "Taking Artificial Intelligence Beyond the Turing Test," Volume 20, Wisconsin Law Review.

72. Remus, Dana, and Frank Levy, "Can Robots be Lawyers? Computers, Robots, and the Practice of Law," Volume 30, Georgetown Journal of Legal Ethics.

73. Rich, Michael (2016). "Machine Learning, Automated Suspicion Algorithms, and the Fourth Amendment," Volume 164, University of Pennsylvania Law Review.

74. Rissland, Edwina (1990). "Artificial Intelligence and Law: Stepping Stones to a Model of Legal Reasoning," Yale Law Journal.

75. SAE (2018). Taxonomy and Definitions for Terms Related to Driving Automation Systems for On-Road Motor Vehicles, J3016-201806, SAE International.

76. Schauer, Frederick (1998). "Prediction and Particularity," Volume 78, Boston University Law Review.

77. Segal, Jeffrey (1984). "Predicting Supreme Court Cases Probabilistically: The Search and Seizure Cases," Volume 78, Issue 4, American Political Science Review.

78. Shaikh, Rafe Athar and Tirath Prasad Sahu, Veena Anand (2020). "Predicting Outcomes of Legal Cases based on Legal Factors using Classifiers," ScienceDirect.

79. Sunstein, Cass (2001). "Of Artificial Intelligence and Legal Reasoning," University of Chicago Law School, Working Papers.

80. Sunstein, Cass, and Kevin Ashley, Karl Branting, Howard Margolis (2001). "Legal Reasoning and Artificial Intelligence: How Computers 'Think' Like Lawyers," Symposium: Legal Reasoning and Artificial Intelligence, University of Chicago.

81. Surden, Harry (2014). "Machine Learning and Law," Washington Law Review.

82. Surden, Harry (2019). "Artificial Intelligence and Law: An Overview," Summer 2019, Georgia State University Law Review.

83. Susskind, Richard (2019). Online Courts and the Future of Justice. Oxford University Press.

84. Tashea, Jason (2019). "France Bans Publishing of Judicial Analytics and Prompts Criminal Penalty," ABA Journal, June 7, 2019.

85. Verheij, B. (2001). "Legal Decision Making as Dialectical Theory Construction with Argumentation Schemes," Proceedings of the 8th International Conference of Artificial Intelligence and Law.

86. Volokh, Eugne (2019). "Chief Justice Robots," Volume 68, Duke Law Journal.

87. Waltl, Bernhard, and Roland Vogl (2018). "Explainable Artificial Intelligence: The New Frontier in Legal Informatics," February 2018, Jusletter IT 22, Stanford Center for Legal Informatics, Stanford University.

88. Webster, David (1978). "The Ages of American Law," Volume 27, Issue 2. DePaul Law Review.

89. White, Edward (2016). Law in American History. Oxford University Press.

90. Wolfram, Stephen (2018). "Computational Law, Symbolic Discourse, and the AI Constitution," in Data-Driven Law: Data Analytics and the New Legal Services (Edward J. Walters ed.).

91. Xu, Nuo, and Pinghui Wang, Long Chen, Li Pan, Xiaoyan Wang, Junzhou Zhao (2020). "Distinguish Confusing Law Articles for Legal Judgment Prediction," Proceedings of the 58th Annual Meeting of the Association for Computational Linguistics.

92. Zhong, Haoxi, and Zhipeng Guo , Cunchao Tu, Chaojun Xiao, Zhiyuan Liu , Maosong Sun (2017). "Legal Judgment Prediction via Topological Learning," Proceedings of the 2018 Conference on Empirical Methods in Natural Language Processing

---

Note: *For supplemental materials depicting the aspects discussed in this chapter, refer to Appendix B, which contains various augmented diagrams, charts, and additional related facets of relevance.*

CHAPTER 12

AI AND LEGAL ARGUMENTATION

Abstract

Legal argumentation is a vital cornerstone of justice, underpinning an adversarial form of law, and extensive research has attempted to augment or undertake legal argumentation via the use of computer-based automation including Artificial Intelligence (AI). AI advances in Natural Language Processing (NLP) and Machine Learning (ML) have especially furthered the capabilities of leveraging AI for aiding legal professionals, doing so in ways that are modeled here as *CARE*, namely Crafting, Assessing, Refining, and Engaging in legal argumentation. In addition to AI-enabled legal argumentation serving to augment human-based lawyering, an aspirational goal of this multi-disciplinary field consists of ultimately achieving autonomously effected human-equivalent legal argumentation. As such, an innovative meta-approach is proposed to apply the Levels of Autonomy (LoA) of AI Legal Reasoning (AILR) to the maturation of AI and Legal Argumentation (AILA), proffering a new means of gauging progress in this ever-evolving and rigorously sought domain.

Section 1: Background on Legal Argumentation

Legal scholars and the legal profession overall have expended much effort and attention toward the formulation and analysis of legal argumentation [5] [31] [32] [42]. This focus on legal argumentation has entailed in-depth research and conceptual examination of what constitutes legal argumentation all told, along with the detailing of the day-to-day practical aspects concerning how to best undertake legal argumentation and how to gauge when legal argumentation is being accomplished well or performed poorly [10] [41] [46].

Taking a brief side tangent for purposes of definitional clarity, there is pervasive ambiguity about the meaning of the phrase "legal argumentation" as to its exact definition and denotations. Likewise, the phrase "legal argument" also has varied connotations. To make this discussion relatively parsimonious, this paper considers that "legal argumentation" shall herein refer to the broadest scope of all facets involved in the act of argumentation within the field of law. Meanwhile, the phrase "legal argument" will be reserved for use when discussing a particular instance or sub-element within the umbrella of legal argumentation. It is hoped that this will enable the discussion to be more readily cohesive and consistent, doing so without any loss of substantive indication or impact. Even if the proposed demarcation is not of satisfaction to some, or could be seen as arguable unto itself, it nonetheless does not undercut or distill the essence of the discussion. Given that brief clarification, the discussion can now continue with that caveat so noted.

Legal argumentation is reasonably viewed as a variant of generic argumentation [18] [68], suggesting that there is a macroscopic realm entailing "argumentation" of any kind or nature and that legal argumentation is an instantiation or incarnation of argumentation into the domain of law. Thus, there is the full spectrum of generic argumentation, out of which there could be argumentation applied in specific disciplines, such as the law, medicine, engineering, and the like.

Some controversy exists over the question of whether generic argumentation is any different fundamentally from the argumentation utilized within any particular domain or discipline.

In other words, generic argumentation might be simply reused within the field of law, for example, and not be structurally or intrinsically any different due to the advent of its use in the legal domain.

There are ongoing debates as to legal argumentation being essentially a subset of generic argumentation or whether it can be construed as a superset. If one asserts that legal argumentation goes beyond the realm of generic argumentation, presumably then it is the case that legal argumentation is a superset. If one asserts that legal argumentation is no more than the application of generic argumentation into the nuances of the law, presumably legal argumentation is a subset thereof.

Whichever side of the debate one takes, it does appear that the efforts to explore, extend, and mature our understanding of generic argumentation provides insights for legal argumentation, and similarly that the efforts underlying the maturation of legal argumentation can be funneled into generic argumentation comprehension. As such, this paper takes no side on this question and merely notes its importance, synergistic effect, and ongoing consideration in such matters.

One could sensibly claim that legal argumentation is more than merely one amongst equals in terms of the instantiation of generic argumentation. Of all the various disciplines that draw upon argumentation, legal argumentation has a most notable history and need for pushing ahead on extending what argumentation consists of and how it can be described and utilized.

Legal argumentation is a vital cornerstone of justice, underpinning an adversarial form of law. This is not to imply that legal argumentation does not appear in and nor serves a crucial role in other forms of law, and merely is noted as especially required and to some degree revered when placed into an adversarial architecture. The adversarial approach places legal argumentation at the front and center of legal matters and therefore heightens interest and priority to the state of legal argumentation.

To bolster legal argumentation, there have been efforts to dovetail the use of computer-based systems into the field of and the everyday acts of legal argumentation. In its simpler form, computers can be a storehouse from which legal argumentation can be undertaken by humans, and otherwise, the computer is serving as a modest aid in a rather mechanistic manner.

The field of Artificial Intelligence (AI) has long sought to intermix with the field of Legal Argumentation, doing so to try and extend the computer capabilities to be a more powerful aid to humans involved in legal argumentation. Indeed, there is extensive research that has attempted to augment or undertake legal argumentation via the use of computer-based automation including especially the AI subfields of Natural Language Processing (NLP), Machine Learning (ML), and Knowledge-Based Systems (KBMS).

An overarching aspiration for AI in the legal argumentation realm would be to have the computer or machine be able to autonomously perform some or all of the aspects of legal argumentation. Ultimately, achieving autonomously effected human-equivalent legal argumentation is a long-sought goal for those in this specialty of AI. Within the legal field, there has been a similar interest, and thus there is a decidedly multi-disciplinary effort involved in these matters. For those interested in technological capabilities, the attention tends to go toward developing AI that can perform legal argumentation. Also, there is a rightful concern and attention toward the societal implications of AI that could perform legal argumentation, including whether this would be considered a form of practice-of-law, and what implications this has for those seeking legal advice and those proffering legal advice.

Returning to the synergistic aspects earlier mentioned, there is an ongoing dance, as it were, entailing the synergistic effects of generic argumentation with legal argumentation, and the synergistic effects of AI with both generic argumentation and legal argumentation. To emphasize, it is not as though AI is somehow a sideline aspect that is solely attempting to implement argumentation (of any kind).

Instead, AI also contributes to the understanding of what argumentation consists of, and thus probes and provides substantive advancement to argumentation, whether it be for generic argumentation or the field of legal argumentation.

There is, in a sense, plenty of synergies to go around. AI as a field is inherently itself enriched by seeking to be an element of and contributor to generic argumentation and also of legal argumentation. This occurs on both a theoretical level of deriving new theories and conceptual gains and also on a practical basis of deploying usable systems. In short, it would seem that each field of inquiry is apt to gain by the deployment of the other into its focal of inquiry.

This paper seeks to contribute to that aspiration and does so by proposing an innovative meta-approach toward applying the Levels of Autonomy (LoA) of AI Legal Reasoning (AILR) to the maturation of AI and Legal Argumentation (AILA), proffering a new means of gauging progress in this ever-evolving and rigorously sought domain.

Doing so provides a well-needed means of measuring progress in the aspiration of integrating AI and legal argumentation. Researchers and scholars can make use of the LoA AILR to AILA to assess progress in the theoretical and conceptual efforts of integration, while practitioners can assess the strengths, weaknesses, and progress in the deployment of such capabilities. This paper also provides a model known as *CARE*, namely Crafting, Assessing, Refining, and Engaging in legal argumentation, which outlines the core facets by which AI is integrated into legal argumentation.

In Section 1 of this paper, the topic of legal argumentation is further introduced and addressed. Doing so establishes the groundwork for the subsequent sections. Section 2 introduces the Levels of Autonomy (LoA) of AI Legal Reasoning (AILR), which is instrumental in the discussions undertaken in Section 3. Section 3 provides an indication of the AI-enablement of legal argumentation as it applies to the LoA AILR. The final section, Section 4, covers additional considerations and recommendations.

This paper then consists of these four sections:

- Section 1: Background on Legal Legal Argumentation
- Section 2: Autonomous Levels of AI Legal Reasoning
- Section 3: Legal Argumentation and AI Enablement
- Section 4: Additional Considerations and Future Research

1.3 Research on Legal Argumentation and AI

As mentioned, legal argumentation is crucial to the field of law, and this is emphasized in the case of resolving legal disputes [9]: "Argumentation is particularly important in law: a legal case typically centres on a conflict between two parties which is resolved by each side producing arguments in an effort to persuade the judge that their side is right. The judge then decides which party to favour, and publishes a decision in which he argues why his decision is justified. Modelling legal reasoning can then be seen, to a large extent, in terms of modelling argument, and so it is unsurprising that attempts to understand legal argumentation have been a key strand in AI and Law."

Of course, legal argumentation has numerous other roles besides solely dealing with particular legal conflicts or disputes and permeates a wide array of legal activities and efforts. In addition, legal argumentation pervades the adversarial process [3]: "Legal reasoning usually takes place in the context of a dispute between adversaries, within a prescribed legal procedure. This makes the setting inherently dynamic and multiparty and raises issues of strategy and choice. For example, there is work on optimal strategies for adversaries in debates with an adjudicator, given their preferences over the possible outcomes of a debate and their estimates of what the adjudicator will likely accept."

There is much discourse regarding whether there is a potential unification theory that might someday be postulated to fully provide a complete semblance of legal argumentation in the law, of which there is doubt cast that such an all-encompassing theory is viable, as will be indicated next.

Consider the pluralistic model of law, which can be depicted as [40]: "I accept the term 'pluralistic' for this descriptive model of legal argument because it reflects the fact that law arises from value choices made by different persons at different times and it acknowledges that there are different ways to determine what choices they made. Heads of administrative agencies, judges, legislators, and the people all make law. There are a variety of methods for interpreting the law they have made, and as a result our interpretations of the law are sometimes contradictory." And as further stated: In their view, the law is not essentially a unitary system that can be explained by a 'grand unifying theory' or 'foundational analysis.' Instead, our system of law is characterized by the fact that multiple legitimate forms of legal arguments exist."

Some are seeking to mathematically or computationally model legal argumentation in the quest of seemingly embodying the law in an axiomatic way. There are serious questions expressed about the efficacy of these approaches in terms of making a key assumption that law is ultimately determinate and calculable. For example, as stated by [40]: "For pluralists, law is inherently indeterminate because valid but contradictory legal arguments potentially exist regarding the interpretation of the law."

Efforts to utilize rule-based non-monotonic logic-based systems for modeling legal argumentation are also called into question [56]: "We also argued that 'traditional' rule-based nonmonotonic logics (whether argumentation-based or not) are of limited use, and that the role of cases, principle, purpose and value should not be ignored, as well as the importance of dynamics, procedure and multi-agent interaction. This holds for the law but also for related areas such as policy making, group decision making and democratic deliberation. More generally, legal applications of logic confirm the recent trend of widening the scope of logic from deduction to information flow, argumentation and interaction."

Part of this can be attributed to what some suggest is a false belief that there are legal specifications that if only found or voiced would then allow for AI to be codified accordingly, as mentioned in [33]:

> "Although it is commonly accepted that legal decisions must be justified in a rational way, there are hardly explicit legal specifications as to what the justification should consist of. One of the important problems in the study of legal argumentation is which standards of legal soundness the argumentation should meet."

According to [33], it is vital to realize that legal argumentation consists of several components, involving philosophical, theoretical, reconstruction, empirical, and practice facets: "The philosophical component attends to the normative foundation of a theory of legal argumentation. In the theoretical component, models for legal argumentation are developed, in which the structure of legal argument and norms and rules for argument-acceptability are formulated. The reconstruction component shows how to reconstruct legal argument in an analytical model. The empirical component investigates the construction and evaluation of arguments in actual legal practice. Finally, the practical component considers how various results forwarded by the philosophical, theoretical, analytical, and the empirical components might be used in legal practice."

This though does not summarily discount the value of mathematical formulation for legal argumentation, noting that one should not necessarily discard the advantages out-of-hand and that such computational models can be of significant benefit [9]: "It is, of course, the case that similar issues underpin one well-established and highly-developed theory: that of formal logic and mathematical proof. It is no coincidence that much of the formal computational treatment of argumentation has its roots in ideas developed from AI inspired contributions to logic and deductive reasoning. So one finds in mathematical proof theory core concepts such as: precisely defined means for expressing assertions (e.g. formulae in a given logical language); accepted bases on which to build theorems (e.g. collections of axioms); procedures prescribing the means by which further theorems may be derived from existing theorems and axioms (e.g. templates for inference rules); and precise concepts of termination (e.g. a sentential form is derivable as a theorem, 'true'; or is logically invalid, 'false')."

But legal argumentation still has extraordinary facets that require going beyond traditional mathematical formulations, of which the intrinsic element that legal argumentation necessitates of *persuasion* opens the matter further, accordingly [9]: "One can summarise the distinction between argumentation and proof by the observation that the object of argumentation is to persuade (to acceptance of a given claim; to performance of a desired action, and so on). Unlike the concept of 'proof'—at the level of deriving a sentential representation of an assertion—whether an argument is "correct" is not a factor, and, indeed, "correctness" may not even be sensibly defined. In contrast, mathematical reasoning, in order to have any value, must be correct where 'correctness' has a strict, formal definition: beyond this requirement, however, notions of "persuasiveness" are unimportant."

Perhaps this is succinctly stated by the assertion in [49]: "But there is more to a legal argument than reasoning or logic. Justices and attorneys bring an interpretive context, argumentative and rhetorical strategies, and other more general models of the domain and the world to an oral argument."

A distinction made by some researchers is that legal argumentation is not a pure logic-based effort and should be seen as one of more so rhetoric-based [40]: "Legal reasoning is not composed of deductive arguments framed for the purpose of proving the truth of a particular proposition but is a species of rhetoric designed to persuade others to accept a particular interpretation of the law. But how is the persuasiveness of a legal argument to be evaluated? What is the yardstick against which we measure the 'correctness' of legal reasoning? There are two fundamental types of challenges to legal arguments: 'intramodal' and 'intermodal' challenges. Intramodal critiques challenge legal arguments on their own terms, while intermodal critiques address the validity or weight to be accorded to each type of argument."

Per the research of [39], persuasiveness is indeed vital to legal argumentation: "Legal reasoning entails a practice of argumentation. The reasons given for the conclusions reached are to be measured by their persuasiveness, not by reference to some established true state of affairs."

Part of the conundrum underlying this ingredient of persuasiveness is that besides being difficult if not indeterminable to model, there are canons of construction related to the law that can essentially land on either side of a legal argumentation case. For example, Llewellyn made this point about the nature of opposing canons [45]: "As in argument over points of case-law, the accepted convention still, unhappily requires discussion as if only one single correct meaning could exist. Hence there are two opposing canons on almost every point. An arranged selection is appended. Every lawyer must be familiar with them all: they are still needed tools of argument."

Some examples of these opposing canons can be illustrative of this matter. Consider this one [45]:

"1. A statute cannot go beyond its text."

And this corresponding and opposite one:

"1. To effect its purpose a statute text may be implemented beyond its text."

Similar examples in [45] demonstrate this same facility of the law and legal argumentation:

"2. Statutes in derogation of the common law will not be extended by construction."

"2. Such acts will be liberally construed if their nature is remedial."

And this one about common law [45]:

"3. Statutes are to be read in the light of the common law and a statue affirming a common law rule is to be construed in accordance with the common law."

"3. The common law gives way to a statue which is inconsistent with it and when a statue is designed as a revision of a whole body of law applicable to a given subject it supersedes the common law."

And so on, including even the role of punctuation [45]:

"24. Punctuation will govern when a statue is open to two constructions."

"24. Punctuation marks will not control the plain and evident meaning of the language."

For adversarial legal reasoning, it has been postulated that there are three levels involved, namely the logic level, argument level, and dialogical level [55]: "Adversarial legal reasoning consists of three levels, the logic level (generates arguments), argument level (organizes argument, identifies attack relations, ascertain acceptability of the arguments for given points in a debate), the dialogical level (how arguments can be deployed in a dispute)." And that this can form the basis for constructing a legal argumentation framework [55]: "A three-level model is proposed, where a formal argumentation framework is built around a logical system and itself embedded in a dialectical protocol for dispute, in such a way that, each time a party adds or retracts information, the argumentation framework reassesses the resulting state of the dispute."

A notable aspect brings up the role of attacks related to legal argumentation. It is insufficient to undertake legal argumentation without also considering the importance and essence of attacks too. Attempts to model the variants of attack include formulations such as denial of the premises, alternative action for same effect, side effects of an action, and so on. In work by [36], the details of fifteen forms of attack are described, though this is a starter list and the researchers mention as such: "However, we consider only the opening stages of an argument, leaving counter-attacks, shifts in the burden of proof, and similar issues to later work."

Research by Dung [18] has highlighted the importance of attacks in legal argumentation:

> "Roughly, the idea of argumentational reasoning is that a statement is believable if it can be argued successfully against attacking arguments. In other words, whether or not a rational agent believes in a statement depends on whether or not the argument supporting this statement can be

> successfully defended against the counterarguments. Thus, the beliefs of a rational agent are characterized by the relations between the 'internal' arguments supporting his beliefs and the "external" arguments supporting contradictory beliefs."

In a means of thinking about legal argumentation, the adversarial approach has perhaps fueled or further bolstered the complexity of ordinary argumentation, as outlined by [56]: "All these aspects of the law, i.e., its orientation to future and not fully anticipated situations, the tension between the general terms of the law and the particulars of a case, and the adversarial nature of legal procedures, make that legal reasoning goes beyond the literal meaning of the legal rules and involves appeals to precedent, principle, policy and purpose, and involves the attack as well as the construction of arguments. A central notion then in the law is that of argumentation."

There is also the need to realize that multiple agents or actors are potentially involved in legal argumentation. This in turn rachets up the complexities [56]: "From this analysis it appears that different kinds of agents, with different functions engage in legal reasoning in different contexts: the addressees of the norms (the citizens), the producers of the norms (the legislators), the appliers of the norms (the judges and administrators), and the enforcers of the norms (the administrators/police officers). The reasoning forms employed in the law may thus not only depend on the nature of the issue addressed but also on the context in which the reasoning takes place."

AI researchers tend to describe argumentation models as being classified or known as COMMA (Computational Models of Argument), and that a cornerstone includes the use of Argumentation Mining (AM) [37]: "The goal of argumentation mining, an evolving research field in computational linguistics, is to design methods capable of analyzing people's argumentation." Furthermore, AM is still an evolving field [37]: "Despite the lack of an exact definition, researchers within this field usually focus on analyzing discourse on the pragmatics level and applying a certain argumentation theory to model and analyze textual data at hand."

There is also the use of Argument Markup Language (AML), such as in the case of the Araucaria system, leveraging elements of XML accordingly: "The argument markup language (AML) defines a set of tags that indicate delimitation of argument components (loosely, propositions), tags that indicate support relationships between those components, and tags that indicate the extent of instances of argumentation schemes. The design of AML builds on results in the theory of argument and its application in AI, and therefore, although similar in spirit, is significantly different from earlier attempts."

Per earlier emphasis, there is not as yet any unifying or unitary theory that has been explicated that could shore-up these varied methods and approaches [69]: "As yet, there is no unitary theory of argumentation that encompasses the logical, dialectical, and rhetorical dimensions of argumentation and is universally accepted. The current state of the art in argumentation theory is characterized by the coexistence of a variety of theoretical perspectives and approaches, which differ considerably from each other in conceptualization, scope, and theoretical refinement."

No singular discipline or specialty is likely to gain notable ground if it does not remain open to other allied disciplines in the cross-boundary multi-headed tentacles of legal argumentation [33]: "The study of legal argumentation draws its data, assumptions and methods from disciplines such as legal theory, legal philosophy, logic, argumentation theory, rhetoric, linguistics, literary theory, philosophy, sociology, and artificial intelligence. Researchers with different backgrounds and from various traditions are attempting to explain structural features of legal decision-making and justification from different points of view."

Recall too that legal argumentation is not an island unto itself and that it presumably in one way or another inextricably entangled with generic argumentation. Note this point about persuasion in argumentation as mentioned in 1917 by Ketcham [44]: "The art of persuading others to think or act in a definite way. It includes all writing and speaking which is persuasive in form." And, going back to 1898 and the work of MacEwan [47]:

> "Argumentation is the process of proving or disproving a proposition. Its purpose is to induce a new belief, to establish truth or combat error in the mind of another."

These underlying elements are acknowledged in today's AI effort towards encompassing even generic argumentation embodiment, since any AI, even that outside of the legal realm and for any nature of human intelligence purposes, must facilitate argumentation [70]: "The field of artificial argumentation plays an important role in Artificial Intelligence research. The reason for this is based on the recognition that if we are to develop robust intelligent machines able to act in mixed human-machine teams, then it is imperative that they can handle incomplete and inconsistent information in a way that somehow emulates the way humans tackle such a complex task."

As stated concisely [70]: "Humans argue. Machines should be able to argue too if we aim to achieve mixed teams in a hybrid society."

Turns out that the legal field, because of its intrinsic requirement for argumentation, provides a valuable testbed for developing AI overall, as revealed in a review of the AI field in this regard [56]: "As can be seen from this review, the development of logical models of legal reasoning nowadays proceeds mostly within AI & law and is very much driven by real examples and applications. We think that the latter is a fortunate development, since it shows that the law is a rich testbed for AI theories of reasoning and argument."

Upon furtherance of this point, the richness of legal argumentation and its keystone role in law are added benefits to the attempts at applying AI [56]: "Law is of vital importance to society, promoting justice and stability and affecting many people in important aspects of their private and public life. Creating and applying law involves information processing, reasoning, decision making and communication, so the law is a natural application field for artificial intelligence. While AI could be applied to the law in many ways (for example, natural-language processing to extract meaningful information from documents, data mining and machine learning to extract trends and patterns from large bodies of precedents), the fact that law is part of society makes logic particularly relevant to the law."

And, continuing [56]: "Since law has social objectives and social effects, it must be understood by those affected by it, and its application must be explained and justified. Hence the importance of clarity of meaning and soundness of reasoning, and hence the importance of logic for the law and for legal applications of AI. This review aims to introduce AI researchers to the law as a rich testbed and important application field for logic-based AI research, with a particularly marked concern for logical models of legal argument."

One subtle but significant aspect of legal argumentation is that it cannot normally be done in a hidden or obscured manner, namely that the expectation is that legal argumentation will be explainable and interpretable. As mentioned in [7]: "Legal decisions must be justified. In law, the answer is not enough: the reasons for the answer must be given in order to guide future decisions, to ensure consistency of decisions, and to attempt to persuade the losing side of why they lost, perhaps leading to acceptance of the decision."

Another consideration is the defeasible nature of the law and thus its impact upon legal argumentation [7]: "Law is defeasible. Legal rules can be overturned by finding that an exception applies, or by finding a conflicting law, or by distinguishing the case so that the rule does not apply."

Recent efforts of AI applied to argumentation include the IBM Project Debater system [5], which makes use of argument clustering, argument summarization, and the mapping of arguments to key points underlying an argumentation. In addition, when coping with a new situation involving an unrehearsed argumentation session, there is the use of "first principles" of reusing prior debates or prior arguments to enact a de novo argument synthesis [10].

Do not though somehow be led into imagining that argumentation is nearly solved, which it is most decidedly not, and likewise nor is legal argumentation.

As aptly stated in [9]:

"Most significantly, however, that the body of theory, techniques, and applications we have discussed is very far from encompassing a final, definitive description of the scope and limits of what argumentation-based approaches can offer to the furtherance of AI as a scientific discipline: many questions remain unresolved, many avenues unexplored, and many applications offer a wealth of possibilities for future work. When people participate in reasoned debate they are engaging in argumentation not demonstration. Thus argumentation, rather than logical demonstration, should be seen as the core technique for justifying claims."

There is a dearth of AI-enabled legal argumentation systems for today's use by the legal profession [3]: "While the theoretical advances on models of legal argument have been impressive and a number of valuable prototype systems have been developed, no systems have been deployed in everyday practice yet."

A somewhat daunting concern is that the ability to have AI fully operate in any substantive autonomous manner as to legal argumentation might be equivalent to the AI problem in its entirety of achieving human intelligence capacities [3]: "Developing artificial tools that capture the human ability to argue is an ambitious research goal, and it may ultimately prove to be as difficult as developing AI in general."

Meanwhile, various attempts at structuring legal argumentation and the modeling of legal argumentation continue, of which some are noted next.

One viewpoint is that there are three pillars involved in AI argumentation facets:

> "The three pillars of the development of argumentation-enhanced intelligent machines are, from my point of view: (i) modeling and reasoning on socio-cognitive components like trust using computational models of argument which are able to deal with incomplete and conflicting information, (ii) mining argument structures in natural language text to detect, e.g., potential fallacies, recurrent patterns, and inner strength, and (iii) analyzing

and understating the role of emotions in real-world argumentative situations (e.g., debates) to inject such information in the computational models of argument to better cast incomplete and inconsistent information when emotions play a role."

One indication is that there are three approaches overall [33] "In the past 30 years three more or less consistent approaches to legal argumentation can be distinguished: the logical, the rhetorical and the dialogical approach."

As recently pointed out in [3], the earlier work by Dung was especially insightful since it illuminates the importance of abstraction in legal argumentation: "Dung's insight was that arguments could be abstract and this freed them from any particular method of generation, whether using a particular logic, particular argument schemes, or case based methods. Once in the framework all arguments were equal. This separated consideration of the status of arguments from the logic that produced them."

In exploring how humans undertake legal argumentation, the work by Huhn [40] postulates that there are five types of legal argumentation: "Five types of legal argument exist: text, intent, precedent, tradition, and policy. Each type of argument may be considered an information set or a category of evidence admissible to prove what the law is." And these are respectively based on differing concepts of the law and justice [40]: "Each type of legal argument is based upon a different conception of justice; that is, a different source of the law. The first four types of legal argument are of ancient lineage, while the fifth, policy analysis, has been expressly acknowledged as a valid legal argument only in the twentieth century."

In terms of what is meant by the fifth type, the policy analysis, here's the indication provided [40]: Policy analysis proceeds in two steps: a predictive statement and an evaluative judgment. The court first predicts the consequences that will flow from giving the law one interpretation or another and then decides which set of consequences is more consistent with the underlying values of the law. In attacking a legal argument based on policy analysis, one may challenge either the predictive statement of consequences or the evaluative judgment.

Policy analysis can be contrasted with each of the foregoing sources of law. Rather than requiring the court to ascertain the value choices made by others, policy analysis invites the court itself to make a policy choice by balancing all of the relevant values and interests affected by the decision to pursue a particular policy."

Finally, before concluding this section of the paper, it is perhaps noteworthy to consider an ongoing question underlying law schools and the training of lawyers, which offers insights into the nature of legal reasoning and human intelligence, all of which are essential to the discussion of legal argumentation.

Per the provocative commentary in [40]:

"Students enter law school expecting to learn 'the law,' that is, rules of law. They conceive law to be a science, a set of determinate rules that govern human behavior. Moreover, students are frustrated when law professors insist the principal purpose of legal education is not learning rules of law, but rather learning 'to think like lawyers.' What exactly does it mean 'to think like a lawyer?' 'To think like a lawyer' is to be adept at legal analysis; it is to be able to predict, argue, and decide what the law is in hard cases. The purpose of legal education is to train students in the mastery of this skill."

The next section of this paper introduces the autonomous levels of AI Legal Reasoning, doing so to then aid Section 3 then explores how legal argumentation automation varies across the levels of autonomy. Section 3 also covers more introspection of the AI intertwining with legal argumentation. Section 4 provides some conclusionary remarks and also an indication of recommended future research.

Section 2: Autonomous Levels of AI Legal Reasoning

In this section, a framework for the autonomous levels of AI Legal Reasoning is summarized and is based on the research described in detail in Eliot [24].

These autonomous levels will be portrayed in a grid that aligns with key elements of autonomy and as matched to AI Legal Reasoning. Providing this context will be useful to the later sections of this paper and will be utilized accordingly.

The autonomous levels of AI Legal Reasoning are as follows:
Level 0: No Automation for AI Legal Reasoning
Level 1: Simple Assistance Automation for AI Legal Reasoning
Level 2: Advanced Assistance Automation for AILR
Level 3: Semi-Autonomous Automation for AI Legal Reasoning
Level 4: Domain Autonomous for AI Legal Reasoning
Level 5: Fully Autonomous for AI Legal Reasoning
Level 6: Superhuman Autonomous for AI Legal Reasoning

2.1 Details of the LoA AILR

See **Figure A-1** for an overview chart showcasing the autonomous levels of AI Legal Reasoning as via columns denoting each of the respective levels.

See **Figure A-2** for an overview chart similar to Figure A-1 which alternatively is indicative of the autonomous levels of AI Legal Reasoning via the rows as depicting the respective levels (this is simply a reformatting of Figure A-1, doing so to aid in illuminating this variant perspective, but does not introduce any new facets or alterations from the contents as already shown in Figure A-1).

2.1.1 Level 0: No Automation for AI Legal Reasoning

Level 0 is considered the no automation level. Legal reasoning is carried out via manual methods and principally occurs via paper-based methods.

This level is allowed some leeway in that the use of say a simple handheld calculator or perhaps the use of a fax machine could be allowed or included within this Level 0, though strictly speaking it could be said that any form whatsoever of automation is to be excluded from this level.

2.1.2 Level 1: Simple Assistance Automation for AI Legal Reasoning

Level 1 consists of simple assistance automation for AI legal reasoning.

Examples of this category encompassing simple automation would include the use of everyday computer-based word processing, the use of everyday computer-based spreadsheets, the access to online legal documents that are stored and retrieved electronically, and so on.

By-and-large, today's use of computers for legal activities is predominantly within Level 1. It is assumed and expected that over time, the pervasiveness of automation will continue to deepen and widen, and eventually lead to legal activities being supported and within Level 2, rather than Level 1.

2.1.3 Level 2: Advanced Assistance Automation for AI Legal Reasoning

Level 2 consists of advanced assistance automation for AI legal reasoning.

Examples of this notion encompassing advanced automation would include the use of query-style Natural Language Processing (NLP), Machine Learning (ML) for case predictions, and so on.

Gradually, over time, it is expected that computer-based systems for legal activities will increasingly make use of advanced automation. Law industry technology that was once at a Level 1 will likely be refined, upgraded, or expanded to include advanced capabilities, and thus be reclassified into Level 2.

2.1.4 Level 3: Semi-Autonomous Automation for AI Legal Reasoning

Level 3 consists of semi-autonomous automation for AI legal reasoning.

Examples of this notion encompassing semi-autonomous automation would include the use of Knowledge-Based Systems (KBS) for legal reasoning, the use of Machine Learning and Deep Learning (ML/DL) for legal reasoning, and so on.

Today, such automation tends to exist in research efforts or prototypes and pilot systems, along with some commercial legal technology that has been infusing these capabilities too.

2.1.5 Level 4: Domain Autonomous for AI Legal Reasoning

Level 4 consists of domain autonomous computer-based systems for AI legal reasoning.

This level reuses the conceptual notion of Operational Design Domains (ODDs) as utilized in the autonomous vehicles and self-driving cars levels of autonomy, though in this use case it is being applied to the legal domain [19] [20] [21].

Essentially, this entails any AI legal reasoning capacities that can operate autonomously, entirely so, but that is only able to do so in some limited or constrained legal domain.

2.1.6 Level 5: Fully Autonomous for AI Legal Reasoning

Level 5 consists of fully autonomous computer-based systems for AI legal reasoning. In a sense, Level 5 is the superset of Level 4 in terms of encompassing all possible domains as per however so defined ultimately for Level 4. The only constraint, as it were, consists of the facet that the Level 4 and Level 5 are concerning human intelligence and the capacities thereof. This is an important emphasis due to attempting to distinguish Level 5 from Level 6 (as will be discussed in the next subsection) It is conceivable that someday there might be a fully autonomous AI legal reasoning capability, one that encompasses all of the law in all foreseeable ways, though this is quite a tall order and remains quite aspirational without a clear cut path of how this might one day be achieved. Nonetheless, it seems to be within the extended realm of possibilities, which is worthwhile to mention in relative terms to Level 6.

2.1.7 Level 6: Superhuman Autonomous for AI Legal Reasoning

Level 6 consists of superhuman autonomous computer-based systems for AI legal reasoning.

In a sense, Level 6 is the entirety of Level 5 and adds something beyond that in a manner that is currently ill-defined and perhaps (some would argue) as yet unknowable. The notion is that AI might ultimately exceed human intelligence, rising to become superhuman, and if so, we do not yet have any viable indication of what that superhuman intelligence consists of and nor what kind of thinking it would somehow be able to undertake.

Whether a Level 6 is ever attainable is reliant upon whether superhuman AI is ever attainable, and thus, at this time, this stands as a placeholder for that which might never occur. In any case, having such a placeholder provides a semblance of completeness, doing so without necessarily legitimatizing that superhuman AI is going to be achieved or not. No such claim or dispute is undertaken within this framework.

Section 3: Legal Argumentation and AI Enablement

In this section, the advent of AI and legal argumentation is explored in several respects. First, a model coined as CARE for Create, Assess, Refine, and Engage is introduced and provided as context for AI Legal Argumentation (AILA) facets. The Toulmin formalism for argumentation is next showcased and discussed, including augmentation that considers the importance of attack vectors, horizontal layers, vertical layers, and recursion. This is followed by an examination of hard cases versus clear cases, providing a four-square quadrant for case difficulty comparison purposes. A persuasion cloud that represents a legal argumentation search space is next shown and used to illustrate the process of identifying a winning argument all told.

A series of figures are included in the discussions to aid in illustrating the matters addressed.

3.1 AI Legal Argumentation and CARE

A model coined as CARE for Create, Assess, Refine, and Engage is shown in **Figure B-1**. This reflects the key activities or processing that an AI-enabled Legal Argumentation (AILA) system would be expected to perform. The wording indicates:

- Create a Legal Argument
- Assess a Legal Argument
- Refine a Legal Argument
- Engage in Legal Argumentation

As earlier indicated in Section 1, the phrasing involving the word "argument" is construed at both a narrow perspective such as an element within a larger overall argument, and can also be interpreted as the totality of the argument that is being forged.

In brief, an AILA is expected to be able to craft anew a legal argument, though this should be understood as not necessarily implying "from scratch" per se. In other words, a new argument might readily be based on prior arguments and not originated from thin air, as it were. Thus, the notion of a new argument is one that is being created anew versus for example examining an existing argument for purposes of assessing the argument. In fact, an additional portion of CARE involves the assessment of a legal argument. This might be undertaken during the crafting of a new argument, or it might occur when seeking to discover counterarguments as part of an adversarial methodology, and so on. Furthermore, it is anticipated that an AILA would be able to refine a legal argument, receiving as input an existing legal argument, and attempt to refine it to bolster its strengths and reduce its weaknesses. Finally, an AILA is expected to be able to engage in a dialogue regarding a legal argumentation.

Note that each of these elements of CARE is anticipated to be interleaving with each other and though listed as seemingly distinct activities or processes are to be considered as intermixing and interoperative.

The CARE model can be aligned orthogonally to the various stages or layers typified in artificial argumentation, such as the research in [3]: "We consider the following five main layers: structural, relational, dialogical, assessment, and rhetorical. Structural layer: How are arguments constructed? Relational layer: What are the relationships between arguments? Dialogical layer: How can argumentation be undertaken in dialogues? Assessment layer: How can a constellation of interacting arguments be evaluated and conclusions drawn? Rhetorical layer: How can argumentation be tailored for an audience so that it is persuasive?"

3.2 Toulmin's Formalism of Argumentation

One of the most commonly cited formalisms for argumentation consists of the argument structure identified by Toulmin [68]. This argument structure is frequently utilized as a core foundation for establishing theories and practical tools for legal argumentation.

As an example of the reuse of Toulmin's argument structure, consider this research by Marshall [49]: "As our representational starting point, we used Toulmin's formalism for logical structure. According to his scheme, a datum is some fact or observation about the situation under discussion that leads to some further observation or fact, the claim. The relation between the two is characterized by a rule of inference, a warrant, that serves to link the information set forth in the datum and claim. A backing supports the warrant with some knowledge structure from the argument's domain. A Toulmin argument structure may also include various kinds of qualifications of the claim (qualifiers) and allow for exceptions (rebuttals). The categories provided by this structure are useful for expressing portions of argument logic."

Here is a rationale for making use of Toulmin's argument structure [49]:

> "What does this work suggest about the essential elements of a tool to support the formulation, organization, and presentation of arguments? First, it suggests that we need

> a system of representations that captures reasoning and allows it to be structured by interpretive information. Toulmin structures and our current system of representations to organize reasoning are a good start. Toulmin structures can also function as the input to reasoning analysis mechanisms such as assumption-based truth maintenance systems. Second, we need a solid understanding of the formulation process."

Figure B-2 indicates the core elements of Toulmin's argument structure.

Figure B-3 augments the core elements of Toulmin's argument structure by emphasizing the importance of attack vectors associated with each element, along with an overarching attack collective. As earlier indicated, robust legal argumentation entails the need to consider attacks that can be waged.

Figure B-4 showcases that the Toulmin argument structure should be considered as multi-dimensional. A legal argument of any substance is likely to have a multitude of horizontal layers and also have vertical layers. These layers contain sub-arguments. Since there is a dependency of the sub-arguments to the encompassing argument(s), it is crucial that the sub-arguments also be given due consideration. There is a recursive facility involved in deriving sub-arguments, such that there are sub-arguments within sub-arguments, and so on.

3.3 Four-Square Grid Case Difficulty Comparison

In **Figure B-5**, a four-square grid of quadrants representing case difficulty comparison is presented.

Along the vertical axis are the two major classifications of legal cases, consisting of hard cases and so-called clear cases. A clear case is denoted as one that is relatively routine, readily commonly understood, and previously experienced (some refer to these as "soft" cases). Hard cases are considered arduous to legally extricate and resolve, are usually one-off's that have not previously been experienced, etc. [38].

Along the horizontal axis is the use of a conventional argument versus an unconventional argument. When combined with the two major classifications of hard cases and clear cases, a four-square grid or set of quadrants is established and can be utilized accordingly. In particular:

- Hard Case – Conventional Argument: *Unconvincing (Deficient)*
- Hard Case – Unconventional Argument: *Inventive (Formative)*
- Clear Case – Conventional Argument: *Convincing (Expected)*
- Clear Case – Unconventional Argument: *Distended (Exorbitant)*

This set of indications is insightful for AILA as to the differences between forming legal argumentation in the instance of a hard case versus a clear case. Of course, it is not necessarily apparent as to whether a given case is a hard case or a clear case until sufficient assessment has been undertaken.

3.4 Legal Argumentation Cloud Search Space

In Figure B-6, a diagram is used to represent the search space involved in examining legal arguments.

This is a cloud in the sense that it is a potentially large search space that needs to be established and utilized by an AILA. While seeking to identify a "winning argument" (based on persuasiveness and other attributes), there is some *n* number of possible legal arguments that can be potentially (exhaustively) identified. There is a need by the AILA to winnow the search space to gauge those legal arguments *m* that are considered in the winning realm. These are contextually dependent and time-dependent.

3.5 Legal Argumentation and LoA AILR

As shown in **Figure B-7**, it is useful to align the evolution of AI-enablement of Legal Argumentation (AILA) with the Levels of Autonomy (LoA) of AI Legal Reasoning (AILR).

For each of the levels of autonomy of AI Legal Reasoning, the impacts upon legal argumentation will be distinctive. A keyword phrasing is used in Figure B-7 to indicate these impacts and consists of:

LoA AILR – Legal Argumentation
Level 0: *n/a*
Level 1: *Mechanistic (Low)*
Level 2: *Mechanistic (High)*
Level 3: *Expressive*
Level 4: *Domain Fluency*
Level 5: *Full Fluency*
Level 6: *Meta-Fluency*

In brief, at Level 0, which consists of no automation for AI Legal Reasoning, the applicability to legal argumentation is considered not applicable ("n/a"), simply due to the by-definition that there is no AI involved at this level. At Level 1, simple assistance automation, the characterization is indicated as "Mechanistic (Low)" since the AI is abundantly unrefined and limited in any substantive practical capacity to the legal argumentation advent, thus considered mechanistic. At Level 2, advanced assistance automation, the characterization is indicated as "Mechanistic (High)" since the AI at this level can modestly assist in legal argumentation but is considered quite preliminary in doing so.

At Level 3, the first substantive impact of AI Legal Reasoning comes to work, and this is characterized by the keyword of "Expressive" denoting that the AI is initially being used as a demonstrative enabler for legal argumentation. Maturing at Level 4, the AI Legal Reasoning is now substantively augmenting legal argumentation, yet does so only within particular legal domains, thus this is characterized as being "Domain Fluency" in its impact. Upon Level 5, encompassing all legal domains, the AI Legal Reasoning has now infused across all legal argumentation and characterized as now being "Full Fluency" in its scope and velocity.

Finally, at Level 6, the superhuman AI Legal Reasoning, the advent of micro-directives would be considered "Meta-Fluency," though keep in mind that Level 6 is a speculative notion and it is not clear as to what the superhuman capacity would bring forth.

To reiterate and clarify, these depictions are not prescriptive and do not intend to predict what will happen, and instead are a form of taxonomy to depict and describe what might happen and provide an ontological means to understand such phenomena if it should so arise.

Section 4: Additional Considerations and Future Research

As earlier indicated, legal argumentation is a vital cornerstone of justice, underpinning an adversarial form of law, and extensive research has attempted to augment or undertake legal argumentation via the use of computer-based automation including Artificial Intelligence (AI). AI advances in Natural Language Processing (NLP) and Machine Learning (ML) have especially furthered the capabilities of leveraging AI for aiding legal professionals, doing so in ways that are modeled here as *CARE*, namely Crafting, Assessing, Refining, and Engaging in legal argumentation.

In addition to AI-enabled legal argumentation serving to augment human-based lawyering, an aspirational goal of this multi-disciplinary field consists of ultimately achieving autonomously effected human-equivalent legal argumentation. As such, an innovative meta-approach has been proposed to apply the Levels of Autonomy (LoA) of AI Legal Reasoning (AILR) to the maturation of AI and Legal Argumentation (AILA), proffering a new means of gauging progress in this ever-evolving and rigorously sought domain.

Future research is needed to explore in greater detail the manner and means by which AI-enablement will occur, along with the potential for adverse consequences encompassing AI-powered legal argumentation. If such AI Legal Argumentation (AILA) is to be productively adopted, the full gamut of legal, economic, societal, and technological ramifications need to be sufficiently examined.

References

1. Alarie, Benjamin, and Anthony Niblett, Albert Yoon (2017). "Regulation by Machine," Volume 24, Journal of Machine Learning Research.

2. Ashley, Kevin, and Karl Branting, Howard Margolis, and Cass Sunstein (2001). "Legal Reasoning and Artificial Intelligence: How Computers 'Think' Like Lawyers," Symposium: Legal Reasoning and Artificial Intelligence, University of Chicago Law School Roundtable.

3. Atkinson, Katie, and Pietro Baroni, Massimiliano Giacomin, Anthony Hunter, Henry Prakken, Chris Reed, Guillermo Simari, Matthias Thimm, Serena Villata (2017). "Toward Artificial Argumentation," AAAI AI Magazine.

4. Baker, Jamie (2018). "A Legal Research Odyssey: Artificial Intelligence as Disrupter," Law Library Journal.

5. Bar-Haim, Roy, and Lilach Eden, Dan Lahav, Roni Friedman, Noam Slonim, Yoav Kantor (2020). "From Arguments to Key Points: Toward Automatic Argument Summarization," Proceedings of the 58th Annual Meeting of the Association for Computational Linguistics.

6. Ben-Ari, Daniel, and D., Frish, Y., Lazovski, A., Eldan, U., & Greenbaum, D. (2016). "Artificial Intelligence in the Practice of Law: An Analysis and Proof of Concept Experiment," Volume 23, Number 2, Richmond Journal of Law & Technology.

7. Bench-Capon, T. (2020). "Before and After Dung: Argumentation in AI and Law," Volume 11, Argument & Computation.

8. Bench-Capon, and Givoanni Sartor (2003). "A Model of Legal Reasoning with Cases Incorporating Theories and Values," November 2013, Artificial Intelligence.

9. Bench-Capon, T., and Paul Dunne (2007). "Argumentation in Artificial Intelligence," Volume 171, Artificial Intelligence.

10. Bilu, Yonatan and Ariel Gera, Daniel Hershcovich, Benjamin Sznajder, Dan Lahav, Guy Moshkowich, Anael Malet, Assaf Gavron, Noam Slonim (2019). "Argument Invention from First Principles," Proceedings of the 57th Annual Meeting of the Association for Computational Linguistics.

11. Braithwaite, John (2002). "Rules and Principles: A Theory of Legal Certainty," Volume 27, Australian Journal of Legal Philosophy.

12. Buchanan, Bruce, and Thomas Headrick (1970). "Some Speculation about Artificial Intelligence and Legal Reasoning," Volume 23, Stanford Law Review.

13. Casey, Anthony, and Anthony Niblett (2016). "Self-Driving Laws," Volume 429, University of Toronto Law Journal.

14. Chagal-Feferkorn, Karni (2019). "Am I An Algorithm or a Product: When Products Liability Should Apply to Algorithmic Decision-Makers," Stanford Law & Policy Review.

15. Chen, Daniel (2019). "Machine Learning and the Rule of Law," in Law as Data: Computation, Text, and The Future of Legal Analysis (Michael A. Livermore and Daniel N. Rockmore eds.).

16. Coglianese, Cary, and David Lehr (2017). "Rulemaking by Robot: Administrative Decision Making in the Machine-Learning Era," Volume 105, Georgetown Law Journal.

17. D'Amato, Anthony (2010). "Legal Uncertainty," Northwestern University School of Law, Faculty Working Papers.

18. Dung, Phan (1993). "On the Acceptability of Arguments and its Fundamental Role in Nonmonotonic Reasoning and Logic Programming," Proceedings of the 13th International Joint Conference on Artificial Intelligence.

19. Eliot, Lance (2016). AI Guardian Angels for Deep AI Trustworthiness. LBE Press Publishing.

20. Eliot, Lance (2020). "The Neglected Dualism of Artificial Moral Agency and Artificial Legal Reasoning in AI for Social Good." Harvard University, Harvard Center for Research on Computation and Society, AI for Social Good Conference, July 21, 2020.

21. Eliot, Lance (2020). AI and Legal Reasoning Essentials. LBE Press Publishing.

22. Eliot, Lance (2019). Artificial Intelligence and LegalTech Essentials. LBE Press Publishing.

23. Eliot, Lance (2020). "FutureLaw 2020 Showcases How Tech is Transforming The Law, Including the Impacts of AI," April 16, 2020, Forbes.

24. Eliot, Lance (2020). "An Ontological AI-and-Law Framework for the Autonomous Levels of AI Legal Reasoning," Cornell University arXiv. https://arxiv.org/abs/2008.07328

25. Eliot, Lance (2020). "Turing Test and the Practice of Law: The Role of Autonomous Levels of AI Legal Reasoning," Cornell University arXiv. https://arxiv.org/abs/2008.07743

26. Eliot, Lance (2020). "Multidimensionality of the Legal Singularity: The Role of Autonomous Levels of AI Legal Reasoning," Cornell University arXiv. https://arxiv.org/abs/2008.10575

27. Eliot, Lance (2020). "Authorized and Unauthorized Practices of Law: The Role of Autonomous Levels of AI Legal Reasoning," Cornell University arXiv. https://arxiv.org/abs/2008.09507

28. Eliot, Lance (2020). "An Impact Model of AI on the Principles of Justice: Encompassing the Autonomous Levels of AI Legal Reasoning," Cornell University arXiv. https://arxiv.org/abs/2008.12615

29. Eliot, Lance (2020). "Robustness and Overcoming Brittleness of AI-Enabled Legal Micro-Directives," Cornell University arXiv. https://arxiv.org/abs/2009.02243

30. Eliot, Lance (2018). "Singularity and AI," July 10, 2018, AI Trends.

31. Feteris E.T. (1999) MacCormick's Theory of the Justification of Legal Decisions. In: Fundamentals of Legal Argumentation. Argumentation Library, vol 1. Springer, Dordrecht.

32. Feteris, Eveline (1999). Fundamentals of Legal Argumentation. Academic Press.

33. Feteris, Eveline, and Harm Kloosterhuis (2009). "The Analysis and Evaluation of Legal Argumentation: Approaches from Legal Theory and Argumentation Theory," Volume 16, Studies in Logic, Grammar and Rhetoric.

34. Gardner, Anne (1987). Artificial Intelligence and Legal Reasoning. MIT Press.

35. Genesereth, Michael (2009). "Computational Law: The Cop in the Backseat," Stanford Center for Legal Informatics, Stanford University.

36. Greenwood, Katie, T. Bench-Capon, and P. McBurney (2003). "Towards a Computational Account of Persuasion in Law," Proceedings of the 9th International Conference on Artificial Intelligence and Law.

37. Habernal, Ivan, and Iryna Gurevych (2017). "Argumentation Mining in User-Generated Web Discourse," Volume 3, Number 1, Computational Linguistics.

38. Hage, Jaap (2000). "Dialectical Models in Artificial Intelligence and Law," Artificial Intelligence and Law.

39. Hermann, Donald (1985). "Legal Reasoning as Argumentation," Volume 12, Northern Kentucky Law Review.

40. Huhn, Wilson (2000). "Teaching Legal Analysis Using a Pluralistic Model of Law," Volume 36, Number 3, Gonzaga Law Review.

41. Huhn, Wilson (2003). "The Stages of Legal Reasoning: Formalism, Analogy, and Realism," Volume 48, Villanova Law Review.

42. Huhn, Wilson (2007). The Five Types of Legal Argument. Carolina Academic Press.

43. Kaplow, Louis (1992). "Rules Versus Standards: An Economic Analysis," Volume 42, Duke Law Journal.

44. Ketcham, Victor (1917). The Theory and Practice of Argumentation and Debate. BiblioLife.

45. Llewellyn, Karl (1950). "Remarks on the Theory of Appellate Decision and the Rules or Canons About How Statutes Are to Be Construed," Volume 3, Number 4, Vanderbilt Law Review.

46. MacCormick, Neil (1978). Legal Reasoning and Legal Theory.

47. MacEwan, Elias (1898). The Essentials of Argumentation. D. C. Heath Publishers.

48. Markou, Christopher, and Simon Deakin (2020). "Is Law Computable? From Rule of Law to Legal Singularity," May 4, 2020, SSRN, University of Cambridge Faculty of Law Research Paper.

49. Marshall, Catherine (1989). "Representing the Structure of a Legal Argument," Proceedings of the 2nd ICAIL.

50. McCarty, Thorne (1977). "Reflections on TAXMAN: An Experiment in Artificial Intelligence and Legal Reasoning," January 1977, Harvard Law Review.

51. McGinnis, John, and Russell G. Pearce (2014). "The Great Disruption: How Machine Intelligence Will Transform the Role of Lawyers in the Delivery of Legal Services," Volume 82, Number 6, Fordham Law Review.

52. McGinnis, John, and Steven Wasick (2015). "Law's Algorithm," Volume 66, Florida Law Review.

53. Mnookin, Robert, and Lewis Kornhauser (1979). "Bargaining in the Shadow of the Law," Volume 88, Number 5, April 1979, The Yale Law Review.

54. Mowbray, Andrew, and Philip Chung, Graham Greenleaf (2019). "Utilising AI in the Legal Assistance Sector," LegalAIIA Workshop, ICAIL, June 17, 2019, Montreal, Canada.

55. Prakken, Henry (1995). "From Logic to Dialectics in Legal Argument," Proceedings of the 5th International Conference on Artificial Intelligence and Law.

56. Prakken, Henry, and Giovanni Sartor (2015). "Law and Logic: A Review from an Argumentation Perspective," Volume 227, Artificial Intelligence.

57. Reed, Chris, and Glenn Rowe (2004). "Araucaria: Software for Argument Analysis, Diagramming, and Representation," Volume 13, Number 4, International Journal on Artificial Intelligence Tools.

58. Reinbold, Patric (2020). "Taking Artificial Intelligence Beyond the Turing Test," Volume 20, Wisconsin Law Review.

59. Remus, Dana, and Frank Levy, "Can Robots be Lawyers? Computers, Robots, and the Practice of Law," Volume 30, Georgetown Journal of Legal Ethics.

60. Rich, Michael (2016). "Machine Learning, Automated Suspicion Algorithms, and the Fourth Amendment," Volume 164, University of Pennsylvania Law Review.

61. Rissland, Edwina (1990). "Artificial Intelligence and Law: Stepping Stones to a Model of Legal Reasoning," Yale Law Journal.

62. SAE (2018). Taxonomy and Definitions for Terms Related to Driving Automation Systems for On-Road Motor Vehicles, J3016-201806, SAE International.

63. Sunstein, Cass (2001). "Of Artificial Intelligence and Legal Reasoning," University of Chicago Law School, Working Papers.

64. Sunstein, Cass, and Kevin Ashley, Karl Branting, Howard Margolis (2001). "Legal Reasoning and Artificial Intelligence: How Computers 'Think' Like Lawyers," Symposium: Legal Reasoning and Artificial Intelligence, University of Chicago Law School Roundtable.

65. Surden, Harry (2014). "Machine Learning and Law," Washington Law Review.

66. Surden, Harry (2019). "Artificial Intelligence and Law: An Overview," Summer 2019, Georgia State University Law Review.

67. Susskind, Richard (2019). Online Courts and the Future of Justice. Oxford University Press.

68. Toulmin, Stephen (1979). An Introduction to Reasoning. MacMillian Press.

69. van Eemeren, Frans and Bart Garssen, Erik Krabbe, Francisca Snoeck Henkemans, Bart Verheij, and Jean Wagemans (2014). Handbook of Argumentation Theory. Springer Berlin.

70. Villata, Serena (2018). "Artificial Argumentation for Humans," Proceedings of the Twenty-Seventh International Joint Conference on Artificial Intelligence.

71. Volokh, Eugne (2019). "Chief Justice Robots," Volume 68, Duke Law Journal.

72. Waltl, Bernhard, and Roland Vogl (2018). "Explainable Artificial Intelligence: The New Frontier in Legal Informatics," February 2018, Jusletter IT 22, Stanford Center for Legal Informatics, Stanford University.

73. Wolfram, Stephen (2018). "Computational Law, Symbolic Discourse, and the AI Constitution," in Data-Driven Law: Data Analytics and the New Legal Services (Edward J. Walters ed.).

Note: *For supplemental materials depicting the aspects discussed in this chapter, refer to Appendix B, which contains various augmented diagrams, charts, and additional related facets of relevance.*

APPENDIX A
TEACHING WITH THIS MATERIAL

The research paper in this book can readily be used as a reading supplemental to augment traditional textbook-oriented content, particularly used in a class on AI or a class about the law.

Courses where this material is most likely applicable encompass classes at a college or university level.

Here are some typical settings that might apply:

- Computer Science. Classes studying AI, or possibly a CS social impacts class, etc.
- Law. Law classes exploring technology and its adoption for legal uses.
- Sociology. Sociology classes on the adoption and advancement of technology.

Specialized classes at the undergraduate and graduate level can also make use of this material.

For each chapter, consider whether you think the chapter provides material relevant to your course topic.

There are plenty of opportunities to get the students thinking about the topics and encourage them to decide whether they agree or disagree with the points offered and positions taken.

I would also encourage you to have the students do additional research beyond the chapter material presented (I provide next some suggested assignments that they can do).

RESEARCH ASSIGNMENTS ON THESE TOPICS

Your students can find research and background material on these topics, doing so in various tech journals, law journals, and other related publications.

Here are some suggestions for homework or projects that you could assign to students:

a) Assignment for foundational AI research topics: Research and prepare a paper and a presentation on a specific aspect of AI, such as Machine Learning, ANN, etc. The paper should cite at least 3 reputable sources. Compare and contrast to what has been stated in the chosen chapter.

b) Assignment for Law topics: Research and prepare a paper covering Law aspects via at least 3 reputable sources and analyze the characterizations. Compare and contrast to what has been stated in the chosen chapter.

c) Assignment for a Business topic: Research and prepare a paper and a presentation on businesses and advanced technology regarding AI and Law. What is trending, and why? Make sure to cite at least 3 reputable sources. Compare and contrast to the depictions herein.

d) Assignment to do a Startup: Have the students prepare a paper or business plan about how they might start up a business in this realm. They could also be asked to present their business plan and should also have a prepared presentation deck to coincide with it.

You can certainly adjust the aforementioned assignments to fit your particular needs and class structure.

You'll notice that I usually suggest that (at least) 3 reputable cited sources be utilized for the paper writing-based assignments.

I usually steer students toward "reputable" publications, since otherwise, they will cite some less reliable sources that have little or no credentials, other than that they happened to appear online was easy to retrieve. You can, of course, define "reputable" in whatever way you prefer, for example, some faculty think Wikipedia is not reputable while others believe it is reputable and allow students to cite it.

The reason that I usually ask for at least 3 citations is that if the student only relies upon one or two citations, they usually settle on whatever they happened to find the fastest. By requiring 3 (or more) citations, it usually seems to inspire them to explore more extensively and likely end-up finding five or more sources, and then whittling it down to 3 if so needed.

I have not specified the length of their papers and leave that to you to tell the students what you prefer.

For each of those assignments, you could end up with a short one to two-pager or you could do a dissertation length in-depth paper. Base the length on whatever best fits for your class, and likewise the credit amount of the assignment within the context of the other grading metrics you'll be using for the class.

I usually try to get students to present their work, in addition to doing the writing. This is a helpful practice for what they will do in the business world. Most of the time, they will be required to prepare an analysis and present it. If you don't have the class time or inclination to have the students present their papers, then you can presumably omit the aspect of them putting together presentations.

GUIDE TO USING THE CHAPTERS

For each of the chapters, I provide the next some various ways to use the chapter contents.

You can assign the below tasks as individual homework assignments, or the tasks can be used for team projects. You can easily layout a series of assignments, such as indicating that the students are to do item "a" below for say Chapter 1, then "b" for the next chapter of the book, and so on.

a) What is the main point of the chapter and describe in your own words the significance of the topic.

b) Identify at least two aspects in the chapter that you agree with and support your concurrence by providing at least one other outside researched item as support; make sure to explain your basis for agreeing with the aspects.

c) Identify at least two aspects in the chapter that you disagree with and support your disagreement by providing at least one other outside researched item as support; make sure to explain your basis for disagreeing with the aspects.

d) Find an aspect that was not covered extensively in the chapter, doing so by conducting outside research, and then offer an expanded indication about how that aspect ties into the chapter, along with the added significance it brings to the topic.

e) Interview a specialist in the industry about the topic of the chapter, collect from them their thoughts and opinions, and readdress the chapter by citing your source and how they compared and contrasted to the material,

f) Interview a relevant professor or researcher in a college or university setting about the topic of the chapter, collect from them their thoughts and opinions, and readdress the chapter by citing your source and how they compared and contrasted to the material,

g) Try to update a chapter by finding out the latest on the topic and ascertain whether the issue or topic has now been solved or whether it is still being addressed, explain what you come up with.

The above are all ways in which you can get the students of your class involved in considering the material of a given chapter. You could mix things up by having one of those above assignments per each week, covering the chapters over the course of the semester or quarter.

SUGGESTED REFERENCES TO EXPLORE

To help get your students started in finding relevant and important additional research papers on the topic of AI and the law, have them take a look at the references cited in each of the chapters.

You could also assign the students to each (or in teams) read an assigned reference from the list, and then have them provide either a written summary and review or do so as part of a classroom presentation.

APPENDIX B
SUPPLEMENTAL FIGURES AND CHARTS

For the convenience of viewing, supplemental figures and charts related to the topics discussed are shown on the next pages

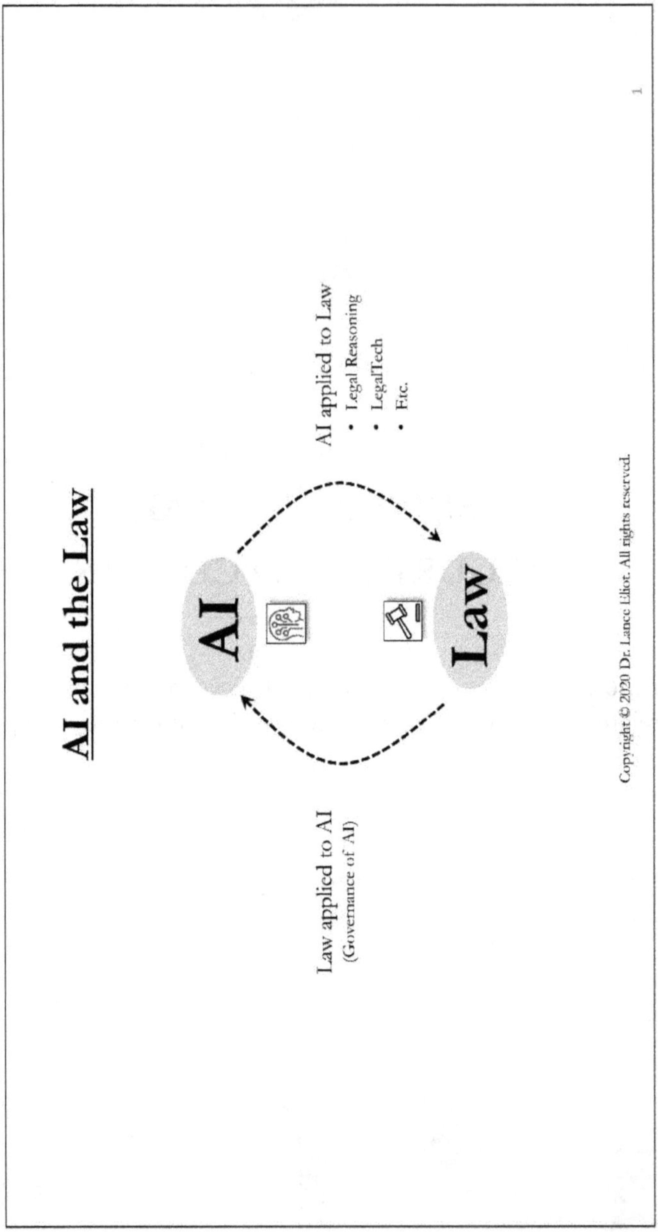

Chapter 1 - Figure 1

AI & Law: Levels of Autonomy For AI Legal Reasoning (AILR)

Level	Descriptor	Examples	Automation	Status
0	No Automation	Manual, paper-based (no automation)	None	De Facto - In Use
1	Simple Assistance Automation	Word Processing, XLS, online legal docs, etc.	Legal Assist	Widely In Use
2	Advanced Assistance Automation	Query-style NLP, ML for case prediction, etc.	Legal Assist	Some In Use
3	Semi-Autonomous Automation	KBS & ML/DL for legal reasoning & analysis, etc.	Legal Assist	Primarily Prototypes & Research Based
4	AILR Domain Autonomous	Versed only in a specific legal domain	Legal Advisor (law fluent)	None As Yet
5	AILR Fully Autonomous	Versatile within and across all legal domains	Legal Advisor (law fluent)	None As Yet
6	AILR Superhuman Autonomous	Exceeds human-based legal reasoning	Supra Legal Advisor	Indeterminate

Figure 1: AI & Law - Autonomous Levels by Rows *Source Author: Dr. Lance B. Eliot* V1.3

Chapter 2 - Figure 1

AI & Law: Levels of Autonomy For AI Legal Reasoning (AILR)

	Level 0	Level 1	Level 2	Level 3	Level 4	Level 5	Level 6
Descriptor	No Automation	Simple Assistance Automation	Advanced Assistance Automation	Semi-Autonomous Automation	AILR Domain Autonomous	AILR Fully Autonomous	AILR Superhuman Autonomous
Examples	Manual, paper-based (no automation)	Word Processing, XLS, online legal docs, etc.	Query-style NLP, ML for case prediction, etc.	KBS & ML/DL for legal reasoning & analysis, etc.	Versed only in a specific legal domain	Versatile within and across all legal domains	Exceeds human-based legal reasoning
Automation	None	Legal Assist	Legal Assist	Legal Assist	Legal Advisor (law fluent)	Legal Advisor (law fluent)	Supra Legal Advisor
Status	De Facto – In Use	Widely In Use	Some In Use	Primarily Prototypes & Research-based	None As Yet	None As Yet	Indeterminate

Figure 2: AI & Law - Autonomous Levels by Columns

Source Author: Dr. Lance B. Eliot

V1.3

Chapter 2 - Figure 2

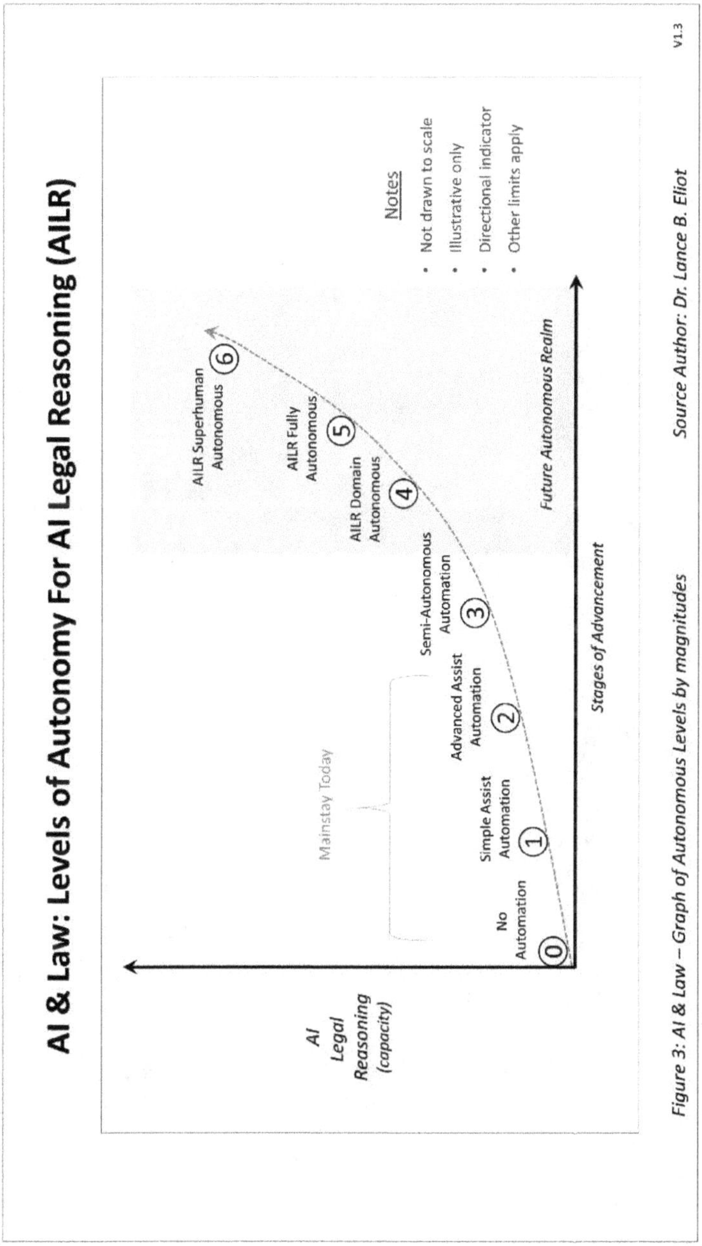

Figure 3: AI & Law – Graph of Autonomous Levels by magnitudes

Chapter 2 - Figure 3

Turing Test and Autonomous Levels of AI Legal Reasoning (AILR)

Strawman Variant

	Level 0	Level 1	Level 2	Level 3	Level 4	Level 5	Level 6
Descriptor	No Automation	Simple Assistance Automation	Advanced Assistance Automation	Semi-Autonomous Automation	AILR Domain Autonomous	AILR Fully Autonomous	AILR Superhuman Autonomous
The Inquirer	n/a	n/a	n/a	Expert Preferred	Expert in Domain	Multiple Experts	Topmost Experts
Human Participant	n/a	n/a	n/a	Expert	Expert in Domain	Multiple Experts	Topmost Experts
AI-Based Legal Reasoner	n/a	n/a	n/a	Minimal	Domain Specific	All Domains	Domains Plus
Queries of the Turing Test	n/a	n/a	n/a	Minimal	Domain Specific	All Domains	Domains Plus
Answers to the Turing Test	n/a	n/a	n/a	Minimal	Domain Specific	All Domains	Domains Plus
Rules of the Turing Test	n/a	n/a	n/a	Minimal	Rigorous	Rigorous	Rigorous
Potential Observers	n/a	n/a	n/a	Open	Law Specialists	Law Professionals	Law & Non-Law
Conclusion Reached	n/a	n/a	n/a	Limited As "Notable"	Domain-Only Pass in AILR	Full Pass In AILR	Exemplary Pass in AILR
Reverse Turing Test	n/a	n/a	n/a	Useful But Not Substantive	Useful In Domain	Useful Overall	Useful Overall

Figure 1: AI & Law – Turing Test and LoA AILR by Columns

Source Author: Dr. Lance B. Eliot

V1.3

Chapter 3 – Figure 1

Turing Test and Levels of Autonomy For AI Legal Reasoning (AILR)

Level	Descriptor	The Inquirer	Human Participant	AI-Based Legal Reasoner	Queries of the Turing Test	Answers to the Turing Test	Rules of The Turing Test	Potential Observers	Conclusion Reached	Reverse Turing Test
0	No Automation	n/a	n/a	n/a	n/a	n/a	n/a	n/a	n/a	n/a
1	Simple Assistance Automation	n/a	n/a	n/a	n/a	n/a	n/a	n/a	n/a	n/a
2	Advanced Assistance Automation	n/a	n/a	n/a	n/a	n/a	n/a	n/a	n/a	n/a
3	Semi-Autonomous Automation	Expert Preferred	Expert	Minimal	Minimal	Minimal	Minimal	Open	Limited As "Notable"	Useful But Not Substantive
4	AILR Domain Autonomous	Expert in Domain	Expert in Domain	Domain Specific	Domain Specific	Domain Specific	Rigorous	Law Specialists	Domain-Only Pass in AILR	Useful in Domain
5	AILR Fully Autonomous	Multiple Experts	Multiple Experts	All Domains	All Domains	All Domains	Rigorous	Law Professionals	Full Pass in AILR	Useful Overall
6	AILR Superhuman Autonomous	Topmost Experts	Topmost Experts	Domain Plus	Domain Plus	Domain Plus	Rigorous	Law & Non-Law	Exemplary Pass in AILR	Useful Overall

Figure 2: AI & Law – Turing Test and LoA AILR by Rows

Strawman Variant

Source Author: Dr. Lance B. Eliot V1.3

Chapter 3 – Figure 2

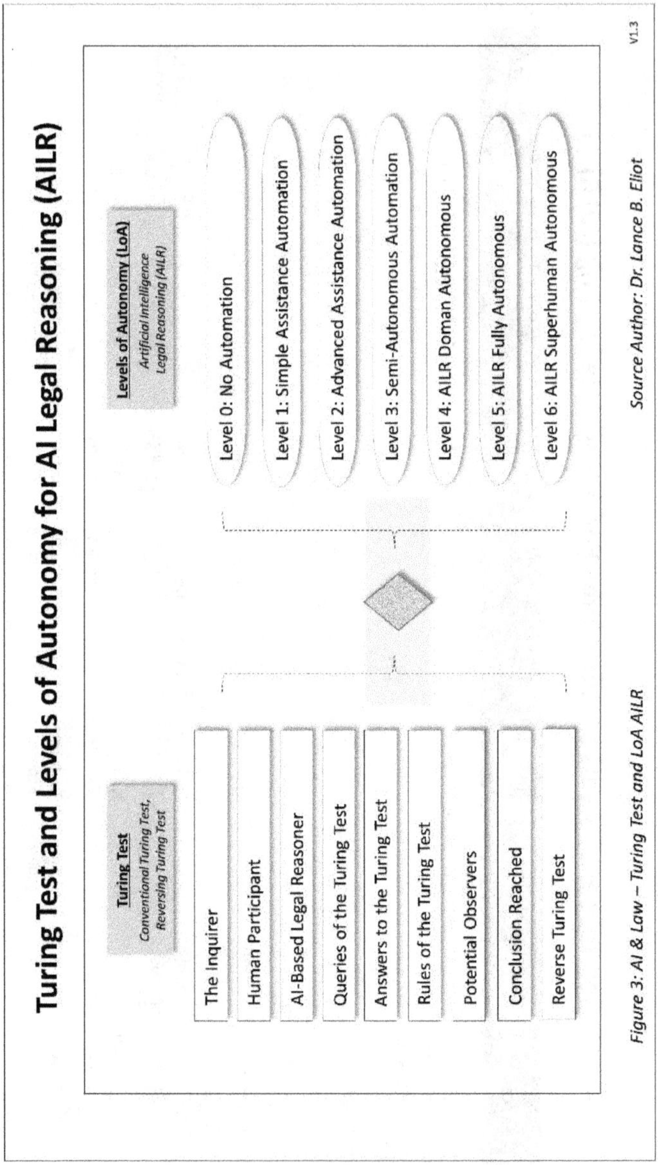
Turing Test and Levels of Autonomy for AI Legal Reasoning (AILR)
Turing Test
Conventional Turing Test, Reversing Turing Test
The Inquirer
Human Participant
AI-Based Legal Reasoner
Queries of the Turing Test
Answers to the Turing Test
Rules of the Turing Test
Potential Observers
Conclusion Reached
Reverse Turing Test
Levels of Autonomy (LoA)
Artificial Intelligence Legal Reasoning (AILR)
Level 0: No Automation
Level 1: Simple Assistance Automation
Level 2: Advanced Assistance Automation
Level 3: Semi-Autonomous Automation
Level 4: AILR Doman Autonomous
Level 5: AILR Fully Autonomous
Level 6: AILR Superhuman Autonomous
Figure 3: AI & Law – Turing Test and LoA AILR
Source Author: Dr. Lance B. Eliot
V1.3

Chapter 3 – Figure 3

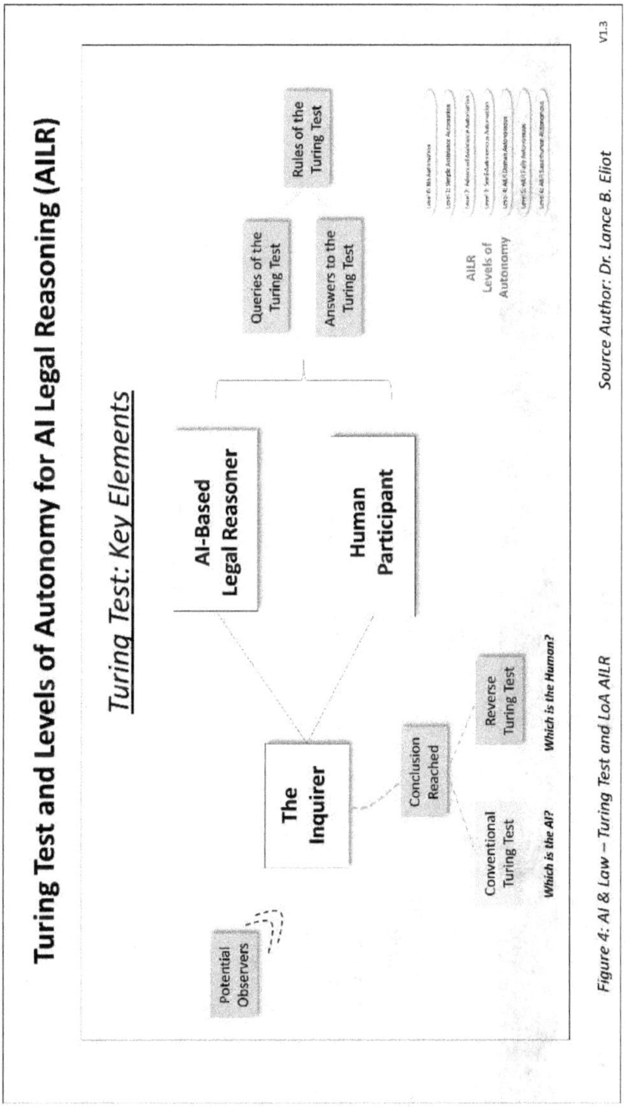
Turing Test and Levels of Autonomy for AI Legal Reasoning (AILR)
Turing Test: Key Elements
AI-Based Legal Reasoner
Human Participant
Queries of the Turing Test
Answers to the Turing Test
Rules of the Turing Test
Potential Observers
The Inquirer
Conclusion Reached
Conventional Turing Test
Reverse Turing Test
Which is the AI?
Which is the Human?
AILR Levels of Autonomy
V1.3
Figure 4: AI & Law – Turing Test and LoA AILR
Source Author: Dr. Lance B. Eliot

Chapter 3 – Figure 4

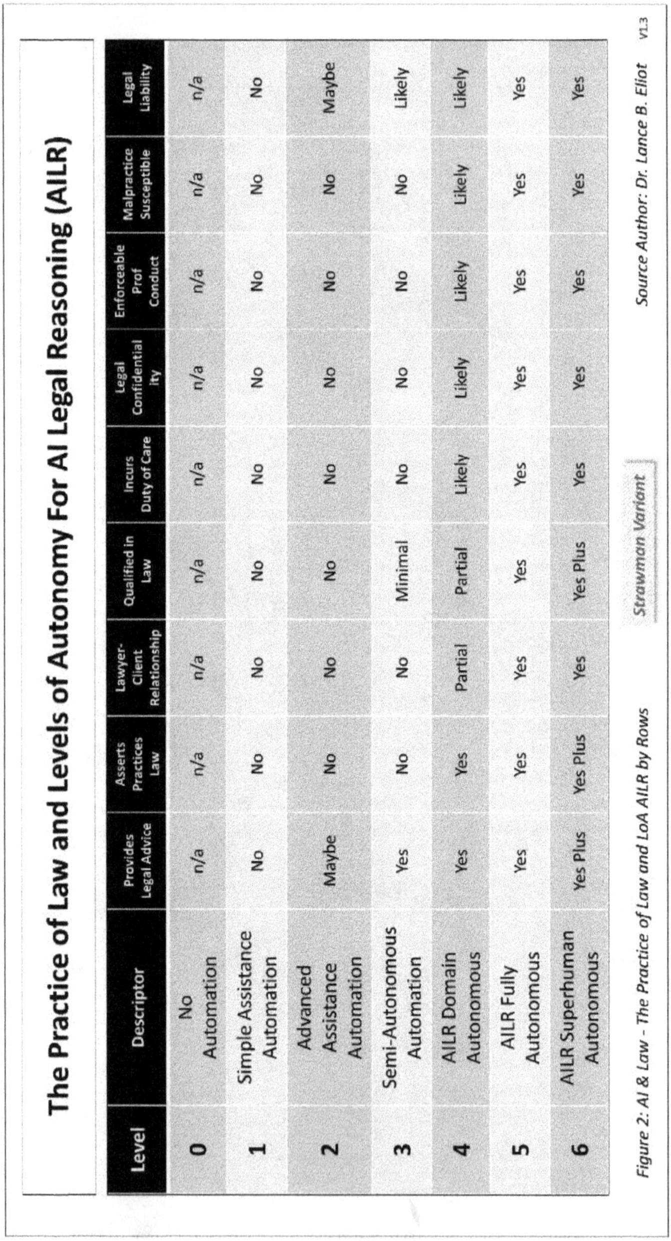

The Practice of Law and Levels of Autonomy For AI Legal Reasoning (AILR)

Level	Descriptor	Provides Legal Advice	Asserts Practices Law	Lawyer-Client Relationship	Qualified in Law	Incurs Duty of Care	Legal Confidentiality	Enforceable Prof Conduct	Malpractice Susceptible	Legal Liability
0	No Automation	n/a	n/a	n/a	n/a	n/a	n/a	n/a	n/a	n/a
1	Simple Assistance Automation	No	No	No	No	No	No	No	No	No
2	Advanced Assistance Automation	Maybe	No	No	No	No	No	No	No	Maybe
3	Semi-Autonomous Automation	Yes	No	No	Minimal	No	No	No	No	Likely
4	AILR Domain Autonomous	Yes	Yes	Partial	Partial	Likely	Likely	Likely	Likely	Likely
5	AILR Fully Autonomous	Yes	Yes	Yes	Yes	Yes	Yes	Yes	Yes	Yes
6	AILR Superhuman Autonomous	Yes Plus	Yes Plus	Yes	Yes Plus	Yes	Yes	Yes	Yes	Yes

Figure 2: AI & Law - The Practice of Law and LoA AILR by Rows Strawman Variant *Source Author: Dr. Lance B. Eliot* V1.3

Chapter 5 – Figure 1

The Practice of Law and Autonomous Levels of AI Legal Reasoning (AILR)

	Level 0	Level 1	Level 2	Level 3	Level 4	Level 5	Level 6
Descriptor	No Automation	Simple Assistance Automation	Advanced Assistance Automation	Semi-Autonomous Automation	AILR Domain Autonomous	AILR Fully Autonomous	AILR Superhuman Autonomous
Provides Legal Advice	n/a	No	Maybe	Yes	Yes	Yes	Yes Plus
Asserts Practices Law	n/a	No	No	No	Yes	Yes	Yes Plus
Lawyer-Client Relationship	n/a	No	No	No	Partial	Yes	Yes
Qualified in Law	n/a	No	No	Minimal	Partial	Yes	Yes Plus
Incurs Duty of Care	n/a	No	No	No	Likely	Yes	Yes
Legal Confidentiality	n/a	No	No	No	Likely	Yes	Yes
Enforceable Prof Conduct	n/a	No	No	No	Likely	Yes	Yes
Malpractice Susceptible	n/a	No	No	No	Likely	Yes	Yes
Legal Liability	n/a	No	Maybe	Likely	Likely	Yes	Yes

Strawman Variant

Figure 1: AI & Law – The Practice of Law and LoA AILR by Columns

Source Author: Dr. Lance B. Eliot

V1.3

Chapter 5 – Figure 2

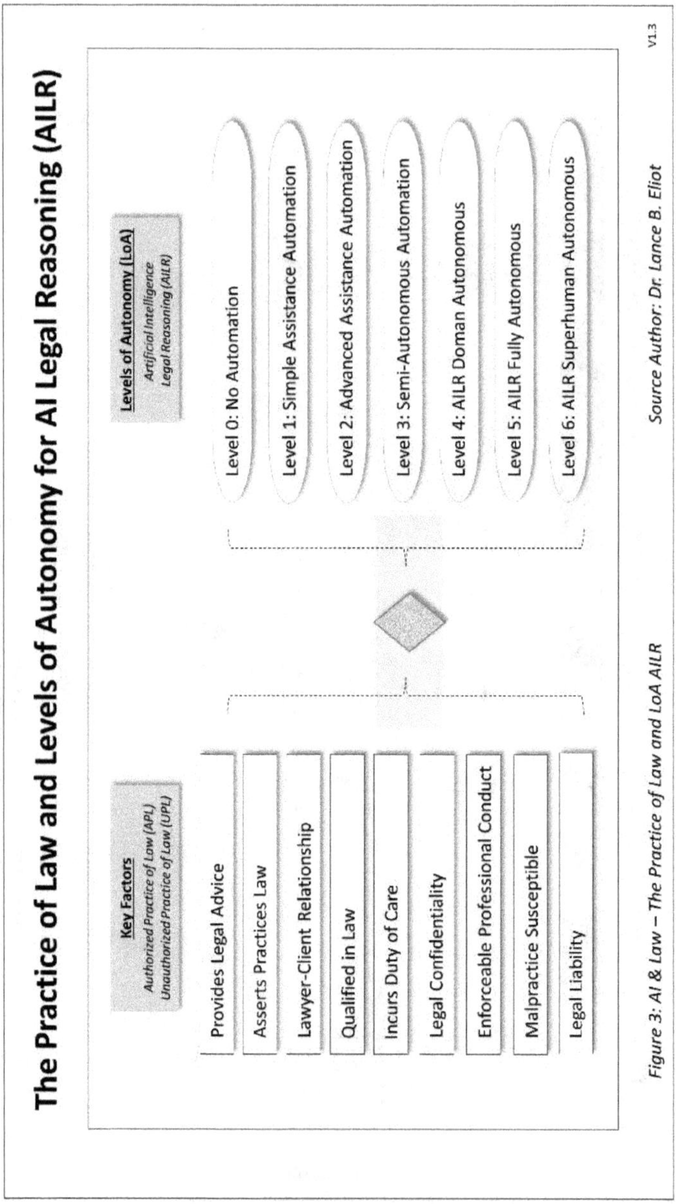

Chapter 5 – Figure 3

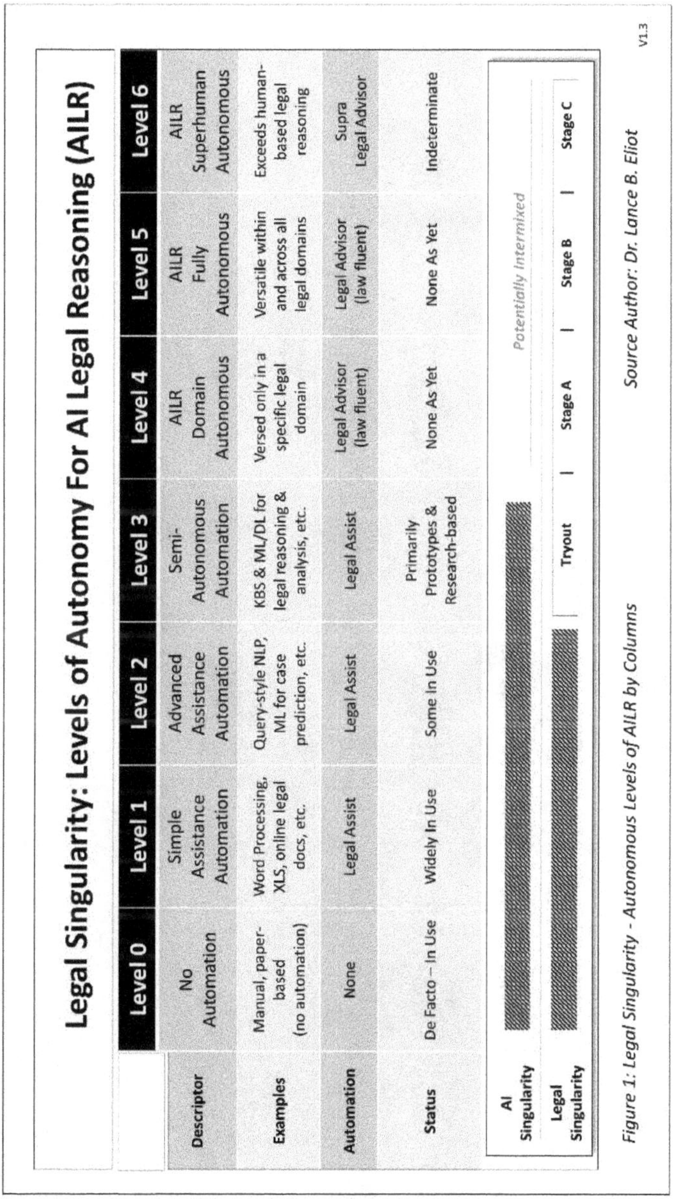

Legal Singularity: Levels of Autonomy For AI Legal Reasoning (AILR)

	Level 0	Level 1	Level 2	Level 3	Level 4	Level 5	Level 6
Descriptor	No Automation	Simple Assistance Automation	Advanced Assistance Automation	Semi-Autonomous Automation	AILR Domain Autonomous	AILR Fully Autonomous	AILR Superhuman Autonomous
Examples	Manual, paper-based (no automation)	Word Processing, XLS, online legal docs, etc.	Query-style NLP, ML for case prediction, etc.	KBS & ML/DL for legal reasoning & analysis, etc.	Versed only in a specific legal domain	Versatile within and across all legal domains	Exceeds human-based legal reasoning
Automation	None	Legal Assist	Legal Assist	Legal Assist	Legal Advisor (law fluent)	Legal Advisor (law fluent)	Supra Legal Advisor
Status	De Facto – In Use	Widely In Use	Some In Use	Primarily Prototypes & Research-based	None As Yet	None As Yet	Indeterminate

Figure 1: Legal Singularity - Autonomous Levels of AILR by Columns *Source Author: Dr. Lance B. Eliot*

Chapter 6 – Figure 1

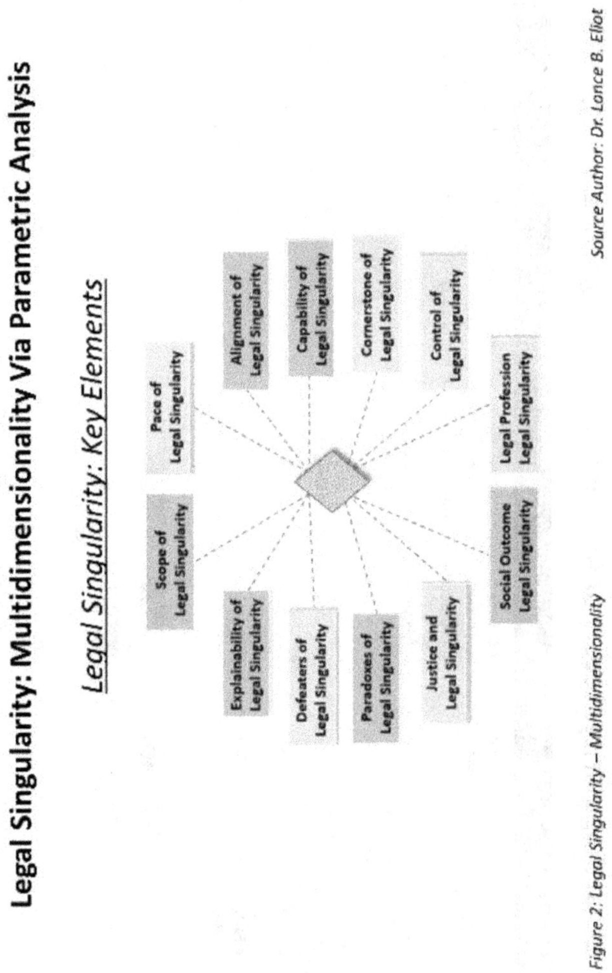
Legal Singularity: Multidimensionality Via Parametric Analysis
Legal Singularity: Key Elements
Scope of Legal Singularity
Pace of Legal Singularity
Explainability of Legal Singularity
Alignment of Legal Singularity
Defeaters of Legal Singularity
Capability of Legal Singularity
Paradoxes of Legal Singularity
Cornerstone of Legal Singularity
Justice and Legal Singularity
Control of Legal Singularity
Social Outcome Legal Singularity
Legal Profession Legal Singularity
Figure 2: Legal Singularity – Multidimensionality
Source Author: Dr. Lance B. Eliot

Chapter 6 – Figure 2

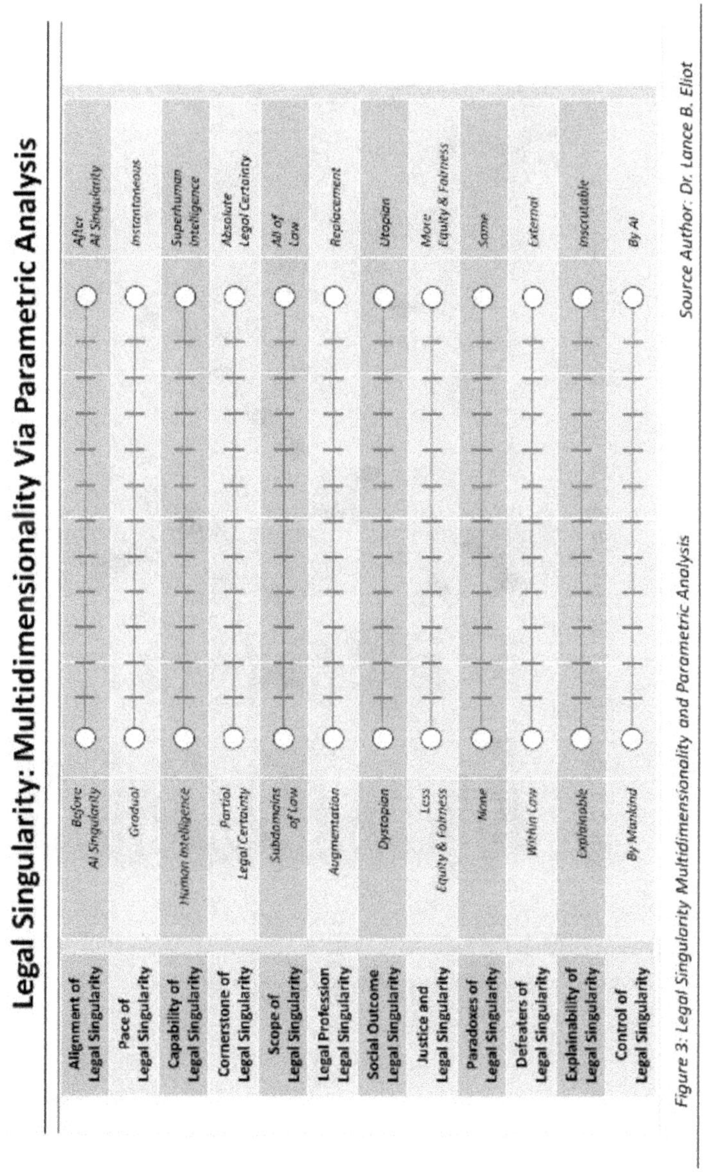
Legal Singularity: Multidimensionality Via Parametric Analysis
Alignment of Legal Singularity
Before AI Singularity
After AI Singularity
Pace of Legal Singularity
Gradual
Instantaneous
Capability of Legal Singularity
Human Intelligence
Superhuman Intelligence
Cornerstone of Legal Singularity
Partial Legal Certainty
Absolute Legal Certainty
Scope of Legal Singularity
Subdomains of Law
All of Law
Legal Profession Legal Singularity
Augmentation
Replacement
Social Outcome Legal Singularity
Dystopian
Utopian
Justice and Legal Singularity
Less Equity & Fairness
More Equity & Fairness
Paradoxes of Legal Singularity
None
Some
Defeaters of Legal Singularity
Within Law
External
Explainability of Legal Singularity
Explainable
Inscrutable
Control of Legal Singularity
By Mankind
By AI
Figure 3: Legal Singularity Multidimensionality and Parametric Analysis
Source Author: Dr. Lance B. Eliot

Chapter 6 – Figure 3

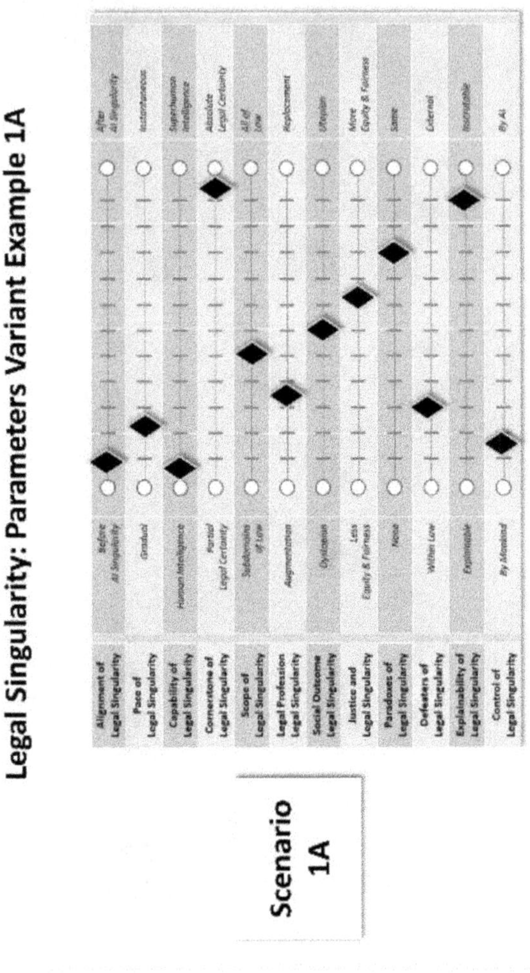

Figure 4: Legal Singularity – Multidimensionality

Source Author: Dr. Lance B. Eliot

Chapter 6 – Figure 4

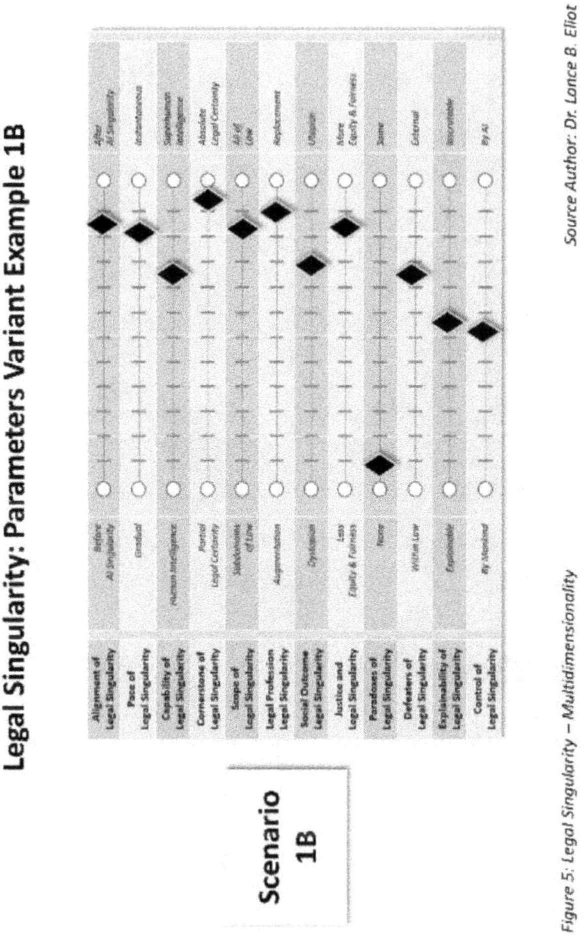

Chapter 6 – Figure 5

Principles of Justice and Autonomous Levels of AI Legal Reasoning (AILR)

	Level 0	Level 1	Level 2	Level 3	Level 4	Level 5	Level 6
Descriptor	No Automation	Simple Assistance Automation	Advanced Assistance Automation	Semi-Autonomous Automation	AILR Domain Autonomous	AILR Fully Autonomous	AILR Superhuman Autonomous
Substantive Justice	*Traditional*	*Traditional*	*Traditional*	Emerging	Phase X Impacts	Phase Y Impacts	Phase Z Impacts
Procedural Justice	*Traditional*	*Traditional*	*Traditional*	Emerging	Phase X Impacts	Phase Y Impacts	Phase Z Impacts
Open Justice	*Traditional*	*Traditional*	*Traditional*	Emerging	Phase X Impacts	Phase Y Impacts	Phase Z Impacts
Distributive Justice	*Traditional*	*Traditional*	*Traditional*	Emerging	Phase X Impacts	Phase Y Impacts	Phase Z Impacts
Proportionate Justice	*Traditional*	*Traditional*	*Traditional*	Emerging	Phase X Impacts	Phase Y Impacts	Phase Z Impacts
Enforceable Justice	*Traditional*	*Traditional*	*Traditional*	Emerging	Phase X Impacts	Phase Y Impacts	Phase Z Impacts
Sustainable Justice	*Traditional*	*Traditional*	*Traditional*	Emerging	Phase X Impacts	Phase Y Impacts	Phase Z Impacts

Figure 1: AI & Law – Principles of Justice and LoA AILR by Columns

Source Author: Dr. Lance B. Eliot

V1.3

Chapter 7 – Figure 1

Principles of Justice and Levels of Autonomy For AI Legal Reasoning (AILR)

Level	Descriptor	Substantive Justice	Procedural Justice	Open Justice	Distributive Justice	Proportionate Justice	Sustainable Justice
0	No Automation	*Traditional*	*Traditional*	*Traditional*	*Traditional*	*Traditional*	*Traditional*
1	Simple Assistance Automation	*Traditional*	*Traditional*	*Traditional*	*Traditional*	*Traditional*	*Traditional*
2	Advanced Assistance Automation	*Traditional*	*Traditional*	*Traditional*	*Traditional*	*Traditional*	*Traditional*
3	Semi-Autonomous Automation	Emerging	Emerging	Emerging	Emerging	Emerging	Emerging
4	AILR Domain Autonomous	Phase X Impacts	Phase X Impacts	Phase X Impacts	Phase X Impacts	Phase X Impacts	Phase X Impacts
5	AILR Fully Autonomous	Phase Y Impacts	Phase Y Impacts	Phase Y Impacts	Phase Y Impacts	Phase Y Impacts	Phase Y Impacts
6	AILR Superhuman Autonomous	Phase Z Impacts	Phase Z Impacts	Phase Z Impacts	Phase Z Impacts	Phase Z Impacts	Phase Z Impacts

Figure 2: AI & Law – Principles of Justice and LoA AILR by Rows

Source Author: Dr. Lance B. Eliot

V1.3

Chapter 7 – Figure 2

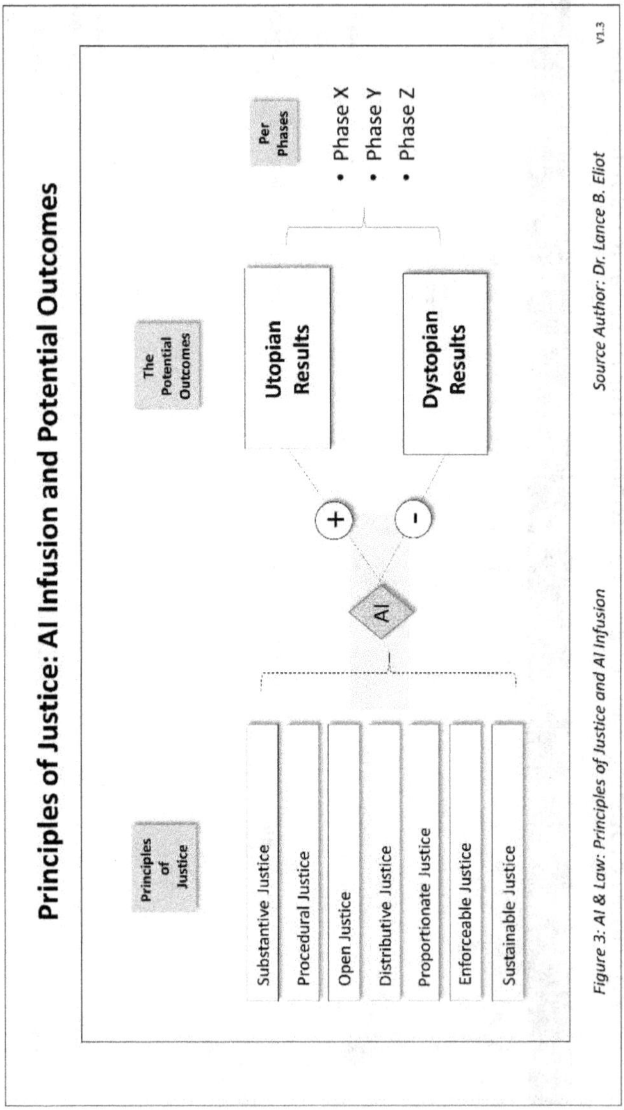

Chapter 7 – Figure 3

Principles of Justice Outcomes and LoA of AI Legal Reasoning (AILR)

Strawman Variant

	Level 4	Level 4	Level 5	Level 5	Level 6	Level 6
	Phase X		Phase Y		Phase Z	
Descriptor	***Utopian***	***Dystopian***	***Utopian***	***Dystopian***	***Utopian***	***Dystopian***
Substantive Justice	Fairer Decisions (law domains)	Unfairer Decisions (law domains)	Fairer Decisions (all of law)	Unfairer Decisions (all of law)	Ultra-Fair Decisions	Ultra-Unfair Decisions
Procedural Justice	Fairer Processes (law domains)	Unfairer Processes (law domains)	Fairer Processes (all of law)	Unfairer Processes (all of law)	Ultra-Fair Processes	Ultra-Unfair Processes
Open Justice	Greater Transparency (law domains)	Lessened Transparency (law domains)	Greater Transparency (all of law)	Lessened Transparency (all of law)	Ultimate Transparency	Utmost Opaqueness
Distributive Justice	Expanded Access (law domains)	Reduced Access (law domains)	Expanded Access (all of law)	Reduced Access (all of law)	Totality of Access	Utter Denial of Access
Proportionate Justice	More Balanced (law domains)	Less Balanced (law domains)	More Balanced (all of law)	Less Balanced (all of law)	Perfectly Balanced	Wholly Unbalanced
Enforceable Justice	Better Enforcement (law domains)	Worse Enforcement (law domains)	Better Enforcement (all of law)	Worse Enforcement (all of law)	Ideal Enforcement	Horrendous Enforcement
Sustainable Justice	Greater Stability (law domains)	Lessened Stability (law domains)	Greater Stability (all of law)	Lessened Stability (all of law)	Completely Sustainable	Entirely Unsustainable

Figure 4: AI & Law – Principles of Justice Outcomes and LoA AILR by Columns *Source Author: Dr. Lance B. Eliot*

V1.3

Chapter 7 – Figure 4

Legal Micro-Directives: Levels of Autonomy For AI Legal Reasoning (AILR)

	Level 0	Level 1	Level 2	Level 3	Level 4	Level 5	Level 6
Descriptor	No Automation	Simple Assistance Automation	Advanced Assistance Automation	Semi-Autonomous Automation	AILR Domain Autonomous	AILR Fully Autonomous	AILR Superhuman Autonomous
Examples	Manual, paper-based (no automation)	Word Processing, XLS, online legal docs, etc.	Query-style NLP, ML for case prediction, etc.	KBS & ML/DL for legal reasoning & analysis, etc.	Versed only in a specific legal domain	Versatile within and across all legal domains	Exceeds human-based legal reasoning
Automation	None	Legal Assist	Legal Assist	Legal Assist	Legal Advisor (law fluent)	Legal Advisor (law fluent)	Supra Legal Advisor
Status	De Facto – In Use	Widely In Use	Some In Use	Primarily Prototypes & Research-based	None As Yet	None As Yet	Indeterminate
AI-Enabled Legal Micro-Directives	*n/a*	*Impractical*	*Incubatory*	*Infancy*	*Narrow*	*Wide*	*Consummate*

Figure 1: Legal Micro-Directives - Autonomous Levels of AILR by Columns

Source Author: Dr. Lance B. Eliot

V1.3

Chapter 8 – Figure 1

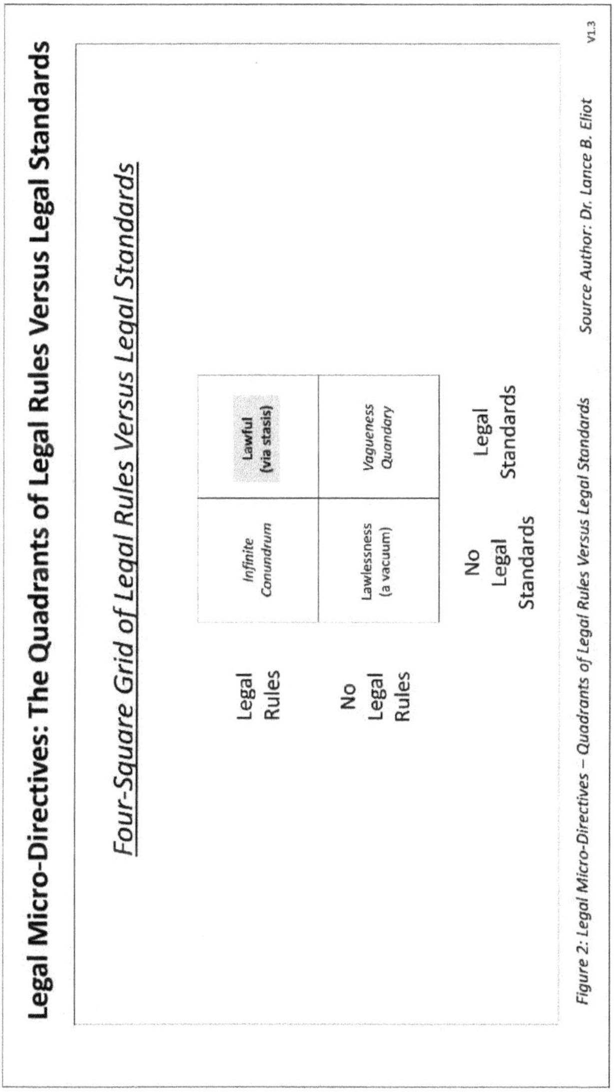

Chapter 8 – Figure 2

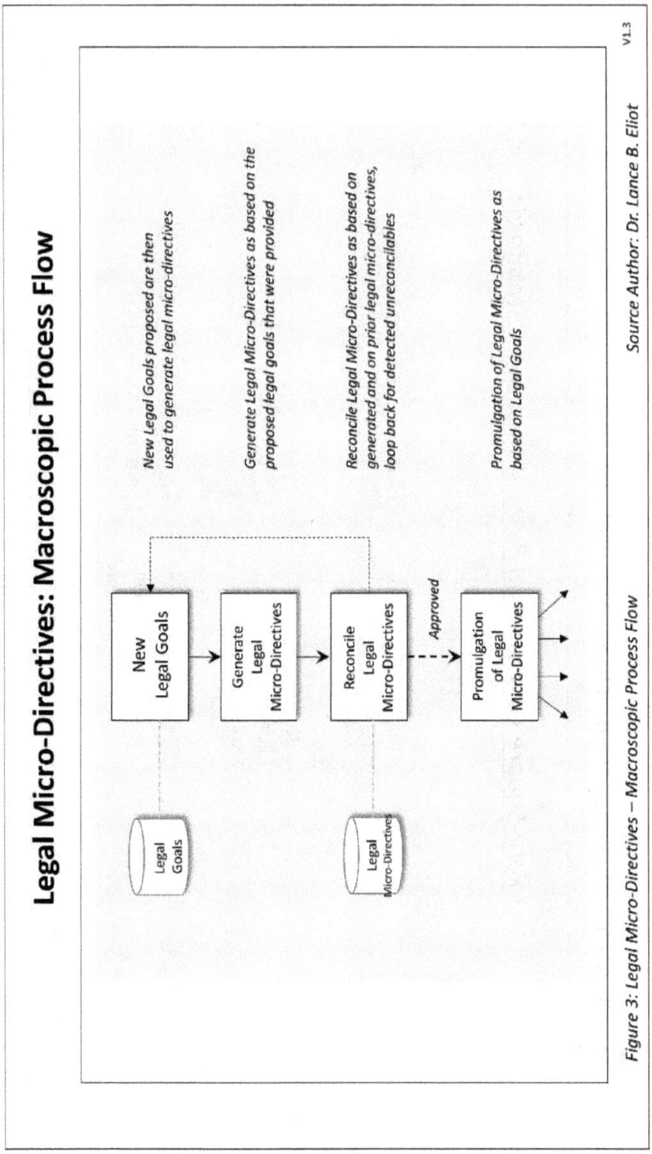

Figure 3: Legal Micro-Directives – Macroscopic Process Flow

Chapter 8 – Figure 3

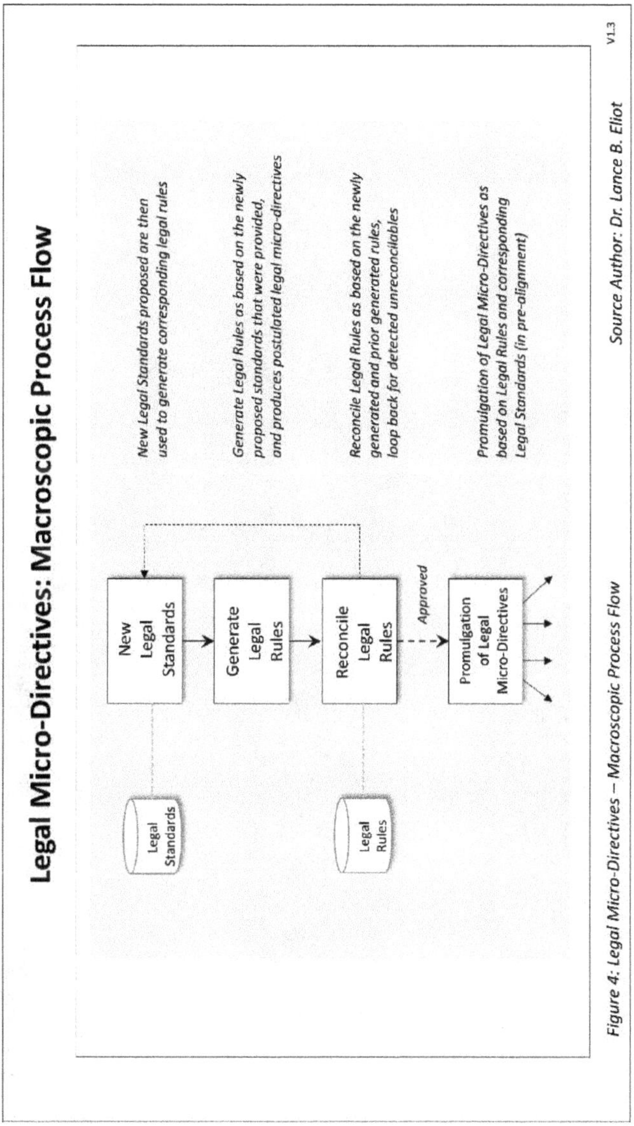

Chapter 8 – Figure 4

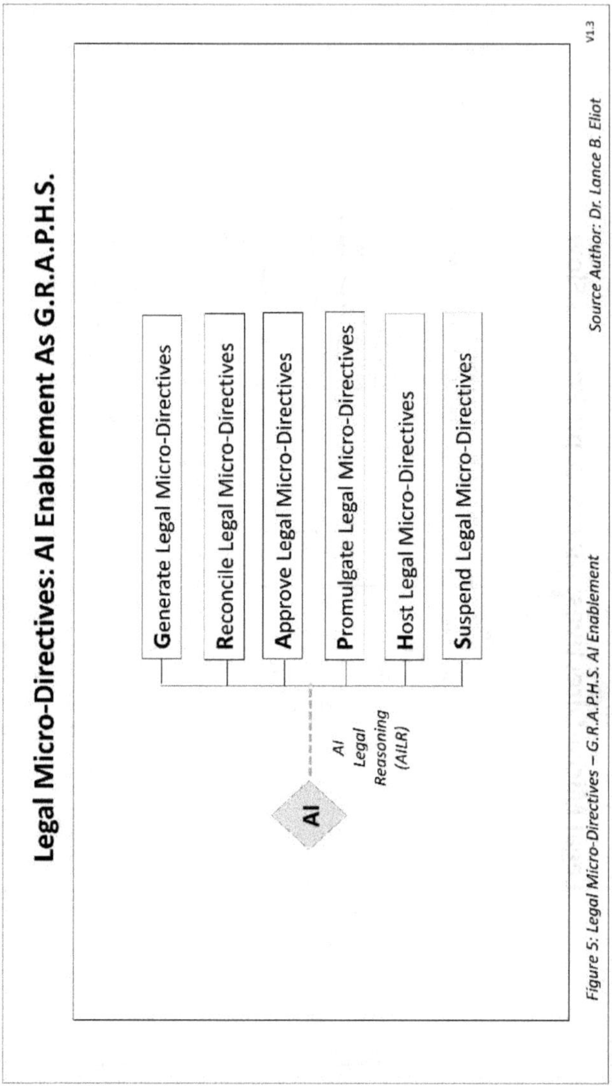

Chapter 8 – Figure 5

Legal Micro-Directives: Brittleness Aspects And Remedies

Brittleness	Description	Potential Remedy
Ripple effect	Change in Standards can produce cavalcade of rules changes	*Reconciliation*
Amalgamation effect	Existing rules become fabric; new rules disruptive to abide	*Disentanglement*
Off-guard effect	Caught off-guard by unexpected appearance of new rules	*Notification*
Propagation effect	Receiving of new rules might encounter propagation delays	*Attestation*
Wariness effect	Wariness toward new rules if all rules seem to be unstable	*Stabilization*
Conflicts effect	Multiple rules that intrinsically conflict with each other	*Harmonization*
Spoofing effect	Spoofing to make illegitimate rules seem as official	*Authentication*

Figure 6: Legal Micro-Directives – Brittleness and Remedies *Source Author: Dr. Lance B. Eliot* V1.3

Chapter 8 – Figure 6

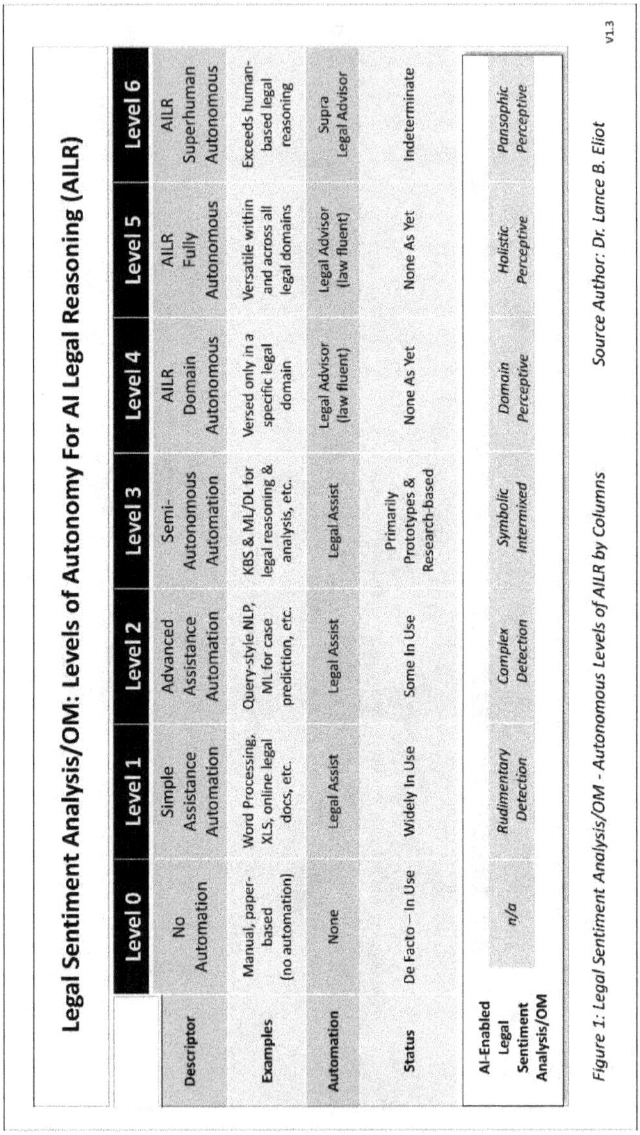

Legal Sentiment Analysis/OM: Levels of Autonomy For AI Legal Reasoning (AILR)

	Level 0	Level 1	Level 2	Level 3	Level 4	Level 5	Level 6
Descriptor	No Automation	Simple Assistance Automation	Advanced Assistance Automation	Semi-Autonomous Automation	AILR Domain Autonomous	AILR Fully Autonomous	AILR Superhuman Autonomous
Examples	Manual, paper-based (no automation)	Word Processing, XLS, online legal docs, etc.	Query-style NLP, ML for case prediction, etc.	KBS & ML/DL for legal reasoning & analysis, etc.	Versed only in a specific legal domain	Versatile within and across all legal domains	Exceeds human-based legal reasoning
Automation	None	Legal Assist	Legal Assist	Legal Assist	Legal Advisor (law fluent)	Legal Advisor (law fluent)	Supra Legal Advisor
Status	De Facto – In Use	Widely In Use	Some In Use	Primarily Prototypes & Research-based	None As Yet	None As Yet	Indeterminate
AI-Enabled Legal Sentiment Analysis/OM	*n/a*	*Rudimentary Detection*	*Complex Detection*	*Symbolic Intermixed*	*Domain Perceptive*	*Holistic Perceptive*	*Pansophic Perceptive*

Figure 1: Legal Sentiment Analysis/OM - Autonomous Levels of AILR by Columns *Source Author: Dr. Lance B. Eliot* V1.3

Chapter 9 – Figure 1

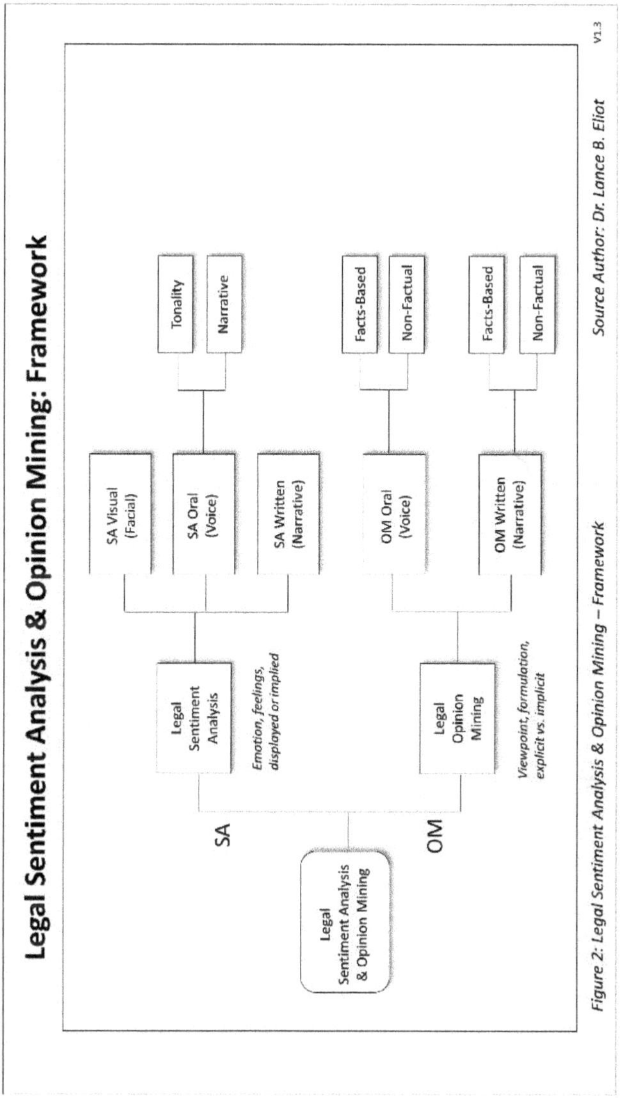

Figure 2: Legal Sentiment Analysis & Opinion Mining – Framework

Chapter 9 – Figure 2

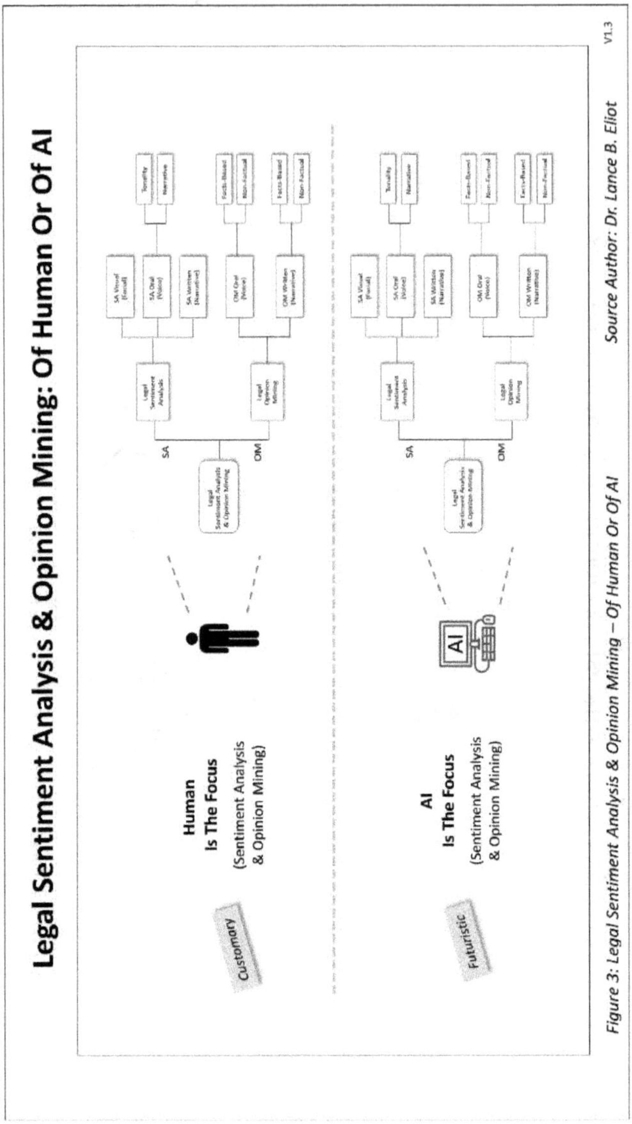

Chapter 9 – Figure 3

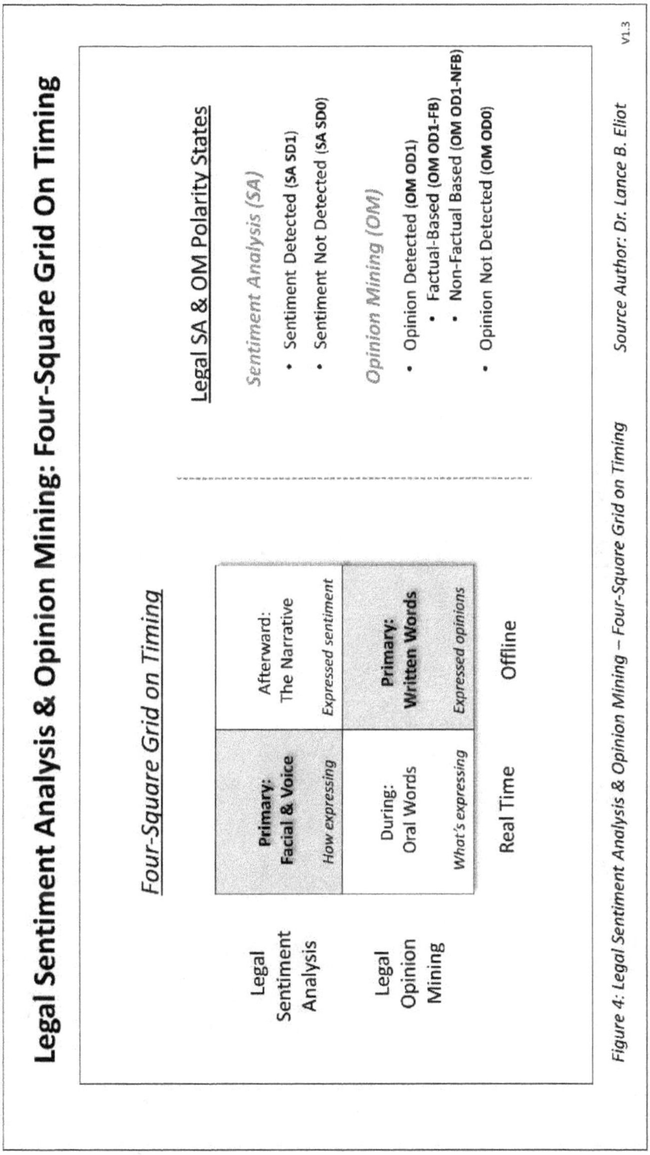

Chapter 9 – Figure 4

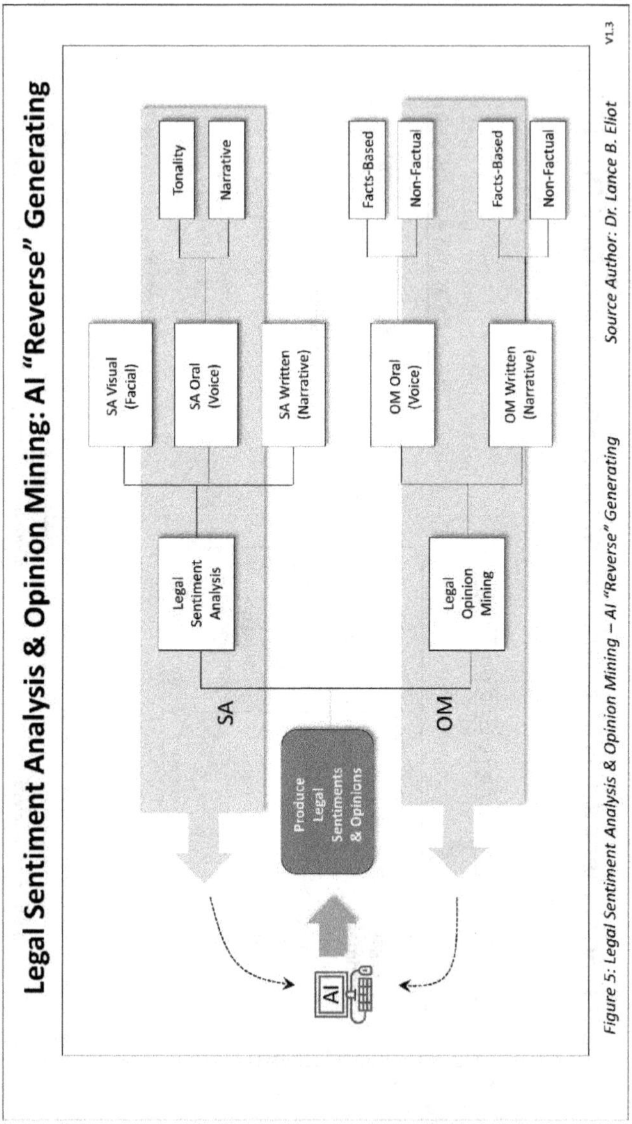

Figure 5: Legal Sentiment Analysis & Opinion Mining – AI "Reverse" Generating

Chapter 9 – Figure 5

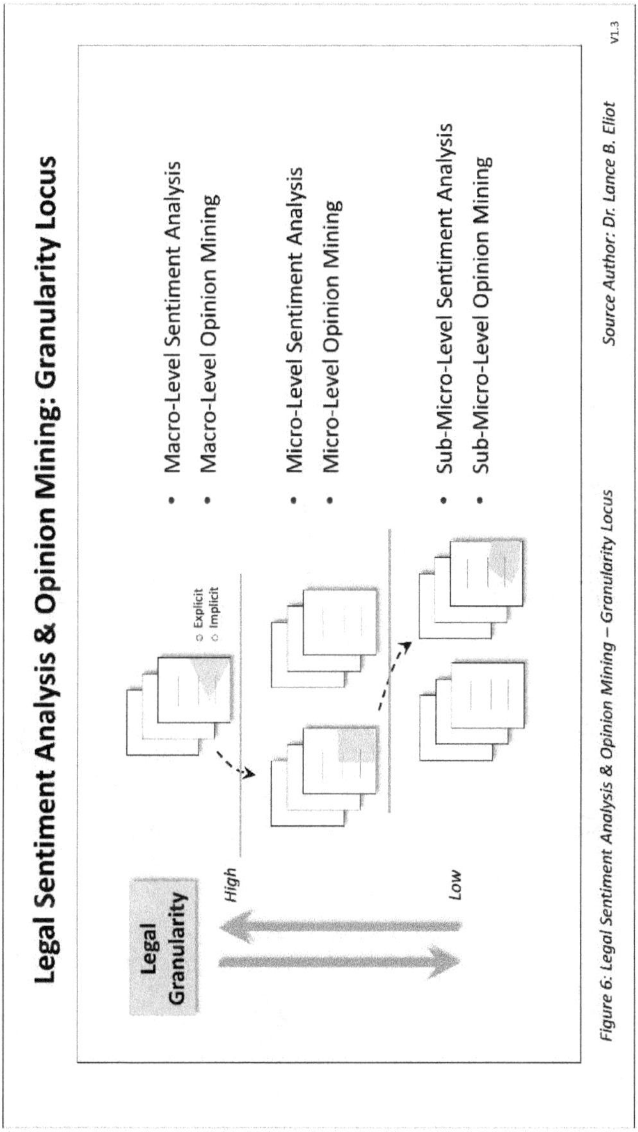

Figure 6: Legal Sentiment Analysis & Opinion Mining – Granularity Locus

Chapter 9 – Figure 6

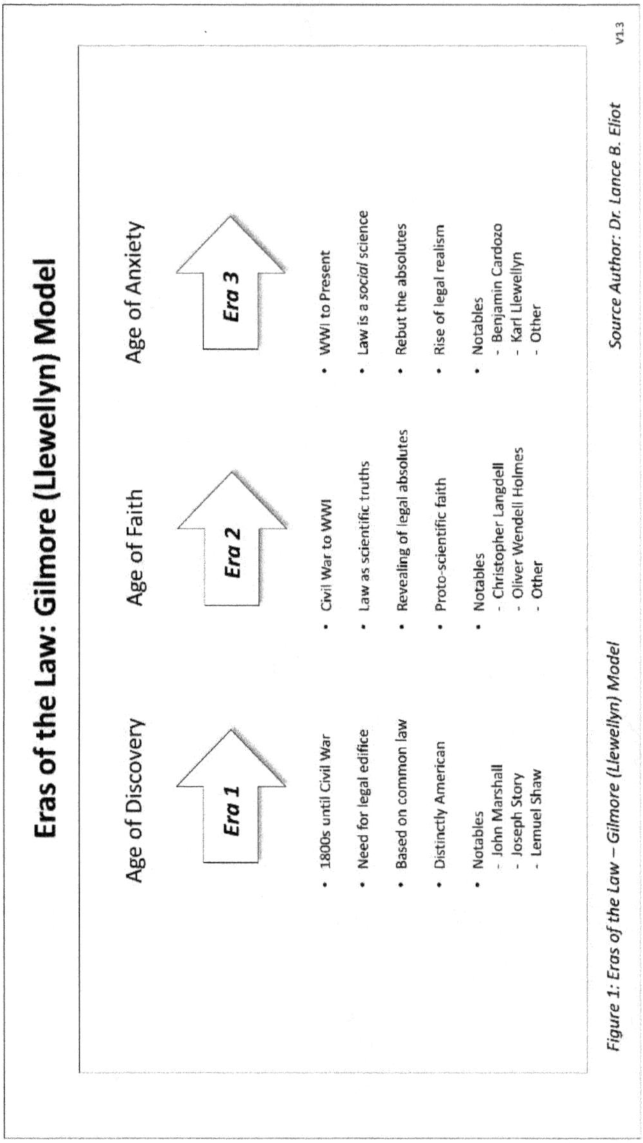

Chapter 10 – Figure 1

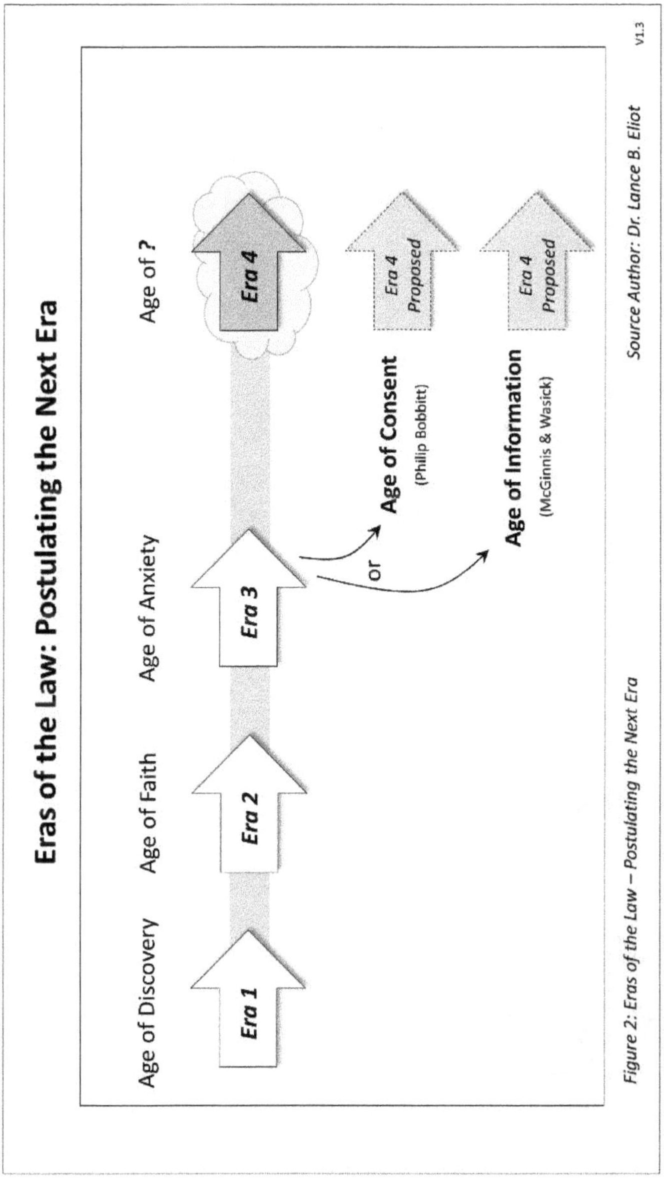

Chapter 10 – Figure 2

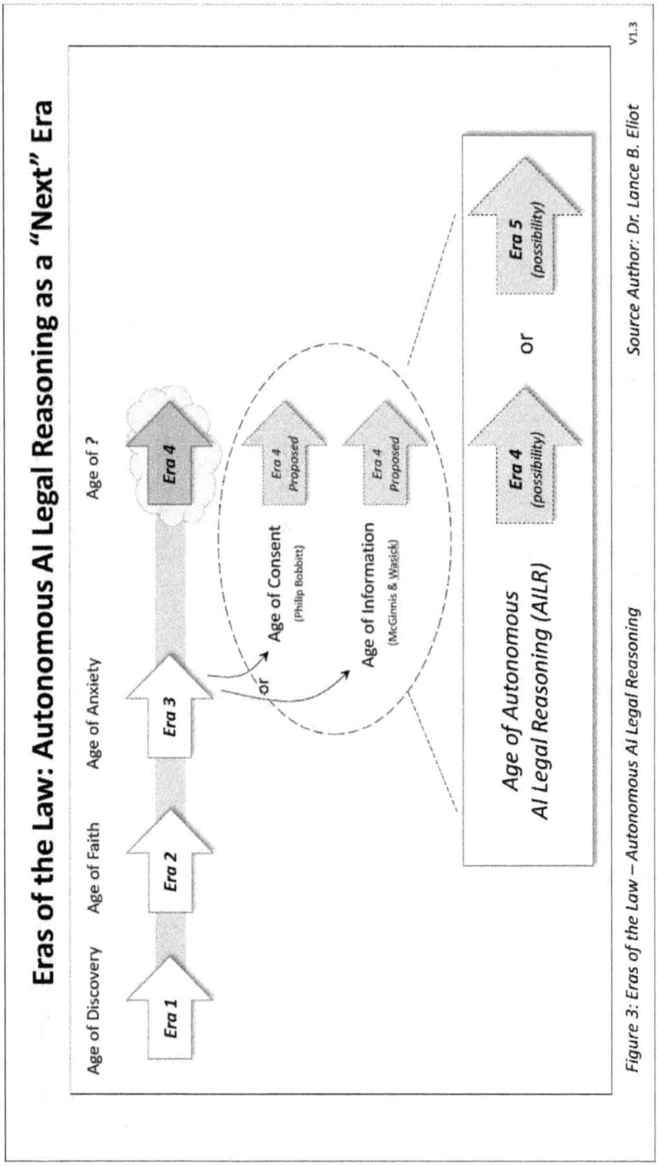

Chapter 10 – Figure 3

Eras of the Law: Levels of Autonomy For AI Legal Reasoning (AILR)

	Level 0	Level 1	Level 2	Level 3	Level 4	Level 5	Level 6
Descriptor	No Automation	Simple Assistance Automation	Advanced Assistance Automation	Semi-Autonomous Automation	AILR Domain Autonomous	AILR Fully Autonomous	AILR Superhuman Autonomous
Examples	Manual, paper-based (no automation)	Word Processing, XLS, online legal docs, etc.	Query-style NLP, ML for case prediction, etc.	KBS & ML/DL for legal reasoning & analysis, etc.	Versed only in a specific legal domain	Versatile within and across all legal domains	Exceeds human-based legal reasoning
Automation	None	Legal Assist	Legal Assist	Legal Assist	Legal Advisor (law fluent)	Legal Advisor (law fluent)	Supra Legal Advisor
Status	De Facto – In Use	Widely In Use	Some In Use	Primarily Prototypes & Research-based	None As Yet	None As Yet	Indeterminate
Eras of the Law by Levels of Autonomy	*In Eras 1, 2, 3+*	*In Eras 3, (4+)*	*In Eras 3, (4+)*	*In Eras 3, (4+)*	*Shape Eras 4 or 5*	*Define Eras 4 or 5*	*Be Eras 5 or 6*

Figure 4: Eras of the Law - Autonomous Levels of AILR by Columns

Source Author: Dr. Lance B. Eliot

V1.3

Chapter 10 – Figure 4

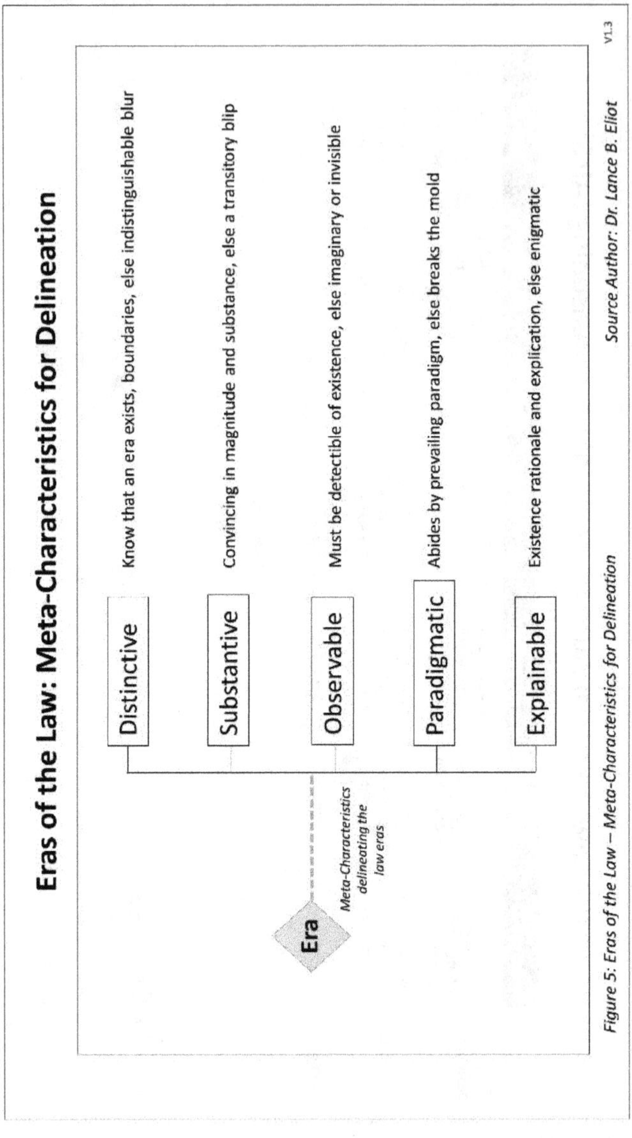

Figure 5: Eras of the Law – Meta-Characteristics for Delineation

Chapter 10 – Figure 5

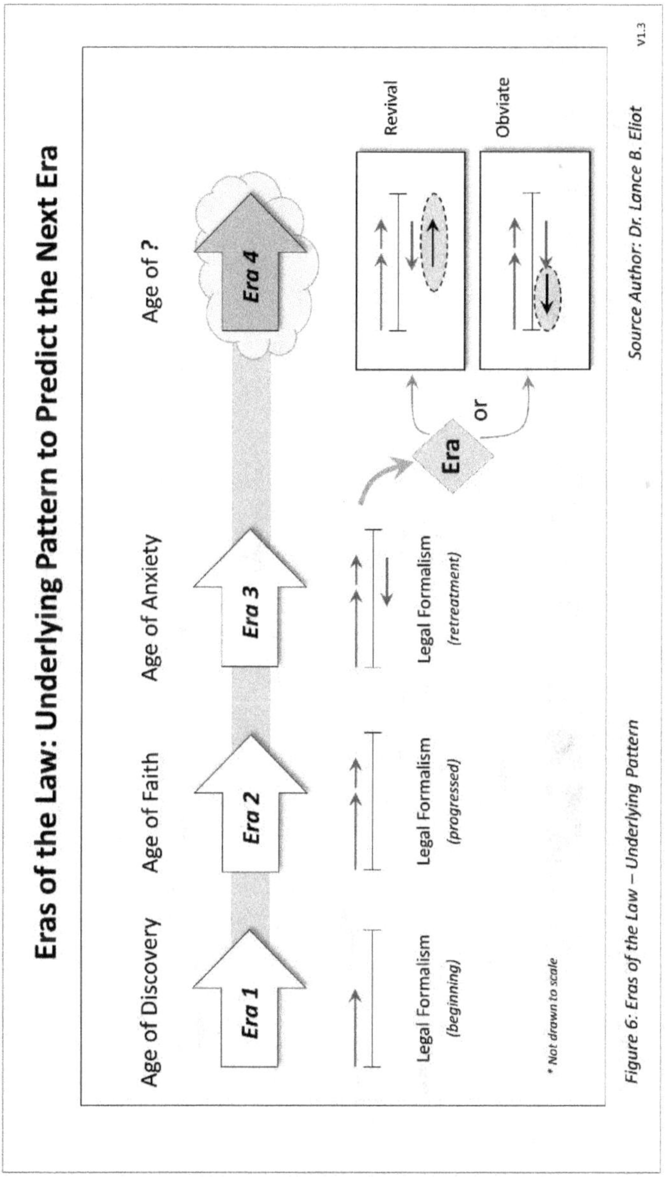

Figure 6: Eras of the Law – Underlying Pattern

Chapter 10 – Figure 6

Legal Judgment Prediction: Levels of Autonomy For AI Legal Reasoning (AILR)

	Level 0	Level 1	Level 2	Level 3	Level 4	Level 5	Level 6
Descriptor	No Automation	Simple Assistance Automation	Advanced Assistance Automation	Semi-Autonomous Automation	AILR Domain Autonomous	AILR Fully Autonomous	AILR Superhuman Autonomous
Examples	Manual, paper-based (no automation)	Word Processing, XLS, online legal docs, etc.	Query-style NLP, ML for case prediction, etc.	KBS & ML/DL for legal reasoning & analysis, etc.	Versed only in a specific legal domain	Versatile within and across all legal domains	Exceeds human-based legal reasoning
Automation	None	Legal Assist	Legal Assist	Legal Assist	Legal Advisor (law fluent)	Legal Advisor (law fluent)	Supra Legal Advisor
Status	De Facto – In Use	Widely In Use	Some In Use	Primarily Prototypes & Research-based	None As Yet	None As Yet	Indeterminate
AI-Enabled Legal Judgment Prediction	*n/a*	*Rudimentary Calculative*	*Complex Statistical*	*Symbolic Intermixed*	*Domain Predictive*	*Holistic Predictive*	*Pansophic Predictive*

Figure 1: Legal Judgment Prediction (LJP) - Autonomous Levels of AILR by Columns *Source Author: Dr. Lance B. Eliot*

V1.3

Chapter 11 – Figure 1

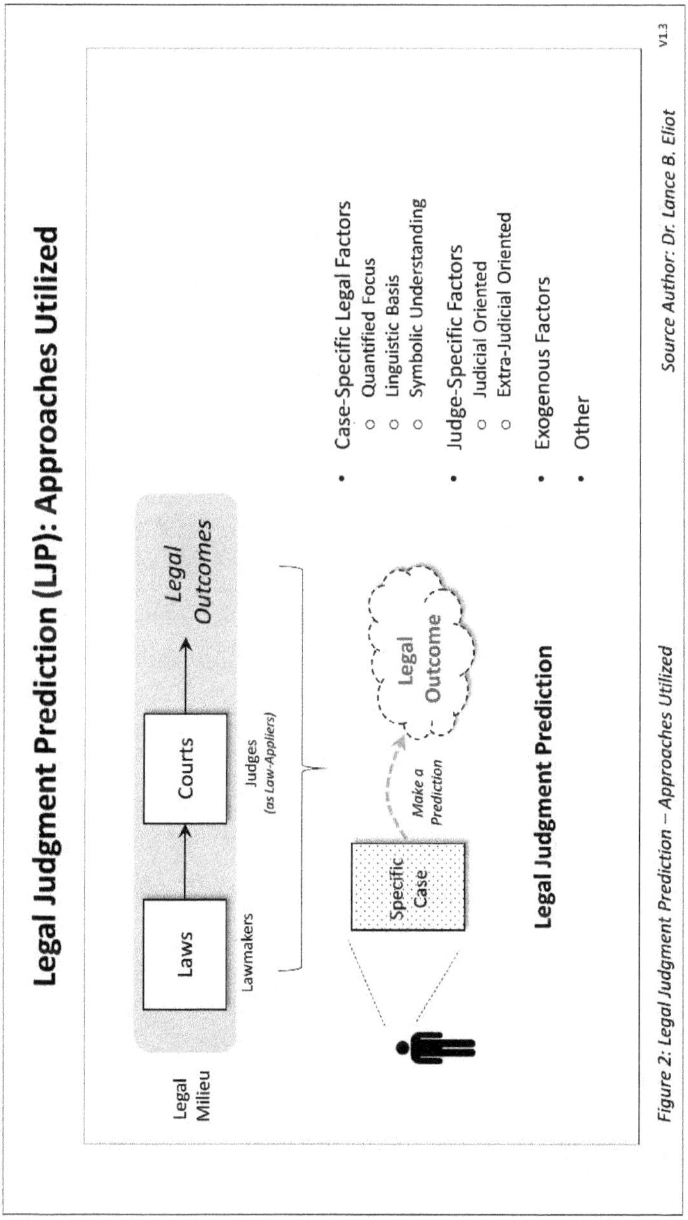

Figure 2: Legal Judgment Prediction – Approaches Utilized

Chapter 11 – Figure 2

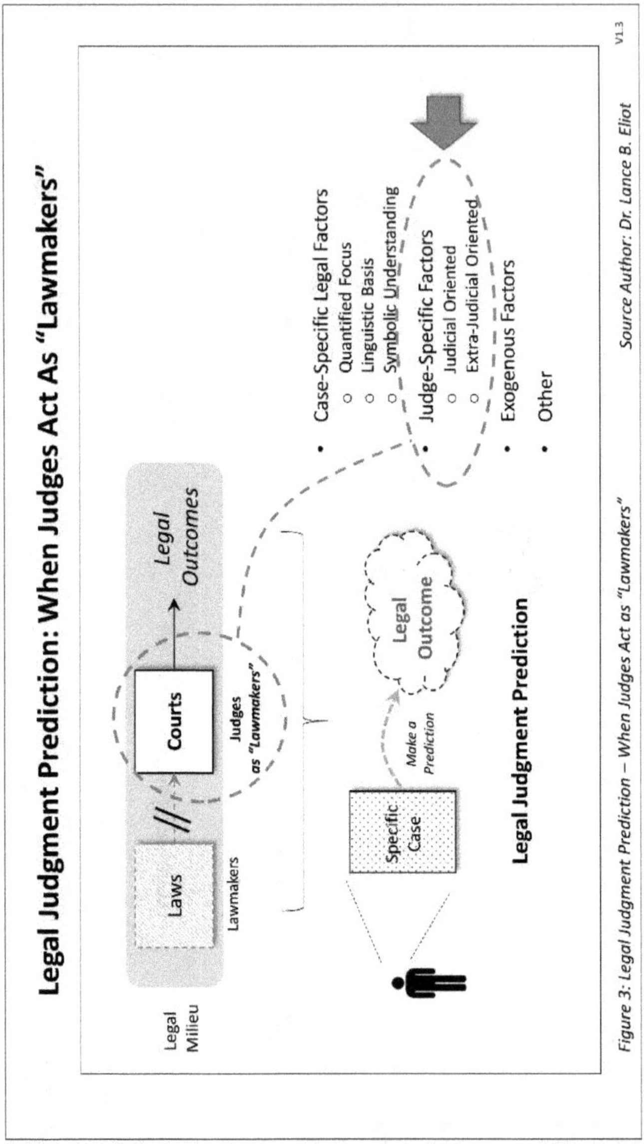

Chapter 11 – Figure 3

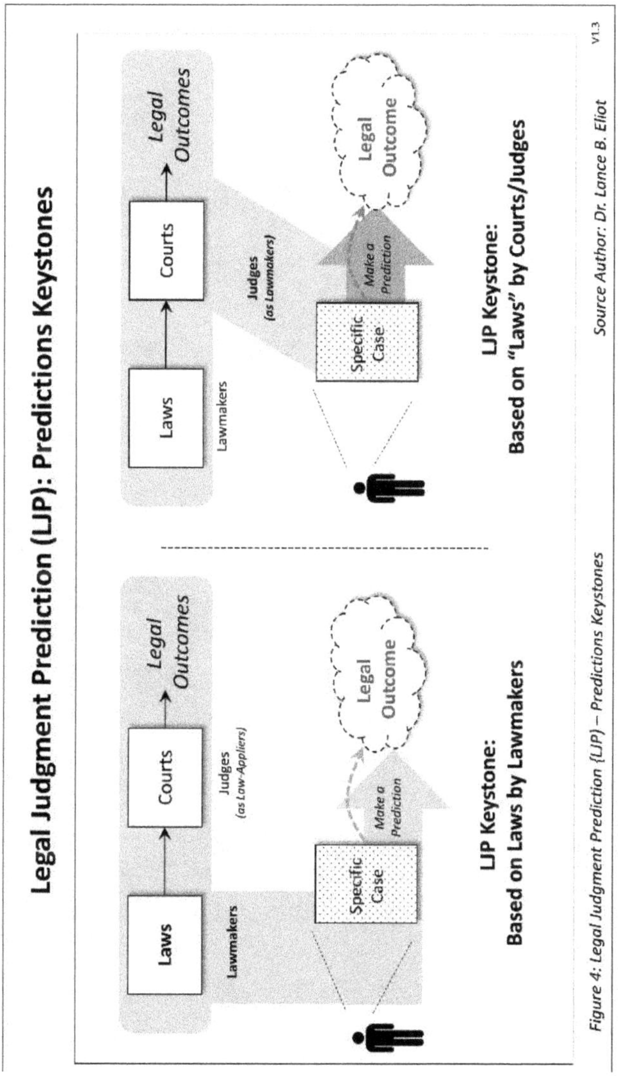

Figure 4: Legal Judgment Prediction (LJP) – Predictions Keystones
Source Author: Dr. Lance B. Eliot

Chapter 11 – Figure 4

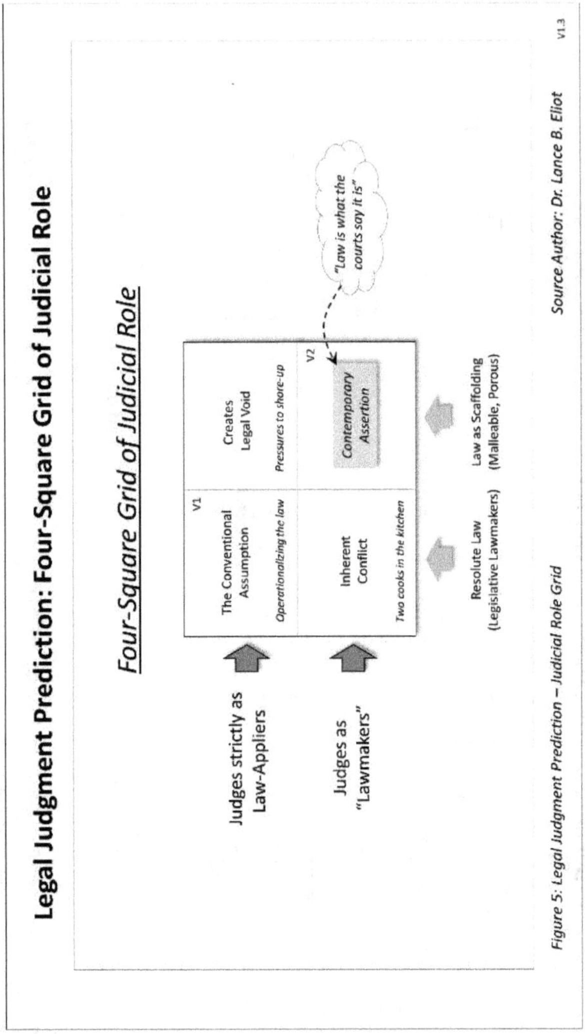

Chapter 11 – Figure 5

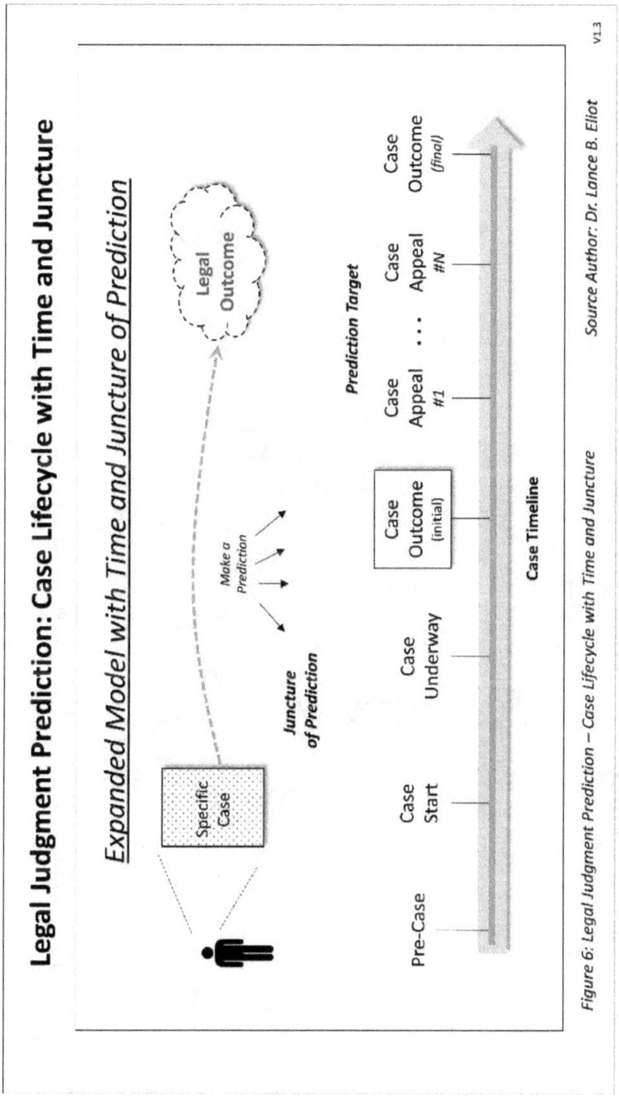

Figure 6: Legal Judgment Prediction – Case Lifecycle with Time and Juncture *Source Author: Dr. Lance B. Eliot*

Chapter 11 – Figure 6

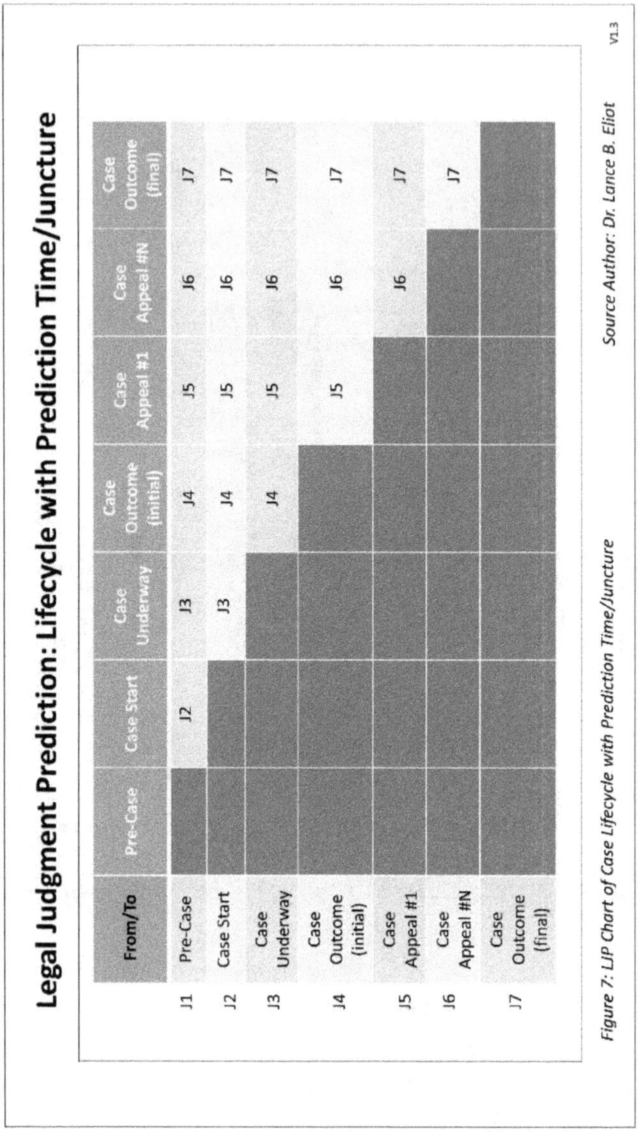

Legal Judgment Prediction: Lifecycle with Prediction Time/Juncture

	From/To	Pre-Case	Case Start	Case Underway	Case Outcome (initial)	Case Appeal #1	Case Appeal #N	Case Outcome (final)
J1	Pre-Case		J2	J3	J4	J5	J6	J7
J2	Case Start			J3	J4	J5	J6	J7
J3	Case Underway				J4	J5	J6	J7
J4	Case Outcome (initial)					J5	J6	J7
J5	Case Appeal #1						J6	J7
J6	Case Appeal #N							J7
J7	Case Outcome (final)							

Figure 7: LJP Chart of Case Lifecycle with Prediction Time/Juncture

Source Author: Dr. Lance B. Eliot

V1.3

Chapter 11 – Figure 7

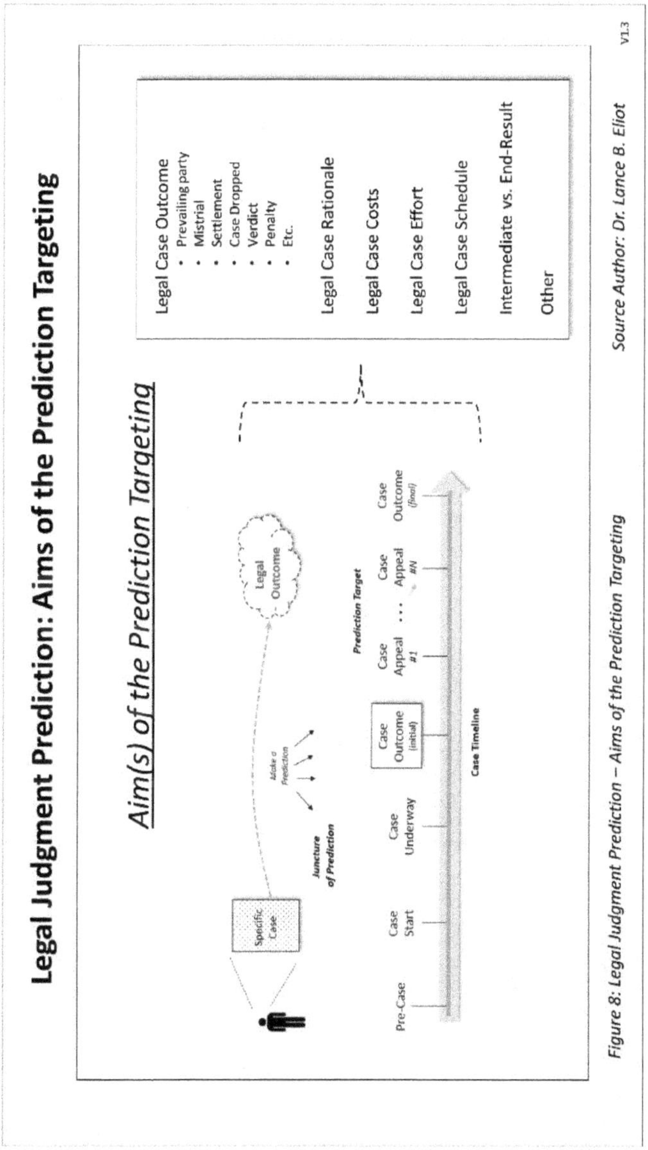

Chapter 11 – Figure 8

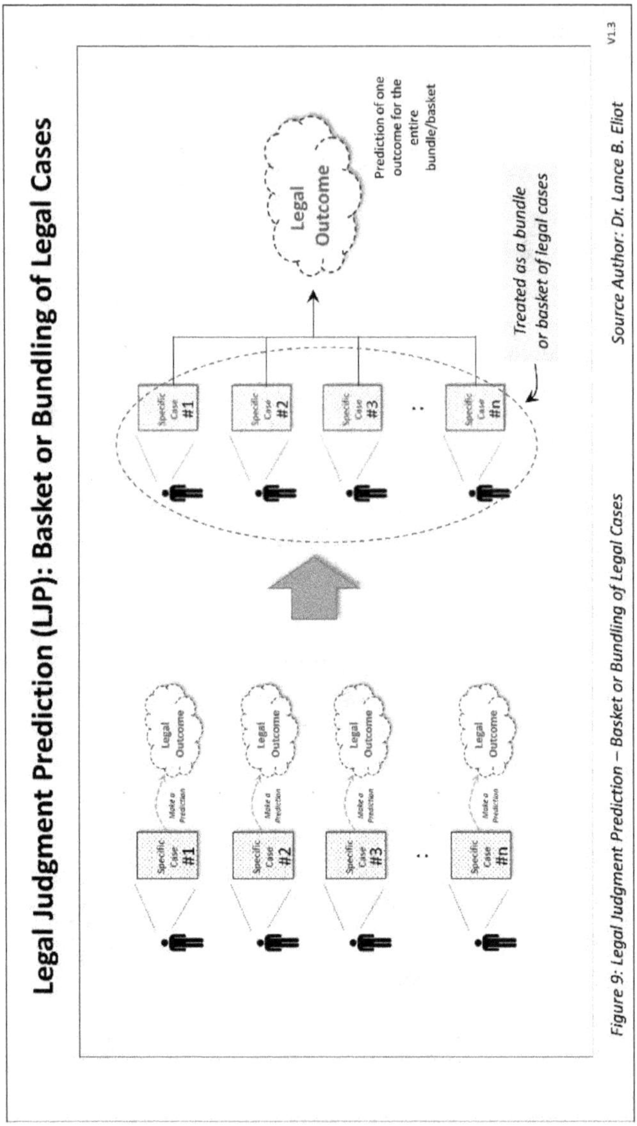

Chapter 11 – Figure 9

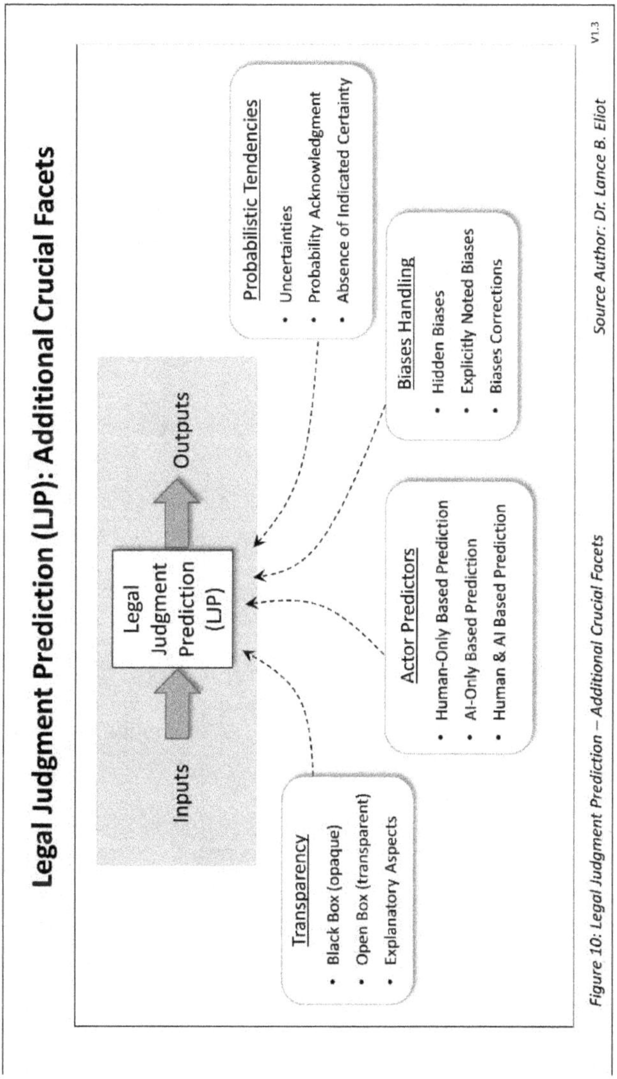

Figure 10: Legal Judgment Prediction – Additional Crucial Facets

Source Author: Dr. Lance B. Eliot

Chapter 11 – Figure 10

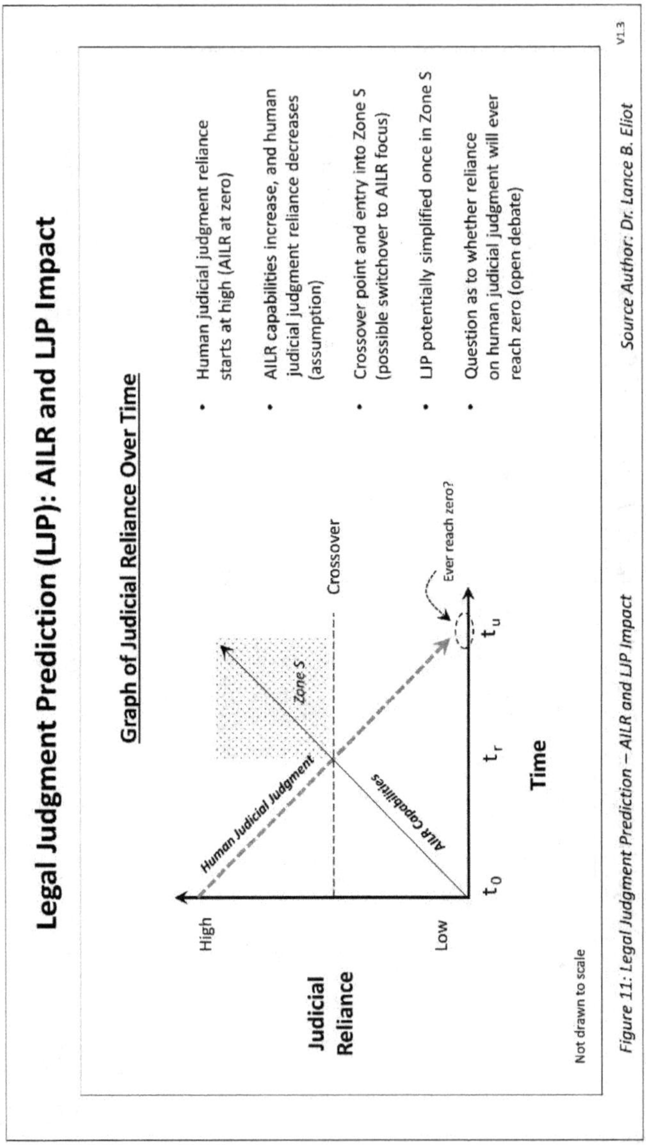

Chapter 11 – Figure 11

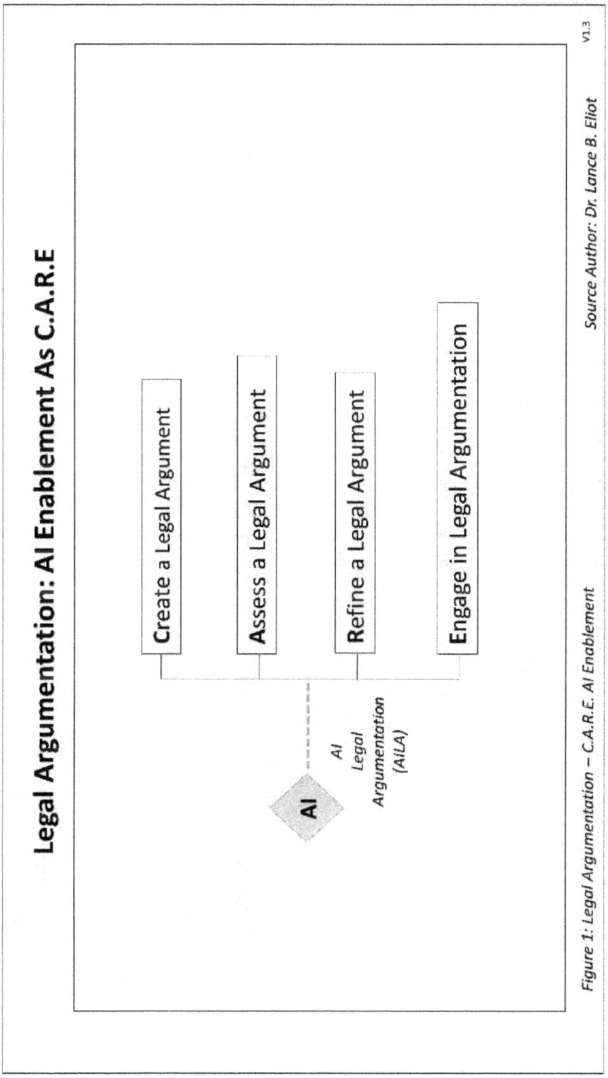
Legal Argumentation: AI Enablement As C.A.R.E
Create a Legal Argument
Assess a Legal Argument
Refine a Legal Argument
Engage in Legal Argumentation
AI
AI Legal Argumentation (AILA)
Figure 1: Legal Argumentation – C.A.R.E. AI Enablement
Source Author: Dr. Lance B. Eliot
V1.3

Chapter 12 – Figure 1

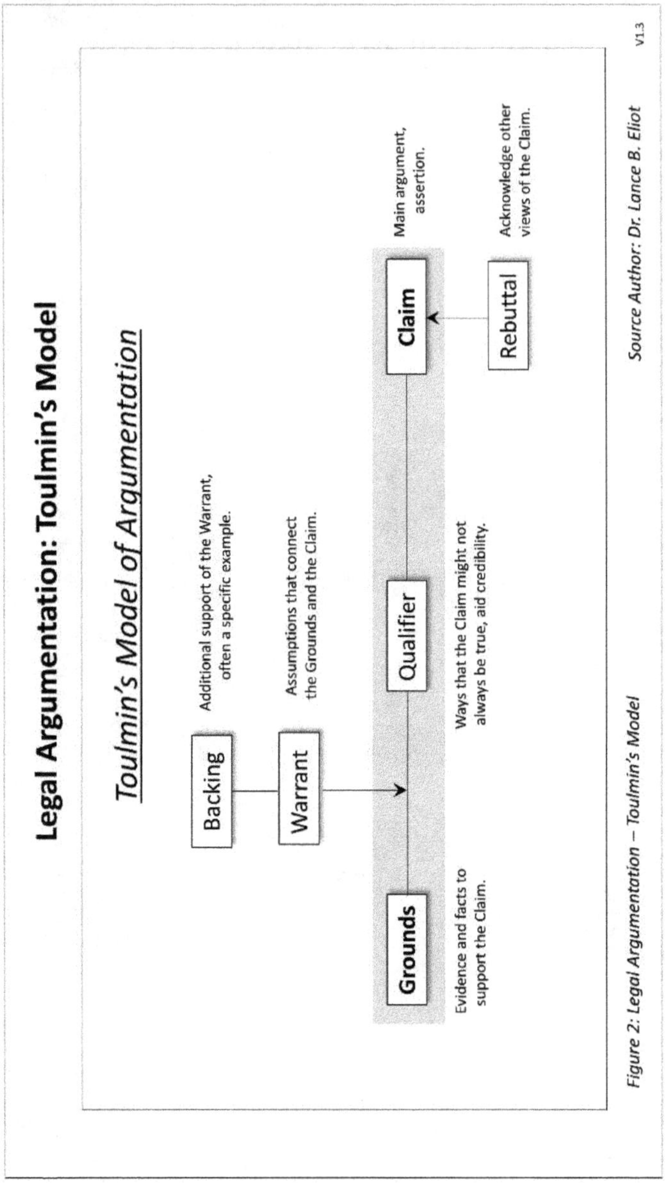
Legal Argumentation: Toulmin's Model
Toulmin's Model of Argumentation
Backing
Additional support of the Warrant, often a specific example.
Warrant
Assumptions that connect the Grounds and the Claim.
Grounds
Evidence and facts to support the Claim.
Qualifier
Ways that the Claim might not always be true, aid credibility.
Claim
Main argument, assertion.
Rebuttal
Acknowledge other views of the Claim.
Figure 2: Legal Argumentation – Toulmin's Model
Source Author: Dr. Lance B. Eliot
V1.3

Chapter 12 – Figure 2

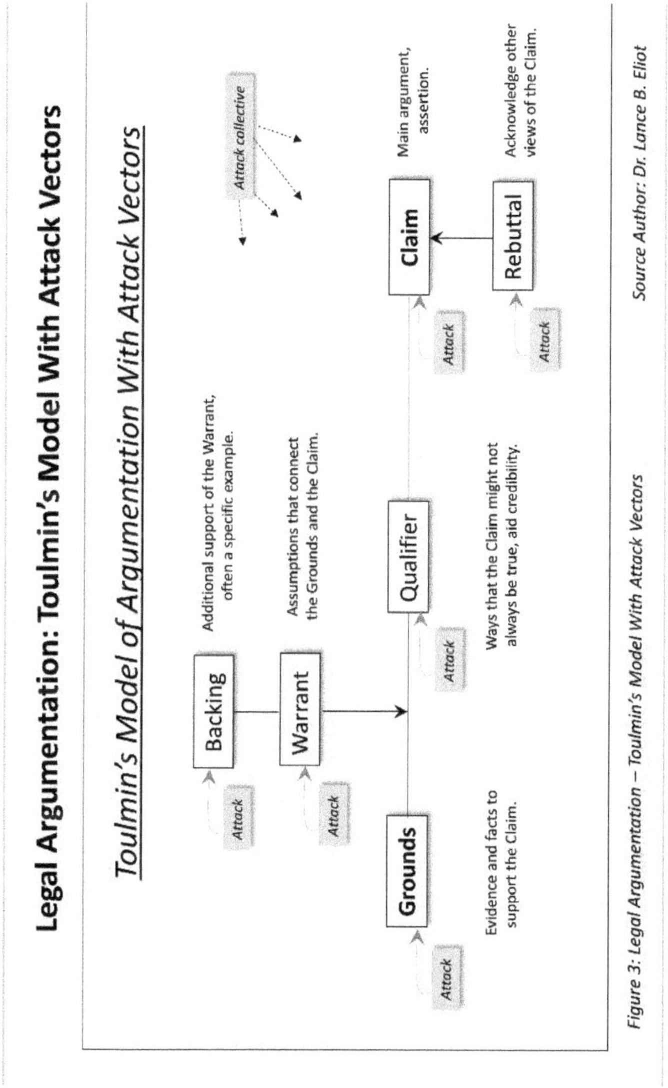
Legal Argumentation: Toulmin's Model With Attack Vectors
Toulmin's Model of Argumentation With Attack Vectors
Attack collective
Backing
Additional support of the Warrant, often a specific example.
Warrant
Assumptions that connect the Grounds and the Claim.
Grounds
Evidence and facts to support the Claim.
Qualifier
Ways that the Claim might not always be true, aid credibility.
Claim
Main argument, assertion.
Rebuttal
Acknowledge other views of the Claim.
Attack
Attack
Attack
Attack
Attack
Attack

Figure 3: Legal Argumentation – Toulmin's Model With Attack Vectors

Source Author: Dr. Lance B. Eliot

Chapter 12 – Figure 3

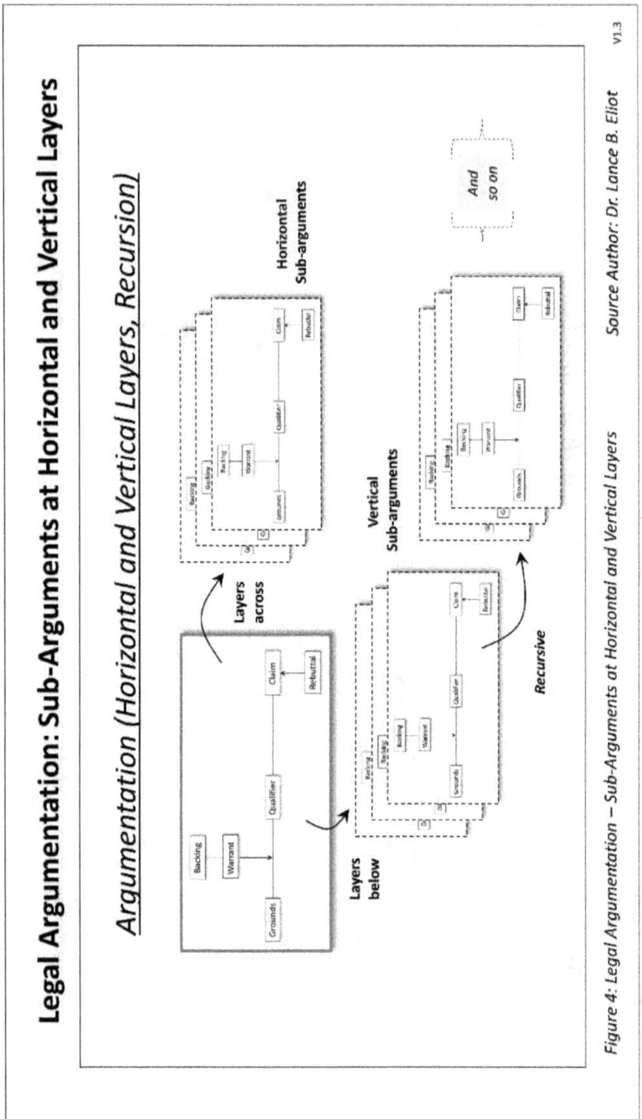

Figure 4: Legal Argumentation – Sub-Arguments at Horizontal and Vertical Layers

Chapter 12 – Figure 4

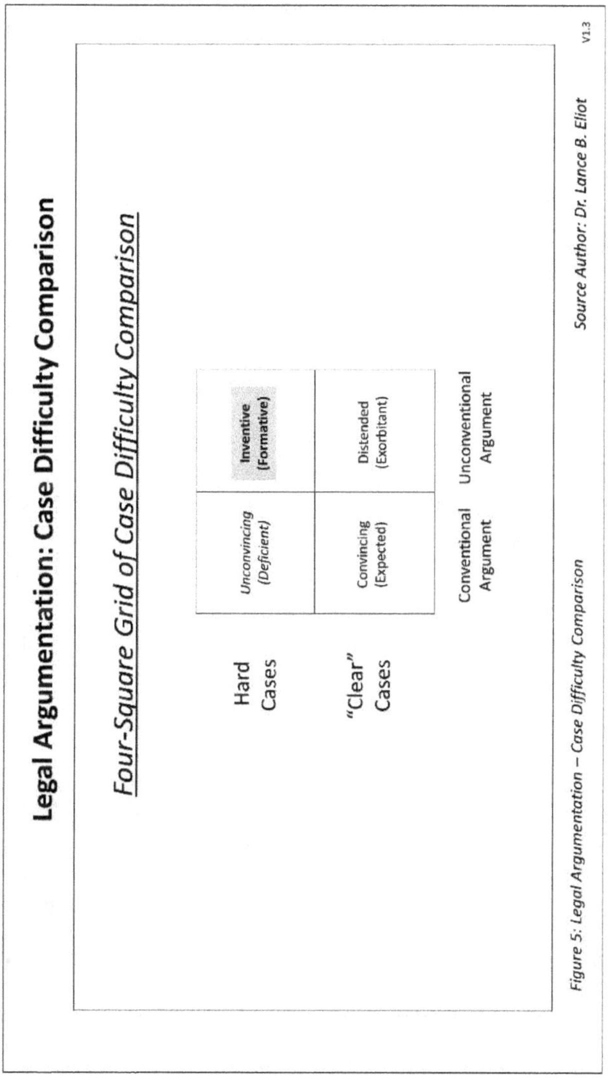

Chapter 12 – Figure 5

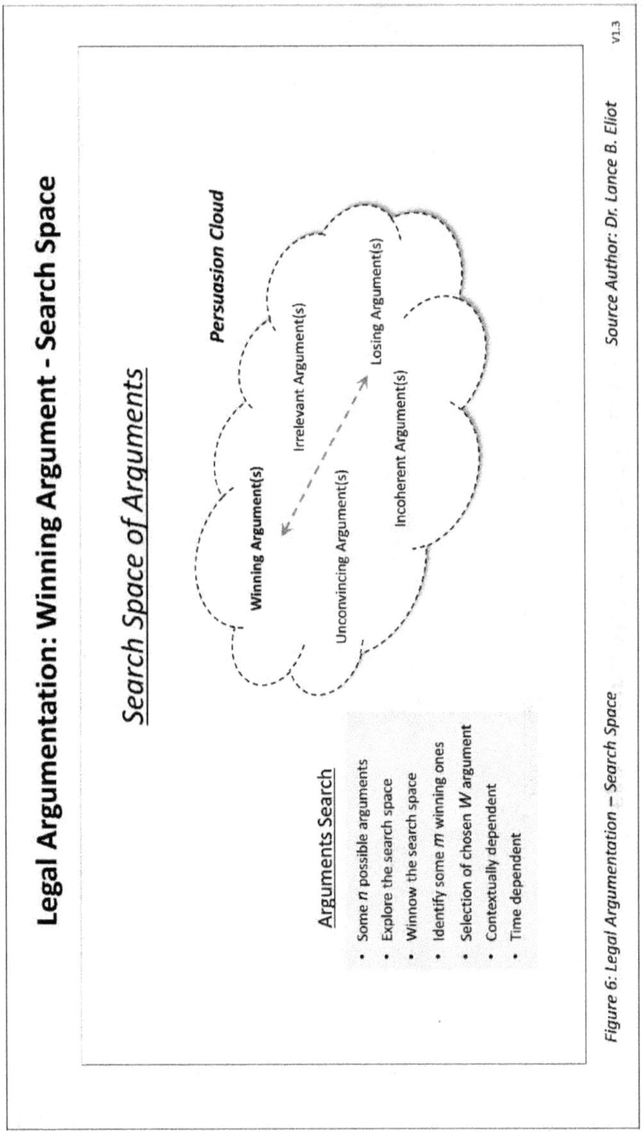

Figure 6: Legal Argumentation – Search Space

Chapter 12 – Figure 6

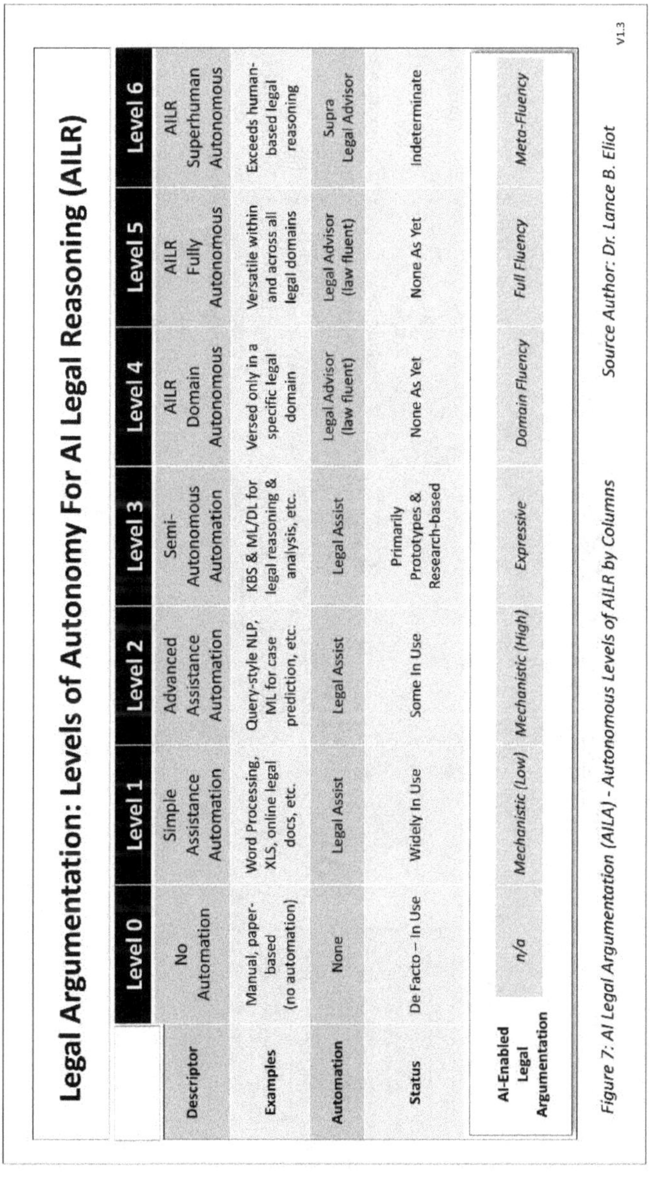

Legal Argumentation: Levels of Autonomy For AI Legal Reasoning (AILR)

	Level 0	Level 1	Level 2	Level 3	Level 4	Level 5	Level 6
Descriptor	No Automation	Simple Assistance Automation	Advanced Assistance Automation	Semi-Autonomous Automation	AILR Domain Autonomous	AILR Fully Autonomous	AILR Superhuman Autonomous
Examples	Manual, paper-based (no automation)	Word Processing, XLS, online legal docs, etc.	Query-style NLP, ML for case prediction, etc.	KBS & ML/DL for legal reasoning & analysis, etc.	Versed only in a specific legal domain	Versatile within and across all legal domains	Exceeds human-based legal reasoning
Automation	None	Legal Assist	Legal Assist	Legal Assist	Legal Advisor (law fluent)	Legal Advisor (law fluent)	Supra Legal Advisor
Status	De Facto – In Use	Widely In Use	Some In Use	Primarily Prototypes & Research-based	None As Yet	None As Yet	Indeterminate
AI-Enabled Legal Argumentation	*n/a*	*Mechanistic (Low)*	*Mechanistic (High)*	*Expressive*	*Domain Fluency*	*Full Fluency*	*Meta-Fluency*

Figure 7: AI Legal Argumentation (AILA) - Autonomous Levels of AILR by Columns

Source Author: Dr. Lance B. Eliot

V1.3

Chapter 12 – Figure 7

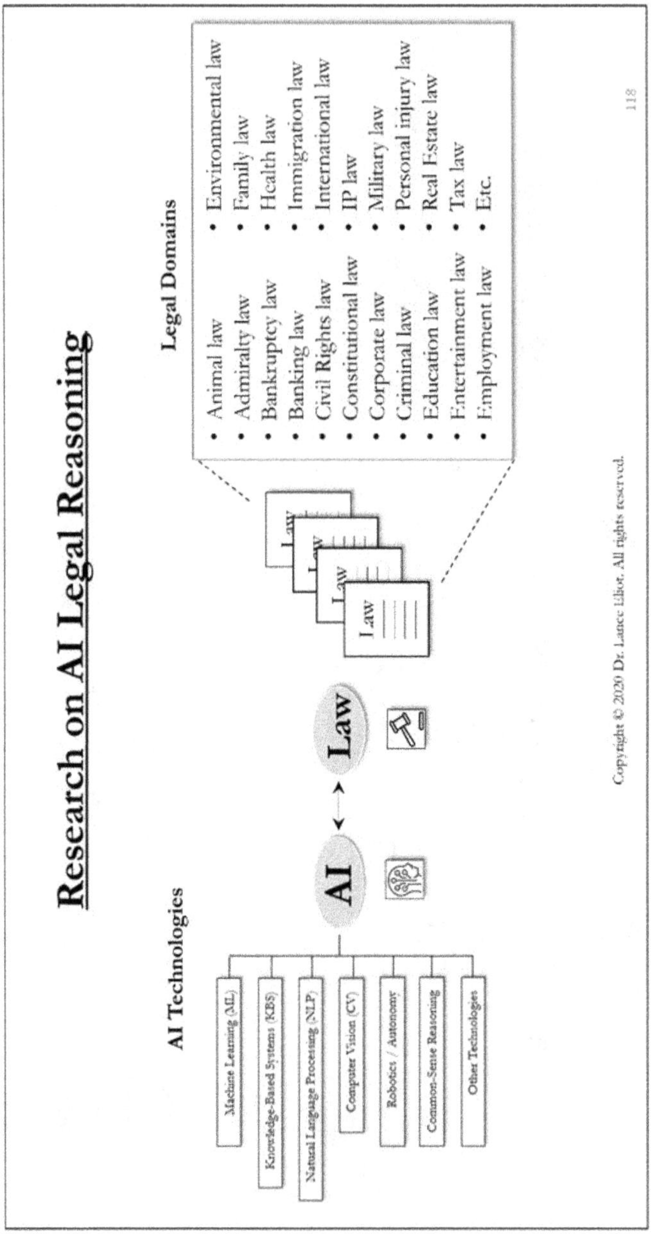

Bonus Figure: Future Research Agenda for AI Legal Reasoning

ABOUT THE AUTHOR

Dr. Lance B. Eliot, Ph.D., MBA is a globally recognized AI expert and thought leader, an invited Stanford Fellow at Stanford University, an experienced top executive and corporate leader, a successful entrepreneur, and a noted scholar on AI, including that his Forbes and AI Trends columns have amassed over 4 million views, his books on AI are ranked in the Top 10 of all-time AI books, his journal articles are widely cited, and he has developed and implemented numerous AI systems.

He currently serves as the Chief AI Scientist at Techbruim, Inc. and has over twenty years of industry experience including serving as a corporate officer in billion-dollar sized firms and was a partner in a major consulting firm. He is also a successful entrepreneur having founded, ran, and sold several high-tech related businesses.

Dr. Eliot previously hosted the popular radio show *Technotrends* that was also available on American Airlines flights via their in-flight audio program, he has made appearances on CNN, has been a frequent speaker at industry conferences, and his podcasts have been downloaded over 150,000 times.

A former professor at the University of Southern California (USC), he founded and led an innovative research lab on Artificial Intelligence. He also previously served on the faculty of the University of California Los Angeles (UCLA) and was a visiting professor at other major universities. He was elected to the International Board of the Society for Information Management (SIM), a prestigious association of over 3,000 high-tech executives worldwide.

He has performed extensive community service, including serving as Senior Science Adviser to the Congressional Vice-Chair of the Congressional Committee on Science & Technology. He has served on the Board of the OC Science & Engineering Fair (OCSEF), where he is also has been a Grand Sweepstakes judge, and likewise served as a judge for the Intel International SEF (ISEF). He served as the Vice-Chair of the Association for Computing Machinery (ACM) Chapter, a prestigious association of computer scientists. Dr. Eliot has been a shark tank judge for the USC Mark Stevens Center for Innovation on start-up pitch competitions and served as a mentor for several incubators and accelerators in Silicon Valley and in Silicon Beach.

Dr. Eliot holds a Ph.D. from USC, MBA, and Bachelor's in Computer Science, and earned the CDP, CCP, CSP, CDE, and CISA certifications

ADDENDUM

Thanks for reading this book and I hope you will continue your interest in the field of AI & Law

---

For my free podcasts about AI & Law:

https://ai-law.libsyn.com/website

Those podcasts are also available on Spotify, iTunes, etc.

For the latest on AI & Law see my website:

www.ai-law.legal

To follow me on Twitter:

https://twitter.com/LanceEliot

For my in-depth book on AI & Law:

AI And Legal Reasoning Essentials

www.amazon.com/gp/product/1734601655/

www.ingramcontent.com/pod-product-compliance
Lightning Source LLC
Chambersburg PA
CBHW071059050326
40690CB00008B/1063
9781736303115